UNIX
For
MS-DOS
Programmers

UNIX
For
MS-DOS
Programmers

Steven Mikes

Addison-Wesley Publishing Company, Inc.
Reading, Massachusetts Menlo Park, California New York
Don Mills, Ontario Wokingham, England Amsterdam Bonn Sydney
Tokyo Madrid San Juan

Many of the designations used by manufacturers and sellers to distinguish their products are claimed as trademarks. Where those designations appear in this book and Addison-Wesley was aware of a trademark claim, the designations have been printed in initial capital letters.

The opinions expressed are solely those of the author and don't necessarily reflect the views of the publisher or any other organization.

Library of Congress Cataloging-in-Publication Data
Mikes, Steven.
    UNIX for MS-DOS Programmers / Steven Mikes.
        p.   cm.
    Includes index.
    ISBN 0-201-17219-4
    1. UNIX (Computer operating system)   I. Title.
    QA76.76.063M525   1989
    005.4'3--dc 19   89-31213
                                                 CIP

Production Editor: Amorette Pedersen
Cover Design by: Doliber Skeffington Design
Set in 10.5 New Century Schoolbook by Benchmark Productions

ABCDEFGHIJ-HA-89
First Printing, May, 1989

To my wife Pati and my daughter Danielle, for your patience and understanding and all your sacrifices that were necessary for me to have the time to write this book.

ACKNOWLEDGMENTS

I would like to thank Chris Williams and Amy Pedersen of Benchmark Productions Inc., for their patience and help in making this book become a reality. I would also like to extend my thanks to William B. Urinoski and Gregg W. White for their technical assistance and input.

TABLE OF CONTENTS

About the Book

This book provides a detailed understanding of the UNIX system from the perspective of the DOS Programmer.

For the experienced DOS developer, this book provides information on the development of applications in the UNIX environment; with comparisons to DOS wherever possible. Knowledge of the DOS environment is used as a foundation upon which a new knowledge of the UNIX system is built.

For those readers interested in simply knowing more about the UNIX system, this book will prove invaluable.

UNIX Overview

UNIX has been in existence for almost 20 years and is probably the most debugged operating system ever written. UNIX is currently installed in hundreds of thousands machines all over the world, and runs on virtually every class and kind of computer, from PC-based microcomputers to the most powerful Cray supercomputers. Both DOS and OS/2 employ concepts and facilities originally developed for the UNIX system.

UNIX, in addition to being a multitasking operating system, is also a multiuser system. It was designed to perform concurrent processing of tasks by multiple, concurrent users. UNIX runs on computer hardware from vendors including AT&T, DEC, IBM, NCR, CDC, Hewlett-Packard, Sun Microsystems, Apple Computer, Apollo, Amdahl, and many others. Over 90 percent of the technical workstation market is running on UNIX-based operating systems.

The UNIX operating system can address as much memory as the hardware is able to accommodate. The file system is designed to become as large as necessary; may be segmented to any configuration imaginable; and is limited in size only by hardware barriers.

Given all of these wonderful things, has UNIX no faults? The answer is yes: its user interface. Users accustomed to a lot of hand-holding, such as with IBM's Structured Programming Facility (SPF) for the mainframe world, are likely to be in for a difficult time when they first encounter the UNIX system user interface. IBM mainframe users adapting to UNIX often find it archaic and user hostile. In comparison to the very hierarchical menu structures and standardized function keys of SPF, the default $ command line prompt of the UNIX shell interface is as cold as ice.

In earlier releases of UNIX, when a user entered something the system did not understand, it would respond with error messages like 'huh?' or simply a question mark. The command line interface has since been dragged into the real world, still leaving a lot to be desired. The main reason is due to the over abundance of user commands. Without a manual as a guide, inexperienced users are as lost as babes in the woods when they encounter the command line prompt. Quite recently, this problem was acknowledged and is currently being addressed.

Several heuristic and ergonomic studies performed by various institutions have arrived at a common conclusion: the best user interface to incorporate into any system is a graphical one, using pictures (icons) instead of or in conjunction with the written word. Good examples of these are the Apple Macintosh or the Microsoft Windows graphical user interfaces (GUI). Actually, this type of user interface was not originated by either of these companies; it was first developed by Xerox Corporation at their Palo Alto Research Center (PARC) during the mid 1970s and much later was licensed to Apple Computer.

With a new graphical standard looming on the horizon, namely the X Window system (or simply X), UNIX is now in a position to provide an excellent GUI, far more powerful than any in existence. AT&T and Sun Microsystems have formed a development effort to deliver UNIX System V Release 4; a major part of which incorporates a new graphical user interface developed using X, called Open Look.

The UNIX system has a sophisticated, powerful, and yet basically simple file system. The DOS and OS/2 file system architecture have borrowed conceptually from the UNIX file system, and on the surface there is a resemblance. The IBM mainframe file system architecture on the other hand, is radically different in concept and function, and provides few common points of reference.

UNIX was designed to be a universal operating system, to run on a variety of different computers. This concept was in contrast to the prevailing idea at the time UNIX was developed, that an operating system should be designed with a specific computer model in mind. The UNIX system broke that mold in the late 1960s.

Audience Assumptions

An understanding of the C language, a basic understanding of PC hardware, and a knowledge of the DOS environment would be helpful to the reader.

It is assumed that you have no familiarity with the UNIX system. For this reason, the text is full of examples and explanation. The main purpose of this book is to impart a thorough knowledge of the UNIX system in an easily understood manner.

What Is To Be Learned

After having completed this book, readers should have an understanding of the following:

- The UNIX Philosophy

- Differences between the DOS and UNIX systems
- UNIX operating system environment
- UNIX file system
- UNIX I/O subsystem
- UNIX development toolsUNIX shell programming
- Internal structure of UNIX applications (processes)
- Fundamentals of multiprogramming environments
- UNIX keyboard and screen techniques
- Memory management and manipulation in UNIX
- UNIX device drivers
- Virtual memory addressing and management in UNIX
- Professional UNIX programming conventions
- Managing software development with sccs
- UNIX system calls and libraries
- UNIX/DOS system call comparisons
- UNIX interprocess communications (IPC)
- UNIX shared libraries
- UNIX communications and networking (UUCP, STREAMS, RFS, NFS, Ethernet, TCP/IP)
- UNIX system administration and security
- An Introduction to the X Window System

CHAPTER 1

INTRODUCTION TO DOS

DOS is by far the most widely installed operating system, running across the range of the Intel 8086 family of processors. It is the current standard in the PC industry, receiving wide acceptance and support from users, developers, and third parties. PCs running DOS are a multi-billion dollar a year industry with an estimated 10 million installed machines in the United States and a growing market overseas.

The acronym DOS stands for Disk Operating System and was originally coined by IBM in the 1960s from the name of their premier operating system for the 360 line of mainframe computers. The references made to DOS in this book have nothing to do with the 360 DOS operating system. It is merely a generic way of referencing the entire DOS family of operating systems for the IBM personal computer (or compatible).

The two principal vendors of DOS operating systems are Microsoft Corporation (MS-DOS) and IBM Corporation (PC-DOS). Compatible versions of DOS are marketed by companies such as Compaq Corporation, Dell Computer, and Tandy Corporation.

1

Review

DOS has advanced considerably since its beginnings in 1981. DOS 1.0 required only 16k of RAM when loaded into memory on a machine with only 64k available. DOS 2.0 required only 24k of RAM (plus the requirements of user-specified device drivers and buffers, etc.), requiring a machine with at least 128k if one was to be productive.

DOS 3.0 (as well as 3.1 and 3.2) required at least 36k of RAM, plus any additional memory requirements for device drivers, buffers, and networking requirements, and usually required a machine equipped with a full 640k of memory.

DOS 4.1 requires more than 36k of RAM and, with today's add-on boards and networking hardware, also requires significant amounts of device driver space. The resident portion of the command interpreter also requires more space and it is not uncommon to see systems that use over 100K of RAM for system overhead. OS/2 is said to require over 900k of RAM for its resident portion. In all fairness, UNIX also requires a large amount of RAM for its system overhead.

Ever popular memory resident software also eats into the amount of available memory for applications, causing the user community to desire a multitasking/multiuser environment capable of addressing more memory than the 640k limitation imposed by the DOS 1 megabyte address space architecture.

Multitasking and The Future

To satisfy the public's quest for multitasking, a number of multitasking environments have sprung up from software vendors, most notably Microsoft Windows which provides multitasking of Windows applications (applications developed specifically for the Windows environment), as well as a windowing environment. The 80286 has evolved into the 80386 which offers the most desktop computing power ever designed but; alas, there was no DOS-based operating system available from Microsoft or IBM that could make use of the hardware's advanced technology.

Microsoft has announced the availability of Windows 386, a product that runs under DOS 3.0 or later, and that does make full use of the

2

protected mode of operation available on a 386 machine. The major problem now, is application programs exceeding the limitations of 640k.

In an environment capable of multitasking, it is likely that many applications would be memory resident concurrently, and it is also likely that the aggregate total of their memory requirements would exceed 640k. To ease the 640k barrier problem, Lotus Development, Intel, and Microsoft corporations have developed jointly a scheme by which memory may be addressable above the 1 megabyte address space that is called extended memory. It is known officially as "The Lotus, Intel, Microsoft Expanded Memory Specification" (LIM/EMS for short).

Another alternative to Expanded memory is something called Extended memory, which basically employs the use of added memory above the 1 megabyte address space, but is accessible in pages of 64k at a time, up to 8 megabytes total.

With the availability of OS/2, memory addressability is no longer a problem, as each individual application will be able to directly address up to 16 megabytes of RAM, the limitation of the 80286 hardware. Under OS/2 Extended Edition running on the 80386 microprocessor, each individual task may directly address up to 1 gigabyte of RAM if it is available.

DOS Architecture

The structure of DOS may be thought of as an architecture consisting of four basic layers. At the heart of the layered architecture is the hardware, which is the physical computer and its physical components such as the microprocessor, the video display screen, the keyboard, disk, and memory storage.

The next layer is the basic input/output system, or BIOS as it is called. This layer is ROM-based, and communicates directly with the hardware layer. The next layer is the DOS kernel and is the part of the operating system that communicates with application programs and provides system functions (or calls) and hardware independence.

The next layer is the command processor shell which is DOS's primary user interface. Its primary function is to provide a method of communication directly from the user and to process DOS commands through a file called COMMAND.COM, the DOS command interpreter.

The last layer is the application layer which is usually a user-developed set of software routines such as end user applications like data base management systems, word processors and editors, spreadsheet programs, and communications programs.

BIOS Layer

This layer is a set of I/O routines used to communicate directly with the processor hardware and peripherals and is system specific for a particular brand of computer. It must be provided by the manufacturer of the particular computer hardware.

When a computer manufacturer claims 100 percent compatibility with the IBM PC, it is the BIOS interface to which they are referring. By providing identical functionality at the BIOS level, the differences at the hardware level become transparent to the end user and to applications that use BIOS calls in order to perform their functions.

The BIOS layer contains the default resident hardware dependent driver modules for such devices as the system clock functions, the system boot disk, the default video display and keyboard drivers. Device drivers are used to communicate with the DOS kernel through I/O request packets. These packets are translated by the individual driver into the necessary command protocol for the particular device/controller hardware.

Some of the most fundamental device drivers are stored in ROM for use by diagnostic programs, standalone programs, and the system initialization (boot) sequence. BIOS routines provide only the most basic access mechanisms for transfer of data to and from the device. For example, for a disk device, BIOS reads and writes in sectors; grouping of data into files is done at the higher level of DOS function calls.

This makes the job of the programmer easier and free of the problems of sector management within application programs. All they need do is refer to devices by a name and issue DOS function calls to perform file related I/O operations. An application program may access a device directly through BIOS calls or via DOS function calls.

As opposed to BIOS calls, when the programmer issues DOS function calls, the program may suffer some degree of performance loss. DOS function calls are recommended to ensure portability across different machine hardware. Not all PC systems have compatible BIOS's; so if an application is written using BIOS specific code, it will not work on another system with an incompatible BIOS. By using DOS function calls the application program will work on any system that uses DOS.

DOS uses BIOS routines to access and control certain devices. By doing this, the application program is insulated from the difficulties of low level I/O management and certain problems that can occur during I/O management. In a sense, the application program makes use of certain error detection and recovery routines built into DOS, and therefore shortens the development time — while also adding program reliability.

There are a few instances where using DOS services is not practical, such as in a communications application that uses the PC's serial port. The serial port may run at speeds up to 19.2k baud (bits per second), but DOS services would fail to properly drive the serial port at even 9600 baud. In such an instance an application program would need to access the serial port directly.

Application programs may access and control devices directly, without the use of DOS or BIOS. These types of applications are usually referred to as device drivers and are specific to the device being accessed, such as a local area network communications board; a specific kind of disk device; or other special function board. By using BIOS, the programmer doesn't need to reinvent the wheel, so to speak, by writing all I/O routines from scratch.

Access and control of devices through BIOS routines are performed through an interrupt mechanism. Basically, each device is associated with a BIOS interrupt number and its own unique handling routine stored in ROM. The interrupt numbers are stored in a special location in memory called the interrupt vector table. By using an interrupt mechanism the programmer may refer to the handler routines without the need to know and remember their respective address locations.

There are alternative ways of accessing devices besides through the use of the interrupt mechanism. DOS uses BIOS interrupts (calls) to access devices. Interrupt driven I/O control is far more effective than a polling method. Imagine the overhead of constantly polling all devices for changes in status instead of letting them inform the operating system as the change occurs.

DOS Kernel Layer

The kernel is the proprietary code that is the very heart of DOS. It performs many functions that include memory management, character device I/O, file and record management, access to the system clock, scheduling and execution of application programs.

This layer communicates an application program's I/O requests to the BIOS layer, unless the program directly accesses a device (a general development no-no), and also provides system functions through the software interrupt facility previously mentioned.

The DOS kernel is not memory resident in ROM, as is BIOS, but must be loaded into RAM during system initialization upon machine power up or during the warm reboot sequence (CTRL-ALT-DEL keys). Special hidden system files on the boot disk are responsible for performing this operation.

The DOS kernel uses memory management functions to provide execution space for application programs, as well as to process application I/O requests. In addition, file management functions within the kernel provide organization of data for access to application programs. The DOS kernel provides limited error detection or correction services. For example, the kernel does not perform any checking to ensure that an application program does not overwrite any areas already occupied by the operating system and its transient components.

The DOS kernel can be thought of as an overall supervisor of things in the system, and is analogous to the UNIX kernel. For those readers familiar with IBM mainframe operating systems such as

VM/370, MVS, or DOS/VSE, the DOS kernel is analogous to the supervisor.

Command Processor Shell Layer

The command processor, or shell, layer provides the primary interface between the user at the computer keyboard/screen console and the operating system. Its main function is to collect and interpret the commands entered at the keyboard or from a command script executed in batch mode, and to then perform the desired execution sequence if the commands pass the syntax checks.

This layer has the responsibility of loading and executing user-provided programs of the media from which it is appropriate to search. The standard shell distributed with DOS is called COMMAND.COM. It must be present in the boot device's root directory, unless it has been redirected through the use of a special variable in a file called CONFIG.SYS, which must reside on the boot device's root directory. If this file is not present, certain defaults are set up and COMMAND.COM is expected to be found in the boot device's root directory. If it isn't, an error occurs and the system initialization fails.

COMMAND.COM's primary function is to display a prompt to the user on the output video display screen and to wait for a response from the keyboard. The user types in a command, and upon pressing the ENTER key, COMMAND.COM begins parsing the command line to determine if the entered command is an internal command that it must perform, or if it is an external command that it must load from disk.

There are two types of external commands; those that are a standard part of the DOS operating system, usually stored in a separate directory; and those that are user applications. Regardless of which external command is being processed, the same loading operation is performed.

If the command line did not contain the specific location of the external command, then COMMAND.COM assumes the program is to be found in the current directory. If the program is not found in the current directory, a special reserved area in memory called the *environment*, is checked for a variable called *path*.

The path variable is a text string containing, in a particular order, the names of disk/directories/subdirectories which will become the location and search order that COMMAND.COM will use in attempting to locate the external command it is trying to process.

If the program is not found in any of the locations specified in the path string, if a path exists, then an error is reported. This does not mean that the program doesn't exist, it means that COMMAND.COM ran out of places to look.

If the external command is found, then COMMAND.COM performs some setup work in preparation for loading the program, loads the program, and transfers control to it. COMMAND.COM appears to the user as the operating system but it is only the command interpreter. It is under the control of DOS and must communicate with it in order to be able to execute other programs.

Other shells can be loaded and executed in place of COMMAND.COM, although for most users it would be unnecessary. An example of an alternative shell would be a command interpreter designed to understand an additional or different set of internal commands, such as one designed to emulate the UNIX shell and which would perform UNIX simulation functions for a UNIX command. An alternate shell is specified by placing the SHELL directive in the file CONFIG.SYS as in the following example:

```
SHELL=BASIC.EXE
```

Popular DOS command shells provide such features as the ability for the user to define the function keys of their keyboard, to enable a help screen to be called upon a special key sequence; or to provide a user friendly display, such as a menu structure on the video screen, as the prompt for those users who find the standard prompt a bit uninviting.

COMMAND.COM actually consists of three different parts. The first part, the resident portion, is loaded into low memory, just above the DOS kernel, buffers, and tables. It contains certain routines, such as a break interrupt handler (CTRL-C and CTRL-BREAK keys), critical error handlers, and termination of other programs (final exit handler).

It is this portion of COMMAND.COM that issues the error messages that the user sees at the console. It is also this portion that contains the necessary routine to reload the transient portion of COMMAND.COM when needed.

The next part is called the initialization portion. This portion is loaded into memory just above the resident portion during system boot up. This portion of COMMAND.COM is responsible for executing and processing of the special AUTOEXEC.BAT file if it exists in the root directory of the boot device. When the processing is done, this portion is terminated and released from memory.

The last part of COMMAND.COM is the transient portion, and it is loaded into the high end of memory. The transient portion of COMMAND.COM issues the user prompt to the video screen and performs both the command line parsing and the execution of all commands. It obtains its input from either the console keyboard or from a batch (.BAT) file and performs the desired execution sequence.

Upon program termination, the resident portion of COMMAND.COM checks to see if the transient portion needs to be reloaded, and if so, obtains a new copy from disk or wherever the environment variable, COMSPEC, points to.

Batch files are identifiable as they have the extension .BAT as part of the file name. These are text files that can be created or modified using any text editor program, and they contain a list of DOS commands or transient programs to be executed by COMMAND.COM.

Transient programs are loaded into a special area of memory before they are executed. Batch files are read and acted upon a single line at a time. Until DOS 3.3, batch files could not be called directly from one another, although they could be daisy chained together, even in a recursive loop. The only way this could be accomplished was to load a second copy of COMMAND.COM which in turn called the second batch file.

If a .BAT file was renamed so that it had a file extension of either .COM or .EXE, it would be loaded into special areas of memory and would cause operating system failure, since batch files contain no binary executable code. The first attempt to load an instruction would fail, and since control of the system is now passed to the program, there would be no way to recover from the attempted invalid operation.

If COMMAND.COM fails for any reason, a reboot usually is required to clear the problem and data may be lost as a result. A reboot with disk files still open may cause file system problems.

The One Megabyte Address Space

DOS was designed to operate within a memory address space one megabyte in size. At the time this was done, the PC only had 64k of RAM available for user applications. In comparison to other popular systems of the day, such as Apple or Commodore, this was par, if not actually better. It was not yet clear if the PC was to become a machine for the individual at the office or, as its name (Personal Computer), seemed to imply, at home. It eventually became both.

The Commodore system was supposed to be capable of addressing more memory than 64k, but the software necessary to perform the bank switching from 64k segment to 64k segment was not available anywhere. The Apple machines also had the same problem and, in fact, have only recently overcome the limited architecture mentality.

Neither Apple nor Commodore could understand why on earth any user would need more than 64k or additional bus slots! As a result, their home markets began shrinking as the IBM PC became more popular at home and with company offices.

Shortly after the PC began to sell, it started setting new hardware and software standards, and in fact, still does so today. Users soon found that they needed more RAM and hard disk drives in order to perform any serious computing on the PC. A new retail market was spawned by the demand for add-in boards that catered to the shortcomings of the early PC hardware design, such as additional memory, serial and parallel ports, and battery backup clock/calendar boards.

Figure 1-1 shows a map of this one megabyte address space.

ROM BIOS
System ROM, ROM Basic, etc.
BIOS Extensions, HD ROM, etc.
Color Graphics Buffer (16k)
RESERVED
Monochrome Buffer (4k)
EGA Buffer (256k)
COMMAND.COM (transient portion)
TRANSIENT USER PROGRAM AREA **(up to 608k)**
COMMAND.COM (resident portion)
Loadable Device Drivers (config.sys)
Disk Buffers (config.sys)
DOS Kernel (loaded at system boot)
SYSINIT   (loaded at system boot)
BIOS from IO.SYS
Interrupt Vector Table (1k)

Figure 1-1: DOS One Megabyte Address Space Map

DOS Boot Sequence

In order to explain the mapping, it is necessary to describe what happens when the PC system boot process is invoked, either at machine power on time, or by the user through a keyboard or software request.

First, the PC usually goes through the ritual of performing power on diagnostics designed to detect any bad memory locations among other things. What actually takes place depends on the bootable ROM of the particular machine. For the purposes of this book, a boot sequence compatible with the IBM standard ROMs is assumed.

The microprocessor (8086 family) hardware is designed to begin execution at the highest end of the one megabyte address space, at address 0FFFF0 hex. This is the location where the bootable ROM routines reside. A machine instruction is issued to "jump" to a routine that begins performing the diagnostics and then loads and executes the bootstrap sequence, also in this area of ROM.

The bootstrap program reads a bootstrap record from a special sector location on the boot device, usually the first hard disk on most modern systems, but possibly an available floppy disk device. Actually, for IBM systems, only the first floppy drive (A:) is used; MS-DOS variants allow for the use of the second floppy device (B:). This special sector is usually the first sector on the disk and contains disk format information as well as instructions to perform the remaining boot sequence.

The sector is read into an arbitrary memory location and control is transferred to it by the ROM-based bootstrap program. (NOTE: This would be an excellent point to place some system security code that could ask for a password sequence and, either continue with the boot or simply lock the system, as the IBM PS/2 does today.)

The bootstrap program then checks to see if the media being booted from contains a valid operating system (DOS). This is done by checking the first sector of the boot disk to see if two files are present: IO.SYS and MSDOS.SYS, if the Microsoft version of MS-DOS is being booted; or IBMBIO.COM and IBMDOS.COM if IBM's PC-DOS is being booted.

If either or both files are missing, then a message is displayed to the video output display device, indicating that the disk is not bootable, and, (if booting from a floppy) to insert a bootable disk into the boot drive. If the boot is taking place from a hard disk and a message like this appears, it indicates there is no operating system present. To solve the problem it is necessary to insert a bootable floppy into the first diskette drive and retry the boot sequence.

When the bootstrap program finds these files present on the boot disk, they are read into memory and control is transferred to IO.SYS (MS-DOS) or IBMBIO.COM (PC-DOS). Some implementations only read in the IO.SYS/IBMBIO.COM file, which in turn reads in the MSDOS.SYS/IBMDOS.COM file.

The IO.SYS/IBMBIO.COM module consists of two parts: the BIOS portion and the SYSINIT portion. The BIOS portion contains device drivers for the console (keyboard/screen), printer, serial port, and block devices; as well as initialization code that runs only during the system boot sequence.

The SYSINIT portion is called by the BIOS code and relocates itself into the high end of memory after determining what the address of that memory is. SYSINIT then loads the DOS kernel (MSDOS.SYS/IBMDOS.COM) into the address space that was previously occupied by SYSINIT before it relocated itself to high memory. Initialization code that is no longer necessary is also overlaid by the DOS kernel at this time.

When the DOS kernel has been relocated, SYSINIT issues a call to the initialization code within the kernel — which in turn begins to set up and initialize internal tables, the interrupt vector table, work areas, buffers, etc. Interrupt vectors 20H-2FH are also set up and initialization routines are executed for any resident device drivers.

The block device drivers are responsible for checking and maintaining the status of their respective equipment and also for preliminary initialization, such as setting up the vectors for hardware interrupts to be serviced.

Upon examination of the block device drivers, the DOS kernel constructs a disk sector block for the largest possible block and returns control to SYSINIT after a copyright message is displayed. At this point, the DOS kernel is initialized, and SYSINIT continues by processing the optional CONFIG.SYS file.

At this time, the CONFIG.SYS file, if present, gives instructions to the DOS kernel telling which loadable device drivers will become memory resident, which command shell interpreter to use, the number of additional I/O buffers to set aside, and the number of file control blocks to set aside, among other things.

Also at this time, all loadable device drivers, such as ANSI.SYS (the standard screen and keyboard driver), and those unique to add-in hardware (clock/calendar boards, extended memory boards, network boards), are loaded into memory in the order of their appearance within the CONFIG.SYS file.

These device drivers call their own initialization routines and are subsequently linked into a device driver list. The initialization code within each driver must notify SYSINIT of its memory requirements, so that enough memory may be reserved. When the device drivers have been loaded, and the other parameters within the CONFIG.SYS file have been processed, all file handles are closed, with the exception of CON, PRN and AUX.

CON is the file handle name for the console (video screen); PRN is the file handle name for the parallel port (also known as LPT1); and AUX is the file handle name for the auxiliary output (also the console under normal circumstances).

CON, PRN, and AUX are reopened by SYSINIT as the standard input/standard output, standard error/standard list, and standard auxiliary devices. This allows for user-supplied character drivers to supersede the BIOS drivers as the standard devices.

After this is done, SYSINIT issues a call to the DOS EXEC function which then loads the COMMAND.COM command interpreter shell (or other if specified in the CONFIG.SYS shell parameter). COMMAND.COM has two portions; the resident portion which occupies low memory, and the transient portion which occupies high memory and is reloadable if necessary.

When COMMAND.COM has been loaded, it checks to see if a special file called AUTOEXEC.BAT exists in the root directory of the boot disk. If it does exist, COMMAND.COM will read and execute each entry within the AUTOEXEC.BAT file a line at a time until the file is exhausted or until another BAT file is executed.

Prior to DOS 3.3, BAT files could only be executed in a serial fashion; that is, they could only be daisy chained, except when loading a secondary copy of COMMAND.COM. In DOS 3.3 it became possible to execute nested BAT files from within one another. As each BAT file completes, control is returned to its caller, and ultimately to DOS.

When the AUTOEXEC.BAT file (or its chain sequence) has completed, then DOS is ready for processing, even though the boot sequence officially ended just prior to execution of the AUTOEXEC.BAT file. Since this file automatically gets executed only upon boot, it was logical to mention it as part of the boot sequence, and may be thought of as a post boot task.

At the end of the normal boot sequence, the DOS one megabyte address space memory map should look similar to the one depicted in Figure 1-1.

DOS and Interrupts

An interrupt is a signal that causes the CPU to suspend processing and transfer control to a special program called an interrupt handler. An interrupt may be generated either by hardware or software. The interrupt handler program is responsible for determining the cause of the interrupt, taking appropriate actions, and for then returning control back to its calling process.

Interrupts are usually caused by events, external to the CPU, that usually require immediate attention. Examples of these might be a signal indicating completion of an I/O sequence such as i. serial communications, a report of some hardware trouble or failure, or other major problems such as a power failure.

For reasons of efficiency, most modern processors are designed to support multiple interrupt types. Information about interrupts such as the type, handler location, and interrupt identification are called interrupt vectors. In the DOS architecture, a special area of memory has been set aside to store interrupt vectors: the interrupt vector table.

Interrupt Types and The Interrupt Vector Table

The DOS interrupt vector table resides at the lowest end of memory, occupying the first 1024 bytes, starting at address 0000 hex and going through 03FF hex. This table contains pointers to the handler routines for the DOS interrupts. Different interrupt types may have precedence over others for special handling. Each interrupt table entry is four bytes long and contains the address (segment and offset) of the corresponding handler routine.

The interrupt types are numbered (in hex) from 0 through 0FF. The interrupts ranging from 0 through 1F are the lowest level type and are used exclusively for internal/external hardware interrupts. The interrupts ranging from 20 through 3F are used by DOS for its software interrupts. The remaining interrupts to the end of the address range for the table (03FF) are available for user software interrupts or for external hardware devices and system device drivers.

During program execution, internal hardware interrupts are generated by events such as the detection of an attempt to perform a mathematical division by zero. In such cases, the handler's assignment is physically wired into the processor hardware and is not able to be modified, as in software interrupts. An external hardware interrupt is generated by an external hardware controller or co-processor, such as a math co-processor or UART communications device.

The external interrupts may be set as non-maskable (NMI) or maskable (INTR) interrupts. NMI interrupts generally are caused by memory fault (parity) errors, power failures, or other catastrophic events. With a device called the Intel 8259A Programmable Interrupt Controller, or PIC for short, it is possible to channel external interrupts. The 8259A is controlled by the CPU and communicates via a hardware circuit (called the INTR pin) by way of signals, allowing interrupts to be enabled or disabled for specific devices, and also allowing for the interrupts to be under program control and adjustable precedence for handling.

Software interrupts may be generated synchronously by application programs through the use of the INT instruction. Basically, an application program obtains control of an interrupt by resetting one of the interrupt vectors. This is done by changing the pointer (address) of the interrupt handler routine to the user supplied code. The interrupt address has a relationship to its interrupt number. Since the table entries are all four bytes long, the interrupt number — when multiplied by four — gives the displacement within the table; its interrupt vector address. Hardware and software interrupts are listed in Table 1-1 and Table 1-2.

Table 1-1: Hardware and ROM BIOS Interrupts

INT	CLASS	ADDRESS	DESCRIPTION
00	Internal Hardware	00-03H	Divide By Zero Trap
01	Internal Hardware	04-07H	Single Step
02	External Hardware	08-0BH	NMI (non-maskable interrupt)
03	Internal Software	0C-0FH	Breakpoint trap (for debuggers)
04	Internal Hardware	10-13H	Overflow Detection
05	ROM-BIOS Software	14-17H	Print Screen
06	Internal Hardware	18-1BH	RESERVED/Invalid Op-Code[*]
07	Internal Hardware	1C-1FH	RESERVED/Processor Extension Not Available[*]
08	External Hardware	20-23H	Timer Tick/Double Exception[*]
09	External Hardware	24-27H	Keyboard Device Input/Segment Overrun[*]
0A	External Hardware	28-2BH	RESERVED/Invalid Task State Segment[*]
0B	External Hardware	2C-2FH	Serial Port Device (COM2)/Segment Not Present
0C	External Hardware	30-33H	Serial Port Device (COM1)/Stack Segment Overr
0D	External Hardware	34-37H	Fixed Disk Device (XT)/General Protection Fau
0E	External Hardware	38-3BH	Floppy Disk Device
0F	External Hardware	3C-3FH	Printer Controller Device
10	ROM-BIOS Software	40-43H	Video I/O
11	ROM-BIOS Software	44-47H	Equipment Configuration Check
12	ROM-BIOS Software	48-4BH	Memory Size Check
13	ROM-BIOS Software	4C-4FH	Floppy Disk/Fixed Disk Driver
14	ROM-BIOS Software	50-53H	Communications Port I/O Driver
15	ROM-BIOS Software	54-57H	Cassette I/O/(AT Auxiliary Functions)
16	ROM-BIOS Software	58-5BH	Keyboard I/O Driver
17	ROM-BIOS Software	5C-5FH	Printer I/O Driver
18	ROM-BIOS Software	60-63H	ROM BASIC/Not present in non-IBM machines
19	ROM-BIOS Software	64-67H	Bootstrap Loader
1A	ROM-BIOS Software	68-6BH	TOD Clock Control
1B	ROM-BIOS Software	6C-6FH	Control-Break Handler
1C	ROM-BIOS Software	70-73H	Timer Control
1D	dummy	74-77H	Points to video initialization table
1E	dummy	78-7BH	Points to diskette parameter table
1F	dummy	7C-7FH	Points to ASCII graphics table (128-255)

*80286 Only

Table 1-2: Software Interrupts

INT	CLASS	ADDRESS	DESCRIPTION
20	Software Interrupt	80-83	General purpose program terminate/(obsolete)
21	Software Interrupt	84-87	DOS Function Call Dispatcher/used by DOS
22	Software Interrupt	88-8B	Terminate vector (pointer only)/used by DOS
23	Software Interrupt	8C-8F	Control-C vector (pointer only)/used by DOS
24	Software Interrupt	90-93	Critical Error vector (pointer only)/used by DOS
25	Software Interrupt	94-97	Absolute Disk Read/used by DOS
26	Software Interrupt	98-9B	Absolute Disk Write/used by DOS
27	Software Interrupt	9C-9F	TSR vector (obsolete)/used by DOS
28-5F	Software Interrupt	A0-17F	RESERVED for DOS/used by DOS
60-67	Software Interrupt	180-19F	Available/User Defined
68-7F	Software Interrupt	1A0-1FF	Stat

Properly handling interrupts in DOS requires special attention. Typically, interrupt handlers must perform specific tasks in order to be certain they won't corrupt the operating system and interfere with other interrupt handlers. In preparation for handling interrupts, the interrupt handler must modify the interrupt vector table:

- If previously enabled, interrupts must be disabled so they don't occur while the vectors are being modified.

- The vector for the interrupt of particular interest must be initialized to point to the correct handler routine.

- If interrupts have been previously disabled, make sure that all other vectors point at a valid interrupt handler routine.

- Enable all interrupts again.

The interrupt handler must also perform the following steps:

- The system context must be preserved by storing the flags, registers, etc., and any other area of memory that will be affected or modified by the handler, to a save area within the handler's own memory area.

- Interrupts that may interfere with the handling of the current one must be disabled, and this is sometimes done automatically at the hardware level.

- Any interrupts that are allowed or necessary should be enabled.

- The cause of the interrupt must be determined by the current handler routine.

- Execute the appropriate logic to handle the interrupt according to its cause, and perform any other interrupt-related processing.

- When finished processing the interrupt, the system context must be restored to the state just prior to the current handler's execution.

- All interrupts disabled or blocked by the current handler must be re-enabled.

- Return control back to the interrupted process.

The process sounds simple and straightforward enough, but it can be difficult and; in fact, writing interrupt handlers and device drivers requires advanced programming skills and expertise in the DOS world.

Reaching Outside The One Megabyte Address Space

As mentioned earlier, the dynamic memory area available to users within the DOS one megabyte address space is limited to a maximum of 640K or, through trickery, sometimes up to 704k. (This is done by accessing unused memory areas within the one meg region.) There is a mechanism through which it is possible to perform bank switched memory expansion, using the Lotus/Intel/Microsoft Expanded Memory Specification. Many companies now provide add-in boards of memory, such as the Intel Above Board or the AST Advantage Board. These boards, and many others like them, allow for applications to make use of memory outside of the limitations imposed by the DOS architecture.

The first add-in board is something called Expanded Memory. Expanded memory uses a special device driver, usually called EMM (Expanded Memory Manager). The LIM/EMS provides the specifications and means for using up to eight megabytes of memory outside of the DOS one megabyte address space. The driver, EMM.SYS (or some form of this name), provides an interface between the user applications and the hardware in a hardware independent manner.

Usually, the vendors of the add-in extended/expanded memory boards will also provide the driver software necessary to make their hardware work on a DOS system. The driver software is basically a character device driver that is linked dynamically into the operating system through specification in the CONFIG.SYS file at boot time.

The EMM driver makes expanded memory available in increments of 16k byte areas called pages, and maps them into an area, called a page frame, that is 64k bytes in size. The page frame resides in expanded memory above the one megabyte address space, the exact location being user configurable, avoiding possible conflicts with other hardware or software drivers.

The EMM driver consists of two major parts: the driver and the manager. The driver has many of the characteristics of standard device drivers, such as initialization and output status functions, and also includes a valid device header. The manager portion is the real interface between applications and the physical expanded memory hardware. Among the many classes of provided services are:

- Allocation management of expanded memory pages.
- Deallocation management of expanded memory pages.
- Diagnostic routines.
- Multitasking capabilities.
- Mapping management of logical pages to physical page frames.
- Hardware and software functionality verification.

In DOS, the software interrupt 67H is provided to allow applications to directly communicate with the EMM. Examples of applications that make use of expanded memory are print spooler programs such as the latest versions of AST Research's SUPERSPOOL program; RAM disk programs such as the VDISK.COM program distributed with DOS; and Microsoft Windows 2.0 which uses expanded memory for the swapping area if it is present.

Extended memory is the second way of accessing memory outside of the DOS one megabyte address space. It is frequently confused with expanded memory. Extended memory, IBM's terminology, is used to reference memory at those physical addresses outside of the DOS one megabyte address space, but accessible to the 80286 while it is running in protected mode.

Recently there have been some vendors, such as Everex Inc., who provide memory expansion boards (for the 80286) that may be used in either expanded or extended mode via their EMM drivers. Up to 16 megabytes may be addressed directly using extended memory.

The DOS File System

The original design of the Personal Computer was a floppy diskette-based model, using removable media that was capable of writing to a maximum of 186k bytes on a single side. Today, the floppy disk is used primarily to introduce new software into the system, perform backups, or create easily transportable disks for loading onto other systems. This is because of the widespread use of hard disks, also called fixed disks.

The hard disk technology has evolved to a state where it is not unusual to find a basic system with a minimum of 30-40 megabytes of hard disk space, as well as a floppy diskette drive capable of 1.4 megabytes of storage on a single 3.5 inch diskette. Recent developments in diskette technology are about to yield a 20 megabyte, 3.5 inch diskette. In describing the file system characteristics, the discussion will center mainly around hard disk-based systems.

Current Drive

In DOS, the concept of the current drive is similar to the IBM VM operating system's concept of the logged drive, although the underlying file systems are nothing alike.

In DOS it is possible to have several disk drives. In fact, it is possible to have a total of 26 drives, physical or logical, with a letter of the alphabet assigned as the reference name for each drive.

Drive A is always the first floppy diskette drive. Drive B, if present, is always the second floppy disk drive. Some systems are limited to only two floppy diskette drives, although on most systems there is a limit of four floppy disk drives, ending at address D. This is very hardware dependent from vendor to vendor. Usually, in today's systems, there are only one or two floppy diskette drives actually installed, even though there are many people with three floppy diskette systems that include a 360k drive, a 1.2 meg drive, and a 1.4 meg drive. In any case, the first fixed disk drive is usually at address C, regardless if there are only one or two floppy diskette drives.

The first fixed disk can never be the B drive. When DOS is booted, the bootstrap program always attempts to load from the first diskette drive. On IBM systems, if the diskette drive is not ready (drive door open), the program proceeds to check all available floppy disk drives until they are exhausted, and then attempts the bootstrap load from the first fixed disk.

Although it is possible to format any hard disk to contain the boot strap and operating system, only the first hard disk may actually be booted from. On IBM and other mainframes, the boot device (called the IPL device) is usually an option that may be set just prior to performing the initial program load, or boot sequence.

When DOS finally has finished booting, the current drive is the boot drive. In the AUTOEXEC.BAT file, a command to change the current drive is permissible and frequently is done either directly or via execution of a subsequent BAT file that does the change.

For the sake of discussion, assume a system with one floppy disk drive (A) and two fixed disk drives (C and D), each of them a 20 megabyte disk drive. If there is no bootable diskette in the A drive, then the system boot occurs from the C drive; otherwise, an error is displayed.

If after the boot sequence, DOS displays the prompt "C", then the current drive is the C drive. This means that in any file operations

specified without a full path name which, includes the disk drive address, the current drive is assumed to be the default.

In order to change to another drive, simply enter the drive letter
followed by a colon and the enter key, as in "d:", which would make
the current drive the D drive and which would display the prompt "D"
in an uncustomized system.

To switch to the A drive is just as simple — enter "a:". From the
time that the current drive is changed to another address, all of the
disk and file operations affect that specific drive, unless the command
syntax includes the specific drive information. This is important when
performing file and directory deletion functions, even more so when
using the DOS format command.

A fully qualified path string name is in the following format:

```
<disk:\path\>command
```

Disk is the disk drive letter, defaulting to the current disk if
omitted. *Path* is the full directory and subdirectory path (also optional
and defaulting to the current directory), where the command may be
found. *Command* is either a DOS command or the name of any executable user program with the extension of COM or EXE, or any
BAT file containing a list of commands to perform.

Directory Paths

DOS has a hierarchical file system, much like that of the UNIX system, although it is not as complex. It resembles an inverted tree
structure, beginning with a root directory. A directory contains only
two things, files and subdirectories. A subdirectory is the same thing
as a directory structure, but appears within another directory. There
is a practical limit within DOS of 255 levels of subdirectories, although four levels are usually adequate.

The parent directory that stores all of the other subdirectories is
called the root directory, analogous to the roots of a tree. It is possible
to store many files and directories in the root directory, but on a well
kept DOS system, the root directory contains only the hidden system

files, the COMMAND.COM program, an AUTOEXEC.BAT file and the CONFIG.SYS file. The rest are subdirectories for the various software products or files the user has. It is possible to place COMMAND.COM in a subdirectory and specify its location in the CONFIG.SYS file using the SHELL directive, as in the following example:

```
SHELL=C:\DOS41\COMMAND.COM
```

In IBM mainframe terminology, a DOS directory is loosely analogous to a PDS (partitioned data set), containing a related set of sequential files. DOS directories should be created for the same purpose — to keep related sets of files apart from unrelated sets of files. If, for example, it was desirable to isolate all of the DOS external commands from the rest of the files on disk, we might create a subdirectory in the root directory and call it "DOS41" (to indicate DOS 4.1). All of the external commands from the DOS distribution diskettes could then be copied into that subdirectory; and the subdirectory name could be added to the search path.

A good reason for separation of files using subdirectories is when installing new software on a system. It is a frequent occurrence for vendors to supply their own recommended versions of AUTOEXEC.BAT or CONFIG.SYS. When copying files from one location to another, DOS does not bother to verify replacement of files with the same name, it just does. So when users install a package that has the vendor's idea of what the AUTOEXEC.BAT and CONFIG.SYS files should contain, they could be in for a surprise, especially if their previous CONFIG.SYS or AUTOEXEC.BAT files contained special information, such as extended memory or network device driver configuration parameters.

DOS File Extensions

DOS uses standard naming convention for files. Users may name their files anything they like, with certain limitations. The file name may be broken into two parts, the file name and the file extension. The file name may be up to eight characters in length and may contain special characters. (It is possible to use white space characters as part of the file name, although this is not a good idea.) A file extension may be added to further classify what type of file it is. The extension is optional for some files and required by others, for instance, all binary executable files must have an extension of either COM or EXE.

The file name is separated from the file extension with the period character, called a dot by most DOS users — as in CONFIG.SYS, pronounced "CONFIG dot SYS". The file extension of BAT is also reserved for DOS use, indicating that this file is to be processed as a command list for COMMAND.COM. The operating system will need to be re-booted if non-executable files are renamed with extensions of either COM or EXE and then executed.

DOS stores certain information about each file entry (32 bytes) in the directory with which it is associated. That information includes: the file name; the file extension; the file attribute; a reserved space; the time the file was created or last modified; the date the file was created or last modified; the starting disk cluster address; and the total file size in bytes.

More detailed information about the location of all subsequent blocks of a file are kept in the disk's special area called the file allocation table, which is insulated from user applications by the access methods. Files may have attributes of *hidden, system, archive, read-only,* or *read-write.* The DOS system files on the boot disk are usually marked hidden, system and read-only.

DOS Customization

The DOS system was designed for ease of customization; however, there are set limitations as to how much it can be customized. For example, a DOS hardware configuration can easily be modified by simply adding in the device. There is no need to regenerate the DOS kernel. The reasons for this are twofold. First, PC's initially were designed to be used as home machines, and as such mandated that they be easy to operate and maintain by the customer (user). Secondly, systems designed to regenerate their kernels require additional overhead, both in startup time as well as in regeneration support utilities. Had the DOS system been designed for dynamic kernel regeneration, the level of technical competence for PC owners would certainly be more than what is required of them today.

Instead of reconfiguring the kernel, DOS uses devices drivers that are specified in CONFIG.SYS, if and when they are necessary. Adding a second hard drive to a PC usually does not require special device drivers, unless the drive has special characteristics that require control logic beyond the basic DOS I/O routines.

Addition of certain other devices, however, usually do require the addition of special device drivers. Examples of these are extended/expanded memory boards, network access boards, and specialized graphics boards. Without the new device's special driver, DOS cannot access the device. Part of a device driver's function is to provide mapping of an address within the DOS standard one megabyte address space, to an address on the device.

As an example of how a UNIX system contrasts with DOS in this area, consider the following. A new disk is added to a DOS system. All the user has to do before the disk is usable, is to execute the DOS command, FDISK.COM, to create a DOS partition table on the disk, then run the FORMAT.COM command to properly format it. After that the disk is ready to be used, unless of course, there are other special considerations that must first be taken care of for that device.

In the UNIX system, similar activities must be undertaken. A disk preparation utility must be executed which constructs the proper file system on the disk. UNIX systems, however, have special device files that must also be present in a special directory before the system can actually write to and read from the disk. There are also several disk partitioning options for which there is no corresponding DOS functionality or need. After the special file requirements have been addressed, a device driver must be loaded (if one that is capable of communicating with the particular device does not already exist in memory) for the kernel to effect I/O to the device. Depending upon the device and the driver software, sometimes it may also be necessary to reboot the system. UNIX device drivers usually check for a response from the device to verify whether or not to load the driver. If there is no response from a device, then the kernel doesn't waste the memory by loading unnecessary drivers.

DOS, on the other hand, simply loads any and all device drivers specified in CONFIG.SYS, regardless if the device exists or not. This can cause serious problems, and indeed, has. As an example, if a device driver is poorly written in DOS so that it attempts to manipulate a device that doesn't exist, it is possible (and likely) that the system will hang during the boot process. One experience that comes to mind was when an expanded memory device driver was given a parameter indicating more memory than was actually available. During the boot process, the driver tried to access the phantom memory and simply hung the system, making it impossible for the boot process to finish. It was necessary to boot from floppy disk so that the CONFIG.SYS file could be changed to indicate the correct memory parameters.

This type of event cannot happen in a UNIX environment; device drivers must perform basic error recovery routines to prevent interference with the operation of the kernel, and are loaded only when all error checking flags are clear.

Another major difference, regarding operating environment customization, is that in DOS, device drivers must be loaded into memory at boot time. In UNIX systems, device drivers may be loaded (and unloaded) at any time. This means that if changes are made to existing drivers specified in CONFIG.SYS, or if new ones are added, DOS must be rebooted before they become effective. This is not necessarily true for UNIX-based device drivers.

Time-Slicing in DOS

DOS users are painfully aware that it is a single tasking operating environment. The PC hardware architecture of the 8086/8088 is capable of performing multitasking operations, it is the DOS operating system architecture and design that causes the problem. The IBM PC/AT, based on the Intel 80286 processor, was originally designed to operate in a protected memory mode, specifically for multitasking, that was never implemented in DOS. Instead, OS/2 was designed and developed for that purpose.

When a program in DOS is loaded and executed, program execution usually does not require 100 percent of the available CPU processing time. An example of this is a word processing or text editing application; the CPU is idle most of the time, even between the keystrokes of the fastest typist. A multitasking system makes use of the idle time between applications, by providing each application with a *time-slice*.

A time-slice is a fixed time interval (usually a couple of microseconds or nanoseconds) in which a program has access to the CPU. After the time-slice interval expires, the next application is given its time-slice, then the next one and so on. This process is repeated in a "round-robin" fashion; each application receives its time-slice until all awaiting applications have had their access to the CPU, and then the cycle is repeated.

Although only a single task actually has the CPU resources at a given instant, computer systems processing instructions at the speed of light and switching time-slices between applications (usually called programs or processes), create an illusion of several tasks running at the same time. Computer hardware doesn't do the task of switching time-slices between processes; it is the job of an operating system component usually called the scheduler, task dispatcher, or supervisor.

Programs are loaded and executed by the DOS EXEC function call. Any program may execute another program by invoking the EXEC function call. The caller program is known as the *parent*, the called program is known as the *child*. Processing of the parent is suspended until the child program is finished. DOS itself is a parent, so when a user application program is loaded, DOS transfers control to it until the application is finished.

If a child program terminates abnormally, sometimes it is likely that DOS will not be able to regain control in order to reload the parent, or if DOS itself was the parent, the system will simply hang and must be rebooted.

To address this problem, a protected memory mechanism was designed into the PC hardware. DOS, however, does not have the program logic to make use of the protected memory features in the hardware.

Multitasking on PCs that are running DOS can be achieved by using terminate and stay resident (TSR) programs such as Borland's SideKick or by using a multitasking application that takes over the PC's resources and acts as the system's task dispatcher/scheduler, such as Microsoft Windows and Quarterdec Systems' DesqView products.

The first method, using TSRs in DOS, is a less than perfect method, to be kind. There are numerous flaws with TSR programs as well as a lack of willingness on behalf of the vendors of such programs, to adhere to a universal TSR standard, despite the fact that there have been attempts by major vendors to do this .

The second method, using a multitasking program as a substitute for an operating system's task scheduler mechanism, has some serious drawbacks in DOS. The basic problem is that existing software, written specifically for DOS, is not mandated to follow any particular rules as to how a program behaves when it has control of the system, even though there are recommended programming conventions and guidelines.

In order for applications to "behave" when they are run under program scheduling systems such as Microsoft Windows, they must be written so that they do not violate any of the basic rules such as how the application uses resources including memory, video hardware, and keyboard devices. Only when a program is developed using the scheduling system's application development routines, is there a guarantee that the application manager's policies will not be violated.

This doesn't mean that other applications will not run under these systems; it just means that when an "ill behaved" application is executed (one that violates the policies and may require special resources that would interfere with the scheduling system), it is treated differently by being loaded and executed using the EXEC function call. In this manner the application takes over the complete system for as long as it is active. When that application terminates normally, the scheduling system regains control and goes about time-slicing to the other applications under its control.

Not all native DOS applications require exclusive use of the system, only certain ones. The type of CPU processor in use also has a direct impact on whether or not an ill behaved application must be loaded as a standalone application under the task scheduling system. For example, Microsoft Windows 386 runs on Intel 80386-based systems in virtual machine mode. This means that applications running under Windows 386 on a system based on the 80386 processor, receive a 640k simulation of the DOS transient program area. Windows 386 is able to manage multiple DOS regions because of the protected memory features of the machine hardware. This would not be possible otherwise.

If an application abnormally terminates (on non-80386 processors), the chances of the task scheduling system making a successful recovery are slim. On systems that provide protected memory and virtual memory management, recovery is usually possible. The reason this is not always true is due to DOS, not the hardware.

UNIX-based implementations make use of the 80286 and 80386 hardware architecture and provide excellent process recovery capabilities. The UNIX operating system itself is rarely ever incapable of recovering if an application process abnormally terminates.

DOS was not designed to run more than one process and, as a result, simply lacks the program logic to do basic functions such as process recovery for abnormally terminated programs, or to prevent one process from overwriting the memory address space of another. In fact, DOS does nothing to prevent an application from writing over any of the writable areas, such as the interrupt vector table or the resident portion of COMMAND.COM, it occupies. Since COMMAND.COM is directly adjacent to the transient program area, it is not uncommon for an application to write over that area, usually resulting in a message that indicates the command processor cannot continue and the system is halted.

OS/2 is designed to prevent this from happening, as well as to provide and enforce application development standards that avoid the possibility of ill behaved applications. In a sense, OS/2 is really just DOS with internal design modifications necessary to implement multitasking. For some reason, probably related to marketing, IBM and

Microsoft have decided not to name the new multitasking, PC-based operating system DOS; choosing instead to call it OS/2.

The UNIX system, in contrast to OS/2, is far more reliable and has had more debugging and enhancement hours spent on it than on any other operating system in the world. Applications developed for OS/2 will run only on PCs; those developed for UNIX are portable to virtually every kind of computer hardware.

DOS Application Development

The DOS application development environment varies between machines and even from developer to developer. Perhaps this is good, because it ultimately produces a variety of software tools from which developers can choose. Perhaps it is bad, from the point of view that there is no *standard* development environment.

There are at least a dozen or more implementations of C compilers, an almost equal number of assemblers and Pascal compilers, and as many Basic interpreters and compilers. The different implementations of each of these introduce additional functions that are not necessarily part of the ANSI specification for C. These additional functions frequently do not adhere to the Kernighan and Ritchie standards. Although they are quite powerful and very useful in the PC environment, it nevertheless makes them non-portable to other environments, including UNIX.

The DOS environment, with its impressively large, installed user base, is rich with software of all types. Most notable, however, are the software development tools which are second to none, including those for the mainframe world. Some shining examples are Borland's Turbo C, Turbo Assembler and Turbo Debugger packages; Microsoft's C Compiler, Macro Assembler 5.1, CodeView debugger, and Windows Software Developers Kit; Greenleaf's C Functions Library packages; and the many fine software development products from Phoenix Associates, to name a few.

Other key parts of software development tools are version control systems, automated compilation utilities, documentation tools, and of course, the most fundamental tool: the text editor with which programmers write their code.

This is perhaps the only area in which UNIX may not be up to speed, depending upon one's point of view. It's not that there is a shortage of good tools, it's just that the available tools do not have the polished user interfaces and advanced functionality that some of the DOS counterparts have. With the advent of X Window, NeWS, and Suntools graphical windowing environments emerging as standards in the UNIX world, this is all changing rapidly.

The only software development tools that are a part of the standard DOS distribution are the DEBUG command (from which assembler programs may be developed, also used for debugging), the LINK command used to generate executables from object code, the EDLIN text editor (functional but retarded by real-world standards), and a handful of other non-essential commands that can be considered developers' tools.

C compilers, assemblers, object library maintenance utilities and automated program generation utilities are all not standard and must be obtained through third party vendors as optional components. This creates a situation where mixing development tools can cause incompatibilities and user interface inconsistencies. The reasons are understandable, not everyone that uses DOS is a programmer and requires programming development facilities.

The same is true of UNIX-based systems; although most UNIX based installations do have an applications development staff. Given that UNIX systems are multiuser, application developers usually share the system with non-programmers. For this reason, most UNIX-based systems usually have the Program Development Set, a set of software development tools (C compiler, pre-compilers, linker, debuggers, and source code version control system), online.

Where the two operating system environments differ greatly is in the tools and naming conventions of the tools. There is no "Turbo" version of anything on UNIX systems. Only in more recent times have there even been tools available, besides those distributed as part of the standard development set. This, too, is changing daily.

CHAPTER 2

INTRODUCTION TO UNIX SYSTEM V

The origins of UNIX date back to 1965, when Bell Laboratories, General Electric, and the Massachusetts Institute of Technology began a joint project for a new operating system called Multics. This new operating system was to provide multiuser, data processing facilities to a large number of concurrent users. By 1969, the Multics operating system was running on a GE 645 computer system, though it fell short of meeting the original goals. As a result, Bell Laboratories decided to withdraw from the project.

Many of the technicians who participated on the Multics project went on to become involved with the development of UNIX.

UNIX is attributed to having been the brainchild of Ken Thompson and Dennis Ritchie, computer scientists working for Bell Laboratories, who had previously worked on the Multics project. Thompson, Ritchie, and a handful of others (Rudd Canaday, Joe Ossanna, and Doug McIlroy) had first drawn up notes and sketches of what was to become the first UNIX file system.

Ken Thompson had written programs that simulated the workings of his proposed file system, simulations of program behavior executing in a demand paging environment, and a simple operating system kernel for the GE 645 hardware. He had also been working on a game called "Space Travel," written in FORTRAN on a Honeywell 635 computer with a GECOS operating system, and had found that it was expensive to run and had experienced some difficulties in controlling the "space ship" in the program.

Thompson discovered a relatively obscure and little-used DEC PDP-7 computer that was immediately enlisted as a development system for the Space Travel game program, and yielded inexpensive computing power as well as a good graphical display. Development of the game enabled Thompson to learn quickly about the internals of the PDP-7 hardware. This development was cumbersome since there was no compiler available and the program had to be cross-assembled from the Honeywell GECOS system, converted to paper tape and read into the PDP-7.

Thompson and Ritchie advanced their designs and began implementing them on the PDP-7. These designs included the first version of the UNIX file system, a set of utility programs, and a process control subsystem. Soon after, the GECOS system was unnecessary as the development system because the PDP-7 system could support itself.

Another member of their team, Brian Kernighan, dubbed the new operating system UNIX, a pun on the original Multics system on which they had previously worked.

The first practical use of the new operating system was meeting text processing requirements of the patent department at Bell Laboratories, which was running on a DEC PDP-11 in 1971.

In looking at the amount of computer power wielded by UNIX, consider that the first UNIX system required only 16k bytes for the operating system; another 8k for user programs; and a disk device with 512k storage, with individual files limited to only 64k each. While this certainly sounds like the true microcomputer operating system, the first true microprocessor did not come until 1971, with the introduction of the Intel 4004 chip that was used mainly in electronic calculators.

The first UNIX operating systems were written in the assembler language native to the machine they ran on. Thompson had begun implementation of a FORTRAN compiler for UNIX, but instead wound up developing a new language called B, (influenced by another language called BCPL — Martin Richards, 1969). The main drawback to B language was that it was an interpretive language, translated into execution code a single line at a time.

Dennis Ritchie (the principal author of C language) developed the interpretive B language into C language that produced machine code and allowed for definition of data structures and declaration of data types. The entire UNIX operating system was converted to C language in 1973, making it the first operating system ever converted to a higher level language from assembly language. It made portability possible to any machine with a C compiler.

The number of UNIX machines gradually increased, at first within Bell Labs, where a UNIX Systems Group soon was assembled for internal support. At the time, AT&T couldn't legally market computer products because of a Consent Decree signed with the Federal government in 1956.

UNIX continued to gain popularity and acceptance within the Bell system, particularly among the OTC's (operating telephone companies). AT&T did not advertise or attempt to market the system in accordance with the 1956 decree; however, it did grant software licenses to universities and a few commercial institutions.

In 1977, UNIX was ported to run on non-PDP hardware, the Interdata 8/32 computer. Rewriting the UNIX operating system in C had paid off, as the port required few major changes. Soon other companies began porting UNIX to new hardware and, along the way, enhanced and customized the operating system until there were many varieties that varied from the basic system. Even within AT&T there were several variants that were ultimately combined into a standard system by Bell Labs, known as UNIX System III.

Actually, the earliest version of UNIX still likely to be encountered is UNIX Version 6; the next oldest is Version 7, and then comes UNIX System III. UNIX System V was developed and released by Bell Labs in January of 1983, from an internal version of System IV that was never released.

There is another major variant of UNIX acknowledged by the user community, known as BSD 4.1 or BSD 4.2, that was developed by the computer science department at the University of California at

Berkeley. The BSD flavor of UNIX contained certain enhancements, such as the "vi" text editor that has found its way to UNIX System V as a standard.

Today, UNIX System V is currently at release level 3, with many additional ports currently under way by companies such as AT&T, Microsoft, IBM, Amdahl, Hewlett-Packard, Sun Microsystems, DEC, Microport, Bell Technologies, and others. UNIX System V Release 4 is scheduled for delivery sometime in early 1989, and will reportedly feature a new graphical user interface, called OpenLook (developed jointly by AT&T and Sun Microsystems, Inc.) The hardware spectrum UNIX runs on ranges from PC microprocessors to the most powerful mainframes, as well as the newer super-micro workstations with near mainframe performance capabilities.

What is UNIX?

UNIX is an operating system; a collection of programs designed to control the interactions of the lowest level machine functions and application programs.

The UNIX operating system controls the resources of the computer, manages them amongst several concurrent users, performs the scheduling of tasks (processes), controls the peripheral devices connected to the system, provides file system management functions, and generally hides the inner machine architecture from the end user. This is accomplished through an architecture that uses layers of software designed for different purposes, as described in the following section.

UNIX Layered Architecture

The UNIX system layered architecture is depicted in Figure 2-1.

At the heart of the layered model is the hardware that is the physical makeup of the computer system. This includes the central processor unit (CPU), random access memory (RAM), a memory management unit (MMU), computer terminals, disk devices, and so on. The next layer is the heart of the operating system, the UNIX kernel which provides the low level interface between the hardware and user layers. The kernel will be discussed later in detail.

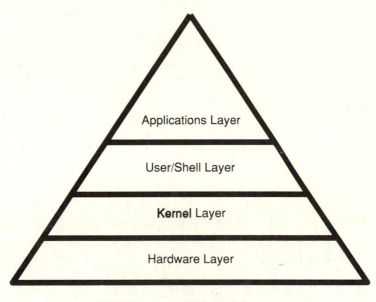

UNIX Layered Architecture

Figure 2-1: UNIX Layered Architecture

The next layer is the user layer which consists of the UNIX command interpreter shell, the external command set, programs such as the editor **vi**, and other utility programs and tools such as **nroff, grep, date, wc, who, ld, as,** and **comp,** to name a few. The final layer is the application layer consisting of the C compiler (**cc**) and other application programs developed by application programmers.

Programs at the user and application layers interact with the UNIX kernel through system calls, a set of routines designed to perform certain system functions. There are a number of system calls available to applications ranging from time and date routines, to enabling programs to share information from separate memory address spaces (known as inter process communications or IPC in UNIX terminology.)

The File System

The UNIX file system is an important aspect of the operating system. The file system is where system and user files are stored on the physical disk media. It is organized into an inverted tree structure with the beginning or root at the very top, branching downward. This structure is depicted in the Figure 2-2.

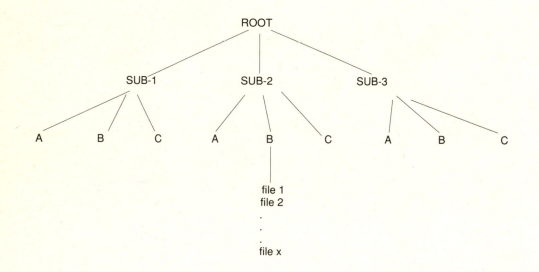

Figure 2-2: UNIX File System Structure

The root directory can contain files, links, or other directories, called subdirectories. The subdirectories are sometimes called **branch nodes,** while files in directories are sometimes called **leaf nodes**. *There is no imposed limit to the number of node levels, except those of* *the physical hardware, although there are certain performance implications to having an excessive number of levels.*

The **path name** is an ASCII text string containing the sequence of directories leading to a particular file or subdirectory. If the objective of a path name is a UNIX file, then the file name is included as part of the path name. The path name in UNIX may be of any length, where each node name is separated by a forward slash character and is from one to fourteen characters in length.

The / character has two purposes in the UNIX system; first, it is the character used to represent the name of the parent or **root directory** of the UNIX file system. Secondly, it is also used as the character that delimits node (directory) and file names.

The characters may be any particular one that a user chooses (of the ASCII character set), even special characters such as non-printable ones that may also have some other function. *(For example, it is possible to create directory or file names containing the backspace character, any control sequence or other special key sequence by preceding them with the backslash \ character, also known as the escape character.)*

In UNIX there is a concept of a current directory, the directory level in which a user is currently active. If users wanted to see the file system information for the root directory, they could either enter a command that contained the specific directory location or they could first change directories so that the root directory was the current directory, and then issue the command with or without the specific directory location.

In UNIX, the **ls** command is used to list information about files and directories, as opposed to the **dir** command in DOS. If users enter the command **ls -l**, the response would be a detailed listing of the files and directories within the current directory. If users wanted to see the file information about the root directory, then they could do one of two things.

First, users could simply enter the command **ls -l** / which indicates the specific directory to provide the listing for; in this case the root directory as indicated by the forward slash symbol /.

The alternative to this involves two steps; first, changing the current directory to become the root directory by entering the command **cd** / which changes directories to the root directory and; second, issuing the list file (**ls -l**) command. In this list file command it would be unnecessary to provide the specific directory location for the **ls** command to list, since the current directory *is* the root directory, the result of having previously executed the **cd** command.

Inodes

The UNIX file system is more than merely a bunch of files and directories. There are certain internals, some of which are important enough for application developers to be aware of, and these are explained here in some detail.

UNIX files are stored on auxiliary storage media, such as hard disk or floppy diskettes. In disk-based files, each file has a unique **inode**, or **information node.** An inode contains information used by processes, such as access information that includes file access permissions, the file's size in characters, file ownership information, and the location *(disk, cylinder, track, and sector addresses)* of the file's data area within the UNIX file system.

It is the UNIX kernel's job to convert path names specified in programs (processes) into the file's individual inode. Static inodes are read in from disk into an in-core inode by the kernel (for performance reasons), where they are manipulated whenever necessary. There are several fields that make up an inode entry. The information contained within the inode fields is somewhat analogous to the DSCB *(Data Set Control Block)* in most IBM mainframe file system architectures. These fields are described below.

File Ownership Field

Identifies the User-ID assigned ownership of the file, including the group ownership that is shared with the individual owner. It also indicates the access privileges for the rest of the user community. The superuser access privileges override any settings in this field.

File Type Field

Specifies the file type of this file; for example, regular, character/block special, directory, or FIFO (as in pipes).

File Permissions Field

Specifies the access level for the three classes of users (user, group, and world). The access level may be read only, write only, read/write, execute, no access, or any combination of these. Directories must have execute permission so users may search for file names within them.

File Access Timestamp Field

This field contains the time and date stamps for the file for creation or last modification dates and times. It also contains the date/time stamp for the last modification of the inode. (This field may be used to validate or to reconcile timestamps of sensitive files.)

Links Field

Specifies the number of links made to this file. This may be thought of as the number of aliases this file has within the file system. Links are explained later.

TOC Field

This field contains the "table of contents" that are the disk addresses of the sectors containing the data for this file. Files are often stored in a fragmented manner; that is, the data is stored in disk sectors that may or may not be adjacent to one another. These sectors are "chained" together by means of sector address pointers which give the illusion of a contiguous byte stream. This field contains the disk block addresses that contain the file's data.

File Size Field

This is the byte count of the file. If the file is 10 bytes in size, starting at offset 0, then the value in this field would be 10.

Inode entries are created or modified by the UNIX kernel when the data contents of the file are written to disk. The inode entries are actually written when the ownership, permissions, or link settings are modified. The inode values of a file may be modified without actual modification of the associated file's data.

The in-core version of the inode contains some different information than the static version on disk, such as:

- In-core Node Status: Indicates if a node is locked; if a process is waiting for the inode to unlock; if the file is a mount point; if in-core version of the inode is different than static version because of changes to the inode data; or, if the in-core version of the inode is different than the static version because of changes to the file's data.

- File System Information: Such as the logical device number of the file system containing the file.

- The inode Number: The linear array address of the inode used by the kernel.

- Pointers to other in-core structures used by the kernel.

- A Reference Count: Indicates the number of instances in which the file is in use (opened).

Other processes are prevented from simultaneous access of an inode if the in-core inode lock is set as active. When such access is attempted by processes that have been locked out, another flag is set so awaiting processes may be awakened when the inode in question has been unlocked. This is a simplified explanation of how the UNIX kernel performs some of its file management responsibilities and how inodes are used in relation to disk blocks.

Directories

A directory in the UNIX file system is a special kind of file containing data entries consisting of inode numbers and filenames for each of the entries within that directory. Each directory entry is 16 bytes in size;

2 bytes for the inode number and 14 bytes for a file name. *(File names are limited to a maximum of 14 bytes in the UNIX system, and may be a minimum of 1 byte.)*

If the inode number of a directory is 0, it indicates that the directory entry is empty; no files exist in that directory. The UNIX kernel manipulates directories in much the same way as it does files, using inode structures. To ensure proper directory modification and construction, processes may read directories, but only the kernel may write directories.

Directory access permissions are similar to file access permissions, they apply the same three levels of user access — owner, group, and world. Read access permission allows the directory contents to be read; write access permission allows the directory contents to be modified *(remove directories and files, create new subdirectories and files)*; and execute access permissions simply allow processes to search the directory for a file or directory name. (It is not possible to execute a directory).

The Superblock

The superblock is used in the UNIX file system to manage the allocation of disk blocks. While it is of no major interest to the average applications developer, there are a few points that should be understood about the superblock.

In the DOS environment, after the machine has been booted and is ready for work, the user may decide to quit working at any time. Typically, in DOS environments, when users quit working, they shut off the computer by switching off the power. This act usually produces disastrous consequences on UNIX file systems.

The reason is that there is information about the file system that needs to be written to disk before the system is shut down. Because of this need, there are special UNIX commands (**shutdown** and **sync**) to perform these functions.

The superblock information is part of what must be updated to disk before the system can be powered off. If this update does not happen, when the UNIX system is booted again, errors will be encountered during the standard file system check. These errors could be discrepancies in the free count and inode allocations that will affect files and directories modified during the last UNIX operating session.

These errors are sometimes difficult to repair, requiring special system administration intervention. In some cases the damage to the file system may be so extensive that it may be beyond normal repair and require extensive recovery management efforts.

The superblock contains the following information:

- The size of the file system.

- Total free blocks in the file system.

- List of the available free blocks in the file system.

- Index of the next free block in the free block list.

- Size of the inode list.

- Number of total free inodes in the file system.

- List of all free inodes in the file system.

- Index of the next free inode in the inode free list.

- Information about lock fields for the block and inode free lists.

- The superblock modification indicator flag.

The superblock is periodically written to disk by the kernel. Imagine what damage may result if the file system is traumatically shut down without first having written the superblock to disk.

Although there is no superblock or functional equivalent in the DOS system, similar results may be obtained on occasion, when the system is powered down during an active application. For example, any files that have been opened during a write operation, may have lost clusters of data sectors, resulting in an incomplete file.

There is no standard way of repairing this type of damage to a DOS file system. The DOS command **chkdsk** can be used to reclaim the lost clusters and to return them to the free list. Special software such as PC Tools and The Norton Utilities may be purchased separately to help with recovering lost clusters of data. Of course, experienced DOS users may also use DEBUG.COM in an attempt to recover lost data.

There is much more to the superblock than is being stated here, but that is mostly of importance to the UNIX system administrator or internals developer, and goes beyond the scope of this book. The superblock was mentioned here to warn of the possible hazards due to an improper shutdown sequence or sudden power failures, events to which DOS developers may not be sensitive.

Regular Files

Regular files are those that are created normally by processes. They contain either data or programs and are stored in a standard manner on disk. Each inode contains a TOC *(table of contents)* that contains the addresses of disk blocks which contain the data portion of the file. The data portion refers to the actual file contents, whether the file is a program or program data.

If file data were stored in contiguous disk blocks, all adjacent to one another, then only the starting block address and the length of the file would be necessary in order to read it. Unfortunately, data stored on hard or floppy disk media are not always stored adjacent to one another. In fact, the more the disk is used — as in creation, modification or deletion of files — the more fragmented the storage area is likely to become.

For this reason, in the UNIX file system it becomes necessary to store the disk block addresses where the data actually resides, within the file's inode entry in the TOC field. The kernel could be made to always allocate contiguous space for files, but the overhead this would cause would make even the fastest hardware seem slow.

Regularly scheduled disk maintenance, designed to compress the fragmented free space into contiguous space, is routinely performed by the UNIX system administrator. In some implementations of the UNIX system, the file system uses methods of storing data and inodes in a manner that doesn't require compression because the data is always in an optimally accessible state. An example of such an implementation is the Hewlett-Packard Series 9000/300 family of UNIX based-micros.

In order to keep the number of index entries in an inode to a minimum, direct and indirect blocks were created. A direct block has a one-to-one relationship with the data block to which it points; that is, the index entry points directly to the data block. A single indirect index entry contains the address of the block that points to the direct blocks. A double indirect block would contain pointers to single indirect blocks, triple indirect blocks would point to double indirect blocks, and so on.

If a logical data block could hold 1024 bytes (1k bytes), and block numbers are addressable as a 4 byte (32 bit) integer, then it is possible to hold up to 256 block numbers. Using this scheme, the maximum number of bytes a file could contain is over 16 gigabytes! The file size is effectively limited to 4 gigabytes because the file size field in the inode is only 32 bits (2^{32}) long.

Regular files are accessed by processes as a character stream by byte offset, with the first byte being at relative byte zero and continuing up to the size of the file. The kernel converts the byte offsets into disk blocks. This is done by converting inode information into logical and physical disk block locations. In the IBM mainframe world, this job would be performed by the access method control programs (SAM, ISAM, BPAM, DAM, BDAM and so on).

Other File Types

There are two other basic file types in the UNIX system: *pipes* and *special files*. A pipe is a file that is read by a process only once, it is temporary in nature. Once the data is read from a pipe it cannot be read again unless the process that created the pipe, re-creates the data to a new pipe.

Pipe files are also known as FIFO (first in first out) files, because their data is readable only in the sequence in which it was created. Pipes are discussed in more detail later in this book.

The remaining file types in the UNIX system are special files of two varieties: block device and character device. These types of files specify devices, not normal files; therefore, their inodes do not reference data. Instead, their inodes contain two numbers: the *major* and *minor* device numbers.

The major number specifies the device type, such as a disk, video display, communications port, tape unit, memory, network interface port, or other device; and the minor number refers to the specific unit number of that device type. Special files are discussed in greater detail later in this book.

Mountable File Systems

Given the flexible structure of the UNIX file system, it is possible to add on to it quite easily. In the DOS system, there is no equivalent concept of a mountable file system. In order to read a diskette in DOS, one simply inserts the diskette and issues the appropriate instructions to read the data from the media.

In the UNIX file system, things are a bit more sophisticated. Not only must removable media such as diskettes be properly mounted before being accessible, and unmounted before removing the media from the drive (diskettes and tape only), but the media must also have been properly formatted and contain a properly constructed file system, usually through the use of the UNIX **mkfs** command. As with every rule, there are exceptions to this one as well; there are certain kinds of disk file formats that do not require that the disk first be mounted, as in *tar* (tape archiver) formatted disk files.

A mountable file system is simply a self-contained file system stored on a media (disk/tape) that may become an optional part of the standard UNIX file system. The standard UNIX file system is the minimum necessary with which to boot the operating system. In the DOS environment, the file system architecture is similar in basic concept, but deviates greatly once investigated beyond the superficial similarities.

For example, in earlier releases of DOS the file system was limited by both logical and physical considerations. With the recent releases of DOS 4.0, Compaq DOS 3.3, and OS/2, these limitations have been overcome. The file system, however, is still accessible only one drive at a time. Each file system must have its own drive associated with it.

In DOS, drives are the physical mechanism, such as a diskette drive or the hard disk drive designed to access the media. A drive is assigned to a file system by means of a drive letter designation, A through Z. The first diskette drive is always reserved as drive A and the first hard disk is usually reserved as drive C. Drive B is optional, but is always a floppy diskette drive. The only instance where drive C is not the hard disk is when a DOS machine is equipped with more than two floppy diskette drives (there is a limit of four.)

In the case of the hard disk, the exterior structure of the file system is similar to the UNIX file system, but does have some major differences. There are usually practical hardware limitations to fixed disk controller devices that provide for no more than two physical, fixed disks in one system. With both fixed disks present, in most cases the C and D drives respectively, each must have a DOS file system on it in order to be readable by DOS. (It is possible to have a hard disk partitioned in a manner that permits non-DOS partitions to coexist with normal DOS partitions. The non-DOS partition is still not accessible to DOS unless there are special device drivers designed for that purpose. This was the basis for many early partitioning schemes designed to overcome file system limitations of DOS's early releases.)

The data is stored in a directory structure similar to the UNIX file system. The file system on one drive cannot be made an integral part of the other, regardless if it is fixed or removable media. In other words, the logical view of the file system is that they are totally separate entities. Some disk controllers, such as certain Western Digital ESDI controllers, offer the capability of treating two drives as a single logical one.

In the UNIX file system, there is no limit to the size of the file system for several reasons. First, there is the concept of *mountable* file systems. This means that even if there were some logical limitations imposed, fixed-disk based file systems could be mounted and unmounted, sharing the same mount points.

An example of this may be in the removable fixed disk technology such as the Bernoulli Box which features two drives capable of addressing 20 megabytes or more for each cartridge. (Bernoulli Box devices also work on DOS machines; however, on a UNIX-based system they could be made to appear as though the combined storage space of the two cartridges was one logical disk.) Another example of this is the more recent development of the 20 megabyte, 3.5 inch floppy diskette.

There is no such limitation in the UNIX system, except that of the hardware. In large UNIX systems, the file system may span several volumes of mass storage devices. An example is UTS *(a UNIX system that is a joint effort between AT&T and Amdahl Corporation, marketed by Amdahl)* running on large Amdahl or IBM mainframes under IBM's VM/370 operating system. (UTS runs native on Amdahl hardware.) In such systems, the typical disk storage capacity for each device is in the gigabytes. It is not uncommon to see literally hundreds of these disk devices (3380's) on a single system.

The media must first be constructed properly, as with the UNIX command **mkfs.** When a file system has been constructed the mount command may be used to add it at any time to the UNIX file system. Only users with sufficient authority, called superusers, may execute the **mount** and **unmount** commands. Before a file system can be mounted, a *mount point* is necessary. A mount point is any empty directory within the UNIX file system. Directories containing files or subdirectories are ineligible as mount points.

Once a file system is mounted, the path to the mount point becomes the path name prefix to any file or directory within the newly-mounted file system. For example, if a directory called *usr2* was created in the root directory of the UNIX file system, it could be used as a mount point for mounting a file system, as long as it remained empty.

After a file system is mounted to *usr2,* any reference to data within that file system would be made by using the path name */usr2* as its root. The **mount** and **unmount** commands will be discussed later in this book.

File Links and Unlinks

A file link is created using the UNIX **ln** command or **link** system call. A link is a way of creating aliases for files in the UNIX file system. The result is a new file name which, when referenced, affects the actual file to which it is linked. It is possible to link directories, but only the superuser may do this. Great care must be taken when linking directories, as it is possible to create a link structure that forms an infinite loop.

If a file has links to it, then any changes to that file affect the users of the links as well. By the same token, if any user modifies a file name that is a link, the original file is affected, and so are all other users of the file and its other links.

It is possible to remove a link from a file or directory by use of the **unlink** command or system call. The ln/link/unlink commands and system calls are documented in the UNIX System V User Reference and UNIX System V Programmer's Reference. Remember, great care should be used when linking and unlinking files.

An Introduction to the I/O Subsystem

The I/O subsystem enables processes to communicate with external hardware devices such as tapes, disks, video displays, keyboards, printers, network hardware, and special programs that control these devices, called *device drivers*. Device drivers are kernel modules designed to handle the low level I/O between a process and the specific hardware it was designed to drive.

There may be one or many drivers for all the different types of hardware in the system. This is particularily true in systems where there is hardware supplied by more than one vendor, such as different disk or terminal devices. Software devices, having no associated physical devices, are also supported; as when memory is used as a device allowing processes to access memory beyond their physical memory address space.

Of particular interest, at this point, are disk drivers and a newer method for implementing device drivers in the UNIX system, called *streams*. Device drivers will be discussed later.

Disk Drivers

A disk driver performs many duties, most notably the transfer of data from the disk media to memory. Disk drivers are the kernel modules that perform the location of the inode, and read in the file data to buffers in memory. They are usually specific for the model of the disk hardware being used.

When application developers write programs that obtain a file handle and issue **open, read, write** and **close** system calls, they are actually making calls to the disk device driver to perform these operations. The disk device driver converts file system addresses to disk sector addresses. It does this in one of the following methods.

First, a strategy procedure obtains a buffer from the buffer pool, in which case the buffer header contains the device and block number. Alternatively, the read and write procedures are provided by the minor device number as a parameter, and perform the conversion using other information in the process' *u area* (user area) to obtain the appropriate block address.

The device number is used by the disk device driver to identify the drive and section to be used for the operation. The disk device driver keeps internal tables that are necessary in order to locate the sector which is the beginning of the disk section. The block number of the file system is added to the starting sector to provide the address of the sector that is used for the target of the I/O operation.

It is sometimes necessary to know about the disk device drivers used, especially when attempting to debug I/O operations. Typically, UNIX application developers do not need to know much about the disk device driver.

Streams

Streams is a recent I/O scheme implemented by Dennis Ritchie AT&T Bell Laboratories to overcome certain inadequacies and drawbacks of device drivers. For example, many device drivers duplicate a lot of functionality, especially network protocol drivers.

A stream is a full duplex connection between processes and device drivers. Streams are implemented using special system calls in a given application.

File System Administration and Maintenance Tools

There are a number of new responsibilities DOS developers must assume if they are to work in a PC-based UNIX environment such as the AT&T 6386 Work Group Station or the Sun Microsystems 386i UNIX-based PC. Part of these new responsibilities will include administration of the system's hard disk. For DOS developers that will be joining a multiuser environment, these responsibilities are assigned to a UNIX system administrator and you need not be concerned, except to know to whom to report problems and requests.

UNIX System V from AT&T provides a menu driven utility program, called *sysadm* (system administration), for the purpose of helping system administrators maintain their systems. Not all implementations of UNIX provide administration tools in an interactive menu driven package. Sun Microsystems provides some administration tools based on their proprietary windowing system, SunTools.

The AT&T sysadm package provides file system maintenance functions that are discussed in a section on system administration later in this book. There is no equivalent functionality in the DOS system, so for those developers who are likely to assume system administration duties for their own development systems, this information will be useful.

Introduction to UNIX System Concepts

The basic philosophy of the UNIX system is to take a tool kit approach to the development of applications. The UNIX system is rich with specialized programs that perform particular functions quite well. According to this philosophy, it is better to build small, specialized applications that can be made to work cooperatively, rather than to make several enhancements to one program — changes that might cause performance problems or incompatibilities with earlier changes.

This philosophy does have its merits; the coupling of generic programs designed for specialized functions reduces application development efforts by elimination of redundant development. For example, a UNIX application that produces output usually does so to a default device known as the *standard output*. Instead of re-developing the I/O routines to write the output to a printer, it is easier to use existing print formatting routines by redirecting the application's output. This fundamental concept was of such importance that the developers of UNIX provided a special mechanism for this purpose: *pipes*.

A pipe provides the coupling facility to make the output of one application available as input to another. Using pipes, it is possible to build applications, even entire systems, by chaining together the appropriate series of programs to accomplish the application goals. Pipes can be used to chain together programs either serially or concurrently (by using another form of pipe called a *tee*). It is possible to implement pipes in a given application either externally at the UNIX shell level, or internally within the application code by using a **pipe( )** system call.

The DOS environment is not very well suited to the UNIX implementation of pipes, primarily because DOS is a single tasking environment. As such, pipes have a limited implementation in DOS, at the shell level. There is no tee function in DOS. Regardless, it should be quite obvious that by using the tool kit philosophy in UNIX application development, there are certain gains to be made in the form of reduced development efforts, modular design, cooperative conformity with other existing applications, and a wealth of development tools to draw upon, just to name a few.

The UNIX philosophy is not solely based upon pipes or tool kits. It is a way of applications development that simply doesn't exist in a DOS environment. This is not to say that tool kits don't exist in the DOS environment — there are many — however, they are provided mostly as third party, vendor-supplied tools. DOS has a limited set of *standard* tools (such as the DOS function calls) for applications developers that are a part of the base distribution. Virtually all implementations of UNIX have additional vendor-supplied development tools, however, there are also sets of standard tools (besides the UNIX system calls) that come with the base distribution package.

Once the fundamentals of the UNIX philosophy are understood and implemented as part of an application's design, the development activities for a project are bound to be reduced, resulting in a better product that makes use of the many UNIX features.

The UNIX Kernel

Keeping with the 'unitized' construction philosophy of the previous section, the UNIX operating system architecture distributes certain functionality to different components. Like the DOS environment, the UNIX kernel is the heart of the operating system. It performs key functions such as memory management and process management and also controls the hierarchical file system, to name a few.

The kernel enforces consistency throughout the file system by treating everything as a file. In UNIX, the kernel views files as streams of bytes, regardless of their source or destination. (Directories in the hierarchical file system are themselves just ordinary files that contain special information.)

System security, non-existent in DOS systems (even in OS/2), is also controlled within the kernel. Users and processes may access data only according to a well-defined set of permissions and rules that are enforced by the kernel. Essentially, the kernel is a sort of driver for the UNIX system.

Device Drivers

Another component of the UNIX architecture is the device driver. A device driver is software that enables transmission of data between a particular device (or class of device) and the computer's memory. Device drivers are controlled by the kernel and; in fact, become part of the kernel during system boot. Some device drivers can be added to the kernel after the system is already running, and there are even some that can be removed without the need for a system reboot.

DOS device drivers are the equivalent of UNIX device drivers, at least in concept. The manner in which UNIX device drivers are controlled by the kernel and the way in which they behave, are quite different than in DOS.

Inherent Security

All implementations of the UNIX system provide inherent security features. These routines are part of the kernel and provide functionality such as file access control (*read, write,* or *execute*) permissions, as well as user login validation. The reason for security within UNIX systems is due mainly to its multi-tasking, multi-user capabilities. Most DOS developers are probably not familiar with the types of security features that UNIX has to offer.

Those new UNIX developers who will be working on their own computers, in which they are the master of their system, should be aware of the available features, as well as the potential hazards involving UNIX security. For those UNIX developers that will be joining an existing UNIX development environment, their primary concern should be limited to understanding how the file and user access permissions work, since it is quite likely that there is already an existing administrator to handle other UNIX security details.

UNIX security is addressed in a separate part of this book; however, it is mentioned here as a simplistic introduction for DOS developers because of the lack of comparable features in the DOS environment. Basically, UNIX users can do pretty much anything they wish to any file that they own. This means if a particular user created a file, or was assigned ownership of that file, that user may do as they see fit with that file, regardless of the access controls that have been set up. This means that if a file has an access permission attribute of read-only, the owner of that file can override the access permission and write over that file, even delete it.

Other users cannot override the access permission settings of a file, with one exception: users that have special authority, called superusers. Superusers have the authority to do whatever they like as far as the security mechanism is concerned. UNIX security is of concern to application developers because there are programming considerations that should be taken into account when designing new applications. There are also security-related UNIX system calls that are possible to make from an application program such as **crypt( )**, a data encryption/decryption routine.

An application may also require references to security-related files and logs such as the master password file, /etc/passwd, that happens to be where all user ID's are stored. Access validation routines in a given application would find this file useful.

It is also possible for a program in UNIX to obtain information about the user ID that is executing the application. This is done through invocation of system calls or forking off other processes designed to return security-related information. In this way, it is possible for an application to control when it is run, and by whom.

An example of such an application is the standard UNIX command called *su*. The **su** (set user) command essentially permits a user to become another user, even the root superuser. Of course, the appropriate passwords must be given to effect the change, but the su command makes use of many of the UNIX system security features.

First, there is a system call, handled by the kernel, that performs the password validation routine. Next, there are calls to perform logging of the su event into a special file so that there is a record of who issued the command, along with a time and date stamp. An application could even go to the extreme of logging each command entered from that point on.

Another example of an application that uses UNIX security features quite extensively is the UUCP data communications system, a standard part of most UNIX systems.

Multitasking

This is really a point to make to DOS developers: UNIX is a multitasking environment. As such, many applications that are developed for UNIX should (and do) take advantage of this fact.

DOS applications must either process serially, or include all processing logic in the primary executable. The exception to this is for TSR *(terminate-and-stay-resident)* applications. There is no TSR equivalent in UNIX, because there is no need for them. It is possible

to run several concurrent applications without any special programming tricks as those required for TSR programs. (This is true for OS/2
also. There are no TSR's in OS/2.)

UNIX application developers have a wealth of good programming
tools designed for use only in a multitasking environment. These tools
include the ability to make applications communicate with each other,
the ability to share common memory address spaces, and other useful
features.

Multiuser

One of the most important fundamentals for new UNIX application
developers to understand, especially former DOS developers, is that
UNIX is a multiuser system. This is significant for several reasons.
Developers in DOS are accustomed to designing applications for a
single user at a time on a PC designed only for that purpose. Their
perceived user base is built on the idea that only one user will execute
the program at a time. Applications designed on such a principle in a
multiuser, multitasking environment can wind up with serious
problems.

Another important point for commercial software developers is that
when a new application is designed for use in a UNIX environment,
the potential market for that application increases dramatically. Instead of the concept of one PC to one user, there is the concept of one
UNIX system with many users. Applications designed for use by a
single user at a time, can't possibly be efficient in a multiuser environment because they don't take advantage of the multiuser, related
functionality that UNIX, and other multiuser systems, have to offer.

Interprocess Communications

Perhaps one of the most important aspects of application development
in the UNIX environment is the idea that processes can communicate
directly with one another. This concept exists only vaguely in the DOS
environment; that is, it is not directly supported by built-in functions
specifically for that purpose.

There are programming tricks that could be used to make multiple processes communicate, but only by an agreed upon convention. The only way it is possible to have more than one process in DOS is to use TSR applications. There have been past attempts to make TSR and normal programs adhere to some universally acceptable convention, without much success.

The UNIX development environment offers a variety of methods for processes to communicate with each other. Signals, pipes, and shared memory are among methods described later in this book. These inter-process communication features can make UNIX-based applications extremely efficient and powerful; more so than similar applications developed in a DOS environment.

Networking Communications

New applications in all development environments must certainly consider how the application will work in a networked environment. Networking of computer systems, ranging from the simplest PCs to the most sophisticated mainframes, is a fact and must be considered as a design factor for new applications. The UNIX system has different types and levels of networked communications.

Basic Networking

The UNIX basic networking utilities (BNU) package, a standard part of the UNIX distribution set, includes such functions as mail, a news facility, messaging between users, the capability of copying data between UNIX systems whether they are directly connected or remote, and the ability to gain access to other UNIX and non-UNIX systems.

The mail, news, and basic file transfer features are built on top of the UUCP Subsystem. UUCP is an acronym for UNIX-to-UNIX Copy.

uucp, uucico, uux, uuto, and cu

The uucp subsystem is capable of file transfers involving either standard ASCII text files or binary files. The underlying mechanism for uucp is called **uucico** (pronounced either you-you-see-ko or you-you-ki-ko).

The **uucico** program is a process that is spawned as the result of having entered one of the uucp commands such as **uucp**, **uux**, **uuto**, or **cu**. These commands gather the information to give to the **uucico** process, which is the real workhorse in the uucp system.

The **uucp** command simply enables users to copy a source file to a target file, the destination usually being on another remote UNIX system. The **uux** command enables users to execute UNIX commands and shell scripts on remote UNIX systems. The **uuto** command is a bit like **uucp,** except that the destination is the name of a user login ID on the remote system, instead of a specific directory pathname.

Finally, the **cu** command is a method for UNIX users to use the communications facilities (if present) of their UNIX system to call other machines. In fact, **cu** is an acronym for *call unix*, although it is possible to call other non-UNIX systems such as CompuServe, GEnie, and even PC-based bulletin board systems.

Area Networking

Networking in UNIX encompasses local, metropolitan, and/or wide area networks, as does any operating systems in use today. The UNIX system, however, uses different methods of interfacing different types of networking strategies. For example, in the PC world the two most popular types of networking are Token Ring networks and Ethernet-based networks; both of which are local area networks (although it is possible to provide wide area networked access to each). The UNIX system does not currently support any of the token ring products available on PCs; although there are a number of possible network scenarios to enable bridging UNIX-based networks to token ring networks.

The primary local area networks widely implemented in most UNIX installations are Ethernet-based, or use AT&T's StarLan product. Ethernet networks are more likely to be encountered by UNIX users and developers. Using the network to carry out the underlying I/O, a number of other file system architectures have been developed to provide better file and file system sharing.

Networking issues, especially file sharing schemes, are of relevant importance to UNIX application developers. The type of networking and file sharing strategy used in a particular UNIX installation could (and usually does) have a direct impact upon how applications behave. If these issues are not addressed before development of an application, developers could be in for some serious redesign efforts should problems develop when networking is introduced to a system in which their application runs.

NFS

Network File System (NFS) was originally implemented by Sun Microsystems, Inc., and has been endorsed by IBM, Hewlett-Packard, Apollo Computer, Apple Computer, and many other vendors of UNIX-based systems, except AT&T. In short, the widest implementation of network file sharing schemes is NFS, and it is therefore, the one most likely to be encountered by the majority of this book's readers.

Even though AT&T strongly advocates its own RFS product, NFS is still used widely within many AT&T sites, primarily on networks involved with development activities associated with Sun Microsystems, such as OpenLook.

NFS is an operating system-independent service that allows entire file systems to be mounted across networks; and then treats those remote file systems as though they were part of the local file system. A major design goal of NFS was to remove any operating system dependencies, along with machine hardware dependencies. NFS also provides crash recovery capabilities, high performance, and transparent access — regardless of the network or operating system.

An example of this is a product available for DOS-based PCs: PC-NFS. PC-NFS communicates to a UNIX-based NFS facility. To the PC, all or portions of the UNIX file system appear as though they were additional local DOS disks. PC-NFS doesn't provide any server features as yet; only NFS client services.

On UNIX-based systems, NFS is integrated with the kernel for reasons of efficiency, even though integration is not mandatory. Of importance to application developers is why and how NFS may affect their applications, and how to implement programming efforts to provide NFS compatibility.

The first part of the question can be answered by considering how an application is designed. The parts most likely to be affected are almost certainly I/O functions; most likely a file system-based I/O. If an application is designed to work with a file using certain file I/O routines there is a possibility that these I/O routines may cause the application to behave in a deranged manner when it is run over a remote file system.

As for how to implement programming efforts for NFS compatibility, this is done by using Remote Procedure Call (RPC) programming language, and External Data Representation (XDR) library routines that are the backbone of Sun's RPC package. The details for each of these is provided by the vendor, and are quite cumbersome. Aside from the library routines, there are entire concepts and philosophies that need to be mastered before programmers can write applications easily using these facilities.

RFS

For those developers that will be using AT&T's UNIX System V, Remote File Sharing (RFS) is likely to be the file sharing strategy in use. RFS provides the same basic capabilities as NFS; although it is implemented in a totally different manner. RFS uses STREAMS protocol, implemented as RFS library calls, to carry out its low level I/O.

The UNIX Shell

The UNIX Shell is analogous to the DOS shell. They both have identical purpose and similar functionality. The UNIX shell, however, is quite more sophisticated than the DOS shell.

For DOS users who understand the concept and purpose of the DOS shell, it should be easy to understand the UNIX shell. As in the DOS system, it is possible in the UNIX system to execute a different shell than the default one supplied with the original UNIX system.

For example, the particular implementation of UNIX being used determines what the default shell will be. It is possible to set the default shell for each individual by modification of a user's entry in the /etc/passwd file. On AT&T UNIX System V, the standard default shell is normally the Bourne shell. On most implementations of Berkeley UNIX (BSD 4), the standard default shell is usually the C shell.

One of the most popular shells is the more recent Korn Shell, or K Shell as it is also known.

Environment Variables

The UNIX shell, regardless of the one being used, uses an environment and special variables, called *environment variables*. The DOS shell was based upon the UNIX shell in its basic function and design. The UNIX shell, however, is far more sophisticated in its ability to manage user sessions and it makes more extensive use of the shell environment and environment variables than does its DOS counterpart. For this reason, the UNIX shell is a fundamental part of all applications development, whereas the DOS shell is largely ignored by most commercially available products.

The chapter on shell programming explains how the environment and special environment variables are used. DOS seems to make use of only a few environment variables, most notably the PATH environment variable. The UNIX system's PATH environment variable, the original prototype for the DOS counterpart, provides the same functionality.

Environment variables can be easily referenced and modified in UNIX, by means of system calls designed for that purpose. The major difference between the UNIX system calls designed for manipulation of environment variables and similar DOS-based C function calls is in functionality. The UNIX system calls are standard across all implementations of UNIX; whereas the C function call counterparts on DOS systems are sometimes compiler implementation dependent.

Also, in the DOS system, because of its single tasking nature and the way in which executables are loaded by DOS, each application inherits a copy of the environment. DOS applications may manipulate the environment while they are running, but when they terminate and have a subsequent program executed, any changes that were made are no longer in effect.

UNIX applications are capable of manipulating the shell environment by modifying existing environment variables and by setting or unsetting new ones. In fact, an application can even start up another shell if so desired, inheriting all of the parent shell's environment. There are, of course, some technicalities behind this; see the chapter on the UNIX Shell.

Shell Scripts

The UNIX shell supports the concept of scripts. UNIX commands can be entered into a file, and executed by entering the name of that file at the standard shell command prompt. UNIX shell scripts are analogous to DOS batch execution files. For a UNIX shell script to be executable, there is no need to follow any particular naming convention as in DOS; instead, the script file must be set with execution permissions. There is a loosely adhered to naming standard for UNIX shell scripts.

To indicate that a command is a UNIX shell script, the extension .sh is added. This is not enforced, and the UNIX shell does not treat files using this naming convention any different than any other ordinary file. It is simply a convention that makes it easier for a user to recognize that a command is actually a shell script rather than an executable binary. Note also that UNIX file naming standards do not enforce specific standards to indicate binary executables, as is the case in DOS.

Programmers and users new to UNIX should understand that the UNIX shell environment is so versatile, and the capabilities of shell script programming are so powerful, it is often the case that new applications can be implemented using shell script programming, rather than more difficult and cumbersome C language development. This is particularly true for customized programming tools. On many UNIX systems there are probably customized development tools already available. In fact, this is a mixed blessing in the UNIX environment.

While on the one hand it is possible to easily and quickly develop customized and powerful tools, on the other it is frustrating to deal with keeping track of the hundreds of custom commands that can result using this capability. Customized shell scripts often are documented poorly , if at all.

Cron Facility

Perhaps one of the most handy features of the UNIX system is the built-in *cron* (chronograph) facility, a feature that provides the ability to perform timed execution of UNIX commands and shell scripts. This feature would have been extremely handy in the DOS environment.

The cron can be used to perform functions as simple as periodically checking for mail, sending reminder messages to a particular destination, mailing out notices when certain events happen, and many other functions limited only by the user's imagination of the user.

The cron is used extensively by UNIX architecture to help in automated management of the overall system, as in the automation of system backups. The UUCP Communications Subsystem also makes extensive use of the cron facility.

System Call Functions

A list of all UNIX System Call Functions is provided in Appendix A. These are of prime importance to UNIX developers. A thorough list of the UNIX system call functions should be referenced in the documentation provided by the vendor of the system on which applications are being developed.

User Interfaces

There are a number of UNIX user interfaces in existence today. The one most universally available is the UNIX command line prompt. It is also accused of being the most difficult one to adapt to. The reasons for this are due to the large number of standard UNIX commands (over 100).

In actuality, the command line interface is probably the most efficient once users gain experience with the set of commands they use the most. It does, however, leave a lot to be desired for beginning users, but no more so than for new DOS users.

Recent studies have concluded that a graphical-based user interface is the easiest and most efficient one to learn for new users, or for users who may not be computer literate. This is supported by the growing number of graphical windowing-based packages that are appearing in both the DOS and UNIX environments.

The UNIX Command Line Prompt

DOS users will find themselves at home with UNIX's command line prompt. The default prompt is actually determined by the system administrator, however, it is usually the $ symbol. As in DOS, the prompt string may be changed to whatever the user desires. The method in which this is accomplished is by setting the **PS1** environment variable:

```
PS1=`logname`; export PS1;
```

This would yield a prompt string that is the login ID of the current user. In DOS the **PROMPT** command is used to set the prompt string; this method is probably easier to understand, but because of DOS' more limited capabilities, it is also less functional.

The UNIX shell simply writes out the prompt string and waits for a command to be entered, the same as the DOS command shell interpreter. When a command has been entered, the shell attempts to execute it. The UNIX shell uses the **PATH** environment variable to determine the execution path search order.

Unlike the DOS shell, the current directory is not automatically the first place the UNIX shell looks for the command. Also, the UNIX shell does not differentiate between shell scripts and binary executables by checking the command file name and extension. (In DOS **.COM** files always take precedence over **.EXE** files if there are identical file names in the same directory. The **.BAT** files are always last on the search list, unless the invoked command was the **CALL** batch file command.)

Shell Script Controlled Interfaces

When UNIX first began to make commercial appearances (and the initial grumblings about the sparse user interface were made), several shell script interfaces were designed to remove some of the perceived hostility. The underlying command execution mechanism was still the same, except that now instead of merely running the basic shell, another shell script was invoked to display menus and more meaningful prompts.

The basic problems with this approach were that they were slow, character-based, tended to behave differently depending upon the hardware used as the access terminal, and most importantly, there was no general agreement upon a standard user interface.

Custom Developed Screens Using CURSES

The next logical development of interface was to convert shell script-based displays (primarily for video screen displays) to faster displays written in C language, using a terminal I/O package known as CURSES. The CURSES package was to solve the inconsistent screen behavior problem, but the problem of a standardized user interface still existed.

Graphical Windowing Interfaces

Finally, a graphical-based windowing user interface was developed, initially released with AT&T's UNIX PC 7300 system. This graphic user interface somewhat resembled the Apple MacIntosh user interface.

The most significant feature this interface had to offer was a menu hierarchy enabled through either a keyboard interface or a pointer device, initially a mouse. Many other vendors of UNIX-based systems have developed interesting and powerful graphical windowing user interfaces; for instance, Sun Microsystems' SunTools, SunView and NeWS interfaces.

Again, the problem of what was to be accepted as an official standard user interface surfaced. Many of the other vendors of UNIX-based systems rejected SunTools for various reasons, but primarily because SunTools was developed for Sun machines and was unavailable for anything else. The answer to this problem began formulating as early as 1984 at MIT — an effort known as Project Athena.

Project Athena is the basis for the **X Window** system. There is still no official, universally standard graphical user interface for UNIX-based systems. However, the X Window system has become quite popular among virtually all vendors, and is the foundation upon which virtually all new graphical windowing interfaces are currently being developed.

AT&T agreed to share in the development of a graphical windowing interface, dubbed as OpenLook. However, when certain business relationships were forged between AT&T and Sun Microsystems, the rest of the UNIX vendor community perceived this as being an unfair competitive edge.

As a result, the Open Software Foundation (OSF) was formed. The OSF decided upon a different graphical user interface standard than OpenLook. The OSF standard is based upon the look and feel that Microsoft Corporation developed for its Windows and Presentation Manager products.

Even within various AT&T organizations, many graphical user interface standards have appeared and are being used to implement new products.

The beauty of the X Window system is that the user interface can be completely controlled by a *window manager*. Also, it is possible to start up different window managers, even though only one window manager can be run at a given time. The real trick for application developers to consider for these graphically oriented environments will be upon which windowing system to build their applications. They will also have to take into consideration which window manager is likely to be used.

The answers to these questions are easy. First, X is almost certainly going to be the standard, mainly because it is available in the public domain from MIT for a nominal charge that covers the cost of the tapes and shipping.

Secondly, applications developed for the X Window system are universally portable across any operating system and machine hardware, as long as there is an X Window display server or development environment available for that system. This means that an X application developed on a UNIX system will probably be easily ported to OS/2 and even to DOS.

There are X Window systems available for DOS on PCs, even though DOS is a single-tasking operating system. X takes over the PC in much the same manner as does Microsoft Windows when it is initiated. X performs all of the multi-tasking and memory management functions on DOS-based PCs, as does Microsoft Windows. Unfortunately, current PC technology and certain limitations of DOS render a severe performance impact upon X Window applications. It is possible, however, to use a PC as a display device *(called an X server)* for X applications *(called X clients)* running on more powerful UNIX-based workstations that are connected over a network.

This last statement hints at what is the true power behind the X Window system: its ability to make applications available to users on multiple and/or dissimilar systems over a network, with complete network transparency.

As to the question of which window managers are likely to be run, developers of X applications need only make certain that the routines exist to respond to a particular graphical icon that may be present for a given window manager. For example, OpenLook and the OSF's window manager user interfaces both send an X client messages about window resizing, movement, circulation, and iconfy/deiconify operations; the only difference is perceived by the end user, not the application. The X client receives the same message notifications of these events, regardless of how it appears to the end user.

An introductory chapter on the X Window System is included as a separate chapter in this book. For DOS programmers considering development on UNIX systems, this is currently the hottest area in demand. Efforts are under way to convert existing applications to incorporate the features and functionality that X has to offer. In doing so, X-based applications will undoubtedly become the most powerful applications available on any type of computer system. Timing for development of X applications is perfect: the current situation is that vendors and customers alike are clamoring for experienced X Window programmers. This means that experienced X developers can command a good income and work on the most interesting projects, and that there is a ready-made marketplace eagerly awaiting good X-based products.

UNIX System Administration

DOS programmers new to the UNIX system who will be working in an environment where they have total control (over their own UNIX-based systems) are in for a shock. There are a number of new administrative chores they will be required to assume for which there is no DOS counterpart. These chores include user account administration, maintaining the UNIX file system, setting up UNIX communications, and administering proper system security.

User Account Administration

This is perhaps the easiest of all of the UNIX system administration functions. The concept is simple. One file is used to contain information about users and other files are used to provide additional information, such as a list of groups and the user IDs belonging to each.

For IBM mainframe experienced developers entering the UNIX environment, the /etc/passwd file is analogous to **SYS1.UADS**, the TSO user ID dataset on MVS systems, and also to the master user directory (known by many names) in VM/CMS systems, usually called **DIRECTORY DIRECT.**

In some UNIX implementations there are automated tools (shell scripts or binary executables) to help administer user accounts, and in others the process is manual, using the file editor to insert changes. The manual method provides maximum opportunity to make mistakes and could result in serious problems if done incorrectly.

One such automated tool, available from AT&T, is the **sysadm** package. This package provides a menu driven interface to handle virtually all of the system administrator's duties by simply responding to the appropriate prompts. It is not a bad tool. The problem is, the **sysadm** package is not universally available, even across different systems provided by AT&T. (For example, **sysadm** is unavailable for UNIX PC 7300 systems.)

File System Administration

Unlike DOS, reading diskettes involves more than simply inserting the diskette into the floppy drive and then issuing the appropriate command. First, the floppy diskette must have a valid file system on it. This is in addition to the diskette having been previously formatted. If both of these conditions have been met, then the floppy diskette file system must be mounted as part of the standard UNIX file system before it can be written to or read.

This is only part of what a UNIX system administrator must be able to do; only superusers are permitted to issue the mount and unmount commands. If any media problems occur within the file system, or if the file system becomes corrupted, the system administrator is expected to know how to deal with the problem.

Normally, a utility program called fsck, (file system check) can be run to determine the nature of the problem, and optionally to repair the damage. The damage is not always repairable, so system administrators must know what other options are at their disposal.

Communications Administration

This is an optional task, depending upon whether or not communications with other systems is desirable. If the answer is no, skip this section.

The main underlying mechanism for external communications on UNIX-based systems is in the UUCP communications subsystem. The administrative work associated with setting up and maintaining a uucp subsystem is not trivial, even to experienced system administrators. Learning about uucp will require time and diligent effort. Perhaps the most complex part of uucp is understanding the concept of *chat scripts* and how they are associated to a particular device.

System Security Administration

For new UNIX developers entering an existing environment with a designated system administrator, the worry is over. If, however, new developers are using UNIX-based systems under their control, then it is necessary to gain an understanding of how the file system access mechanism works, and how the UNIX kernel enforces UNIX security. If this system is to have multiple users, concurrent or not, it will be even more necessary to understand UNIX system security administration.

The concept that is of most importance, concerning UNIX system security, is the permissions settings of certain key UNIX files and directories. Some persons who have acquired either the responsibility of maintaining system security, or the authority of changing permissions have ended up in serious trouble because they did not understand the ramifications of the changes they made. The worst situation likely to occur when an ignorant-but-authorized user makes file access permissions changes is that the system may be rendered incapable of operating, and it may become necessary to reinstall UNIX from the original distribution media.

In multiuser systems, this could have ominous consequences for the person making the changes. UNIX system security administration has been the subject of many books. It requires special attention and should be given serious consideration by the person(s) charged with this responsibility.

UNIX: The User's Point of View

When introducing someone to UNIX for the first time, a description of its features is necessary, but somewhat difficult, as there is a lot to remember. One of the best ways to continue this introduction, perhaps, is to describe what takes place from the user's point of view.

To be able to use the services of a UNIX system, a user must have a UNIX login account; that is, a user ID previously set up by the UNIX system administrator (the person generally responsible for setting up user accounts). A user ID is necessary because UNIX is designed to support multiple concurrent users accessing the system, and therefore, needs a way to differentiate between users. DOS was designed for access by a single individual at a time and doesn't support a multiuser environment, hence the lack of built-in security.

Logging In

Once your user ID has been issued, customarily the initials of your first, middle, and last name, you will be able to log into the UNIX system to which it has been added. A password is usually required, but in some cases a first time user may not have one. This is alright because users have the ability to create or modify their password at any time. We will assume that our user ID is tsm and that the password is go4it.

The first thing that needs to be done is to locate the terminal to be used for a login session. On the AT&T 6386 system, the main keyboard and monitor serve as such a device, although there may be additional terminals connected to a UNIX system that are not the main console. UNIX doesn't require a dedicated console device to be active while the operating system is running, as do certain mainframe operating systems which constantly display information to a special operator console.

On the 6386's main monitor screen there should be a prompt which reads as follows:

```
login:
```

The login prompt means that the UNIX system is waiting for some-one to enter their user ID from the keyboard. Our response is tsm and appears as follows:

```
login: tsm
```

The characters "tsm" are followed by the enter or return key, depending on what key is used to issue a carriage return/line feed (CRLF). On PCs this is called the enter key. Certain terminal devices use an enter key or return key; or sometimes, if equipped with both, either one. Upon entering the user ID, the next prompt asks for the user ID's password, and appears as follows:

```
login: tsm
Password:
```

At this point we enter the password, "go4it" as follows:

```
login: tsm
Password: go4it
```

When the password is actually being entered the characters are *not* echoed back to the screen for security reasons. In the previous ex-ample they appear only for sake of clarity; in a real login situation they would not appear. Upon entering the password, it is validated against an entry in a special system file. If it has been successfully validated then access is permitted to the system; otherwise, an error message ("Login incorrect") is printed and the login prompt reappears.

When access is granted, the user is in contact with another com-ponent of the UNIX operating system; the UNIX Shell. The shell is a layer of software between the user and the operating system designed to interpret commands entered by the user. It is the operating system that actually manages the execution of user commands; the shell is the mechanism used to collect the instructions.

If the login was successful, the standard shell prompt character is displayed (the $ character) and appears as follows:

```
login: tsm
```

```
Password:
$
```

In certain systems other things may appear before the prompt string, such as a welcome notice, message of the day, news, or some other information. In DOS there is a special file called the AUTOEXEC.BAT file which automatically executes upon completion of the boot sequence. In UNIX, there is a file with a similar function, but execution occurs every time the user logs into the system. On UNIX System V, this file is called the *.profile* file; on BSD versions this is known as the *.login* file.

.profile/.login

This file, if present in the user's home directory, may contain a list of UNIX and shell commands that are executed immediately upon login. Traditionally, this file contains login setup information, such as for setting up UNIX environment variable values, terminal characteristics, and other login configuration tasks. Once .profile/.login finishes execution, the UNIX shell issues the prompt string and is ready to process user commands. (On BSD versions of UNIX, the .cshrc file is also executed immediately following the .login file.)

UNIX has a rich command language, with most of the commands capable of several options. These commands need to be examined closely and are described in detail in the user reference manual, entitled "UNIX System V - User Reference Manual."

UNIX Directories and Files

Since login has been completed, the system is waiting for further instructions. A look at the file system is in order. Remember the concept of the current directory mentioned earlier. Being "in" a directory means that if no path names (full or partial) are specified as part of the commands entered, then the command assumes action on those files within the current directory. It is the same as on DOS systems.

Users may change "out" of a directory "into" another one using the change directory command, **cd**. When the change directory command is issued, the result is that the user is no longer "in" the original directory, but "in" the target of the change directory command, if that target exists.

There is another concept called the *home directory*. The home directory is the directory within the file system hierarchy that has been assigned to a specific user when their account was created, and by convention, is usually named the same as their user ID. This directory is the default location of the user's current directory upon completion of login.

In home directories, users have full access permissions and control over all files and subdirectories they create. To illustrate the concept of the home directory, imagine that a UNIX system has five users whose IDs are: *tsm, jen, llw, akl, wbu*. In the traditional UNIX environment, the home directories for these users would appear in the */usr* directory, giving */usr/tsm* for the user tsm; */usr/jen* for user jen; and so on. Figure 2-3 on the next page illustrates this point.

The ultimate or beginning of all the directories is called the *root directory*. It is owned by a special ID called *root* which is the main system administrator user ID. For all intents and purposes, root can be thought of as the super being of users, and in fact is referred to as the *superuser.*

The root directory contains several files and subdirectories, of which */usr* is one. The /usr directory contains several subdirectories, and traditionally contains the home directories of the system users, although this varies from system to system. The system users' home directories may be kept anywhere the system administrator likes. Users may create or modify entries only in directories for which their ID has adequate permissions to do so, not at all like DOS, which has no equivalent feature.

In order to manipulate directories and their contents, there are a few basic commands users need to know. These include the **pwd** command which informs the user what their current directory is; the **ls** command which displays information about directories and files; the **mv** command which is used to move files from one location to another and rename them if moved within the same directory; the **cp** command which copies a file and duplicates its contents to the specified target location; the **rm** command which is used to delete or remove files; the **mkdir** command which is used to create directories; and the **rmdir** command which removes directories.

The next chapter expands upon these and other commands in detail.

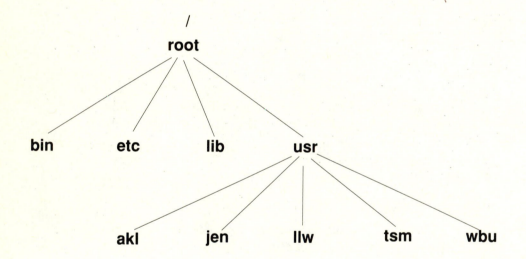

Figure 2-3: User Home Directories

CHAPTER 3

ESSENTIAL UNIX COMMANDS FOR USERS

Users and developers in the UNIX environment usually have a set of standard commands that they are accustomed to working with regularly. The number of commands may be confusing to new users. It is important for the user to understand that there are a few commands that are absolutely necessary for day-to-day use, and that there are also some rather exotic commands that provide even more powerful capabilities.

There are many types of tools: those to prepare the source code, those to create the executable modules with, and tools which are used to shorten both the amount of development effort expended and the time necessary to do it. There are also standard tools designed to reduce the amount of actual coding a developer does so they do not constantly re-invent the wheel, and utilities which make the development process more professional and manageable.

These commands and tools are described in detail in the "System V Interface Definition", a three volume set of reference manuals published by AT&T, considered to be the authoritative definition of UNIX System V standards.

The following is a list of essential commands and tools that programmers and users of UNIX System V would be wise to learn and use (in some cases they also apply to other UNIX systems, such as A/UX, AIX, HP/UX, Sun/OS, BSD 4.3, and so on).

as

This is the common assembler command used when assembling assembler language source files into object files. On occasion, developers may be required to write assembler modules, particularly when constructing specialized subroutines which may be called from C language programs. In order to test these, they may be assembled so they can be properly debugged.

Two versions of the **as** command are described in the UNIX System V User Reference Manual, a version specifically for the DEC PDP-11 assembler, and the non-PDP version, which is discussed here. The **as** command has several option flags, some of which are described here. For a complete understanding of the **as** command's option flags, the reader should reference the UNIX System V Interface Definition.

- -o flag: This flag is followed by the name which the user wishes to call the output object file. The default name for the output file, if the -o flag is not specified, is the name of the input file with a .o suffix appended to it.

- -R flag: This flag removes the input source statement file upon completion of the assembly.

- -V flag: The assembler's version number is included in the output written to the standard error device.

awk

The **awk** filter is a pattern scanning program that reads files a line at a time. It derives its name from the initials of its originators; Alfred Aho, Peter Weinberger, and Brian Kernighan. The topic of **awk** could easily be the subject of an entire book and, in fact, is: in Aho's book, *The AWK Programming Language*, Addison-Wesley, 1988.

The **awk** control statements are actually a processing language that is quite powerful. As each line is read from the file, a pattern specified in the **awk** control statement is compared with the data found in the file record. If there is a match, then the action specified with the associated pattern is performed. The simple general form of the **awk** command is:

```
awk 'program' filename(s)
```

The program is the **awk** control statement containing the pattern to be scanned for and the resulting action to be performed in case of a match. There may be several **awk** control statements containing the pattern/command sequence and several files may be processed as well, making this a very powerful and handy developer's programming tool. The **awk** command may receive input from a file containing several control statements by using the -f option, in the general form:

```
awk -f cntlfile filename(s)
```

The pattern or the program action of the control statement are optional fields. When the pattern is omitted from the control statement, then every input line is affected by whatever **awk** program action was specified. If the program action is omitted, then the default is to print the lines matching the pattern specified to standard output (which may be redirected using one of the redirection operators).

Each input line to **awk** is automatically separated into fields, which are separated by either white space or tab characters. A specific delimiter character may also be specified using -F option (must be a capital F character) followed by the single delimiter character. If, for example, the delimiter character were the *hat* or *caret* character (symbolized as ^), then the value for the -F option would be as follows:

```
awk -F^ 'pattern(s)/command(s)' filename(s)
```

The **awk** command is capable of using symbolic substitution for the fields of an input line as variables $1, $2, $3, etc., through $n which represents the number of the last field. The following example illustrates how **awk** uses input line variables:

```
who | awk '{print $1 $3 $5}'
```

This simple **awk** program will display the first, third, and fifth fields of every output line from the **who** command. The **who** command produces the following output line for each user currently logged on to the UNIX system:

```
userid    ttyaddr    month    day    hours:minutes
```

The first field is the user ID field and is treated by **awk** as $1; the second field is the device number located in the /dev directory for the terminal device the user is logged on through, and is equated to $2 by awk. The third field is a date field indicating the month as a three character abbreviation and is the $3 **awk** line variable; the fourth field is another date field indicating the date the user logged into the system (two digits) and becomes the $4 variable; and the last field is the timestamp consisting of hours and minutes separated by the colon character (hh:mm) and equates to $5.

The **awk** command example above would then produce output in the following form:

```
userid    month    hh:mm
```

The **awk** program, as demonstrated, can be quite simple to use and may be constructed into a sophisticated processing language that performs data handling functions which do not need to be rewritten for every new application.

Instead, the application may invoke **awk** through a system call, and in doing so provides flexibility to modify the control statements if they are input to **awk** as a separate file.

banner

The **banner** program is used to create posters. It echoes the input character string back to the standard output in poster sized block letters. When executing long shell scripts, it is extremely useful to use as a means of indicating what is happening.

Another useful purpose is to emphasize something by making the output a **banner** created poster, as in a response to a query. The input string is limited to 10 characters; if it is longer and the string is contiguous, it is truncated at the tenth character. If the string contains blanks, the blanks serve as delimiters that appear on separate lines in the output.

The output of **banner** is usually directed to a video display device, but may be redirected to a file instead.

```
banner Hello World
banner Hello World > hello.world
```

cb

This is the C beautifier that is a very handy program for UNIX developers to use. It takes a C language source code file as input and produces a "beautified" version as its output, which is still valid code and capable of compilation without errors.

The beautification process involves reorganization of the code using indentation and new lines to make the program more readable. The -s flag converts the code to the style standards as described by Kernighan and Ritchie in *The C Programming Language*, 1978.

All output from **cb** is written to the standard output and may be redirected to a file if desired. The following is an example of the command line to enter in order to beautify a program and produce the output to a new file:

```
cb -s oldsource.c > newsource.c
```

It is customary to perform beautification on a program only after it has been debugged and is working properly.

cc

This is the command used to invoke the UNIX system C language compiler. It has many flags, some of which are briefly explained below; for a detailed explanation the reader should refer to the compiler documentation appropriate for their UNIX system. The general form of this command is as follows:

```
cc option(s) file(s)
```

The command line may contain either one or several options that are flags used by the compiler as instructions on how to handle the input file. Either one or more files may also be present on the command line, separated by at least one white space.

Input filenames may be fully qualified pathnames; the .c file identifier must be included in the filename. The default name of the output file is a.out, unless otherwise specified on the command line using the -o flag.

The flags most developers should know about initially are as follows:

- -c flag: his causes the link edit phase of the compilation process to be suppresed, forcing the object file (filename.o) to be produced. Normally the .o file is deleted during the compilation process.

- -g flag: This flag causes the compiler to produce the information necessary for use with the symbolic debugger program (sdb).

- -o flag: Changes the default name of the executable module produced as output from a.out to the specified name following the flag, for example, -oname or -o name.

- -O flag: This flag generates optimized object code. This is mutually exclusive with the -g flag.

- -S flag: Generates the assembler language output (filename.s) for all corresponding .c files being compiled.

There are several other flags that may be referenced in the UNIX System V Interface Definition.

chgrp

This command is used to change the group ownership attribute for a file. The general form of this command is:

```
chgrp new_groupname file_name
```

When a file is created, it is assigned certain ownership values, such as the ID of the owner (default is the creator of the file, also known as *user*), the group ownership value (default is the group to which the owner belongs when the file is created), and certain other access permission values that are derived from defaults associated with the owner's umask values at file creation time.

There are many instances where it becomes necessary to change any of these values; the **chgrp** command is used to assign a new group ownership. The group must exist, otherwise a diagnostic message is returned. The group ownership value does not apply to super-users. In order to change the group ownerships, the user must be authorized and must be a member of the group to which the file allows modification permissions.

The new group to which group ownership is being assigned may be any group, as long as it already exists (usually maintained by the system administrator). Once the group ownership has been reassigned, access for the group level is restricted to members of the new group. The group level access permissions previously set remain in effect.

chmod

The **chmod** command is used to change the access mode values associated with a file. The general form of the **chmod** command is:

```
chmod value filename
```

The access mode value of a file defines, among other things, the access permissions granted to the file's owner, group, and the rest of the world (referred to as 'other') and whether or not the file is executable. Access mode values apply to directories and subdirectories as well as to files, so the term "file" mentioned for this topic is interchangeable with either. (Access mode values do not apply to superusers!)

There are three types of users who may access a file: the file's assigned owner; users belonging to the group associated with the file; and the rest of the world (other). Within each of these categories of users, it is possible to define just how the file may be accessed; that is, read, write, or execute (represented by the characters r,w, or x). When the user lists the detailed information about a file (ls -l), one of the things returned are the file access mode permissions, which are depicted as:

```
rwxrwxrwx
```

This triad of rwx characters runs from left to right. The first group refers to the owner, the next refers to the group access, and the last refers to other (the rest of the world). Other information may also be provided (such as an indication that the entry is a directory or a file), but it is not relevant to the **chmod** command.

Numeric values can be used to set the access permissions each group within the mode permissions triad may have. The **chmod** command uses numeric values for each of the triads; for example, if the owner, group, and other permissions were to allow read, write, and execute permissions, the numeric value to specify when to use the **chmod** command would be 777. If instead of allowing full access for group and other, it were desirable to keep full access limited only to the owner, the numeric value would be 700.

As you can see, the three digit number has a positional relationship that corresponds to the rwx triad group. The first number (left most) corresponds to the owner field, the second number (middle) corresponds to the group field, and the last number (right most) corresponds to the field reserved for other. (Actually, it is possible to specify a four digit number and this process is discussed in the chapter on system administration and security.)

An alternative method of specifying the mode value to the **chmod** command is by using alphabetical characters. The alpha characters r,w, and x (for read, write, and execute) may be used in conjunction with the characters u,g, o, and a. The u character refers to the owner of the file, the g character refers to the group, the o character refers to other (all other users), and the a (all) applies the changes to all three (u,g, and o).

The characters +, -, and = are also used in the assignment process; the + character means to add the permission value(s) to the right of it; the - character means to remove the permission value(s) to the right of it and the = character means to reset (no permissions at all) the permission values for the users specified to the left of the character. Examples of this are listed below:

```
chmod a+rw filename
chmod uo-x filename
chmod a= filename
```

The first line in the example sets read and write permissions on for all users of the file called filename. The second line turns off execution permissions for the owner and other, but not for group. The last line resets all attributes to off (no permissions at all) for the owner, group, and other. In order to manipulate this file, the owner must first **chmod** it to the appropriate permissions.

chown

This command is used to reassign ownership of a file from one user to another. The general form of the **chown** command is:

```
chown newowner filename
```

In order to change the ownership value of a file, users must be authorized; they must own the file or they must have superuser privileges. Non-superuser authorized users, once the file ownership has been changed, are bound to the access permissions defined for the file.

If users accidentally change ownership to another user, they must either get the new owner to change ownership back, or get an authorized superuser to reset the ownership (usually done by the system administrator).

cmp

This command is used to compare two files. The purpose is the same, the functions are similar, but the actual implementations are different. Two files are compared for equality. If the contents of both files are identical, there is no comment displayed and an exit code of zero is returned.

If the contents of the files differ, the line number and byte offset of the differing file is echoed to the standard output as the default action, for each occurrence.

The **cmp** command has two option flags that may be specified. The -l (long) flag produces a tabular listing containing the decimal byte offset and the octal value of the first and second input files for each byte that differs in either file. This can produce a lot of output if the files being compared are large.

The second flag is the -s (short) flag which produces only the return code. Obtaining return code values from commands executed in a shell script are discussed later.

cp

The **cp** command is used to duplicate files in the UNIX system. The general format is:

```
cp file1 file2
```

File1 is the input to the copy operation and file2 is target output produced. File1 and file2 must be different names; if they are the same name then a diagnostic message is issued indicating that they are identical, and the file is not copied on top of itself. If file2 previously existed, it is overwritten by the contents of file1.

The **cp** command assumes that users know exactly what they are doing and does not attempt any confirmation before overwriting existing files, so this command must be used carefully to avoid accidental modification to existing files.

cpio

This command is quite powerful and useful for several functions, including creating backups. Its name stands for "copy input to output" and it is particularly powerful when combined with the **find** or the **ls** command in a compound command statement. It can be used to write to disk or tape devices, or to create sequential files containing the contents of entire directories that can be used as transmission files in telecommunications. Because of its flexibility and usefulness, it is essential that users and programmers understand this command.

It has three basic modes that are determined by the option flags -o, -i, and -p. The -o flag indicates that the **cpio** command is to create a special output file, which will ultimately be read as input to **cpio** using the -i flag. The output file created using the -o flag is a sequential file and can be manipulated with other commands, such as **pack** and **unpack**.

The file may also be transmitted over a communications link, such as the transmission file for **uucp**, or copied across file systems. It may even be copied to another UNIX system across a local area network link such as Starlan or Ethernet. The contents of such files are usually multiple files and/or directories.

If, for example, the current directory was /usr/tsm on a UNIX system called *rambo*, and it was desirable to copy all of the files and subdirectories to another UNIX system called *omega*, there are several ways to go about it. In this example, it is assumed there is no direct link to the remote system, omega, and that the file must be transmitted by a modem connection using serial communications.

This means that the **uucp** command will actually transmit the data, but **cpio** must be used to create the transmission file. The **find** command is incorporated into a compound command with the **cpio** statement as follows:

```
find /usr/tsm -print | cpio -ocv >  tranfile
```

In this example, the **find** command begins in the /usr/tsm directory and prints the file names to the standard output, working its way through any and all subdirectories encountered from that level on down.

The standard output is piped as input to the **cpio** command; creating an output file called tranfile, which is a sequential file of all the files and directories within the /usr/tsm directory.

The -ocv flag settings indicate that **cpio** is to create an output file (o); that the header information is to be written in ASCII characters for portability (c); and, that as each entry is being processed, it will be listed on the screen (called the verbose (v) option).

Once this is done, the output file, tranfile, may be transmitted by the **uucp** command. A standard practice that should be used when transmitting large files with **uucp**, is to pack them prior to transmission. This reduces the amount of data to transmit, therefore reducing transmission time. Packed files may be unpacked at the destination when the transmission file has arrived. See the **pack** and **unpack** commands later in this section for an explanation of how to do this. Also, see the **uucp** command for details on data transmission to remote UNIX systems.

The next mode of **cpio** is the input (-i) mode. This mode instructs **cpio** that a file which was created with the -o flag of **cpio** is to be read as input. There are several other possible flags to be used with the -i flag; for the sake of brevity only those pertinent to this specific example are discussed here.

In this example, assume that the input file had been transmitted to our system from a remote UNIX system and that it has already been unpacked. The target directory where the tranfile contents are to be restored is called /usr/wbu, and it already contains some files and directories.

It would be necessary to make /usr/wbu the current directory before invoking the **cpio** command. Using the name tranfile from the previous example, the following command line would then be used to read it and restore the files and directories it contains:

```
cpio -iduvm <  /usr/spool/uucppublic/tranfile
```

The flags (-iduvm) may appear in any order, but by convention the -i should be the first in the string, if for no other purpose than to make it easy to see what operation **cpio** is performing. The -d flag indicates that any directories which do not exist in the target are to be created; the -u flag indicates that all files in the input file are to be restored, replacing any identically named files in the target directory.

The default restoration activity for a file when the -u flag is not specified is that the newer of the two files is kept; this is determined by the file's time/date stamp in the inode information. The -v flag is the verbose indicator that causes the filenames to be listed on the screen as they are processed; the -m flag indicates that the time/date information of the restored file's inode is to be preserved intact without any modification. Processing time for **cpio** may be significantly reduced by omitting the verbose (-v) flag for either the -i or -o modes.

The redirection operator indicates where the input file for **cpio** is to be located, in this case the fully qualified pathname /usr/spool/uucppublic/tranfile.

The directory /usr/spool/uucppublic is a directory open to access by anyone and where **uucp** can deposit data without worrying about file access permissions (see **uucp** for more information). Any existing files with identical names are replaced unconditionally if the -u flag was specified or only if the file being restored is newer and the -u flag was not specified (the default).

The -p (for pass) mode allows for mass copying; performing in and out processing in a single operation. This is handy for copying directories from one file system to another or for making duplicates of entire directory trees. An example of this is as follows:

```
find /usr/tsm -print | cpio -pduvm /usr/wbu
```

This command sequence will first execute the find command to provide the list of files and directories for input to **cpio**. The target location for **cpio** to place the output is a directory called /usr/wbu. In this example, all files with identical names that already exist in the target directory are replaced because the -u flag was specified.

The target directory may be another file system, such as a floppy disk that has been properly mounted, or any other properly mounted file system.

cut

The **cut** command is used to selectively extract information from an input file. Each input line is separated into fields that are separated by a delimiter. The -d flag is used to specify what the delimiter character is; the default delimiter is a single white space character. The -f flag is used to indicate which fields are to be cut.

For each line of input, the **cut** command produces an output line containing the field(s) specified in the -f flag. Assuming that a listing of all user ID's and their names was desired, the following command could be used:

```
cat /etc/passwd | cut -d":" -f1,5
```

This example types out the contents of the /etc/passwd file and pipes it to **cut**, which in turn echoes the user id (field #1) and the user's name from the comments field (field #5) separated by the delimiter character. The delimiter character is a colon and is specified in the -d flag. The **cut** command is frequently used in conjunction with a grep statement in a compound command statement.

date

This command simply echoes back the system date. The format of the output is:

```
Day  Mon  dd  hh:mm:ss  TZ  yyyy
```

Day represents a three character abbreviation of the current day of the week, the values are the first three characters of the weekdays, Sunday through Saturday.

Mon represents a three character abbreviation of the current month, the values are the first three characters of the months of the year, January through December. The two characters, dd, represent a two position decimal number ranging in value from 1 to 31, depending on the current date.

This is followed by a time stamp field represented by hh:mm:ss, which indicates the current hour, minute, and second when the date command was entered. The next field, TZ, is a three character field that indicates the time zone in effect. For the continental US, the possible values are EST, CST, MST, or PST, depending on which time zone has been set for the machine by the system administrator. The last field, represented by the characters yyyy, indicates a four digit field that is the current year.

ed

This is the standard text editor distributed as part of all UNIX systems. Although it is quite primitive by most word or text processing standards, it is still quite useful. Unfortunately for most UNIX environments, there is not yet a very rich set of text editing programs available, as there is for the DOS environment. This is changing rapidly.

In UNIX System V, for example, there are only two editors available that are part of the standard distribution: **ed**, the standard line editor; and **vi**, which can be thought of as a full screen implementation of **ed**.

Like it or not, at some point in time, UNIX users are likely to use the **ed** editor. Without a manual or some documentation to aid the user, **ed** can be less than user friendly (even downright frustrating) with its obvious lack of built-in aesthetics. However, in the hands of a true craftsman, even the cheapest instrument can be made to sound sweet, and so can the **ed** editor when used by an expert.

The **ed** editor provides most of the capabilities found in more exquisite text editors, such as block manipulation, global and limited scope of operations, etc., although in the real world it is not common to see many programmers using **ed** (especially when **vi** and **emacs** are available).

The **ed** editor would be very useful if the user had established a remote communication session with a UNIX system over a terminal device that used a hardcopy printer type of display mechanism, instead of a CRT screen device. The **vi** editor is also capable of being invoked over such a device, although the full screen operations would not be valid since the cursor movement to any portion of the screen is no longer valid.

The **ed** command is documented in the UNIX System V Interface Definition, and there are tutorials on **ed** in the documentation that is part of the standard UNIX distribution package. Curious developers can investigate these further in their UNIX documentation.

egrep

The **egrep** command is part of the **grep** family of pattern search commands. It performs an extended pattern search on files. The **egrep** command works like to the **grep** command, however, it accepts regular expressions that the **grep** command does not.

An example of how the **egrep** command works is as follows:

```
egrep Bil+ /etc/passwd
```

This example would list all entries containing the string "Bil" anywhere in the line for the /etc/passwd file. The output is echoed to the standard output. Another way to do this would be as in the following:

```
cat /etc/passwd | egrep Bil+
```

This form would be slower since it involves two operations, first to type the output and then to filter it in the **egrep** command. Another example of how the **egrep** command works is as follows:

```
egrep 'Bil+|Ste+' /etc/passwd
```

This example is asking the **egrep** command to filter out all entries that contain the strings "Bil" or "Ste" from the /etc/passwd file. Multiple files may be specified as follows:

```
egrep 'Bil+|Ste+' /etc/passwd  /etc/opasswd  /usr/entries
```

In this example three files were specified: /etc/passwd, /etc/opasswd, and /usr/entries. If there was a match for any of the files, the format of the reply is filename:entry, where filename is one of the filenames specified on the command line and entry is the actual line entry in the file that contains the search pattern. They are separated by a colon (:) character.

env

This command is used to obtain a list of the user's shell environment's contents. The contents are the strings that make up the environment variables and their values.

When the **env** command is executed without any option flags for the purpose of listing the environment values, it is called obtaining the current environment. A form of the **env** command allows for modification of the environment, prior to execution of other commands. To set or to change a variable, the following form of the command could be entered:

```
env variable=value
```

The result would be first to modify the environment and then to display it to the standard output. The variable is set to the value specified. Environment variables may be set, without using the **env** command, by entering variable=value on the command line. The result of setting variables using the **env** command is temporary since the modified envrionment is inherited only for the current command. A command may be executed as part of the **env** command as follows:

```
env variable=value command arg(s)
```

Using this form of the **env** command, the environment is modified first (variable=value) and then the command is executed using the inherited environment. After the command finishes execution, the environment is restored to its original state prior to modification.

fgrep

The **fgrep** command is another **grep** family command accepting only fixed strings as the pattern search argument. It is sometimes called "fast grep" since no time is spent evaluating expressions as in the **egrep** command. Its functions are the same as those of **grep** and **egrep** and it produces similar output.

find

This command is an easy and powerful way of locating objects in the UNIX file system. The UNIX **find** command has many option flags, of which only a few are mentioned here. See the UNIX System V Interface Definition for a full explanation of these flags.

The purpose of the **find** command is to search out file names matching the boolean expression specified on the command line. If no expression is provided, the default is to affect all files encountered. The search operation begins at the specified directory level (which is not optional); if no depth is specified then a diagnostic message is returned.

The search operation begins at the specified depth level and continues through the entire remaining subdirectory paths. Thus, if the starting depth was at the root of the file system, the entire file system would be searched for the occurrences of the specified item. This is a handy way to locate one or more items if the user is not sure where they exist or to check for duplicate named items in different directories. If, for example, users wished to locate a file called *Systems*, the following command could be entered:

```
find / -name Systems -print
```

This example instructs the **find** command to begin searching at the root of the file system, locate all occurrences of files named Systems, and print the results to the standard output. Meta characters are also supported as part of the item name, as in:

```
find / -name Sys* -print
```

This command line would produce a report of any file with the first three characters matching "Sys." If the depth of the search is to be limited, the user may accomplish this by making their current directory the beginning of the search path or by specifying the specific starting point. The following command line could be used if the user's current directory is to be the beginning of the search path:

```
find . -name Sys* -print
```

The following command line could be used to specify the starting point of the search path:

```
find /usr/tsm -name Sys* -print
```

If the entire contents of the file system were to be listed, the following command could be entered:

```
find / -print
```

By now it has become apparent that the -print option is used to direct the information to the standard output, and that the -name option is used to identify the pattern for which to search.

Another handy option is the -cpio option which automatically invokes the **cpio** command after the items have been located. For example, if users wish to create a backup of their directory to a diskette already mounted as /mnt and containing a file system, the following command might be entered:

```
find . -print -cpio /mnt/filename
```

This assumes that the current directory is already set to the desired directory. An equivalent of this command line (same assumptions) would be:

```
find . -print | cpio -ocv >  /mnt/filename
```

or

```
find . -print | cpio -pduvm /mnt
```

Of the above two command line examples, the first is the functional equivalent of the previous example. There is a major difference between the results of these two commands; have they become apparent yet? In the second of the above two lines, the output will be readable; that is, the output produced by the **cpio** command are all the files and directories from the **find** command.

They are not created as a single sequential file, but are created as mirror image files and directories in the /mnt directory. In the first of the two lines, the output would be a sequential file indicated by filename, and it would need to be processed by the -i mode of the **cpio** command in order to restore it back into readable files and directories. Other flags allow the find command to locate objects by their access permissions, file types, user ownerships, links, file size, dates, and other information.

grep

The **grep** (get regular expression) command is the base of the **grep** family of commands (**grep**, **egrep**, and **fgrep**). It is a filter that scans input files for matching patterns. When a match is encountered, the line containing it is written to the standard output, unless it is overridden by one of its option flags. Multiple files may be processed concurrently by specifying their names on the command line, although it is usually done on a single file at a time. The general form of the command is as follows:

```
grep options  expression  file(s)
```

The option flags are:

- -c flag: Produces the line count for the number of matches found.

- -i flag: Instructs grep to ignore the distinction between upper and lower case during comparisons.

- -l flag: Specifies that only the file names are to be displayed if a match is found. Useful when processing a large number of files.

- -n flag: Turns on line numbering which is included in the display of the matching lines.

- -s flag: Causes suppression of error messages arising when encountering nonexistent or unreadable files.

- -v flag: Instructs **grep** to print all but the matching lines to the standard output.

The expression should be enclosed within single quotes, ultimately evaluating to the pattern that is searched for. More than one file may be searched at a time by specifying the names on the command line, separated by white space. If users want to see their entry in a file, such as in the /etc/passwd file, it is not necessary to list the entire file, or to edit the file. The following command could be entered and would produce the desired information:

```
grep 'tsm' /etc/passwd
```

The following command is equivalent to the preceding example:

```
cat /etc/passwd | grep 'tsm'
```

While this produces identical results, it is slower because two separate processes are involved; first **cat** and then **grep**. The output of **cat** becomes a temporary file which is then piped to **grep**. This is additional overhead since **grep** could have directly read the /etc/passwd file.

Using the pipe makes it necessary to read the entire file again; first by the **cat** command and then by **grep**. Sometimes pipes are the only solution for obtaining input from a previous process.

The UNIX System V Interface Definition (SVID) entry for the **grep** command makes the statement that future versions of the **grep** command will contain the combined functionality of **egrep** and **fgrep**; and those two commands will be discontinued.

kill

This is the command used to terminate active processes in the UNIX system. There is no DOS system equivalent function because DOS is a single tasking system. A user must be authorized to kill a process. Only those processes started by a user may be terminated by that user. The superuser has authority to kill any process, including process 0.

The **kill** command sends a signal to the process about to be killed; the default is signal 15, terminate. The signal value is indicated in the command as an option flag, as in -15 for signal 15. The -9 flag is an immediate and certain kill; if the user is authorized to issue the **kill** for a process, there is no other validation, the process is immediately killed.

The general form of the **kill** command is as follows:

```
kill -signal# PID
```

The -signal# is the signal number sent to the process. The default is SIGTERM (signal 15) if none is specified; SIGKILL (signal 9) causes immediate unconditional termination. The PID is the process ID to kill.

This may be obtained using the **ps** command (documented later in this section), or when a background process is started by the user at the command line, the process ID number is echoed back to the terminal. An example of how to kill a process, assuming that the PID is 137 and the user is authorized to do so, is demonstrated in the command line below:

```
kill -9 137
```

Process ID number 137 would then be terminated immediately and released from memory.

ld

This command is used to combine multiple object files into one executable module. It is the linkage editor command. When multiple objects are combined into a single executable, all external symbols are resolved. The loader program (**ld**) generates the necessary symbol table used for symbolic debugging (**sdb**). The general form of this command is as follows:

```
ld options filename(s)
```

There are several option flags. The -m flag instructs **ld** to provide a link edit map as part of the output; it is displayed to the standard output. The -o flag is used to specify the name of the resulting output module and to override the default name of a.out. The -s flag strips symbol table entries previously used by the sdb command and produces a more compact execution module.

Refer to the UNIX System V Interface Definition entry for the **ld** command or to the UNIX System V User Reference Manual for a more thorough explanation of the option flags. Additional suggested reading on the **ld** command and related information may also be found in the UNIX System V Programmer Guide and in the Link Editor User Guide, both of which are normally provided as part of the standard documentation distributed with the UNIX System V distribution set.

lint

The **lint** program is used to perform precompilation syntax checking of C language source code. In addition to syntax checking, **lint** also attempts to identify items in the source code that may be potential problems, non-portable, or otherwise wasteful (such as unused variables). The general form of the **lint** command is as follows:

```
lint options file(s)
```

While there are several options, only those most likely to be used are specified here. The -h flag is used to suppress heuristic tests that identify potential bugs, wastefulness, or suggest improved style. The -n flag suppresses non-portability information and the -p flag enables stricter checking to test portability of the code to other versions of C.

Use of this command will help UNIX programmers reduce the time it takes to develop C applications. In some implementations other than UNIX System V, the functionality of **lint** is included as part of that system's C compiler. Additional reading on the **lint** command and related information may be found in the UNIX System V Programmer Guide.

ln

This command is used to create links (aliases) to another file. When a link is created to a file or to another link, all changes to the links are actually changes to the file to which they are being linked. Links may be made to other links, although files may not be linked across file systems. Only the superuser may link directories. Links may be removed using the **unlink** or **rm** commands, though great care should be used. An example of the **ln** command is as follows:

```
ln /usr/tsm/.profile myprofile
```

This **ln** statement creates an alias of myprofile for the /usr/tsm/.profile file. Any reference to the file myprofile is actually a reference to /usr/tsm/.profile. The link may be removed with either of the following command lines:

```
unlink myprofile
rm myprofile
```

make

This is the utility used to automate the program generation process for UNIX developers. It works by reading an input file with the special file name of makefile, which contains a list of dependencies. When any of the items in the dependency list are modified, the **make** utility determines which specific modules need to be recompiled and linked, rather than recompiling every module for the program. The **make** utility accepts several option flags:

- -e flag: Indicates that environmental variables are to override assignments within the makefile.

- -i flag: Causes the return codes of commands invoked by the makefile to be ignored.

- -k flag: Causes work on the current entry to be abandoned, but all non-dependent processing is continued.

- -n flag: Indicates that the commands in the makefile are to be listed only, no execution takes place.

- -p flag: Causes all macro definitions and target descriptions to be printed.

- -q flag: The question flag causes the make command to return either a zero or non-zero return code, depending whether the target file is up to date or not.

- -r flag: Causes built-in rules to be bypassed.

- -s flag: Indicates silent mode which supresses the printing of command lines.

- -t flag: Causes the target file time/date stamps to be brought up to date.

mkdir

This command is used to create directories and is a required fundamental that all UNIX system users should understand. An example of **mkdir** is as follows:

```
mkdir newdir
```

This example creates a new directory, called newdir, in the current directory. At this point, it is assumed that the reader is already familiar with the concept of UNIX directory tree structures. The following example shows how to create a directory at a specific location:

```
mkdir /usr/tsm/newdir
```

mv

The **mv** command is used to move a file from the source location to the destination. It works very much like the **cp** command, except that the source is deleted after the file has been copied. The **mv** command should be used with caution. If the target file already exists, **mv** will overwrite it unconditionally. Also, if several files are being moved at the same time, the target must exist; otherwise, the **mv** command will issue a diagnostic. An example of the **mv** command is as follows:

```
mv /usr/tsm/mbox /usr/wbu
```

In this example, the file being moved is /usr/tsm/mbox, and the destination is a directory, /usr/wbu, that previously existed. At the end of the operation, mbox no longer exists in the /usr/tsm directory.

od

This is the octal dump command (actually, a general dump command), that reads a file and displays the contents in octal, hexadecimal, ASCII, decimal, or any combination of these. An offset within the file where the **od** command begins displaying the data may also be specified. The format is determined according to the option flags which are:

- -b flag: displays bytes in octal format.

- -c flag: displays bytes in ASCII format.

- -d flag: displays words in unsigned decimal format.

- -o flag: displays words in octal format.

- -s flag: displays words in signed decimal format.

- -x flag: displays words in hexadecimal format.

The general form of the command is as follows:

```
od -options file
```

The -options are one or more of the above option flags. If none is specified, then the -o flag is the default. The file is the name of the file being dumped. If none is specified, the standard input is the default. When the standard input is being used as the input source, a CTRL-D terminates the input line. Users should experiment with this command in order to observe the many possible combinations of output. The output may be redirected to a file if desired.

pack

This command reads an input file and produces a compressed version as output. It is used in conjunction with the **unpack** command that performs the opposite function of **pack**. The original input file(s) are replaced by the packed output files and their names are appended with the characters ".z," indicating (by convention) that they have been compressed. Compression will not occur for any of the following reasons:

- file cannot be opened for some reason

- file is already packed

- no benefits derived as a result of the packing

- the input file is empty

- the .z output file already exists

- the .z file cannot be created for some reason

- input file has links to it
- input file name specified is a directory
- invalid input file name specified
- I/O errors during packing process

The output file name must adhere to standard UNIX naming conventions and allow for inclusion of the .z character string which is automatically appended; otherwise, the process will fail. Character files, (such as ASCII text files) normally benefit the most from packing. They are compressed into a binary format on a byte-by-byte basis using a minimum redundancy compression code, often achieving compression greater than 70 percent.

Binary files, such as load modules (programs), usually achieve less than 15 percent compression since they are already in a binary format. Generally, the larger the file, the more compression is likely to occur. Files that occupy less than three disk blocks receive little or no benefit from being packed.

Some interesting uses of the **pack** command are: when creating files to be used to transport data media that has limited available space (such as diskettes) or for data transmission over some communications media (such as a switched telephone, direct line, or local area network connections).

By packing the transmission file(s), the transmission time may be reduced. This, of course, assumes the receiving system is capable of unpacking the files. The **pack** command may force compression of files by specifying the -f option flag. The only other option flag is the - flag, which acts as a toggle.

The first occurrence of the - flag (without anything immediately following) sets an internal flag that displays certain statistical information which includes the compression percentage, among other things. The next occurrence of the - option flag negates the first one, and so on.

This command is particularly useful when combined with certain other commands in a procedure. If it were desirable to transmit an entire directory, along with its subdirectories and their subsequent files, users could accomplish this through the following steps.

First, the **find** command may be used to obtain the list of which files and directories to affect. Next, these files would be piped to the **cpio** command which may be used to create a sequential file containing the directory structure. This process could easily produce a huge output file. Before transmitting this file to its destination, or copying it to a diskette or tape, it could be packed and reduced substantially.

The following is an example of such a procedure. It assumes a user (tsm) wishes to create a transmission file of the home directory and all subsequent files and directories.

```
find /usr/tsm -print | cpio -ocv > tranfile
pack -f tranfile
```

The first line uses the **find** command to create a list starting at user tsm's home directory and pipes it to the **cpio** command, which in turn produces a sequential output file called tranfile. This file contains all the information for the **cpio** command to reconstruct the /usr/tsm directory and all its files and subdirectories. The second line unconditionally packs tranfile (because the -f option flag was specified), producing a new file called tranfile.z, which may then be used as the transmission file for some communications transfer, such as **uucp** or **uuto**.

Once the file arrives at the destination, the process is reversed. The packed transmission file is placed in its target directory and is then unpacked. After that, the **cpio** command is used to reconstruct the directories and files contained in tranfile. The following example demonstrates how this process may be accomplished:

```
mv /usr/spool/uucppublic/tranfile.z /usr/wbu
cd /usr/wbu
unpack tranfile.z | cpio -iduvm </usr/wbu/tranfile
```

This example assumes that the transmission file, tranfile.z, was placed into the /usr/spool/uucppublic directory, making it necessary to relocate the file to another target directory. In this case, the target directory is the home directory of a user ID, called wbu. After moving the transmission file there, the current directory becomes /usr/wbu, as indicated in the **cd** command.

With /usr/wbu as the current directory, the file is unpacked, using the **unpack** command. The tranfile.z file is replaced with the unpacked version of the **cpio** file, tranfile. Next, the **cpio** command is used to create the files and subdirectories which existed in the /usr/tsm directory of the sending system. (Caution should be used in this type of operation. If there are any files in the directory to which the cpio input file is being restored, they may be overwritten. See the **cpio** command for additional details.)

There is no standard DOS equivalent command for this standard UNIX feature. There are, however, public domain utility programs (**arc**, **pk**, and **pkx**) that perform similar functions, although they are limited in certain functions.

ps

The purpose of the **ps** command is to report the status of processes that are active in the UNIX system. For those who are knowledgeable in the IBM mainframe operating system MVS, this is the UNIX system's counterpart of the MVS "**d a,l**" (display activity) command.

The **ps** command has several option flags. The flags -e and -f are of most interest to developers, since they report all information available for all processes. These flags are usually specified as -ef, which produces eight columns of information as follows:

- UID column: Identifies the user ID of the owner of the process. The ID corresponds to the login name of the user, as specified in their /etc/passwd entry.

- PID column: Identifies the process ID number, which is necessary to know for any action that may be taken for the process, such as a **kill** command.

- PPID column: Identifies the parent process, indicating how the process was originally initiated. (Only process 0 is its own parent.)

- C column: Indicates the amount of processor utilization for scheduling.

- STIME column: Indicates the time the process was started. Certain processes may have a date instead of a time, indicating that they are system startup processes created by process 0.

- TTY column: Indicates the controlling terminal associated with the process, and may contain the ? character, meaning the process has no controlling terminal. The value in this column has a corresponding entry in the /dev directory.

- TIME column: Indicates the total execution time the process has accumulated since it was started.

- COMMAND column: Describes the name of the process by indicating the command it is executing, as well as its arguments.

An easy way to determine what someone may be up to is to issue the **ps** command and search for any lines containing the **ed**, **vi**, or **emacs** (if available) commands. They may contain enough information to determine which files they are editing. An example of how this can be done is as follows:

```
ps -ef | egrep "vi|ed|emacs"
```

This line may produce output indicating processes that may not be performing any of the commands being searched for. Since the **egrep** command is itself a process, and contains the very items being searched for, it will appear in the output. Since the **ps** command is also a process, and the UNIX system is a multitasking operating system, the displayed information may no longer be valid by the time it appears on the output, if things have changed.

Users are encouraged to experiment with this command and its option flags, which may be referenced in the UNIX System V Interface Definition, or in the UNIX System V User Reference Manual.

pwd

This command is used to display the current directory, and is actually an acronym for *print working directory*. It has no option flags and merely echoes back the current directory (UNIX path name). If any error message is returned, it may be an indication of possible file system trouble and should be reported to the UNIX system administrator.

```
$ pwd
/usr/src/cmd/vi
$
```

In the preceding example, the $ represents the UNIX command line prompt. The first line indicates the user entering the **pwd** command and the second line is the response which assumes that the user is in the directory called "/usr/src/cmd/vi" (which, in UNIX System V, is the location for the source code to the **vi** editor). In the third line, after pwd is finished the shell returns back to the user prompt string (indicated by the environment variable PS1).

rm

This command is used to remove files from the UNIX file system. The option flags are the -f, -r, and -i. The default action, when no flags are specified, is to attempt removal of the specified objects. If the specified file name is a directory, an error is displayed — unless the -r flag was specified. The -r flag (recursive) indicates that directories and their entire contents (including any subdirectories and their contents) should be removed.

Normally, users must have write permission to directories containing files (or subdirectories) that are being removed. The superuser overrides any such requirements. Files in a directory need not have write permission to be removed. If a file doesn't have write permission, a message indicating the actual file permission values is printed and the user is prompted for a response to proceed with the removal.

Only a response beginning with the character "y" will effect removal of the file.

If the -y flag was specified, no prompt appears and the file is unconditionally deleted. (Users must still have write permissions to the directory!) The -i flag is the opposite of the -f flag; it creates an interactive dialogue for every file, regardless of access permissions. It verifies the deletion before taking place. Only a response beginning with the character "y" will allow for deletion of the file in question.

If the -f and -i flags are both specified, the -i flag takes precedence. If the specified file is the last link to a file, the link and file are both removed!

Beware of entering wild card characters, as they can have disastrous consequences! When entering the following command be absolutely certain of the current directory in which it is executed:

```
rm -r *
```

This is especially true if the user has superuser privileges!

rmdir

This command is used to remove only those directories that are empty, and is a relatively safe way of removing directories. Assuming the directory called "/usr/src/cmd/junk" contains no files, the following command line may be entered to remove the directory from the file system:

```
rmdir /usr/src/cmd/junk
```

In this example, *junk* must be a directory and not a file, otherwise a diagnostic error message will appear.

SCCS

SCCS is an acronym for Source Code Control System, a feature that may not necessarily be a standard part of all UNIX systems. As the name implies, SCCS is used to manage source code updates. It is actually a collection of programs that make up the system, and not a single module.

It is used for storing text source files, fetching versions of a source file, controlling update access to source files, identifying source files, and keeping track of change information (who, when, where, and why changes were made). The following information is not intended to be a full tutorial of SCCS. A full tutorial may be found in the UNIX System V Programmer's Guide. The covered material is designed to provide UNIX developers (who may not yet be familiar with SCCS) with a basic understanding of what SCCS can do and how it works.

SCCS appears to be intimidatingly sophisticated at first, but, as with most UNIX development tools, it becomes easy to use and understand after some practice and it becomes an invaluable timesaver. In fact, it may at some point save the developer much grief and many hours of tedious program reconstruction in the event anything ever happens to a source file. The uses for such a control system are obvious.

Say, for example, that a problem is reported with some program in the field and the program version ia many levels old. One of the first questions likely to be asked is "What version of the program are you using?" The support personnel should have the ability to reproduce the problem with the version of the program being reported. With SCCS this is accomplished easily. Programs are usually maintained by several programmers during their existence. Different people have different habits when documenting changes, not all are necessarily good. SCCS becomes an invaluable tool for keeping track of such changes.

It should be noted that SCCS is capable of maintaining source code for programming languages other than the C language. In fact, any text file can be administered using SCCS. Perhaps SCCS should have more properly been called Version Control System.

The changes, called *deltas* in SCCS terminology, are stored in special files called *s-files* and are assigned an SCCS identification (SID) string that can have up to four components. The release and level numbers of the file are the first two components, and they are separated by a period.

The initial value of the release and level numbers is 1.1; the second update is 1.2; the third is 1.3, and so on. Although the release number may be changed at any time, it is usually reserved to represent major changes to the file.

The commands that make up SCCS are listed below, and may be referenced in the UNIX System V Programmer's Guide for additional detail.

- admin: Initialization of SCCS files.

- cdc: Changes delta commentary.

- comb: Combines delta files into a single delta file.

- delta: Applies the actual changes (delta's) to the source file (s.) under SCCS control.

- get: Obtains the source file (s.) under SCCS control; also provides file information.

- help: Reports information about SCCS error messages.

- prs: Formatted print out of portions of the source file (s.) under SCCS control.

- rmdel: Removes deltas that may have been made in error, from the source file (s.).

- sact: Reports data about currently active source files under edit.

- sccsdiff: Does comparison of any two SCCS source files (s.) and reports any differences between them.

- unget: Undoes the get -e command if the file has not been changed with the delta command.

- val: Performs validation of an SCCS source file (s.).

- vc: Version control filter.

sed

This command is the stream editor. It is a less powerful version of the **awk** command and is actually a powerful filter. It is useful when the functionality of the **grep** family of commands is too limited.

Sometimes it is useful to "edit" large files from a shell script. A shell script can be made extremely intelligent through the use of the **sed** command. The **sed** command copies lines of input from the specified input file(s) and produces edited output lines to the specified output file. The default input, if no file is specified, is the standard input; the default output is the standard output, unless a filename is specified.

The **sed** command is driven by commands describing what editing action is to occur. These commands may be grouped together into a file called a script file, which may be created using any text editor, such as **vi**. The -f option flag is used to instruct sed to receive its editing script from a script file. The achievable level of functionality using the **sed** command is that of the **ed** editor.

As a simplified example of what the **sed** command is capable of, assume that it is necessary to modify a C language source code file so that all occurrences of the string "dts" become "DTS." Assume that the name of the file being modified is called "dts.c" and that it is in a directory called /usr/src/dts. The following **sed** command may be entered from the command line by a user:

```
sed s/dts/DTS/g /usr/src/dts/dts.c  /usr/src/dts/DTS.c
```

What this command is likely to do is to substitute "DTS" for all occurrences of "dts" in file /usr/src/dts/dts.c and to write the output to a file called /usr/src/dts/DTS.c.

The file name specified in the output was converted to upper case manually by the programmer, not by **sed**. If no filename is specified for the output, the file is echoed to the standard output. In either case, the input file remains unchanged. The input file and output file should be different names.

Since **sed** works one line at a time, if the input and output files were the same, the output file would be truncated to a length of 0 upon opening the file for output. This is why the target file of /usr/src/dts/DTS.c was created. A subsequent **mv** command could be used to move the DTS.c file to the new name of dts.c.

sort

The **sort** command, as the name implies, is used to produce sorted output files. It can sort multiple input files and merges the sorted output into a single file, which by default is the standard output. An output file may be created either using the redirection character on the command line, or through the specification of the -o option flag. This command has several option flags, some of which are discussed here. The general form of the command is:

```
sort option(s) file(s)
```

If a minus sign (-) appears in place of a file name or if the file name is omitted, the standard input is used as the source. Multiple sort keys are supported, although the default assumes only one. The default collating sequence is ascending according to ASCII lexicographic conventions. Some of the option flags necessary with which the reader should be familiar are as follows:

- -c flag: Checks to see if a file is already sorted to ordering specifications; output is produced only if records in the file are out of sequence.

- -m flag: Assumes the specified input files have been previously sorted and only merges them to the output.

- -u flag: Performs comparison of the specified files and produces only a single output line (sorted), even for those lines that are identical in all input files. This guarantees unique output, duplicity is avoided.

- -o flag: Specifies the name of the output file. The general format is -ofilename or -o filename, where filename is the name of the output file. This is an alternative to using output file redirection.

- -d flag: Specifies that the sort is to use *dictionary order;* that is, only letters, spaces, tabs, digits, etc. are to be compared, in dictionary collating sequence.

- -f flag: Ignores case differences, "folds" lower case to upper case for comparisons.

- -i flag: Instructs sort to ignore all characters in the file that are outside of the ASCII range. Only the ASCII values 20H through 7EH are eligible for non-numeric comparisons.

- -r flag: Indicates the collating sequence is to be reversed.

- -t flag: Identifies the character to be used as the field delimiter for the input lines. The default field delimiter is a white space (blank) character.

- +n flag: n indicates the field number on which to begin sorting, the default is 1 so a value of +1 would be field 2.

- -n flag: n indicates the beginning of the field number on which to end sorting. If this is omitted, sort assumes the comparison to the end of the input line. If -n were a value of -4 then the sort would compare up to the end of the fourth field.

Some examples of the **sort** command are shown in the following lines:

```
sort file1 file2
sort -o sorted file1 file2
sort -urf file1 file2 > sorted
ls -l | sort -r +5 -7
ls -l | sort -o sorted -r +5 -7
ls -l | sort -r +5 -7 > sorted
```

The first example will sort files named file1 and file2, producing all sorted lines on the standard output. The second example performs the same function, but writes the output to a file called sorted, as specified in the -o option flag.

The third example uses the redirection method of storing the output to the file called sorted; while the option flags, -urf, indicate only unique records are to be written in reverse order and that case differences are to be ignored.

The fourth example pipes the output from the **ls** command and sorts the lines in reverse order for fields 6 through the end of field 7. This happens to be the date information produced by the long form of the **ls** command (month and date), and is one way of displaying the files in chronological order by most recent modification date. In this example the output is directed to the standard output.

In example five, the same function is accomplished, but the output is redirected to a file called sorted, as specified by the -o option flag. In example six the same function is again performed, but the output is saved to the file name which is sorted through the use of the redirection character.

spell

This is the UNIX system spelling checker utility. Spell checking may be performed on any text file. The **spell** command uses its own dictionary, as well as a user-provided list of words (auxiliary dictionary). By default, the input to **spell** is obtained from the standard input. The general format of the **spell** command is as follows:

```
spell option(s) +auxfile file(s)
```

Options are the following option flags:

- -b flag: Indicates that the British form of spell checking is to be used. The British spell certain words differently than the Americanized versions of the same English language words; for example, colour instead of color; centre instead of center; programme instead of program; and many words sometimes use *is* instead of *iz* as in *standardisation/standardization.*

- -v flag: Verbose; causes all words *not* in the dictionary lists to be printed to the standard output, as well as seemingly similar words that were logical derivations of the suspected misspelling.

- -x flag: Causes all possible iterations of the suspected misspelling to be printed with the = character.

- +auxfile: Names a user-provided text file containing a list of words (sorted in ascending order) that will be used as a user dictionary and which will be searched when words are not found in the standard dictionary.

Multiple files may be specified for the **spell** command, but the output is concatenated (in sorted order) to the standard output, which may be redirected to a file.

The UNIX **spell** command is adequately functional but, admittedly, leaves a lot to be desired when compared to similar utility programs available for DOS environments and even third party add-on word processing software packages for UNIX environments.

stty

The **stty** command may be used to inquire about the state of certain terminal characteristics, as well as for setting their values. All users logged on to the UNIX system, regardless of whether or not they are on a locally attached device (such as the primary monitor and keyboard considered to be the master console of the UNIX workstation), have certain terminal characteristics.

These characteristics may include such information as connection type and speed, special characters (backspace, kill, line deletion, character deletion, end of file, end of line, break key, etc.), flow control data, and communication line characteristics. When this command is entered with no arguments, it echoes back a summary of setting information. If the -a option is specified, then a full report of the setting information is returned.

The -g flag formats the setting information into fields that are separated by colons. These fields may be manipulated by other commands, such as other **stty** commands. There are many options that can be set using the **stty** command.

The settings likely to be of immediate interest are: how to change the backspace character, parity and line speed settings; and, how to reset the erase and kill characters to their default values.

The following examples explain how to accomplish this.

```
stty -a
```

This command will provide a long listing of all changeable **stty** values and their current settings.

```
stty erase '^H'
```

116

This example sets the erase character to the backspace character.

```
stty kill '#'
```

This example sets the kill character to the "#" character.

```
stty ek
```

This example resets the erase and kill characters to their standard defaults of "#" and "@", respectively.

```
stty parodd
```

This example selects odd parity; -parodd is the logical opposite of odd (even parity).

```
stty cs8
```

This example indicates that a character is 8 data bits; the values are cs5-8, the default is 7.

```
stty 4800
```

This example will reset the baud rate to 4800 for terminals connected via a serial communications port.

```
stty ixon
```

This example indicates that XON flow control is to be enabled; -ixon would disable XON flow control processing.

```
stty ixoff
```

This example indicates that XOFF flow control is to be enabled; -ixoff would disable XOFF flow control processing.

tr

This is the command used to translate characters in a file. It is not as sophisticated as **sed** or **awk**, but is quite useful, nevertheless. Some of the most common reasons for the use of the **tr** command are to perform case translation for text files, to perform simple string substitutions, and to perform simple pattern editing. The simplest form of the command is:

```
tr str1 str2 < filename
```

This example indicates that all occurrences of str1 in the specified file in filename are substituted to str2, and the results are written to the standard output. Another variation of this is:

```
tr str1 str2 < filename > filename2
```

This example indicates that the output is to be saved in a file indicated by filename2. If it is desirable to convert lower case to all upper case characters in a file, the following example would work in UNIX System V:

```
tr \[a-z\] \[A-Z\] < filename > filename2
tr '[a-z]' '[A-Z]' <filename> filename2
```

Ranges are specified by using the hyphen between the range values, which are enclosed within escaped brackets. In this example, all lower case characters in filename are converted to uppercase and are written to filename2.

Numeric ranges are permissible as well. There are three possible option flags for the tr command. The -d flag specifies that the values specified in the first editing argument are to be deleted from the output text.

For example, if for some reason someone wanted to produce a text file that contained no vowels, the following example could be used:

```
tr -d "aeiouy" < filename > filename2
```

The file indicated by filename2 would then contain words with only consonants. The -c flag performs substitutions.

unpack

The **unpack** command is the logical opposite of the **pack** command. It performs decompression on files that have been compressed using the pack command. The .z that was appended to the filename by the **pack** command is removed by **unpack**. Examples of the **unpack** command are as follows:

```
unpack myfile.z
unpack myfile
```

The first example line unpacks a file called myfile.z and, after removing the .z qualifier, leaves behind the unpacked file now renamed to myfile. The second line produces identical results; the .z qualifier is optional when specifying the input file name to the **un-pack** command. If the .z qualifier is omitted, **unpack** assumes it. If no file exists with the .z qualifer, an error will occur.

vi

This command invokes the visual editor, which is a full screen display oriented text editor. It is a descendent of the **ed** line editor and is primarily driven by keyboard commands. This editor lacks some of the features and glitter that are to be found on the editing programs available for the DOS or IBM mainframe environments, but **vi** is still a powerful and useful tool.

Once users get accustomed to it, it can be quite easy to use. The most serious problem with **vi** is that without an instruction manual it is practically useless since the user interface doesn't offer any clues as to its usage. The user interface is not intuitive and there is no built-in help facility.

In the **vi** editor it is possible, however, to accomplish almost anything that most other editors can do, and even several things which most other editors cannot.

With **vi** it is possible to insert, delete, move, and copy blocks of text that may be anything from a single character to an entire range of lines. It is possible to limit the range of changes or make them global. The **vi** editor also has the ability to do pattern search/replace operations on a limited or global basis. Text may also be deleted and moved to a new location (cut and paste operations) within the file, and data can be imported from other text files.

Additionally, **vi** is capable of editing any kind of file, text or binary. One of the most important features of **vi** is the ability to undo changes if necessary. The **vi** editor can also edit one file and create the output to a different file, leaving the original intact. It is possible to execute UNIX commands without ever leaving the file being edited because **vi** allows the invocation of a sub-shell, without termination of the edit process.

If a file is lost due to an interrupt, the -r flag of **vi** may be used to attempt recovery of that file. Several files may be edited (serially) by specifying them on the command line. When each file is written (or terminated using the q command) the **:n** command will bring up the next file.

wc

The **wc** command is also called the word count command. It can count and report the number of characters, words, and lines in the specified file(s). If no input files are specified, then the standard is the default (terminated by a CTRL-D to close it.) If no option flags are specified, the default is to provide all (characters, words, and lines) information to the standard output that may be redirected. There are three option flags that may be specified:

- -l flag: Only the number of lines are reported.

- -w flag: Only the number of words are reported.

- -c flag: Only the number of characters are reported.

Examples of the **wc** command are as follows:

```
wc  $HOME/mbox
wc  -c  $HOME/.profile
wc  -w  /etc/passwd
wc  -l  /etc/passwd
wc  -cl  $HOME/.profile
```

The first example line will execute the **wc** command and report the number of characters, words, and lines for a file called mbox (located in the user's home directory). In the second example line, **wc** will report only the number of characters for a file called .profile in the user's home directory.

In the third example line, the **wc** command will echo back only the number of words for the /etc/passwd file, while in the fourth line **wc** reports only the number of lines for the same file. In the last example line, **wc** will report the characters and lines for the user's .profile file in their directory.

who

The **who** command is used to determine the number and identities of the users currently logged in to the UNIX system. Besides the user's name, the **who** command can also report the user's time of login; the login terminal (/dev entry); the user's command interpreter PID; and other information, all by reading a file called /etc/utmp which is dynamically modified as each user logs in or out of the system.

The **who** command also performs an additional special function when the phrase "am i" or "am I" is specified in place of the option flags. The result is that the **who** command will echo back information about the user ID associated with the terminal fromwhere the command was entered. This can be useful when in a room full of terminals it is desirable to know the ID of the user who is logged on to a terminal that may be unattended. There are several option flags that may be specified, some of which are listed below.

- -a flag: This option produces a report with all options specified.

- -H flag: Produces column headings for the output of who.

- -s flag: Reports only the user ID, login terminal ID, and login time fields (default).

- -b flag: Echoes back the date stamp information since the last system boot.

- -q flag: Echoes back the number of users currently logged on.

- -l flag: Reports the lines waiting for users to log in.

Examples of the **who** command are as follows:

```
who
who am i
who -a
who -aq
who -Ha
who -Haq
who -Hb
```

CHAPTER 4

UNIX AND DOS COMPARISONS

The File System

In both UNIX and DOS files refer to the standard definition of a collection of data organized in logical order. In both operating system environments, files are stored in a structure called the file system. A file system is a collection of files organized in a specific fashion, such as a tree structure. The file system is usually integrated into the operating system and the operating system controls access to the files it contains. In mainframe terminology, this access is controlled by a mechanism known as the access method; in UNIX and DOS this is built into their kernels.

The UNIX and DOS environments use a hierarchical file system resembling an inverted tree structure, with the beginning or root at the very top, and branching downward. On the surface, the file systems of both environments appear to be similar. To a certain degree they are, but it is a superficial similarity. They use a lot of the same terminology, for instance, they both use the term *directory* to refer to a node within the structure. In both systems, directories contain files and/or other directories. The general hierarchy is also the same. UNIX file systems, however, contain certain files that are not present in the DOS environment, such as special files used to refer to I/O devices connected to the computer — as in the UNIX directory /dev.

The DOS file system was modeled from the CPM file system, which in turn was modeled originally from the UNIX file system; this partly explains the similarity. The DOS file system is much simpler than in the UNIX system. Without getting into details of the UNIX file system at this time, potential UNIX developers simply need to know that if they understand the basic structure and function of the DOS file system, they will have no difficulty with the UNIX file system. The real differences to the user, regarding the file system, are at the command execution level for the commands used to view and manipulate files and directories.

File System Commands

In DOS, the **dir** command is used to view the contents of a directory, the UNIX counterpart would be the **ls** command. Both commands allow for optional parameters to be specified in the command line, but their forms are slightly different. By convention, command line arguments used for the standard DOS commands, including the **dir** command, use the form "**command/arg**", where **command** is the actual command to execute, and **arg** is the actual argument to be passed. The forward slash character (/) is used as a delimiter (called the *switch* character) to indicate an argument that follows. Multiple "**/arg**" parameters on a single command line are permissible.

The UNIX form is similar, but the switch character is slightly different. By convention, any of the following forms are acceptable:

```
command -arg ... -arg
command -arg arg ... arg
command -arg1arg2arg3...
```

The following example illustrates some of the equivalent forms of the **ls** command and the **dir** command in DOS.

DOS	UNIX	FUNCTION
dir	ls -l	list directory entries
dir /w	ls -x	list entries across screen
dir \auto*	ls -ld /auto*	list entry using wildcard
dir /p or dir | more	ls -l | more	list entries and pause

UNIX and DOS have slightly different, but functionally identical, commands used to create and remove directories. To create directories in either UNIX or DOS, the **mkdir** command is used and to remove directories, the **rmdir** command is used. The DOS form of these commands also have aliases, **md** and **rd**. In both systems, the target directory must be empty before it is possible to remove it.

In UNIX the **rm** command is used to remove files, while in DOS the **del** or **erase** commands are used. The **cp** command is used to copy files in UNIX, and in DOS the **copy** command performs the equivalent function. To move or rename a file in UNIX the **mv** command is used, while in DOS the **rename** command is used. There is no built-in way to move a file in DOS. In the UNIX system it is possible to assign an alias for a file by creating a link to an existing file name using the **ln** command; there is no DOS equivalent for this UNIX capability.

In UNIX, the **cat** command is used to view the actual contents of printable files, while in DOS it is the **type** command. Output from the **cat** and **type** commands can be redirected in either UNIX or DOS, using the standard redirection facilities built into both environments. In UNIX systems, an alternative to **cat** is the more filter (on some systems this is the pg filter). DOS also has a more filter.

File System Navigation

UNIX and DOS file systems both support the concept of a *current directory* or the directory location within the file system hierarchy that is considered the current position of the user. This means that if no full path information is supplied as part of the command arguments, the resulting action of a command will affect the files in the current directory first, and then any other directory paths specified in the PATH environment variable.

125

Navigation through the file system hierarchy is achieved through the use of the change directory command in both UNIX and DOS. In DOS this is the **chdir** command, in UNIX it is the **cd** command. The DOS **chdir** command also has an alias of **cd.**

Another important thing for all users of a hierarchical file system to know is what their current directory is. In the UNIX system the standard user prompt string normally does not display any information to indicate this, although it is possible to modify the prompt string environment variable so that it provides the path name of the current directory.

In DOS this is done through the PROMPT environment variable using built-in features that provide drive and path information. To obtain the current directory in UNIX the user enters the **pwd** command; in DOS users enter the **cd** command with no arguments. In both cases the current directory is echoed back. If the **cd** command is entered with no arguments in the UNIX environment, the current directory is set to the user's HOME directory.

A HOME directory, also called the *login* directory, contains files belonging to the user. This is normally the default directory that the user starts out in after login and is considered to be that user's home base within the file system.

It is known as the HOME directory because of the UNIX environment variable, HOME, that is usually set to the path name for a user's login directory.

Directory Entry Contents

The DOS file system stores information such as the file name, file size in bytes, the creation/last modified date stamp, creation/last modified time stamp, and other attributes (read, write, file/directory) for each entry in the directory. The UNIX file system stores the entry's attributes, number of links, owner id, group id, file size in bytes, creation/last modified time/date stamp, and the file/directory name.

It is evident that the amount of information about a directory entry in UNIX file systems is considerably more than in DOS directory entries. This is because the UNIX file system was designed for concurrent multiuser access. The output of the **ls -l** command will print the detailed form of the directory entry listing. The first field of this output is used to determine the entry type and its access permissions. An example of this field is as follows:

```
drwxrwxrwx
0123456789
```

Type and Access Permissions

The second line of the previous example is not part of the normal output, but is placed there for illustrative purposes to indicate the positioning of the characters on the line above. If the first character, in position 0, is a "d" it means the entry is a directory. If it is a "-" then it is an ordinary file. If this character is a "b," "c," or "p," this indicates the file is a special file used by the UNIX operating system to perform I/O operations.

The next group of characters, positions 1 through 3, indicate the owner's access permissions to this file; the characters *rwx* are used to indicate *read, write,* and *execution* permissions. If a "-" appears in either of these positions it indicates the absence of that type of access permission. The access permission of *x* indicates that the file is an executable file, such as a binary executable command or a shell script file. Files that do not have this set permission will not be allowed to execute, regardless if they are actually binary executable programs or shell scripts. DOS, in contrast, uses the file name itself as the mechanism to determine if files are executable and how they will be treated.

The three positions, 4 through 6, indicate the access permissions for the group level. The last three characters in positions 7 through 9 indicate the access permissions for all other users of the system. The three access levels indicated here are referred to as *user, group,* and *other*. The types of access permissions for all three levels are the same. The DOS file system does not have any corresponding functionality since it was designed as a single user system, security access permissions weren't a consideration.

Links

The information regarding links refers to the number of aliases of this file. (Aliases for files are different from command aliases.) If file modification is performed using any of its aliases, it is the original file that is actually affected. Care should be taken using the **rm** command with linked files; if the alias was the last link to a file in UNIX, the file may be removed as well. There is no DOS equivalent of UNIX links.

User (Owner) Access Permissions Field

The user field identifies the owner of the entry. Owners are free to change the access permissions for the entry (for any access level) to whatever they like. The superuser may access this file in any mode, overriding the owner's access permissions. File ownership is either automatically set when the file is created by the owner or assigned via the UNIX **chown** command. Only the owner and the superuser may reassign file ownerships.

The access permissions are set automatically by the owner's *file creation mask* when the file is created, and may be reset at any time via the UNIX **chmod** command. In UNIX-based systems it is possible to specify the default file creation mask; this is the default set of access permissions for all newly created files, and is done by setting the *umask* system variable with the **umask** command. If the umask system variable is not specified either in the user's .profile (K-Shell or Bourne Shell) or .cshrc (C Shell) file, a default value is used — one that was established previously during login processing.

There is no DOS equivalent for the concept of file ownership and access permissions, although file attributes such as read only, write only, read/write, hidden, system, or archive may be set using the DOS **attrib** command.

The group access permissions field is used to identify the group to which the owner belongs, or the group ID authorized to access the file according to the settings of the group access permissions. This field defaults to the group the owner belongs to when the file is created, and may be subsequently modified using the UNIX **chgrp** command.

Users not belonging to the group specified in this field may only access this entry according to the access permissions set for all remaining users (other), while users that are members of this group may only access the entry according to the settings in force. There is no DOS functional equivalent for this feature.

The file size field indicates the entry's size in total number of bytes, and is the functional equivalent of the file size information provided in the DOS **dir** command. The creation/modification — date/time stamps field contains a date and time stamp of the creation or last modification date information, and is the functional equivalent of the information found for files in the DOS file system — though the exact format of the date information differs.

The file name is is the UNIX file or directory name for the entry. It is identical to the equivalent directory information in the DOS file system, except that file and directory names adhere to the standard naming conventions used in the UNIX file system.

File Access and Manipulation

There are basically two forms of file manipulation: external manipulation such as moving, deleting, and copying; and internal manipulation as in modification of the contents of a file. The external manipulation commands previously have been introduced in the section on File System Manipulation.

The internal manipulation techniques involve the use of text editing or word processing programs, or other utility programs and commands designed to alter the contents of files, such as pipes and filters.

There are two standard text editors distributed with UNIX-based systems. They are **ed** and **vi**. The **ed** editor is a simple and relatively easy to use text editor. It is completely command line-based and does not use any full screen editing features. This editor was designed and written at a time when full screen editing was not yet popular. Without a prior understanding of the **ed** editor or a manual, it is next to impossible to use, as are most other command-based editors.

Ed is remotely similar to the DOS system's **edlin** program. Actually, it more closely resembles the IBM VM/370 original CMS editor,

edit. The **ed** editor can be learned in a relatively short period, however, it is quite primitive when compared to other text editors available in the UNIX and DOS systems.

The **vi** editor is a bit more advanced and is the favorite of many true blue UNIX developers. It is a full screen editor packed with a lot of powerful features, and is also documented in the UNIX System V distribution documentation. It is still largely a command line-based editor, and from a user interface point of view, may even appear primitive in comparison to certain text editors available in UNIX, DOS, and other environments.

Memory Management and Usage

This is an area where the UNIX and DOS systems differ sharply. The actual management by the UNIX and DOS kernels is different because the design of each operating system is different; for example, one is single user, single-tasking and the other is a full multi-programming environment. In the UNIX system there are a number of concurrently executing processes, each requiring amounts of memory.

In the DOS system, once the application gains control of the machine's resources (including memory) it may do as it sees fit. This means that no area of memory is safe from being disturbed by the application, not even the areas already occupied by resident dormant programs or even those areas used by the operating system. It is, therefore, easy for an application to corrupt the operating system by writing over portions of it while it is executing.

There is no built-in management to ensure that applications do not modify areas of memory already in use by other processes. This is true for all versions of DOS, regardless of the machine type and despite any capabilities built into the hardware to specifically deal with this problem.

DOS does not have any memory management functions to protect one process from another because it was designed as a single tasking operating system. The assumption was that only one application would ever be active in a DOS environment at a time (with the exception of the PRINT background program).

The fact that multiple processes can even occupy memory in DOS is the result of attempts to circumvent the limitations imposed by a single tasking environment. DOS also does not perform any of the other forms of memory management, such as swapping or paging of processes *(or their dormant segments)* out of memory so that another process may use the memory slots; again, because it is not a multi-programming environment.

The UNIX system, however, does perform all of these memory management tasks. It is because the UNIX system is a multi-user, multi-tasking, full multi-programming environment that these memory management functions are a fundamental part of the operating system.

The UNIX system provides features such as memory protection, swapping, paging, allocation and deallocation of memory buffers for processes, and making certain that processes properly return memory buffers when they have terminated. This is a new concept for DOS developers to understand and is of great importance if they are to write efficient applications that make the most use of the available resources.

Basic Swapping

If, in a hypothetical UNIX system, the hardware is limited to a maximum of six megabytes of real memory; and there are processes active which required eight megabytes of memory, not all of them could reside in memory at once. One or more would have to be swapped out to *secondary storage*, the UNIX term used to describe the area where the swap region is located, usually a special section of a hard disk within the file system.

The area of memory where processes must execute is called *primary memory*, known as RAM (random access memory) by most DOS developers, and as main memory by most IBM mainframe programmers. It is inevitable that primary memory will be exhausted in any multi-programming environment, making it necessary to swap dormant processes out to secondary memory until they become active again.

There is a memory management subsystem within the UNIX system that decides which processes are eligible for swapping. It keeps track of the available primary memory and, when necessary, will write processes out to a secondary memory device, called the swap device.

The memory vacated by swapped processes is then made available for the requesting process. When a swapped process needs memory, if the memory is available it is given to that process. If the memory is unavailable, then another process is swapped, and the vacated memory is assigned to the requesting process.

A process must be resident in primary memory, at least partially, in order to execute. The memory management subsystem also manages the parts of the process that have been swapped out to secondary memory. This is sometimes referred to as *virtual address space management*.

There are three major functions performed in swapping: management of the swap space on the swap device, swapping processes out of primary memory, and swapping them back in.

The swap device is a block device, usually a section on a hard disk. The kernel allocates swap space in groups of contiguous blocks — as opposed to a block at a time — the method used for ordinary files. Processes having been swapped out and residing in the swap space will eventually be swapped back into memory; their swap space is considered to be temporary, not static as in normal files.

Since the speed of the swapping process is critical, I/O is performed much faster for multiblock operations than for single block operation, hence the reason for allocation of a group of contiguous blocks for the swap space. An in-core table, called a *map*, is kept by the kernel to efficiently track the amount and location of free blocks for the swap space.

The map is updated by the kernel as the blocks are used and freed. The specific details of how this is done are not necessary for the application developer to know, unless their applications are systems internals that may have something to do with the swap space map.

The newer implementations of UNIX systems allow for multiple swap devices, usually on separate physical drives. In such a system, the kernel would select which swap device to use in a linear fashion, one after the other in a round robin fashion. The swap device must contain enough contiguous memory to become eligible to store the swap data.

Swap devices may be created and removed dynamically by the UNIX system administrator. If a swap device is removed, it goes into a *quiesced* state in which all remaining process are eventually swapped back in to primary memory. Swapping is not performed to the device and eventually it goes completely dormant when it is empty; only then may it be removed.

Swapping Processes Out of Primary Memory

Processes may be swapped out of primary memory and into secondary memory by the kernel. For example, if a **fork( )** system call was made by a process, space must be allocated in primary memory for the child process. If sufficient space exists, there is no need for swapping, however, if there is insufficient space then swapping occurs to accommodate the child process.

It is also possible for an active process to require additional memory if the stack capacity is naturally increased. In this case, swapping would be necessary only if there was insufficient space available in primary memory for the dynamic growth to occur. The kernel decides which process(es) will be swapped out.

Other instances that may cause swapping to occur are if a **brk( )** system call was made to increase the size of a process; or when the kernel is swapping in a previously swapped out process and memory is needed to accommodate it, but may not be available. If necessary, the kernel will lock a process into memory to prevent its being swapped out while a swapping operation is already in progress. All hardware I/O operations must have been completed before swapping can be resumed.

The kernel keeps track of virtual address maps of swapped processes, so that when they are swapped back into memory they can be properly reconstructed by reassigning the correct virtual addresses for the process.

Swapping Processes Back Into Primary Memory

The swapper, process 0, is the process that is responsible for performing swapping of processes. Only the swapper may bring a process which has been swapped out, back into primary memory. When there is no swapping to be done, the swapper goes to sleep for an interval, until awakened by the kernel, and reenters its endless loop of performing swap management.

Process 0 is itself non-swappable, and executes at a higher execution priority than other processes. When it awakens, it checks to see if there are any processes that are swapped out which are eligible to be swapped back in. This state is the *"ready to run but swapped out"* state, and there may be several processes that are eligible. The one that has been swapped out the longest is selected.

If there is enough free memory available it is allocated for use by the process being swapped in. The process is read in from the swap device and the swap space occupied by the now swapped-in process is released. If there is insufficient memory available, one or more processes are first swapped out until there is sufficient memory and then the process is swapped in.

As soon as this is done, the swapper goes on to the next waiting process that is in the "ready to run but swapped out" state, and repeats the exercise until either there are no more processes eligible to be swapped back in (in which case the swapper goes to sleep until awakened by the kernel), or there is no more memory available and there are no processes eligible to swap out.

A process that is in a *"ready to run"* state must be resident in primary memory for a minimum of two seconds before it is eligible to be swapped back out. Processes that are waiting to be swapped back in must have been swapped out for at least two seconds before they are eligible to be swapped back in. Certain processes are not swapped out because they occupy no physical memory. Other processes that are likely candidates for being swapped out undergo a selection criteria

based on current status, time already in memory, and other information used by the swapper's selection algorithms.

It is a good idea for UNIX developers to be familiar with swapping
strategies and how the swapping mechanism works, since the applications they develop may take advantage of execution characteristics to
minimize swapping.

Demand Paging

The UNIX System V architecture also supports paging, which is when
only segments of a process are swapped out in sections called *pages*. A
memory page of a fixed size is transferred from primary memory to
secondary memory (and vice versa), instead of the entire process. The
benefit of this is that the entire process need not be memory resident
for it to execute, only the portions that are referenced, otherwise
known as its *active pages*. When the process references pages not resident in primary memory, the kernel will retrieve them upon demand.
This is called *demand paging*.

Greater flexibility is achieved using demand paging. The amount of
time it takes to transfer a few pages is far less than the time necessary to swap out an entire process. This also allows the process to
exceed the size of the available real memory. For example, if the system is equipped with only eight megabytes, a process that was 16
megabytes in size could still execute. Not all of its pages would be
memory resident at the same time.

Swapping is supposed to be less overhead, but there are differing
opinions on this subject. This type of virtual memory management
has been around for over 15 years in the IBM mainframe world and is
commonly known as Virtual Storage.

Most IBM mainframe developers should be familiar with the concepts of virtual storage management, such as in MVS, or VM. The
basic concepts of swapping and paging in the UNIX system are somewhat related to the methods used by these operating systems, although certain terms and swapping strategies are different.

Memory Management For Programmers

To allocate and release memory within the application program, both UNIX and DOS; use the C language family of memory management subroutine calls. These are built-in functions of the C compiler and may be implementation dependent, but usually adhere to the Kernighan and Ritchie standards used in virtually all UNIX-based compilers.

Standard memory functions such as *malloc( )*, *calloc( )*, *realloc( )*, and *free( )* should adhere to the System V Interface Definition (SVID) published standards if the compiler implementation is to be considered fully compatible with the UNIX System V C compiler.

For the most part, these functions are fully implemented on the Microsoft, Lattice, and C86 compilers for the DOS environment. Developers should check their compiler documentation to verify its compatability with the UNIX System V C compiler for these functions. If the memory functions are implemented fully , then it is not necessary to learn any more about how memory is managed from within an application program.

If there are differences between the UNIX System V C compiler and other implementations, then it would be a good idea for the developer to understand those differences and understand how the UNIX System V C compiler implements these functions.

Keyboard and Screen I/O

Another major difference between the UNIX system and DOS is in the way I/O is performed with peripheral devices such as video screens, printers, disks, and keyboards. In DOS, certain devices are *memory mapped*, such as the video display. A developer may write a program that can access data in the memory area reserved for the video display.

In the UNIX system, all peripheral devices are treated as files, for which there are corresponding entries in a special directory called **/dev**. Programs may read or write directly to or from these files. Certain peripheral devices in the DOS system have a similar counterpart, such as CON:, LPT1:, and COM1:. These are remotely similar and do not provide the same flexibility as do the entries in the /dev directory of the UNIX system.

The UNIX developer may write a program that reads the standard input device and writes to the standard output device. Either of these may be redirected to an entry in the /dev directory, making it possible to read and write to any device that is part of the UNIX system, including the keyboard and video displays of any user.

Since there is no multiuser capability in DOS, this is a rather new concept for some DOS developers to grasp. For example, it is possible for a program to monitor the data of a user's screen by redirecting the standard input to the /dev entry for a particular terminal screen, and to write the output to another screen by redirecting the standard output to the /dev entry for that device.

The application program would read from *stdin* and write to *stdout*, the redirection would take place during execution when invoked at the command line.

Batch Files Versus Shell Scripts

In the DOS operating system, there is a feature that allows users to batch together, in a file, DOS commands that are read by a batch interpreter and executed a line at a time. DOS developers will recognize this as the batch file facility that only reads and executes files having a file extension of .BAT. The batch facility of DOS, by comparison to the UNIX shell is severely limited.

Shell scripts in UNIX systems are the fundamental backbone used for developing powerful tools, and so the functionality of the shell must be powerful also. The single most important difference is that the UNIX shell makes extensive use of the environment. The DOS batch file and shell make limited use of the environment.

Editors and Wordprocessors

The lack of an efficient editor and wordprocessor may be the only weak areas of the UNIX system to date.

DOS is the most widely installed and used operating system in the world. This means that there are more software developers for DOS than for any other single operating system environment and that there are generally more applications available, especially text editors and word processing software.

Some of the best of these DOS applications have had several years in the market place to mature and become commercially successful, creating a demand for excellence and commercial polish. Without detracting from any of the products in this category available in the UNIX environment, it was only recently that UNIX-based systems began to make use of high resolution color display technology for commercial availability. Many vendors of popular and successful products began porting their applications to UNIX systems. In many cases, the product was enhanced beyond the capabilities of their DOS predecessors, or in some cases, a completely new product was developed.

This is not to say that the products available under UNIX are any less functional or professional. However, for the DOS developer learning the UNIX system, it may be necessary to learn how to use new tools, including a text editor. It is likely that a developer's favorite DOS word processor or text editor program don't exist in the standard UNIX environment, or at least for a particular implementation of UNIX.

Many of the basic or standard text processing tools that are available in the UNIX environment, although quite powerful, have a command-line user interface, heavily dependent upon numerous commands and control sequences and a lot of keyboard activity.

The menu, function key, and mouse driven word processors available in DOS, offer more user friendliness, simplified command sets, and commercial flash.

Only recently has there been graphical screen oriented windowing text processing software available in the UNIX world; software that is intuitive and easy to use, as well as powerful. As an example, most UNIX-based systems still rely on **nroff** and **troff** to perform special text formatting functions. The formatting control commands must be embedded directly into the ASCII text manually by the creator of a text file.

In contrast to other non-UNIX environments, such as the Apple Macintosh and DOS systems, desktop publishing systems have provided much more advanced (graphically oriented) ways of doing the same thing with products such as Aldus PageMaker. UNIX-based systems also have desktop publishing systems, but they don't have anywhere near the general recognition or market popularity that PageMaker or Ventura Desktop Publisher do.

This point is not worth belaboring, since it is largely a matter of personal opinion. It is likely that a new developer to the UNIX environment will have to learn how to use text processors such as **vi** or **emacs**.

If developers have no fear of doing this, they may be in for a pleasant surprise, once they experience the power of UNIX-based applications. If a DOS developer has only had limited experience with text processing programs such as **edlin**, then they will certainly agree that the **vi** or **emacs** editors are far superior. If a developer has traditionally used menu driven or extremely user friendly programs in the past, such as the IBM mainframe program development tool called SPF, then they may be in for a shock.

CHAPTER 5

UNIX PROCESSES

The material presented in this Chapter shows how the UNIX kernel interacts with processes and serves as a point of reference for those developers familiar with the internal counterparts in DOS.

The data processing term "program" is generally defined as a collection of computer instructions that are executed in a particular order to produce a particular result. Sometimes programs require data for input in order to perform calculations, comparisons, or other computational processing tasks. In the DOS environment, when the program executes, the entire facilities of DOS and the computer hardware are at the complete disposal of the program — for the duration of its execution. In the UNIX environment, the operating system performs the task of making the required machine and program resources available to the application program. It does this through the implementation of *process management*.

In UNIX the term *process* is used interchangeably with the term *program*. A process may be thought of as a program, but it is in fact, more than just a program. Because of the single tasking nature of DOS, the program is the process.

In the UNIX system a process is actually the *program execution environment*, consisting of three parts, also called *regions* or *segments*:

- the text or instruction segment
- the user data segment
- the system data segment

It is through the use of the process environment that the UNIX kernel manages and keeps track of all processes.

In the DOS environment, a program's *program segment prefix* (PSP) is the closest counterpart to the information contained within a UNIX process. In the DOS system the PSP is an area constructed by the DOS **EXEC** function; similar to the concept of process construction and control by the UNIX kernel. In the UNIX system, the kernel loads executable modules through an **EXEC** system call, which in turn sets up the process text, data, and stack segments for the program.

The actual contents in UNIX processes and DOS program PSP's are quite different. The general structure of DOS programs and a UNIX process are similar enough: both have a segmented architecture containing instruction, data and stack segments. The similarity ends when control is passed to the program by the operating system, since the execution environments are designed differently.

In the DOS environment, once **EXEC** has finished loading and the application program is executing, it is in control of the machine until the program terminates or is interrupted externally, as in the use of the BREAK key or a system re-boot.

Since several processes are executed concurrently in the UNIX system, the kernel needs a way to identify one process from another. This is done through the use of a process ID number, or the PID. Every process in UNIX has a parent; the process that was responsible for creating it (called the *parent process*). A process created from a parent process is called a *child process.* The creation of processes is accomplished through the **fork( )** or **exec( )** system calls. Processes may have only a single parent process, but may have many child processes. All processes must have been created from a parent process, with the exception of process 0.

Process 0 is created during the UNIX system boot process. When the boot process is complete, process 0 then forks a new child process called process 1, also known as *init*. Process 0 then goes on to become the *swapper* process that schedules the allocation of memory to other processes. Process 1, init, is the process whoes job it is to initiate all new processes and is the grand ancestor of all other UNIX processes.

UNIX provides a method of terminating processes through the **kill** command. A process may be executing in either foreground or background. A foreground process communicates to the user's terminal screen and has control of the keyboard to the extent that, while the foreground process is active, no other foreground processes can communicate through the I/O devices it controls. Background processes, however, run asynchronously to what is happening in the foreground. This means that while it is running, other background and foreground processes may also be running.

If a process is to be killed, the PID must be known in order to terminate the correct process. It can be obtained in one of two ways. The PID is echoed back to the screen when background processes are initiated from the user's terminal. If the PID is not known, then the user may first issue the **ps** (process status) command which displays information on all active processes, including their PIDs. All PIDs are guaranteed to be unique.

In the UNIX kernel, there is a component called the *process control subsystem* that is responsible for inter-process communication, process scheduling (process 0), and memory management. Before going into more detail on the process control subsystem, a look at the process architecture is in order.

Process Segments

This segment contains the machine executable code of the process which, in effect, is the program that gets executed. The code contained in this segment also manages the size of the program stack. This segment is analogous to the DOS *code segment*, and is the source of information that most debugging tools use to display program instructions.

User Data Segment

The data segment contains data values that have an initialization value at the beginning of the program, and other information that the kernel needs in order to allocate space for uninitialized data items. The kernel initializes these values to zeros. This segment is analogous to the DOS *data segment* and may be used to examine the values of variables or constants during program execution in most debuggers.

System Data Segment

This is also called the stack region; created by the kernel at execution time. Its size is dynamically adjusted during execution. This area consists of elements called stack frames which are pushed onto the stack when the process calls a function, and are popped off the stack when the function(s) complete. The stack pointer is used to indicate the depth of the stack. Stack frames contain function parameters, local variables, and recovery data (such as the states of program counter and stack pointer when the function call was made) which are necessary to pop back to the previous stack frame.

A UNIX process may execute in either of two modes: kernel or user. A separate stack is generated for each mode. The user stack contains local variables, arguments, and other information for functions executing in user mode. The kernel stack contains stack frames for kernel mode functions. The stack construction in both modes is the same, although they are used for different purposes.

The system data within this segment contains information such as open file descriptors, accumulated CPU execution time, and the name of the current directory. Various system calls are necessary for a process to modify its system data. Child processes inherit most of the system data attributes in this segment from their parent processes.

Other Process Related Memory Areas

A process table is maintained by the kernel that contains entries for each process. The *u* area (user area) is an area allocated for each process that contains data which is used and modified only by the

UNIX kernel. The kernel process table points to another area called the *per process region table,* which contains entries that point to other entries in a region table, used to describe the attributes of a region (such as text or data, shared or private, and data region location.) Regions are contiguous areas of memory within a process' address space, such as the previously mentioned text, data, and stack segments.

If a process issues the UNIX **exec( )** system call, regions are allocated for text, data, and stack segments after the process's old regions have been freed. If a process issues the UNIX **fork( )** system call, the address space of the old process is duplicated by the kernel, allowing for processes to share regions. When the **exit( )** system call is issued by a process, all regions used by the process are freed by the kernel.

States and Transitions

A process can be in one of are nine possible states at any given time. The states are listed below.

- User execution mode

- Kernel execution mode

- Not executing, but ready when kernel schedules it

- Sleeping in main memory

- Ready for execution when swapped back to main memory for scheduling by the kernel

- Sleeping and swapped out of main memory to auxiliary storage

- In transition from kernel to user mode, but the kernel has preempted and switched its context to schedule another process

- Newly created process in a transition state; not sleeping/not ready to run; the starting state for all processes

- Zombie state, executed a system exit call, no longer existing; the final state of all processes

Processes transform from one state to another during their lifetime, but may not go through every one of the nine possible states. After the process has been started by a parent process, through the invocation of a **fork( )** or **exec( )** system call, it may be in a ready-to-run state and can then be selected by the kernel for execution (kernel running state). It is the kernel, not the process, that has control over changes in process status.

Process Contexts

Process contexts are made up of the contents of various memory locations associated with the process, such as the contents of the user address space, the contents of the system hardware registers, and other information such as relevant kernel data structures. It can be said, that a process' context is the state of its text, global and user variables, system hardware registers in use by the process, the contents of the user and kernel stack, and the contents of its process table slots within the process' u area. The term *state*, as used here, implies the actual contents or values of the various registers and memory areas.

User Address Space

This level of context contains the text, data, user stack, and shared memory belonging to the process. The process is sharing its address space in memory (although portions of these may be paged or swapped out and they are still considered part of the user level context).

Process Text

The process text is the machine executable form of the program that is loaded in from the secondary storage device on which it is stored. This refers to the output of the fully compiled and ready to execute program instructions which make up the process. These instructions are executed one at a time by the CPU when the process is active in memory.

Process Data

The process data is the input or output data used or created by the process. Processes may read or write their own data, but may not access those of another process. Other mechanisms are provided to share data between processes.

User Stack

Processes may execute in either user or kernel mode. Depending on which mode the process is active in determines which stack the process will use. The process uses the user stack while in user execution mode and contains arguments, variables, and other data used by the process.

When a special instruction is executed by the process, it switches to kernel execution mode, executing kernel instructions by using the kernel stack. The user and kernel stacks are located in the stack region of a process which is created automatically by the kernel. Stack sizes are dynamically modified by the kernel when necessary.

The logical record entry, which is pushed onto the stack by a called function, is referred to as a stack frame. Stack frames are popped off of the stack when the called function returns back to its caller. The stack pointer is a special indicator used to determine the current location within the stack (called the stack depth), and is actually a special register.

Shared Memory

Shared memory makes it possible for processes to communicate directly with one another. Processes can share portions of their virtual address space, and by reading and writing to that shared memory area, provide a means for other processes to do likewise. This is implemented at the application level through the use of UNIX system calls such as **shmget( )**, **shmat( )**, **shmdt( )**, and **shmctl( )**.

The **shmget( )** system call is used to create a shared memory region or to return the address of an already existing one. The **shmat( )** system call is used to attach the shared memory region to the virtual address space of a process. The **shmdt( )** system call performs the logical opposite of the **shmat( )** system call; it detaches the shared memory region from the process' virtual address space. The **shmctl( )** system call is used to control the assorted parameters used with the shared memory.

System Hardware Registers

This context is comprised of the following components:

- The program counter which specifies the next CPU instruction that is a virtual address either in the kernel or the user address space to execute.

- The PS (processor status) register that specifies the status of machine hardware pertaining to a process.

- A stack pointer that indicates the location of the position (next entry) within the user or kernel stack, depending upon which execution mode the process is in.

- GPR (general purpose registers) contents created during the process' execution.

System Context and Kernel Data Structures

Processes may have only one static part of a system context during its execution period, but may have many dynamic parts that are pushed and popped to and from a stack by the kernel when certain events occur. The system context contains the process table entry that is a kernel data structure used to define the state of a process, and keep other control information. This table contains fields accessible to the kernel and includes the following entries:

- Process state field that indicates the state the process is currently in.

- Process and u area location information used by the kernel to locate this information either in primary or secondary storage. These fields are used during a context switch when the process changes states, and also for paging and/or swapping. This information also includes the process size necessary for the kernel to be able to allocate the correct amounts of memory.

- Multiple user identifiers (UID's) that are used to effect processing privileges, as in process signalization.

- Multiple process identifiers (PID's) that are used to specify the relationships which processes have with each other.

- An event descriptor field created when the process enters the sleep state.

- Process scheduling information that is used by the kernel to determine the order in which processes change states.

- A signal event counter to keep track of received signals not yet handled by the process.

- Various other timer fields that are used by kernel process scheduling algorithms, process accounting, process execution time, and kernel resource utilization.

The system context also uses the u area (user area) that contains information about process states. This information is contained in the following fields:

- Process table entry pointer that is used to identify the corresponding entry in the process table for the u area.

- UID entries that are used to determine the process' privileges, as in access permissions.

- User and Kernel execution mode timer fields that are used to accumulate the execution time for each of these modes.

- An array used to determine how the process will respond to certain signals.

- An optional field used to determine the login terminal associated with the process. *This may not exist for some processes.*

- An error field counter used by the process to keep track of errors during system calls.

- A field to contain the return values of system calls and which may be used to determine if the system call was successful.

- Parameter fields used in I/O operations and which contain information such as location of the source and destination data fields, file offsets used in I/O operations, and size of the data to transfer.

- Information about the process' current directory and other file system information relating to the process.

- The user file descriptor table that is used to keep track of the number of open files in use by the process.

- Fields containing restrictions or limitations for the process; such as the size the process may be allowed to grow to, or the maximum number of bytes the file may write to a file.

- File creation mask information that contains the default file permissions used when the process creates new files.

- Pregion entries, region tables, and page tables that define the mapping of the virtual storage addresses to real address locations in physical memory. The kernel uses these areas to determine which parts of a process' virtual address space are not resident in memory.

- Stack frames of the kernel stack for kernel procedures when a process is executing in kernel mode. All processes must have a private copy of the kernel stack even though they all execute the identical kernel code. The kernel needs this information to be able to restore the kernel stack contents and stack pointer location when processes resume kernel mode execution.

- Dynamic portions of system level context, containing information about subsequent layers organized into a logical LIFO stack. Each of these system context layers provides the data necessary to restore the context of the previous layer.

Controlling Processes: Process Creation

In the UNIX system, invoking the **fork( )** or **exec( )** system calls will create a new process. Refer to the UNIX System V Programmer's Reference Manual for the correct syntax of these system calls according to the specific machine used.

Upon spawning the process, the kernel allocates a slot in the process table for the new process. It then assigns the child process a unique process ID number and makes a copy of the parent process' context. Afterwards, file and inode table counters are incremented for all files associated with the child process. Then the kernel returns the PID number of the child process to its parent process, and gives the child process a PID value of 0.

During the creation of the process, any paging or swapping that is necessary is also performed according to the standard algorithms associated with the spawning activity.

Process Signals

Signals are used to notify processes of the occurrence of asynchronous events. A process may receive signals from either the kernel or another process. The **signal( )** system call is described in detail in the UNIX System V Interface Definition (SVID) and the UNIX System V Programmer's Reference/Guide manuals.

The following are the major types of signals:

- Process termination signals
- Signals to indicate exceptions caused by the process
- Signals associated with system call exceptions and indicating unrecoverable conditions
- Signals sent because of other error conditions during a system call (unexpected errors)
- Signals generated by a process executing in user mode
- Signals indicating terminal or peripheral device activities
- Signals generated when tracing process execution

Process Sleep

A process has the ability to temporarily suspend its own execution for a specific time interval. Unlike interrupt handlers which cannot enter a sleep state, processes may do this from within their own control logic through the use of the **sleep( )** system call. A process may decide to go to sleep so that it can wait for an event to occur and wake it up.

Examples of such events are: waiting for completion of some I/O to a terminal, printer, disk, or other peripheral device; waiting for other processes to terminate; waiting for the availability of some system resource; or virtually any other event that can be detected and cause the process to be awakened.

Going into a sleep state is preferable to a *busy wait* because the process becomes totally dormant, entering a sleep state in which the process does nothing. Processes in a busy wait would be active constantly because of timed polling sequences that require CPU resources and a small amount of overhead.

By going to sleep, the kernel awakens the process when the event it is waiting for, has occurred. It is possible for several sleeping processes to be waiting for the same event to occur, in which case the kernel would wake them all up. When a process is awakened from its sleep state, it does not execute immediately, it undergoes a state transition from "sleep" to "ready to run" and thus becomes eligible for execution scheduling by the kernel.

When a process enters sleep state, the kernel can schedule other processes for execution. The kernel switches contexts to the new processes as necessary. When wakeup events occur, sleeping processes resume execution after they are awakened and rescheduled by the kernel. The process may be swapped out during its sleep cycle.

If there is more than one process sleeping on an event, and the occurring event causes them all to be awakened (if they are waiting for a resource to be unlocked and it is locked by another process which has also been awakened), then the remaining processes are put back to sleep. This continues until each awaiting process has gotten the awaited resource.

152

If a process is sleeping on an event that may not occur, the kernel may interrupt the sleeping process by sending it a signal instead. If, for instance, a process is awaiting input from a peripheral device that may have failed for some reason, it will wait until the device becomes reactivated.

The kernel may be able to detect such problems and awaken the sleeping process by sending it a signal. If a sleeping process is awaiting some event such as an I/O event for a failed device, the kernel can cause the hung process to complete with an error code by sending a signal to the sleeping process.

Process Address Space Manipulation

System calls are used to manipulate the address space of processes. The process region table is used to describe information about the region. The kernel must have this information to know when it performs manipulation of the process address spaces data. The elements of the region table contain the following information:

- Inode pointer indicating the file loaded into the process region
- The region type (text, shared memory, private data, stack)
- The region size
- Address of region within memory
- Region status (any combination of): locked, in demand, being loaded into memory, loaded into memory (valid)
- Reference count indicating the number of other processes referencing the region

Region Locking/Unlocking

Process regions may be locked and unlocked by the kernel, just as the file system performs locking/unlocking upon inodes. This occurs independently of the allocate/free operations.

Region Allocation

New regions are allocated by the kernel if the **fork( )**, **shmget( )**, or **exec( )** system calls are made. A region table entry (a kernel data structure) is made for every newly allocated region by removing the first available entry from the free list and placing it on the active list.

The region is locked and is marked shared or private. The inode field of the region table entry is set to point to an executable file (if one exists) associated with the process, indicating the region to the kernel and allowing other processes to share that region if necessary. The inode reference count is incremented for each access by other processes.

Region Attachment to a Process

New or existing regions are connected to a process address space when they are attached by the kernel during the **fork( )**, **shmat( )**, or **exe( )** system calls. Regions may be attached to a process address space so they can be shared between processes.

Region Size Expansion/Contraction

Processes may grow or shrink in size by expanding or contracting their virtual address space. This is accomplished via the **sbrk( )** system call. The process' stack is automatically increased with the number of procedure calls. The stack size is also automatically adjusted when procedure calls return. It is the job of the kernel to insure that virtual addresses of process regions do not overlap in memory when regions are expanded. The kernel also insures that the size of a process never exceeds the maximum permissible virtual memory space. When a process region contracts, the unused memory is freed and made available for reuse.

Loading Regions

UNIX System V supports demand paging in which files are mapped by the kernel into a process' virtual address space. This is accomplished via the **exec( )** system call. The process may read physical pages upon demand. Loading a region means to copy the contents of a file into the appropriate region of a process' virtual address space, such as text regions which contain the actual machine instructions that make up the process. The kernel performs the loading operation.

Region Detachment from a Process

The **exec( )**, **shmdt( )**, and **exit( )** system calls are used by the kernel to detach regions from a process. The region is freed if the region reference count is zero and there is no need to have the region in memory any longer.

Freeing a Region

The kernel frees regions that are no longer attached to processes. The freed regions are returned to the list of free regions. For regions having an association with inodes, the inodes are also released. Various resources used by a region (page tables and memory pages) are released by the kernel when the region is freed. The region reference count must be a value of zero before these resources can be released.

Region Duplication

When a **fork( )** system call is made, the kernel must duplicate the regions of the parent process for the child process. For regions having shared memory or shared text, the region reference count is incremented for each sharing process. The parent and child processes may share the regions, making it unnecessary to duplicate the parent process' regions.

If, however, the region is not a shared region, then it must be duplicated. In this case a new region table entry is allocated by the kernel, as well as a page table and primary storage space for the duplicated region.

Process Termination

At the user level, processes may be terminated by entering the **kill** command. The user must either own the process they are attempting to kill or have superuser privileges.

At the program level, process termination occurs during execution of the **exit( )** system call. The exiting process enters zombie state, after which all of its resources are surrendered and its context is eliminated. When a C program returns from the main function the **exit( )** system call is executed. The default status of the **exit( )** system call is the value zero.

CHAPTER 6

THE UNIX SHELL

The UNIX shell is the primary contact for developers and users since it lies directly between them and the machine internals. The shell is an integral piece of the UNIX system, designed to allow users to communicate with it in terms which the users can understand. It is a very flexible, powerful, and programmable user interface designed to carry out user provided instructions. These instructions may come from either a terminal keyboard, a shell script running as a process, or may be invoked through a system call from an application program executing as a process.

The UNIX Shell Environment

The shell uses an *environment* that is similar in concept to the DOS shell's environment. The environment is an area in memory that contains a list of shell variable values and which is created for every user upon login. It may be used by the shell or processes to obtain the values of shell variables, such as the path to a user's home directory, information to compute time offsets from GMT (Greenwich Mean Time), the user ID of someone logged onto a terminal, and many other things.

There are three types of environment variables: *user variables*, *Shell variables*, and *read-only Shell variables*. These are the variables that may be declared, initialized, read, and modified either directly at the command line or from within a shell script. These variables are traditionally thought of as environment variables by most users, but to be more precise, they are *user* variables.

Shell variables are those declared by the UNIX Shell, but are accessible to users for reading and modification. Read-only shell variables are also declared by the shell and may also be read by users, but they may not be modified by users.

This should not be confused with the ability to make a user variable read-only. A user may create a user variable, initialize it to a value, and make the variable read-only. Once the variable has been declared read-only, users may not change its value. An example of this is shown below:

```
X_WINDOW_LIB=/usr/lib/X11
X_WINDOW_SRC=/usr/src/X11.3
readonly X_WINDOW_LIB
```

In this example two user variables are defined and initialized, but only one of them is made read-only: the X_WINDOW_LIB variable. Its value cannot be modified for the duration of the login session.

Environment variables may be added to the user's shell environment at any time, including in the user's .profile file where users traditionally perform customization of their login environment. In the Bourne shell, the default shell distributed with UNIX System V, the way to create a shell variable is simple. The user enters a command from the terminal or writes a shell command statement in a shell script file in the following manner:

```
VARIABLE=value
```

In this example, VARIABLE is the name the user wishes to give the shell environment variable, and value is the value assigned to the variable via the equal = character. To declare a shell environment variable without any value, simply leave off the value. By convention, environment variables are usually entered as uppercase characters, although they may be anything the user wishes. Users may obtain a list of their variables and their current values by typing a command to their terminal as follows:

```
env
```

All commands typed on the terminal command line must be followed by either a return key or enter key depending upon which is available for the hardware being used. The result of this command is to echo back the contents of the shell environment variables and their values. Another way to determine the value of an individual shell variable is to use the **echo** command. The format for this is as follows:

```
echo $VARIABLE
```

The $ character causes the **echo** command to display the value of VARIABLE, which is the name of an environment variable. If no such variable exists, then nothing is echoed back. To remove an existing variable from the environment, the **unset** command is used and takes the following form:

```
unset VARIABLE
```

This removes the entry from the environment. Any reference to VARIABLE will not produce results since it no longer exists in the environment. The equivalent method of doing this in the DOS environment, is to set the environment variable to a null value using the DOS set command:

```
set variable=
```

Setting the variable to a null value is also supported in the UNIX shell, but produces different results; the value is null but there is still an entry in the environment for VARIABLE.

There are a few standard environment variables having special usages that developers need to know about. These are listed in alphabetical order and are discussed in the following paragraphs.

EDIT Variable

This optional variable is used to identify the pathname where the default editor is to be found. If a user enters $EDIT on the command line, it should invoke the editor as though they had entered the actual editor command:

```
$EDIT xxx
```

Assuming the default editor was /usr/bin/vi, (as it usually is for UNIX System V) then **vi** would go into full screen edit on a file called xxx.

HOME Variable

This variable is one of the most important variables and every user has one created for them by the shell when they log in. It may be modified at any time and contains the directory path name considered to be the home directory of the user. A home directory is usually owned by the user just logging in.

When a user enters the UNIX **cd** (change directory) command without a target directory, the default action is to change to the directory specified as the path name value of the HOME variable. Thus, "cd" and "cd $HOME" are functionally the same. There is no DOS equivalent for this variable.

LOGNAME Variable

The LOGNAME variable's initial default value is a character string of the user's ID set up by the shell at login. This may also be changed at any time. There is no DOS equivalent for this variable.

MAIL Variable

This variable is optional and is typically used by the UNIX **mail** command to determine where to deliver mail for a user. In some systems, this is a standard variable created by the shell, on others it is optional depending upon the system administrator. It may be modified, but the **mail** command must have sufficient access permissions to be able to write to whatever new target is specified. There is no DOS equivalent for this variable.

PATH Variable

This environment variable is similar in function and form to the DOS PATH environment variable. (There is no **path** command in UNIX.) It specifies the default execution path for UNIX commands. Commands are located using the value specified in the PATH variable if the command does not exist within the user's current directory. The main differences are as follows. In UNIX the shell is case sensitive and the PATH variable must be in all uppercase; in DOS, all variables automatically get translated to uppercase by the command interpreter, COMMAND.COM. The PATH variable in UNIX environments is used to locate only executable programs; in DOS it may also be used to locate files of any type. This variable may be modified at any time.

PS1 Variable

This variable is used to specify the user's prompt string value, and is roughly the functional equivalent of the DOS **prompt** command/environment variable. The DOS **prompt** command has some built in features enabling users to set color attributes via the ANSI.SYS terminal driver, and also providing users the ability to construct a prompt string containing the current drive and directory path values.

While it is possible to accomplish this in the UNIX shell, there is no built-in facility to do this with the PS1 variable. The prompt string may be anything a user wishes, including embedded commands, special control sequences and characters, or any constant, even the value of another variable. This variable may be standard on some systems, and is not standard for others. The default string is established by the system administrator and is usually the **$** character. The following are examples of various prompt strings:

```
PS1="$LOGNAME: "
PS1="`echo $LOGNAME`@`uname`[!]: "
PS1="$"
PS1="[!]: "
```

The second and fourth lines of the preceding example require the Korn shell to work properly. These will provide a number, embedded within the left and right square brackets, that corresponds to the number of commands entered thus far by a user. Using the Korn shell it is possible to retrieve a command from a command history file by entering ESC-K. The command most recently executed is retrieved to the command line and is capable of being edited by users before it is entered. The number of commands stored in the command history file is specified by another Korn shell environment variable (HISTSIZE). The number appearing within the square brackets in the example reflects how many commands have been entered up to that point.

The following is an example of how to set the PS1 variable so that it reflects the current directory each time a user changes to another directory. (K-Shell is required, this will not work for the Bourne or C shells.)

```
function c {
   cd $*
   PS1="`pwd`>"
}
alias cd=c
```

By adding the lines specified in this example to a .profile, users should experience a prompt string similar to the DOS prompt string when using "`prompt $p$g`".

PS2 Variable

This variable is similar to the PS1 variable, but it displays its prompt string under slightly different circumstances. The PS1 variable is displayed when the shell is ready to receive a command from the user at the terminal.

The PS2 prompt is displayed as an alternative prompt to let a user know that it is waiting for the user to finish entering a command that was continued from a previous line. This is the secondary prompt string. The customary default value of this is the greater than symbol ">", but may be changed to anything the user likes, such as:

```
PS2="continued: "
```

SHELL Variable

This variable identifies the absolute path name of a user's shell. This variable is optional and by default is usually undefined, depending upon the system administrator. Its value for the UNIX System V Bourne Shell is /bin/sh; for those systems using the C Shell the value should be /bin/csh. The more recent Korn Shell, or K-Shell as it is sometimes called, would be /bin/ksh. DOS systems use the **shell** command as an entry in the file CONFIG.SYS to specify a different command shell.

TERM Variable

This variable is optional, but should be defined by users in their .profile file. It is used by several UNIX commands and facilities when writing their displays to terminals. If the value of the TERM variable is unset, or incorrect for the hardware being used, programs such as **vi** will not function correctly. If, for example, the terminal being used was either a DEC VT100 terminal or a device capable of emulating one, then the following command line would set the TERM variable correctly:

```
TERM=vt100;export TERM
```

The **export** command will be explained later. For a list of the valid terminal types that may be used, refer to the documentation concerning the UNIX System V system file called terminfo or, as an alternative, take a look in the directory called /usr/lib/terminfo. This subdirectory contains several subdirectories of its own (a through z and 0 through 9), each of which contains several terminal characteristic files for terminal types beginning with the letter that the directory is named after. For example, all terminals beginning with the letter **v** are named for the directory called /usr/lib/terminfo/v. There is no DOS equivalent for this variable.

TZ Variable

This is a UNIX System V environment variable used to determine the time zone in which the machine a user is logged into is physically located. The machine could be in California and the user in New York — the TZ would be set to PST, not EDT. Certain processes that provide time and date information may use this variable to compute the offset from GMT (Greenwich Mean Time) to determine what a user's time zone is. The default time zone is determined by the UNIX system administrator. There is no DOS equivalent for this variable.

UMASK Variable

This is an optional UNIX System V environment variable, that may be used by certain processes and UNIX system and/or shell facilities to determine what a user's default file creation mask is set to. This value is normally set using the **umask** command. The mask is actually a three digit octal number that is subtracted from the default system file creation mask (usually the value 777). Each position of the

umask corresponds to the owner, group, and other users — as each of these relates to the standard UNIX file access permissions feature.

If a **umask** of 077 was specified, then the resulting file would have an access permission value of 700, indicating that the owner of the file had full read-write-execute permissions, while the group and all other users could not even read it. (The **chmod** command is closely related to the umask value; it can be used to alter the file access permissions of any file, provided that a user has sufficient authority to do so.) See the UNIX **umask** command later in this book for additional information.

The Shell: Command Language Interpreter

The UNIX shell's primary job is to receive instructions from the user. It does this by displaying a prompt to the terminal device and awaits a keyboard response (the same as DOS does). Also, shell services can be invoked by a process via the **system( )** system call.

The shell is considered a command interpreter because it translates and executes each command one line at a time. Almost every modern computing environment having either an operator or other user facility available, employs the use of some sort of interpretive command interface.

For example, the DOS system uses the COMMAND.COM shell while in the IBM mainframe world there are several. For VM systems there are the CMS (Conversational Monitoring System) and CP (control program) interfaces. For MVS systems there are several; TSO (Time Sharing Option), ISPF (Interactive Structured Programming Facility), VSPC, ROSCOE, Librarian, and Panvalet. There are many others that include special command interpreters for the system operator consoles and subsystem consoles such as IMS, CICS, and OmegaMon.

The thing that all of these systems have in common is that they receive input from a keyboard device which must be parsed for executable commands.

There is a special file in UNIX System V called .profile (.login for Berkeley implementations of UNIX.) This shell script, if it exists, is executed after login processing has finished. Another file, /etc/profile, is executed for all users upon login, regardless of whether a user has a .profile shell script in their home directory or not.

Once /etc/profile is finished executing, a user's own .profile script is executed, but only if one exists. A prototype .profile script that all users receive when their user account is first set up by the UNIX system administrator, resides in the file /etc/stdprofile. Assuming the correct method of creating a user account was used, this file is copied to a the new user's home directory as their .profile script. Later when a user has logged into their account, they are free to modify their profile script any way they like.

In UNIX System V, the shell is referred to by its name, the Bourne shell, (named after its creator Stephen R. Bourne). Berkeley implementations of UNIX use a different shell, called the C shell, which derives its name from its C language-like capabilities. A third shell, the Korn shell (named for its creator David Korn) is also widely used in both Berkeley and System V implementations of UNIX. It has not yet been made a standard part of the official distribution for UNIX System V, though this is likely to happen. The Korn shell incorporates many features of both the C and Bourne shells as well as providing its own enhancements.

I/O Redirection

The UNIX shell is capable of redirecting its output from stdout to wherever it is instructed. It can also do the same for its input, redirecting its input from stdin to some other source such as a file or alternate device. This is possible through the use of characters that have a special meaning to the UNIX shell: the > and < characters.

Redirecting Output

The output of a process may be redirected using the > redirection character. When added to the command line during invocation of a process, it instructs the shell to redirect the output to the destination to the right of the > character. Usually, this is a normal file, but may also be a special file such as a device entry in the /dev directory.

Normally, stdout is directed to a user's terminal. The output can be redirected to a disk file so that it may be manipulated by a subsequent process or even printed.

If a continually running process is always writing messages to a screen, its output may be sent to a disk file to create a log file of sorts. The output may also be redirected to another user's screen if so desired. The general format of the redirection operation is as follows:

```
command > targetfile
```

This may be thought of as "the output of the command goes to the target file name specified by targetfile." The value of targetfile may be any standard UNIX path name containing a file name that adheres to UNIX file naming standards. If the file previously existed, it will be overwritten using this method. If the existing output file should not be overwritten, but appended to, then the use of two consecutive output redirection characters (no spaces in between) must be used:

```
command >> targetfile
```

The command may be any standard UNIX command, or user developed program producing output to stdout, the standard output. The output of **command** is appended to **targetfile** in the preceding example.

If a user wishes to send the output to a terminal screen, such as a screen dedicated for monitoring the output of a long running process (tape operator console and communications console) then it is possible to redirect the output to the entry for a specific device in the /dev directory. The specific device name must be known. For example, if the output of a process were to be directed to the device considered to be the system console, then the following command would be entered:

```
cat /etc/motd > /dev/console
```

The result of this example would type a file called motd located in the /etc directory and display its contents to the device defined as the console. If a user were logged in on an asynchronous port at device tty103, then the following command could be entered to display the contents of the motd file to that user's terminal:

```
cat /etc/motd > /dev/tty103
```

Beware of using the **cat** command to display the contents of files to other users' terminals. An old practical joke played upon unsuspecting users is to use **cat** to display binary executable files to their terminals. This causes the recipient's terminal to seemingly go crazy until **cat** has finished displaying the file.

Files can be redirected within DOS to a limited degree. Appending files using the >> characters is also limited to certain commands.

A process may receive input from a file, a terminal keyboard, a memory buffer or some other logical input source. In the cases of normal files and terminal keyboards it is fairly straightforward. In the case of an alternative input source there are several options. For example, one process may produce data to be fed as input to another, as in pipes or compound command statements.

Compound command statements are multiple UNIX commands that are *stacked* onto the command line and separated by the semicolon ";" delimiter or that are command statements containing other embedded UNIX commands.

The following is an example of the latter, using some simple UNIX commands:

```
PS1="`uname -n`:`echo $LOGNAME`>"
```

In this example the prompt string is set up to contain the system name and current user ID separated by a colon and is terminated with the greater-than character. If this command were entered on a system named omega and the user ID was tsm, then the prompt string would end up as "omega:tsm>."

The previous example's compound statement contains three commands. First there is the prompt string assignment (PS1=); but before that occurs, the system name is obtained by execution of the command within the first set of back quotes (uname -n). After the **uname** command has executed, its output is substituted in the position occupied on the command line (the first position after the opening double quote and before the colon character).

The next UNIX command then is executed — which is also between a pair of back quotes (echo $LOGNAME). This command echoes the value of an environment variable that is substituted in the command line location in the same manner as the first substitution. At this point the prompt string is complete and the PS1 variable has been set to its new value.

Piping File Output

The output of a process may be redirected to another process by using a pipe. When a process' output is piped into another process, the receiving process may only read the data in a FIFO (first in, first out) order, and it may only do so once. The character symbol used to depict a pipe is the vertical bar which, on some keyboards, appears as a split vertical bar, and on others is a solid vertical bar. An example of a pipe in action is as follows:

```
echo `uname -a | cut -d' ' -f5`
```

The object of this example is to obtain the computer type by using information from the **uname** command. The -a option of the **uname** command provides the full information that is piped as input to the **cut** command.

The -d option of the **cut** command indicates that the delimiter is the value between the single quotes; in this example it is a single white space character. The -f5 option of the **cut** command indicates that it is the fifth field that is to be selected for cutting and which will become the result echoed back by the **echo** command. The fifth field of the **uname** command with the -a option should be the type of computer the command is being executed on, such as 3B15, 3B2, 6386, IBMPC, HP9000, SUN3, or the VAX2000.

CHAPTER 7

SHELL PROGRAMMING

One of the most important features of the UNIX command shell interpreter is its ability to make commands interact with one another through the use of pipes, filters, and redirection operators. The use of *compound statements* on a command line provides sophistication and power for constructing advanced programming tools. A wealth of tools already exist and they are available to incorporate into new applications. This saves unnecessary time and effort in developing new functions.

In the UNIX system, one method of interprocess communications involves the use of pipes. In a simple UNIX command the output is sent to a file referred to as stdout, which is usually attached to the control terminal associated with the command. The output, of course, can be redirected to a disk file using special redirection operators and pipes.

Theoretically, there is no limit to the number of pipes on a command line. In practice, however, most systems limit users to about twenty or thirty processes. Two or more commands connected by pipes can be used to form compound statements. It is the compound statement that can make a command line entry extremely powerful, especially if there is a succession of compound statements executed from a disk file. Such files are called *commands* or *shell scripts*.

Shell scripts are user created ASCII files that contain UNIX and/or shell commands which may otherwise have been entered at the command line prompt. Shell scripts can be created to do just about anything users do themselves when sitting at a physical terminal, including, manipulating results and acting out entire command sequences.

Developing new applications in UNIX doesn't always require a 100 percent compiled language solution. This is a deviation from the traditional way that new applications are developed in the DOS system. Commercial applications rarely use or interact with any of the existing commands or batch programming facilities of the DOS system.

UNIX applications almost always use the advanced resources available, including those external to compiled programs. This is an important concept for new developers coming from the DOS environment to understand and accept if their applications are to compete in the UNIX world.

Commands Within Commands

In the previous chapter, a command line was entered that executed three commands on a single command line. In addition, the result of the second command became a parameter to the third command. In the last chapter the concept of compound statements was mentioned; these are actually commands within commands.

Using pipes and redirection is a simple form of compounding command statements. Another method is by the using the back quote character (represented as: ` ). Enclosing a command within a pair of these back quote characters ( `command`) instructs the shell to execute the command string first and to redirect the standard output from that command into the command line. This results in a value being produced, one that is treated as a parameter to another command on the command line. This may sound confusing, but it is actually simple:

```
echo `uname -a | cut -d' ' -f5`
```

What actually happens is that the **echo** command is used to echo characters to the standard output. Before it can do so, however, the commands within the back quotes are executed so they will produce some characters upon which the **echo** command operates.

The commands in the string "uname -a | cut -d' ' -f5" are executed before the **echo** command. In reality, the **uname** command is actually executed first, producing a line of characters which, among other things, contains the name of the UNIX machine on which this command is running. This line contains multiple fields separated by white space, much like the words in this sentence. The human mind has been conditioned to read by separating the words in sentences using white space as a delimiter.

The second command to be executed (**cut**) receives the output generated from the **uname** command via the pipe character. The purpose of **cut** is to select specific fields from the record it is reading and to echo those as its output. In this example there is only one field to be cut. The -d option means that the delimiter being used is enclosed within the normal single quote characters, in this case, a white space. The -f5 parameter indicates that it is field 5 in the output from the **uname** command that is to be returned.

The next character is the ending back quote, terminating the command execution string. The result from the **uname** and **cut** operations is now substituted in place of the back quote pair and becomes the argument for the **echo** command to send to the standard output.

This type of compound shell command is quite common in powerful shell scripts. Just using the information presented so far, readers have the ability to construct powerful single word macro's that in turn may be entered into a shell script.

In order to make proper use of commands executed within commands by using the back quotes, readers should become familiar with all of the commands used in the example. It is possible to nest as many commands within pairs of back quotes as a user likes, although they rarely go beyond two or three levels. This is due mostly to the complexities of nested compound command statements and because it is usually possible to accomplish the objective without getting too complex.

Another important aspect of command substitution is that shell variables themselves may be set up so that they execute commands. For example, to define a variable called DIR to give a long listing of the current directory, the following line would suffice:

```
DIR="ls -las"
```

In order to find out what the value of the DIR variable is, simply type:

```
echo $DIR
```

The response should be:

```
ls -las
```

The variable may also be used by entering it on the command line as though it were a command:

```
$DIR
```

The result should be a long listing of the current directory. Although this is a simplified example, the possibilities should be obvious.

Shell variables can also contain other shell variables as part of their content. When this happens, the second variable is substituted with its value. The following example should make this point more clear:

```
HOME=/usr/tsm
USRBIN=$HOME/bin
INFORMIX=$USRBIN/informix
```

In the first line of the example, the HOME variable is set to the string "/usr/tsm." The second line uses the value of the HOME variable and appends the string "/bin" to it, resulting in the string "/usr/tsm/bin." The third line uses the value of the USRBIN variable and produces the string "/usr/tsm/bin/informix." It is possible to use and reuse shell variables within other variables. They may also be used on the command line:

```
cd $INFORMIX
```

This is identical to having entered:

```
cd /usr/tsm/bin/informix
```

The shell uses its symbolic substitution capabilities to provide users with a powerful way to make the shell script more generic.

Variables and Substitution

A shell script may receive arguments from the command line when it is invoked at a terminal, or they may be passed on through a call from one shell script to another. (These arguments are not to be confused with the command line option flags that are processed by the UNIX Shell that interprets and executes the shell scripts.)

There are nine command line arguments which the UNIX Shell stores in argument variables named $1 through $9. There is a $0 argument variable, which when echoed from a shell script, will result in displaying the last command used to invoke the shell script, and may be thought of as a variable whose value is the name of the current shell script.

When a shell script is invoked at the command line the first argument beyond the shell script name ($0) is pointed to by $1, the second is pointed to by $2, and so on. Any argument variable which has no corresponding command line argument has a null (0) value. For example, if there were no command line arguments passed to a shell script when it was invoked, then $1 through $9 all have null values. If two arguments were passed, then $3 through $9 all have null values.

The following example depicts the contents of a simple shell script using the $1, $2 and $3 variables; a listing of the command being executed and its result is also provided. (The prompt string in this and several subsequent examples is tsm:)

```
tsm: cat echoargs
echo 'The name of this shell script is' "$0"
echo ' '
echo 'args='"$1" "$2" "$3" "$4" "$5" "$6" "$7" "$8" "$9"
tsm: echoargs /tsm /usr/bin /etc
The name of this shell script is echoargs
args=/tsm /usr/bin /etc
tsm:
```

The first part of the example executes the **cat** command, displaying the contents of the shell script called echoargs. The second part of the example executes the shell script with three command line parameters. These parameters are echoed to the screen; the remaining argument variables, $4 through $9, are not echoed since they all contain null values.

Another special variable is the $* variable, used to reference all argument variables $1 through $9. The following example should make this clear:

```
tsm: cat echoall
echo 'The name of this shell script is' "$0"
echo ' '
echo 'args='"$*"
tsm: echoall /tsm /usr/bin /etc
The name of this shell script is echoall
args=/tsm /usr/bin /etc
tsm:
```

Again, since the argument variables $4 through $9 have no values, they are not displayed. Only arguments having non-null values are echoed. The argument variables $1 through $9 could be considered the approximate shell counterpart to the argv parameter in the function **main( )** of C language programs. Another argument variable that may be of use, and is the approximate shell counterpart to the argc paramter of the **main( )** function of C programs, is represented by the

$# symbol. This variable contains the number of argument variables ($1-$9) having non-null values. The value is a decimal number indicating the actual number of parameters passed to the shell script — $0 is not included in the count.

Should it become necessary to specify more than nine parameters to a shell script, there is a way to do it. The first nine parameters are referenced by the argument variables $1 through $9. The tenth variable may be obtained by performing a *shifting* operation. Using the **shift** shell command, each parameter is moved down the list by one position; the parameter value for $2 is now referenced by $1, $3 becomes $2, and so on. The $9 variable now contains a new value: the parameter which was formerly the tenth argument on the command line.

The former $1 value is no longer capable of being referenced, and may be thought of as having fallen off into the bit bucket. Each time a shift operation is performed, $1 goes off into the abyss and $9 becomes the newest argument in the parameter list. As this is done, the $# variable is also decremented to provide an accurate argument count. The following illustrations should clarify this point:

```
$1 $2 $3 $4 $5 $6 $7 $8 $9 arg10 arg11 arg12
shift
$1 $2 $3 $4 $5 $6 $7 $8 $9 arg11 arg12
shift
$1 $2 $3 $4 $5 $6 $7 $8 $9 arg12
shift
$1 $2 $3 $4 $5 $6 $7 $8 $9
shift
$1 $2 $3 $4 $5 $6 $7 $8

$ cat shifter
while [ "$#" -ne 0 ]
do
echo "$1" "$2" "$3" "$4" "$5" "$6" "$7" "$8" "$9"
shift
done
```

```
$ shifter a b c d e f g h i j k l m
a b c d e f g h i
b c d e f g h i j
c d e f g h i j k
d e f g h i j k l
e f g h i j k l m
f g h i j k l m
g h i j k l m
h i j k l m
i j k l m
j k l m
k l m
l m
m
$
```

Sometimes it is necessary to construct a string using both characters from a substitution and a string constant. For example, if a user variable called file was defined, then in order to reference it in a shell script $file would be correct. To append the character "x" to the end of that variable, then $filex would be incorrect. The following example should clarify this:

```
file=/usr/tsm/book/chapter13/chapt13.a
cp $file ${file}x
```

The second line of this example would translate to:

```
cp /usr/tsm/book/chapter13/chapt13.a
/usr/tsm/book/chapter13/chapt13.ax
```

If the { } pair had been omitted, an error would have resulted, since the variable $filex had not been declared or initialized to a value. The { } pair is used in this case to assure exclusivity.

It is also possible to provide a default substitution value. An interesting variation of the ${ } construct allows the use of the colon dash character sequence, :-, to be contained within the { } pair.

When this construct is used, the item to the left of the :- indicates a variable whose value should be used if it is not null; otherwise, the value to the right of the :- indicates the literal value to be used:

```
tsm: TERM=vt100
tsm: echo ${TERM:-4410}
vt100
tsm: TERM=
tsm: echo ${TERM:-vt100}
vt100
tsm: echo $TERM

tsm:
```

Yet another variation of this construct uses the equal sign (=) instead of the hyphen. It works almost like the previous example. Should the parameter value to the left of the := be a null, then the default literal to the right of the := is used and assigned to the parameter value to the left of it.

```
tsm: TERM=
tsm: echo ${TERM:=vt100}
vt100
tsm: echo $TERM
vt100
tsm:
```

The next iteration uses the question mark (?) in place of the equal sign. This construct determines if the parameter value on the left is null and can write a message to the standard error output (usually the control terminal associated with the command).

If there is a value to the right of the question mark, then the message is what is written to stderr. If there is no value, then the shell will generate a message. This construct is used to ensure that variables necessary for script execution have non-null values. The following example illustrates how this works:

```
tsm: TERM=vt100
tsm: echo ${TERM:?}
```

```
vt100
tsm: TERM=
tsm: : ${TERM:?"No terminal defined"}
TERM: No terminal defined
tsm: :${TERM:?}
TERM: parameter null or not set
tsm:
```

The following example will indicate which of the variables being checked are null or not set:

```
tsm: : ${TERM:?}
tsm: ${HOME:?} ${INFORMIX:?} ${STARLAN:?}
sh: INFORMIX: parameter null or not set
sh: STARLAN: parameter null or not set
```

The remaining form of the ${ } construct uses the plus character (+) in place of the question mark. If the left parameter is *not* null, then the literal value to the right is used. If the left parameter value *is* null, then no substitution takes place, the null value is honored. The following example demonstrates this:

```
tsm: TERM=vt100
tsm: echo Terminal type is: ${TERM:+"4410"}
Terminal type is: 4410
tsm: TERM=
tsm: echo Terminal type is: ${TERM:+"4410"}
Terminal type is:
tsm:
```

Variables and Sub-Shells

Variables declared within a shell script are known only to that shell level unless they are made global. This is done using the shell **export** command. The parent shell for all users is their login shell. When a shell script is executed, it is considered a sub-shell which has no knowledge of variables local to the parent shell, unless they have been exported specifically. If the first sub-shell declares some local variables without exporting them, subsequent sub-shells are also unaware of those variables.

Sub-shells cannot change the values of variables belonging to their parent shells, even when those variables have been exported. This is because when a variable is exported, sub-shells only receive a copy of those variables and may not modify the originals. When the sub-shell has completed execution, all of its variables are destroyed. Variables may be exported at any time, prior to or after they have been assigned a value. The general format for the **export** command is:

```
export variable-1 ... variable-n
```

It is customary to declare and initialize variables before exporting them, unless a sub-shell reassigns a new value. If the **export** command is entered without arguments, then a listing of all currently exported variables is produced. Commonly exported variables include:

```
CDPATH
EDITOR
ENV
HISTFILE
HISTSIZE
HOME
LANG
LOGNAME
LOGTTY
MAIL
PATH
PS1
PS2
PUBDIR
PWD
SHELL
TERM
TIMEOUT
TZ
UMASK
```

The techniques used to pass arguments between shell scripts involve the use of all the methods discussed up to this point. Suppose that a shell script is invoked as follows:

```
cmd1 red green blue white black cyan
```

The arguments are assigned to the positional parameters $1 through $6; remember that $0 is the name of the shell being executed, in this example its value is cmd1. If the cmd1 shell executes another shell script (cmd2) from within its own code, in order to pass its arguments to cmd2 the following call must be made:

```
tsm: cmd2 $1 $2 $3 $4 $5 $6
```

When cmd2 receives control its own $1 through $6 argument values now become the values "red green blue white black cyan," the same as for cmd1. If a variable called COLOR had been declared and initialized in the cmd1 script, in order for cmd2 to be able to test its value, it would need to have been exported before the call to cmd2:

```
(this is in the cmd1 script)

COLOR=$3
export COLOR
echo $COLOR
cmd2 $1 $2 $3 $4 $5 $6
echo $COLOR

(this is in the cmd2 script)

echo "Color=$1"
echo "COLOR=$COLOR"
COLOR=$6
echo "COLOR=$COLOR"
```

Assuming that the arguments passed to cmd1 were the colors listed previously, then the value for the variable COLOR is blue when it is declared and initialized. The result of the echo command will also be blue. The next statement is a call to cmd2, in which all of the original arguments are passed directly to cmd2. When cmd2 receives control, the value of $1 is echoed back to the screen, which results in the line "COLOR=red." The next echo statement in cmd2 would result in the line "COLOR=blue," since the COLOR variable in cmd1 was set to blue and subsequently exported, and was unmodified before the call to cmd2.

The next statement in cmd2 modifies the value of the variable COLOR to the value of $6, cyan and the subsequent echo statement results in the value "COLOR=cyan." Assuming that cmd2 is done now, control returns back to cmd1, its parent shell. The next instruction to be executed by cmd1 is an echo command to see what the value of the variable COLOR is. Remember that cmd2 had modified the value of its copy of the variable COLOR to contain the value "cyan."

However, when cmd1 assumes control again, its value of the COLOR variable is still blue, even though in cmd2 it was exported. This is due to the previous statement that sub-shells may not modify inherited variables belonging to their parent shells. Another limitation of sub-shells is that they may not change their current directory. This should be done by the parent shell before the call to the sub-shell is made.

There is a way to make the commands of a sub-shell appear to be executing within the current shell. Through the use of the dot (.) shell command. Its purpose is to execute the contents of the file name specified (to the right of the . character) within the current shell script. The general format of this command is:

```
. filename
```

There should be a space between the filename and the . character. If no space appears, then the current shell assumes that the . character is part of the file name and an error message will result. Using this subtle change in the same shell script, the results are quite different.

```
cmd1 red green blue white black cyan
```

```
(this is in the cmd1 script)

COLOR=$3
export COLOR
echo $COLOR
. cmd2 $1 $2 $3 $4 $5 $6
echo $COLOR

(this is in the cmd2 script)

echo "Color=$1"
echo "COLOR=$COLOR"
COLOR=$6
echo "COLOR=$COLOR"
```

Another interesting shell feature is the capability to transfer control over to a sub-shell, without returning to the parent. When the sub-shell is finished, there is no return to the parent; instead, the sub-shell simply terminates execution and control is returned back to the user's login shell. This is accomplished through the use of the **exec** shell command, the general format is:

```
exec filename
```

The file name is the name of an executable shell script and once it completes, all shell processing is completed and control returns back to the login shell.

Other Useful Shell Features

There are three types of quotes that the UNIX shell recognizes; single quotes, double quotes, and the back quote. Although the back slash is not actually a quote, it too, is discussed here. Quotes can be used to contain items separated by whitespace, so that they may be treated as a single object; otherwise, they could appear as multiple objects.

The following examples demonstrate this:

```
grep Steven Mikes /etc/passwd
grep: can't open Mikes
/etc/passwd:tsm::100:1:Steven Mikes:/usr/tsm:
tsm: grep 'Steven Mikes' /etc/passwd
/etc/passwd:tsm::100:1:Steven Mikes:/usr/tsm:
tsm:
tsm: echo Hello    There                    All!
Hello There All!
tsm: echo 'Hello    There                    All!'
Hello    There                    All!
tsm:
```

In the first example, the **grep** command complained that it couldn't open a file called "Mikes"; it treated the string "Mikes" as the file to scan through, instead of as part of the scan argument.

Since the **grep** command supports multiple search files, it was able to open /etc/passwd and find the string "Steven" in it; the reason for the appearance of the second output line from **grep**.

The next example shows how **grep** would respond to the name enclosed within single quotes; it reports back every entry that exactly matches the string between the single quotes. Had the string contained Steve Mikes, and not Steven Mikes, there would not have been a match (unless of course there was an entry in the /etc/passwd file that did contain that exact string).

In the first echo example, there are three arguments separated by several spaces; yet in the response, they are each separated by only a single space. In the second echo example, the arguments are all enclosed within single quotes and the number of spaces between them are retained in the subsequent response.

Arguments contained within the single quotes are treated as literals and parameter substitution does not occur. This includes any of the $var constructs as well. If $1 through $9 or any variable name were attempted to be substituted within single quotes they would be treated as literals:

```
tsm: echo $?
0
```

```
tsm: echo '$?'
$?
tsm:
```

Double quotes on the other hand, do perform parameter substitution. The following example illustrates this:

```
tsm: echo "The value of '$?' is: $?"
The value of '0' is: 0
tsm:
```

Evidently, it performed too well. The $? variable was also substituted even though it was within its own set of single quotes. So how would literals be mixed with substitution variables? This is why the back slash character is included in the discussion. When the back slash character precedes some special character, such as the $ which is used to denote a substitution variable, it is interpreted as a literal instead:

```
tsm: echo "The value of \$? is: $?"
The value of $? is: 0
tsm:
```

When enclosed within a pair of double quotes, certain special shell characters are not interpreted as literals (unless preceded by a back slash); namely, the back quotes, dollar sign character ($), and the back slash itself.

Remember that back quotes have a very special meaning to the UNIX shell. This is another form of substitution; the command sequence appearing within the back quotes is executed first. The result that this produces is then substituted in place of the actual command string, the resulting value is then treated as the argument value.

This is one of the most useful features of the UNIX shell and can be quite a powerful aide when developing personalized tools. It is possible to nest as many command executions enclosed within back quotes as is necessary; be sure, however, that the back quote pairs all match up properly, otherwise some unpredictable results could occur.

Making Decisions

It is necessary to make decisions in every programming language, and the UNIX shell is no exception. The shell provides several methods for making decisions, some are logically neater (easier to use and understand) and may produce quicker results than others. Also, the shell is used for testing one or more conditions using an *if-then-else* construct. An example of its form is as follows:

```
if test "$TERM" = vt100
then
echo "Terminal type is a vt100"
fi
```

The argument of the **test** command is an expression that evaluates to either true or false. If the expression evaluates to true, **test** returns an exit value of 0; otherwise, false evaluations result in a non-zero exit status. In the previous example, the expression is a parameter substitution value, $TERM, which is compared for equality with a literal string *vt100*.

First, the $TERM variable is substituted with the user environment variable's value. Then that value is compared against the string *vt100*. If the result of the comparison is equal, **test** returns a 0 and the if condition is true; otherwise **test** returns some non-zero value and the result of the comparison is false.

A frequent error made by many shell programmers is not enclosing shell variables within double quotes. Doing this will circumvent problems that might arise if the shell variable being tested has a null value. In such a scenario, unquoted shell variables having a null value are substituted with nothing, producing a situation where the **test** command interprets this occurrence as an incorrect number of arguments being given it.

It is generally a good idea to use the standard of enclosing variables within double quotes to avoid any problems. The **test** command can be used to determine if a variable has a null value or not:

```
test "$var"
```

This example will return true if the variable is not null, and false if it is null. The **test** command is a built-in feature of the UNIX shell and has a number of option flags, two of which may also be used to determine whether a variable is null or not. These are the -n and -z flags.

When the -n flag is used, **test** returns a zero if the value of the variable is non-zero; when the -z flag is specified, **test** returns an exit status of zero if the variable is null:

```
tsm:  TERM=
tsm:  test  -z  "$TERM"
tsm:  echo  $?
0
tsm:  test  -n  "$TERM"
tsm:  echo  $?
1
tsm:
```

Another interesting twist appears in the following example:

```
tsm:  TERM=
tsm:  [  -z  "$TERM"  ]
tsm:  echo  $?
0
tsm:
```

If something like this is encountered, don't be alarmed, this is only the **test** command in disguise. Most UNIX programmers and professional users prefer this method to the verbose form of test. (Perhaps it is because it looks a bit more cryptic and implies an advanced level of shell language programming skill.)

This construct is handy for use in conjunction with file operators. There are a number of these operators that may be used to determine such things as whether the file is a directory or ordinary file; if the file is readable, writable, or executable; or if it has a non-zero length. The following examples demonstrate how the file operators are used with this form of the **test** command:

```
[ -d /etc/passwd ]
[ -f /etc/passwd ]
[ -r /etc/passwd ]
[ -s /etc/passwd ]
[ -w /etc/passwd ]
[ -x /etc/passwd ]
```

The -d operator returns true if the file is a directory; the -f operator returns true if the file exists and is an ordinary file; and the -r operator returns true if the file exists and is readable by the inquiring process. The -s operator returns true if the file exists and has a file size greater than zero bytes; the -w operator returns true if the file exists and is writable by the inquiring process; and the -x operator returns true if the file exists and is executable by the inquiring process. When the logical negation character (!) is placed in front of any test expression, it will negate the result of the evaluation for that expression.

Another alternative to the long hand form of the if statement is to use the && and || constructs. The following example should make it clear how the && construct works:

```
[ -z $TERM ] && TERM=vt100
```

is the same as writing:

```
if [test -z "$TERM"]
   then
   TERM=vt100
fi
```

The argument to the left of the && characters is the expression to be evaluated. If the result of the evaluation is a zero value, then the command to the right of the && characters is executed; otherwise, for non-zero evaluation results the command gets skipped. The && characters may be thought of as the "*then*" within the *if-then* sequence.

The || construct works almost the same, except that the || characters act as the *"else"* in an *if-then-else* sequence. Consider the following example:

```
[ -z $TERM ] || export TERM
```

It is the same as writing:

```
if [test -z "$TERM"]
   then
   :
   else
   export TERM
fi
```

This construct can be very handy to perform error handling:

```
some command sequence || call to error handler
```

There is also another form of decision making available in the UNIX shell that very closely resembles the switch/case construct of the C language — the **case** command. The following example illustrates the usage of this command and how it works:

```
case $TERM
   in
      vt100)   echo "TERM=vt100";;
      tv970)   echo "TERM=Televideo 970";;
esac
```

The **case** construct uses a special terminator, similar to the *if-fi* construct, called **esac** (case backwards). Each possible matching pattern appears after the **in** statement, followed by a right parenthesis and any commands to be executed for this condition. The last command to be executed is terminated by using a double semicolon sequence. The pattern to be matched may be a single character or an entire string, numeric or alpha. A range may also be used as follows:

```
case $answer
   in
      [0-1] )   echo "digits";;
      [a-z] )   echo "lower case alpha";;
      [A-Z] )   echo "upper case alpha";;
      * )   echo "any other character";;
esac
```

The logical OR symbol may also be applied as in the following example:

```
case $answer
in
1 | 2 | [5-9] )   echo "You answered either a 1, 2, 5,
6, 7, 8, or 9";;
esac
```

Shell Functions

UNIX System V Release 2 (and later) supports shell functions. It is possible to create intricate shell programs with callable functions that are executed the same way ordinary shell commands are — by entering its name. Functions are defined by creating a name followed by a left/right pair of parentheses (to indicate it is a function) and any commands that this function is to execute are enclosed between a left/right pair of curly braces:

```
name()   {   command1; ... commandn; }

name() {
   command1
   ...
   command2
}
```

Functions cannot be passed on to sub-shells, they exist only within the shell in which they are defined. When a function has completed, it may return a value to its caller using the return command, quite similar to the way the **return( )** function of the C language works. The caller may then act according to the results of the return code.

Trapping Events

The **trap** command may be used to trap certain events, such as the BREAK key to prevent early termination of a shell. The general format of the trap command is as follows:

```
trap "commands" signal
```

The commands are enclosed within double quotes that are separated by semicolons. The signals capable of being trapped are any of the standard signals supported in the UNIX system. Entering the trap command with no arguments produces a list of any traps changed by the current shell. Signals may be ignored by trapping the signal of choice, and assigning a null command sequence (""):

```
trap "" signal
```

In order to reset a trapped signal back to its original handler, omit the command sequence. The following example resets signal 0 back to its default:

```
trap 0
```

When a shell script is executed, normally the command lines are hidden from the user. This makes debugging difficult, so in order to see what is happening, there is a technique available. To invoke debugging, the **-x** option must be specified as the parameter to the UNIX shell, followed by the shell script name that is to be debugged (and any of its arguments). This invokes the debugging feature of the UNIX shell, writing each shell script line to the terminal so it can be observed for errors. This output may be redirected to a file if desired. The following examples would invoke the -x option for a shell script

called test6 and three arguments, first using the Bourn shell and then
using the Korn shell:

```
sh -x test6 red green blue
ksh -x test6 red green blue
```

Shell Script Background Execution

Being that the UNIX system is multitasking, as well as multiuser, it
would be inconvenient if it were not possible to execute a shell script
without having to wait for it to complete. The UNIX shell provides a
way to execute shell scripts, while users are free to continue as they
like, even log off if necessary. All that needs to be done is to append
the & character to the command line used to invoke a shell script:

```
test6 red green blue &
```

The shell script test6 would now be running in the background.

CHAPTER 8

KEYBOARD AND SCREEN HANDLING

In DOS, keyboard input (at the lowest levels) is handled through a hardware interrupt that may be controlled by an application program. In UNIX it is possible for a process to receive and manipulate keyboard input from multiple terminals. The kernel actually does this when validating logins from the many terminals connected to it.

Terminals

The term *terminal* is actually a reference to a node in a communications network, its origins most likely being the pioneer days of the first true communications networks when the teletypes used by Western Union were called teletype terminals. Since the early days, the term has been used to describe everything from a *dumb* terminal to an intelligent node with a keyboard and display, used to receive and display data. (Early terminals did not have video screen displays, instead they had paper displays that were mechanical contraptions similar in concept to typewriter carriages.)

The modern use of the term implies a combination of a keyboard and a video display device such as a Cathode Ray Tube, hence the modified term *CRT terminal*. The UNIX system came to light in the late sixties, when most CRT terminals were dumb devices; that is, they could be driven only by the system to which they were connected and they had no processing power of their own. Intelligent terminals, on the other hand, have local processing abilities provided by a microprocessor capable of localized logical processing and providing a method of communication with a remote host.

Today, both dumb and intelligent terminals are used to communicate over local and wide area networks such as Ethernet, Starlan, IBM Token Ring, and SNA. They also communicate over dialed serial communications such as bulletin board systems and remote dialup communications. In UNIX, as with most other systems, the terminal is the hardware interface between the user and the computer hardware.

A terminal is usually thought of as a single device, though it may actually be two separate devices: the keyboard and the video display. This is particularly so in the IBM PC, in which the keyboard plugs into a special port on the PC's motherboard and the video display device requires a separate controller board that plugs into an available bus slot, also on the PC's motherboard.

In this type of hardware environment the terminal is a logical entity consisting of the two separate pieces of hardware that are sometimes from different manufacturers. The more conventional terminal is usually an integrated device with both pieces provided by the same manufacturer.

In mainframe computer systems there is a *master console* used by the system operator as the primary terminal to control the system. The term *console* is sometimes used in place of *terminal*, implying that a console device has greater authority than terminal devices. In UNIX there is a special device in the /dev directory reserved as the system console, called /dev/console. In the DOS system, there are five reserved file handles:

- File Handle 0: Used as stdin (standard input) which is part of the CON: device and is the PC's keyboard.

- File Handle 1: Used as stdout (standard output), also part of CON: and is the PC's video display.

- File Handle 2: Used as stderr (standard error) which defaults to CON: and is also the PC's video display.

- File Handle 3: Used as stdaux (standard aux), the standard auxiliary device.

- File Handle 4: Used as stdprn (standard printer), the standard printer output port (LPT1 - LPT4).

When a DOS program opens file handles 0, 1, or 2, a **read( )** function obtains input from the PC keyboard and **write( )** functions output to the PC video display screen. In the UNIX system it is possible to have several terminals connected to the computer system, any of which may be possible to address from a given process. There are literally hundreds of different types of terminals in existence, many of which are supported in UNIX through terminal device drivers, programs designed to drive a specific terminal type.

Terminal Device Drivers

Before a data string may be written to a physical terminal from a process or other terminal, it must first be processed by a terminal device driver that is a part of the UNIX kernel. The device driver may either pass the data unmodified through to the terminal device, or may modify the data stream as necessary. Modification frequently performed by a terminal device driver is the translation of newline (LF) characters into a two character sequence: carriage-return-line-feed (CRLF).

This means that a character commonly referred to as a newline or line feed (CTRL-J or octal 012) is replaced with two characters: carriage return (CTRL-M or octal 015) and line feed. The purpose of such a substitution is so that each new line begins on the left side of a terminal screen. On a video display screen it is possible to issue a new line (CTRL-J) request from the keyboard without repositioning the cursor position to the beginning of the line, as is the case for most full screen oriented text editors (**vi** and **emacs** for example).

Since terminal users frequently make typing errors, the terminal device driver allows for the handling of backspace, character and line deletion, and cursor up/down/left/right positioning. Note that the positioning performed appears on the video screen, yet the mechanism for performing the operations is derived through the keyboard; implying that terminal I/O is treated as an integrated function.

Certain terminals may be "programmable"; that is, they may be made to perform special display formatting of the output, such as reverse video and blinking. In order to do this, it is customary to send a sequence of *escape* characters preceding or embedded within the text to be displayed. Such escape sequences must be dealt with by the specific terminal driver so that they may be handled properly. For this command to be effective, escape sequences are used to instruct the ANSI.SYS terminal driver to display the data properly. If the ANSI.SYS driver is not loaded at DOS boot time (specified in CONFIG.SYS), the escape sequences are interpreted incorrectly and curious results may occur.

The same is true for UNIX terminal drivers; in order for data to be displayed properly on the screen, the correct driver must be used for the particular terminal type. The **vi** editor performs interesting and sometimes destructive results if the incorrect driver is specified for a particular terminal type. The UNIX shell uses the environment variable TERM to determine which terminal driver to use for a particular user when writing output to the screen. If no TERM variable is specified, certain defaults are assumed, and generally work for simple unformatted displays.

Control Terminals

A *control terminal* is a terminal associated with a process and its subprocesses (through their standard file descriptors) — for their lifetimes. Since the DOS environment is a single tasking, single-user system and usually has only one display associated with the machine hardware, there is no concept of a control terminal in DOS. When a key is struck on the terminal considered by any and all processes as their control terminal, they all receive the SIGINT signal. A control terminal is inherited by any subprocess across **fork( )** system calls. Should a process require access to its control terminal, it may do so through the standard file descriptors or the /dev/tty*xx* entry. A process may disassociate itself with its control terminal by using the **setgpgrp( )** system call.

Primarily Used for Data Transmission

The basic job the terminal device driver must perform is the transmission of characters from the physical terminal hardware (keyboard/screen) to a process, and vice versa. A user may be entering data via the keyboard, mouse, or other input mechanism while data is being displayed to the screen. For this reason the terminal driver must be capable of processing these I/O activities simultaneously and asynchronously of one another. To accomplish this, the terminal driver stores the input data from the **read** function to an input buffer and also stores data to be written to an output buffer using the **write** function.

When data is being written to the terminal screen, or when a process is running, the keystrokes entered by a user are saved in a type-ahead buffer and are processed when time becomes available. The problem with a such a type-ahead buffer is that it is possible to lose characters and cause input errors. The type-ahead buffer can be configured as a large ring buffer with logic to determine when it is full; but there is no way to detect a loss of input characters.

In DOS, an unmodified type-ahead buffer is limited to only 16 bytes. This limits the possibility of lost input characters. It also limits the whole concept of type-ahead buffer usability. A more practical approach would be a method of "editing" the type-ahead buffer with a command line recall feature, or even a "flush buffer" key sequence. The UNIX system will echo back characters entered into the type-ahead buffer, as opposed to the DOS system which will not. By not echoing back the characters entered into the type-ahead buffer, the possibility of typographic errors increases.

Another irritating quirk of the DOS type-ahead buffer is that all commands are stacked in sequence. If users suddenly realize that they made a mistake and wish to interrupt the current process, the normal method to do so would be to enter a CTRL-C through the keyboard. If they slip and enter anything else, the current process will complete and only then will the corrected second CTRL-C sequence be executed.

The typing mistake is interpreted as a command and is acted upon accordingly (usually resulting in another error). Afterwards, the "real" CTRL-C sequence is executed (producing a delayed reaction affecting whatever is active after the current process has finished).

The Computer/Terminal Link

There are four nodes that make up the link between the computer and terminal hardware, which are:

- **The Program Node:** This node generates output characters, interprets input characters, and interacts with terminals using the read/write system calls, special library function subroutine calls from a screen management package (such as Curses or X Window), or through high level standard I/O library calls. All I/O is performed through the fundamental low level primitives, **read** and **write.**

- **Terminal Device Driver Node:** The terminal device driver is code that is incorporated into the UNIX kernel. It is usually hardware specific, permitting the system to properly access the terminal hardware. The primary function of the driver is receiving input and delivering output characters to the terminal, mapping of characters if necessary, logical processing of terminal escape sequences for formatting purposes, and any other end user features such as line editing or special type-ahead buffering capabilities.

- **Keyboard Node:** This node is the keyboard part of a terminal. Although a terminal is traditionally thought of as a single device, it consists of two distinct and logically separate components. The terminal driver communicates with the keyboard node by storing characters entered through it into a keyboard input buffer.

- **Screen Node:** This node is the screen part of a terminal. The terminal driver communicates with the screen node by maintaining a separate output buffer from which characters are written to the screen.

The UNIX Terminal

In the UNIX system, terminals are identified as special files in the /dev directory, and are treated as character devices. They have names such as:

```
/dev/console
/dev/consoles
/dev/contty
/dev/tty
/dev/tty01
/dev/tty02
. . .
/dev/ttynn
```

The term *tty* refers back to the "teletype" terminals and is used interchangeably with the term "terminal." Actually, in the UNIX system the tty entry in the /dev directory is an entry defining a communications port. Any type of terminal may be connected to a port and defined through the TERM environment variable. When a user logs into a particular terminal, the kernel changes access permissions for the terminal to those of the user, since the user "owns" the terminal during the session.

The first three standard file descriptors in the UNIX system are the same as for the DOS system: file descriptor 0 (stdin) is the terminal keyboard for the control terminal; file descriptor 1 (stdout) is the terminal screen for the control terminal; and file descriptor 2 (stderr) is the terminal screen for the control terminal.

Normal I/O

The definition of "normal" is the default terminal settings that are in effect prior to user modifications with the **stty** command. I/O programming should be as device independent as possible, because it isn't always possible to know in advance if terminals, files, or pipes are already in use. There are four basic I/O system calls: **open( )**, **read( )**, **write( )**, and **close( )**.

open( ) System Call

This is the system call used to open files. One of its parameters is used to specify how the file is to be opened: read-only, writeable, or both. The **creat( )** system call may also be used to open terminal files. However, since the special file must already exist in the /dev directory, the **open( )** call is better, especially since **creat( )** will open the file in write only mode and terminals are usually opened as read/write devices. Terminal I/O is unaffected by the **lseek( )** system call.

read( ) System Call

This system call is used to obtain characters from the keyboard portion of the terminal, and behaves quite differently for terminal files than for ordinary files. Characters are not returned until an entire line of data is ready and only a single line is returned at a time. This is true even if only a single character was requested. There are special characters that may be entered at any time on the input line and which can modify the data to be read, such as the erase (#) character or the kill (@) character.

For this reason, the line cannot be assumed to be in its final form until a special "end of line" character is received. This special character is called the newline character and is represented as the ASCII ^J (CTRL-J) or octal 012 value. The integer value returned by the **read( )** system call is the number of bytes actually read.

An alternative to the newline character is the EOT character, ASCII ^D (CTRL-D) or octal 004. When this is entered, the line is read regardless of how many characters are in the input buffer, or whether or not there is a newline present.

write( ) System Call

This system call is used to send characters to the video screen component of the terminal. It will send the specified number of bytes to the device identified by the file descriptor, the first argument in the calling parameter list. The file pointer is incremented by the number of bytes that were actually written (which may differ from the number of bytes requested).

close( ) System Call

This system call is used to close the file indicated by the specified file descriptor, which must have been opened previously. The result is that data buffers are written to the file and are flushed and closed.

NON-Blocking Terminal I/O

A **read( )** system call will wait for data if the line is not ready when the call is issued. The process cannot do anything until the I/O has completed. This is referred to as *blocking*. In normal files the data is either available as the next character or when the end of file (EOF) has been reached. NON-blocking may be set when issuing the **open( )** or **fcntl( )** system calls by specifying the O_NDELAY (no delay) flag. In this case, if the line isn't available, the function returns immediately with a byte transfer count of zero. This is almost identical to an end of file condition that may be generated by users entering a CTRL-D, and must be taken into account when using non-blocking I/O.

One possible solution is to use some other character or character sequence to indicate the equivalent of EOT, such as CTRL-X, CTRL-Z, or ESC. A possible use for non-blocking input would be if it were desirable to monitor the input streams from multiple terminals. Since it would be possible for characters to be transmitted on a totally random basis, it would be impossible to predict when a particular terminal may send a character. For this reason, blocking I/O is not used because while waiting on a particular terminal, it's likely that data from other terminals may be ignored.

The non-blocking method allows for polling of all terminals, one at a time. If there is no data available, the **read( )** system call will return a zero value indicating this, and polling just continues. To prevent excessive monopolization of the CPU, the process could be put to sleep between polling cycles if no data were read from any terminal.

RAW Terminal I/O

The **ioctl( )** system call may be set up for unmodified access to the data stream. Before this can be accomplished, however, certain flag settings must first be reset. Raw I/O should have the following attributes:

- Punctual Input: ICANON is cleared and MIN and TIME are both set.

- Character Mapping Off: Output processing is suspended by clearing OPOST in c_oflag. INCLR, ICRNL, and IUCLC must also be cleared for input and ISTRIP should be cleared to obtain all eight data bits.

- Flow control must be disabled by clearing IXON.

- No Control Characters Allowed: BRKINT and ISIG must be cleared.

- Echo must be disabled by clearing ECHO.

An example of how this might be done is in the following function.

```
void set_raw_mode() /* set raw mode on for terminal I/O
*/
{
struct termio termbuf;
if(ioctl(0,TCGETA, &termbuf) == -1)
syserr("ioctl error!\n");
save_termbuf=termbuf;
termbuf.c_iflag &= ~(INLCR | ICRNL | IUCLC | ISTRIP |
IXON | BRKINT);
```

```
termbuf.c_oflag &= ~OPOST;
termbuf.c_lflag &= ~(ICANON | ISIG | ECHO);
termbuf.c_cc[4]=5;
/* MIN */
termbuf.c_cc[5]=2;
/* TIME */
if(ioctl(0,TCSETAF, &termbuf) == -1 )
   syserr("another ioctl error");
}
```

ioctl( ) System Call and Terminal Characteristics

This system call can be used to control a terminal device from a program. This is done by using the **ioctl( )** system call in conjunction with *termio* structures.

termio Structures

The information stored in a termio structure can be thought of as the current state or context of a terminal. It contains information about such things as line speed, character length, and flow control and is represented by various state flags for each terminal device. A termio structure contains several fields that may be obtained and manipulated using the **ioctl( )** system call.

A properly written application that manipulates terminal parameters via **ioctl( )** calls saves the current settings before any modifications. When the program is finished it should then restore those original settings before final termination. The following code fragment example illustrates this basic point:

```
#include <termio.h>
struct termio old_termbuf, new_termbuf;
int term_fd; /* file descriptor to terminal affected */
 .
 .
 .
/* save original terminal state */
ioctl( term_fd, TCGETA, &old_termbuf );
```

```
/* initialize fields in new_termbuf to new values */
.
.
.
/* modify the terminal state */
ioctl( term_fd, TCSETA, &new_termbuf );
/* restore original terminal state */
ioctl( term_fd, TCSETA, &old_termbuf );
exit();
```

All terminal modification operations should use the general guidelines demonstrated in the preceding example; first save the original terminal state, proceed with modification of terminal characteristics using a different termio structure, and restore the original terminal state before final exit.

line speed

A terminal's line speed can be reset by accessing the c_cflag field within a termio structure. This is done by ORing certain constant values defined in the termio.h header file and assigning the result to the c_cflag field. The following code fragment example changes the terminal line speed from its current setting to 9600 baud:

```
#include <termio.h>
struct termio old_termbuf, new_termbuf;
int term_fd; /* file descriptor to terminal affected */
.
.
.
/* save original terminal state */
ioctl( term_fd, TCGETA, &old_termbuf );
/* initialize fields in new_termbuf to new values */
new_termbuf.c_cflag |= B9600; /* set baud rate */
/* modify the terminal state */
ioctl( term_fd, TCSETA, &new_termbuf ); /* changes are
now in effect */
.
/* other processing /*
```

```
.
/* restore original terminal state */
ioctl( term_fd, TCSETA, &old_termbuf );
exit();
```

parity value

The parity value can be set by using other flags in conjunction with
the c_cflag field of a termio structure. The following example sets the
parity to odd with parity checking enabled:

```
#include <termio.h>
struct termio old_termbuf, new_termbuf;
int term_fd; /* file descriptor to terminal affected */
.
.
.
/* save original terminal state */
ioctl( term_fd, TCGETA, &old_termbuf );
/* initialize fields in new_termbuf to new values */
new_termbuf.c_cflag |= (PARENB | PARODD); /* set parity
values*/
/* modify the terminal state */
ioctl( term_fd, TCSETA, &new_termbuf ); /* changes are
now in effect */
.
/* other processing /*
.
/* restore original terminal state */
ioctl( term_fd, TCSETA, &old_termbuf );
exit();
```

Data Flow Control Flags

Use the c_iflag field of a termio structure to set flow control options
(c_iflag |= VALUE). There are three input control flags associated
with flow control:

- IXON: When specified, XON is enabled (CTRL-Q) and incoming data is received.

- IXANY: When specified, any character acts as XON character.

- IXOFF: When specified, XOFF is enabled (CTRL-S) and incoming data is halted.

Character Translation/Mapping

Use the c_iflag field of a termio structure to set character translation options (c_iflag |= VALUE). There are three input control flags associated with character mapping:

- INLCR: Translates newline to carriage-return (LF to CR) when specified.

- IGNCR: Ignores carriage return when specified.

- ICRNL: Opposite of INLCR, carriage-return to newline (CR to LF) translation.

Terminal Control Characters

The following table describes the values for the c_cc array member of a termio structure. This elements in this array are the values for the terminal control characters.

Table 8-1: Termio Structure Values

SYMBOL	VALUE	DESCRIPTION
VINTR	0	Interrupt Key
VQUIT	1	Quit Key
VERASE	2	Erase Character
VKILL	3	Kill Character (line erase)
VEOF	4	End-of-File Character
VEOL	5	End-of-Line Character (optional)

The following example demonstrates how to change the values of any of these keys:

```
include <termio.h>
struct termio old_termbuf, new_termbuf;
int term_fd; /* file descriptor to terminal affected */
.

.

.
/* save original terminal state */
ioctl( term_fd, TCGETA, &old_termbuf );
/* initialize fields in new_termbuf to new values */
new_termbuf.c_cc[VQUIT] = 033; /* ESC key = QUIT */
new_termbuf.c_cc[VERASE] = 177; /* DEL key = character
erase */
new_termbuf.c_cc[VKILL] = 043; /* # key = line kill */
/* modify the terminal state */
ioctl( term_fd, TCSETA, &new_termbuf ); /* changes are
now in effect */
.
/* other processing /*
.
/* restore original terminal state */
ioctl( term_fd, TCSETA, &old_termbuf );
exit();
```

Basic Windowing

Windowing is nothing more than setting all or part of a physical
terminal's screen to allow displays. It is important to note that many
windows or simply one window may be opened on a screen. Windows
are given names (handles) and are then referenced by that name.
Unique screen display attributes may be set within a window. The
size of a window does not necessarily have to correspond to a given
screen's physical dimensions.

Windows can be thought of as view ports containing all or a portion
of the entire display. For windows containing only a portion of the
entire display, the rest of the display may be viewed by scrolling up
and down or left and right using specialized controls that are manipu-

lated by users from either the keyboard or through some form of input device such as a mouse.

Another characteristic of most modern windowing systems is that windows can overlap one another, obscuring all or part of other windows. Usually, windows can be moved around the screen. There are three main windowing systems used in UNIX-based systems today: curses, X Window, and NeWS. Of these, curses is the oldest and provides limited character-based windowing; nevertheless, it is still widely used and has even been ported to the PC environment in various implementations .

The X Window System, described later, has gone on to become the new standard for graphical windowing systems because of the extreme portability across a variety of computer hardware and operating systems that it provides.

NeWS, for Networked Window System, is Sun Microsystems' answer to X Window. NeWS provides similar functionality. Efforts are underway to make NeWS available for processors besides those from Sun.

Curses

Curses is a terminal-independent library of C subroutines designed to let programmers control terminal I/O in an easy fashion. It is the highest level of screen control because it optimizes cursor manipulation. The curses routines update the screen in a random access method, data located anywhere on the screen can be manipulated by going directly to that data's location, as opposed to updating in a sequential manner and thus eliminating the need to manipulate and update unchanged screen data.

The curses library lets the programmer create window data structures, control screen video attributes, and allows keyboard input. Note that many of the curses routines are macros defined by the preprocessor and should be used carefully. Note also that curses routines are not linked automatically to programs and therefore, must be named in the command line when creating the program:

```
$ cc -o progname progname.c -lcurses
```

The curses library was created in the 1970s to standardize programmed instruction for different types of CRT terminals in the UNIX environment. (This predates graphical terminals and workstations by several years.) The idea was that these functions could address most of the different terminals by referencing a file describing the individual terminal characteristics. Since that time, curses has become a standard in most UNIX environments.

For DOS users familiar with the Lattice C curses Screen Manager Library, the UNIX curses Library is fully compatible, and programs can easily be ported between them. For a more detailed description of the curses functions, refer to the UNIX System V Programmers Guide or Volume 3 of the UNIX System V Interface Definition.

Basic curses Program Structure

All programs using the curses library must have the following basic structure:

```
#include curses.h
main()
{
                initscr();
                /*main program*/
                endwin();
                exit(0);
}
```

The header file curses.h must be included in all programs using curses. The **initscr( )** function must be called before any other curses subroutines. Its function is to determine the terminal type from the TERM environment variable and to initialize certain curses data structures. The **endwin( )** function should be called prior to program exit to restore the terminal's original state and to place the cursor in the lower left corner of the screen.

Modes

The terminal modes for I/O are usually set after the call to **initscr( )**. None of the mode setting subroutines accept parameters.

echo( ) / noecho( )

These functions allow programmers to turn on or off the terminal driver's echoing to the terminal. The default state is *echo on*. The function **noecho( )** disables this automatic echoing.

nl( ) / nonl( )

These functions allow programmers to enable or disable carriage-return/newline mappings. When enabled, carriage-return is mapped on input to newline and newline is mapped on output to newline/carriage-return. The default state is *mapping enabled*, and **nonl( )** is used to turn this mapping off. It is interesting to note that while mapping is disabled, cursor movement is optimized.

cbreak( ) / nocbreak( )

Canonical processing (*line at a time* character processing) is disabled within the terminal driver when calling **cbreak( )**, allowing a break for each character. Interrupt and flow control keys are unaffected. The default state is *nocbreak*, which enables canonical processing.

raw( ) / noraw( )

These functions are similar to the **cbreak( )/nocbreak( )** functions, except that interrupt and flow control keys are also disabled or enabled.

savetty( ) / resetty( )

The current state of the terminal can be saved into a buffer reserved by curses when calling the **savtty( )** function. The last saved state can be restored via the **resetty( )** function.

Curses I/O Functions

The following are a few of the many curses library functions.

addch( )

This function adds a character to a window at the current curser position.

```
#include curses.h
main()
{
WINDOW *win;
                initscr();
                addch('e');
                refresh();
                endwin();
}
```

mvaddch( )

This function moves a character into a window at the position specified by x and y coordinates.

```
#include curses.h
main()
{
WINDOW *win;
int x, y;
                x=3; y=10;
                initscr();
                mvaddch(x, y, 'e');
                refresh();
                endwin();
}
```

addstr( )

This function adds the specified string to a window at the current curser position.

```
#include curses.h
main()
{
WINDOW *win;
                initscr();
                addstr("This is a string example.");
                refresh();
                endwin();

}
```

mvaddstr( )

This function moves the specified string into a window located at the position specified by the x and y coordinates.

```
#include curses.h
main()

{
WINDOW *win;
int x, y;
x=3; y=10;
                initscr();
                mvaddstr(x, y, "This is the string example.");
                refresh();
                endwin();

}
```

printw( )

This function outputs formatted strings at the current cursor position and is is similar to the **printf( )** function of C, in that multiple arguments may be specified.

```
#include curses.h
main()
{
WINDOW *win;
   char *word = "example";
   int number = 1;
     initscr();
     printw("this is just %d %s of a formatted string!
\n",
        word, number);
     refresh();
     endwin();
}
```

mvprintw( )

This function outputs formatted strings at the line specified in y and
the column specified in x. Multiple arguments may be given.

```
#include curses.h
main();
{
WINDOW *win;
   char *word = "example";
   int number = 1;
   int x=3; int y=10;
     initscr();
     mvprintw(x, y, "this is just %d %s of a formatted
string! \n",
        word, number);
     refresh();
   endwin();
}
```

move( )

This function moves the cursor to the line/column coordinates given.

```
#include curses.h
main()
{
WINDOW *win;
int line=3; int column=10;
                initscr();
                move(line, column);
                refresh();
                endwin();
}
```

getyx( )

This function is used to determine and return the current line/column location of the cursor.

```
#include curses.h
main()
{
WINDOW *win;
int y,x;
                initscr();
                getyx();
                refresh();
                endwin();
}
```

getch( )

This function is used to read a single character from the keyboard, and returns an integer value. It is similar to the C standard I/O function **getc**.

```
#include curses.h
main()
{
WINDOW *win;
int in_char;
```

```
                    initscr();
                    in_char = getch();
                    refresh();
                    endwin();
    }
```

inch( )

This function returns the character from under the current cursor position of a terminal's screen, in an integer format.

```
    #include curses.h
    main()
    {
    WINDOW *win;
    int in_char;
                    initscr();
                    in_char = inch();
                    refresh();
                    endwin();

    }
```

mvinch( )

This function is used to get the character under the cursor location specified as x and y coordinates. The value returned is an integer.

```
    #include curses.h
    main()
    {
    WINDOW *win;
    int in_char;
                    initscr();
                    in_char = mvinch(3, 10);
                    refresh();
                    endwin();
    }
```

clear( )

This function completely clears the terminal screen by writing blank spaces to all physical screen locations via calls to **erase( )** and **clearok( )**, and is completed by the next call to **refresh( )**.

```
#include curses.h
main()
{
WINDOW *win;
                    initscr();
                    clear();
                    refresh();
                    endwin();
}
```

erase( )

This function is used to insert blank spaces in the physical screen and, like **clear( )**, erases all data on the terminal screen, but does not require the call to **refresh( )**.

```
#include curses.h
main()
{
WINDOW *win;
                    initscr();
                    erase();
                    refresh();
                    endwin();
}
```

clrtobot( )

This function is used to clear the physical screen from the current cursor position to the bottom of the screen, filling it with blank spaces.

```
#include curses.h
main()
{
WINDOW *win;
                initscr();
                clrtobot();
                refresh();
                endwin();

}
```

clrtoeol( )

This function allows the programmer to clear the physical terminal screen from the current cursor position to the end of that physical screen line by filling it with blank spaces.

```
#include curses.h
main()
{
WINDOW *win;
                initscr();
                clrtoeol();
                refresh();
                endwin();

}
```

delch( )

This function deletes the character under the current cursor position, moving all characters on that line (located to the right of the deleted character) one position to the left, and fills the last charactor position (on that line) with a blank space. The current cursor position remains unchanged.

```
#include curses.h
main()
{
```

```
WINDOW *win;
                    initscr();
                    delch();
                    refresh();
                    endwin();
}
```

mvdelch( )

This function deletes the character under the cursor position at the line/column specified in y/x. In all other aspects, it works the same as the **delch( )** function.

```
#include curses.h
main()
{
WINDOW *win;
                    initscr();
                    mvdelch(3, 10);
                    refresh();
                    endwin();
}
```

insch( )

This function is used to insert the character named in 'c' to be inserted at the current cursor position, causing all characters to the right of the cursor (on that line, only) to shift one space to the right, losing the last character of that line. The cursor is moved one position to the right of the inserted character.

```
#include curses.h
main()
{
WINDOW *win;
                    initscr();
                    insch('e');
```

```
                          refresh();
                          endwin();
    }
```

mvinsch( )

This function inserts the character named in 'c' to the line/column
position named in y/x, and otherwise works identically to the **insch( )**
function.

```
#include curses.h
main()
{
WINDOW *win;
                          initscr();
                          mvinsch(3, 10, 'e');
                          refresh();
                          endwin();
    }
```

deleteln( )

This function allows the deletion of the current cursor line, moving all
lines located below up one line and filling the last line with blank
spaces. The cursor position remains unchanged.

```
#include curses.h
main()
{
WINDOW *win;
                          initscr();
                          deleteln();
                          refresh();
                          endwin();
    }
```

insertln( )

This function is the opposite of the **deleteln()** function, in that it allows the insertion of a blank-filled line at the current cursor line, moving all lines located below down one line. The bottom line is lost, and the current cursor position is unaffected.

```
#include curses.h
main()
{
                initscr();
                insertln();
                refresh();
                endwin();

}
```

refresh( )

This function is used to update the physical terminal screen from the window buffer and all changes made to that buffer (via curses functions) will be written. If the buffer size is smaller than the physical screen, then only that part of the screen is refreshed, leaving everything else unchanged.

```
#include curses.h
main()
{
WINDOW *win;
                initscr();
                /* curses function call(s) here */
                refresh();
                endwin();

}
```

wrefresh( )

This function is identical to the **refresh( )** function, except that the refresh operation is performed on the named window.

```
#include curses.h
main()
{
WINDOW *win;
                initscr();
                /* curses function call(s) here */
                wrefresh(win);
                endwin();
}
```

initscr( )

This function call must be present in all programs calling the curses functions. It clears the physical terminal screen and sets up the default modes. It should be the first call to the curses functions when using the library to initialize the terminal.

```
#include curses.h
main()
{
WINDOW *win;
                initscr();
                /* curses function call(s) here */
                refresh();
                endwin();
}
```

endwin( )

This function call should be present in any program using the curses function, and should also be the last function call of that program. It restores all terminal settings to the original state prior to using the

initscr( ) function call and it places the cursor to the lower left hand portion of the screen and terminates a curses program.

```
#include curses.h
main()
{
WINDOW *win;
                    initscr();
                    /* curses function call(s) here */
                    refresh();
                    endwin();

}
```

attrset( )

This function call allows the programmer to set single or multiple terminal attributes. The call **attrset(0)** resets all attributes to their default state.

```
#include curses.h
main()
{
WINDOW *win;
                    initscr();
                    attrset(A_BOLD);
                    /* sets character attributes to bold */
                    ...
                    /* curses function call(s) here */
                    attrset(0);
                    /* resets all attributes to default */
                    refresh();
                    endwin();

}
```

attron( )

This function is used to set the named attribute of a terminal to an *on* state.

```
#include curses.h
main()
{
WINDOW *win;
                    initscr();
                    attron(A_BOLD);
                    /* sets character attribute bold to on */
                    ...
                    /* curses function call(s) here */
                    refresh();
                    endwin();

}
```

attroff( )

This function is the opposite of the **attron( )** function and will turn off the named attribute of a terminal.

```
#include curses.h
main()
{
WINDOW *win;
                    initscr();
                    attron(A_BOLD);
                    /* turns on the bold character attribute */
                    ...
                    /* curses function call(s) here */
                    attroff(A_BOLD);
                    /* turns off the bold character attribute */
                    refresh();
                    endwin();

}
```

standout( )

This function sets the attribute A_STANDOUT to an *on* state, and is nothing more than a convenient way of saying **attron** (A_STAND-OUT).

```
#include curses.h
main()
{
WINDOW *win;
                    initscr();
                    standout();
                    ...
                    /* curses function call(s) here */
                    refresh();
                    endwin();
}
```

standend( )

This function, like **standout( )**, is just another way of saying **attroff** (A_STANDOUT), meaning that the A_STANDOUT attribute is set to an *off* state. Actually, this function resets all attributes to the *off* state.

```
#include curses.h
main()
{
WINDOW *win;
                    initscr();
                    standout();
                    ...
                    /* curses function call(s) here */
                    standend();
                    /* end of attribute settings */
                    refresh();
                    endwin();
}
```

Attribute Values

The following is a list of the terminal attributes that may be set on or off using the curses library. It is important to note that all of these attributes may not be available to the physical terminal, depending upon the given terminal's characteristics.

- A_STANDOUT: This attribute allows the terminal to display characters in highlight, bold, or some other fashion (depending upon that terminal's characteristics).

- A_REVERSE: This attribute allows the terminal to display its characters in reverse video.

- A_BOLD: This attribute allows the terminal to display its characters in bold lettering.

- A_DIM: This attribute allows the terminal to display characters at less intensity than normal.

- A_UNDERLINE: This attribute allows the terminal to display characters with a horizontal line beneath them (underlined).

- A_BLINK: This attribute allows the terminal to display blinking characters that will appear and disappear at a rate depending upon the terminal characteristics.

CHAPTER 9

THE UNIX I/O SUBSYSTEM

Processes perform peripheral device I/O through the UNIX I/O subsystem which is a collection of kernel modules called *device drivers*. Device drivers perform the lowest level interface functions between a process and the physical hardware. When a process writes output data and the output media is a particular disk device, the kernel invokes the appropriate device driver to perform the actual transfer of data from computer memory to the physical track and sector location on the disk device.

The list of I/O devices includes terminals, printers, disks, tape units, and even network and communications hardware. In many instances, there may be devices from different manufacturers that behave similarly but which need to be treated as different device types. Each device may require its own unique device driver. Sometimes, the device driver may be sophisticated enough that only a single driver is necessary for each of the device types.

Aside from the physical hardware devices, UNIX also supports software devices such as memory so that a process may access physical memory outside of its own address space. A process may read memory areas in the system as input, before displaying them to a physical output device.

In this chapter, the makeup of device drivers is discussed in more detail. Knowledge of how device drivers work and how they are written is not essential to general application developers, however, it is a good idea to understand how an application performs its I/O processing.

Special Files

There are five types of files supported in UNIX System V:

- Plain Files
- Directories
- Block Special Files
- Character Special Files
- FIFO Special Files

Plain files are files created by UNIX users and usually contain data such as ASCII text created by an editor, binary files that are user data, or executable programs.

Directories contain information (time and date stamps, file size, filenames, and access permissions) about the files and sub-directories that are associated with a particular directory.

Block and character special files refer to device drivers that perform I/O to peripheral devices (previously mentioned) and are represented by an entry in the directory /dev. These special files refer to the portions of the UNIX kernel that provide a path to operating system features.

Lastly, FIFO special files (also called named pipes) provide the ability for unrelated processes to communicate by exchanging data. The output from program A may become the input to program B which, in turn, may become the input to some other program.

In UNIX System V Release 2, there are certain subdirectories that were added to the /dev directory to provide organization. For example, the /dev/dsk and /dev/rdsk subdirectories refer to special files used in conjunction with hard disk devices while the subdirectories /dev/mt and /dev/rmt contain entries (also special files) that are associated with magnetic tape devices.

Device Types

There are two basic device types in the UNIX system, *raw* devices (also called character), and *blocked* devices. Character devices obtain *byte streams* of an arbitrary length and may or may not support random access. Block devices do support random access and transfer data in fixed blocks, typically 1024 bytes in size. The part of the disk media where file data resides is called a *partition* or *disk slice*. In UNIX System V, these disk slices are blocked into 1024 bytes. Block device drivers are similar and vary at the low level control of their particular devices.

Character devices include terminals, modems, and printers; while block devices include disks or tapes. Every device is represented by a UNIX *device file* in the /dev directory. Block devices may also have a character device interface. Such block devices are represented by two device files in the /dev directory, one for the block special device file name and one for the character special device filename. (File systems can only exist on block devices.)

The UNIX system uses two operating system configuration tables to map the devices to the device specific peripheral driver code. These are called the character device and block device tables. Both tables and the device specific driver code are maintained within the kernel and use an integer called the *major device number* as an index.

The major device number is stored in the special file's inode. A second integer, called the *minor device number*, is also stored in the special file's inode and is used to identify which particular port is to be used (for devices that support multiple peripheral ports).

For a communications board that supports four ports, they would all share the same major device number and each individual port would be addressed by a unique minor device number; in this case, 0 through 3. Access to devices from programs is accomplished by invoking one of the **open( )**, **read( )**, **write( )**, **close( )**, or **ioctl( )** system calls.

Device (System) Configuration

In order to install, modify, or remove devices from the UNIX kernel, a system administrator specifies certain installation dependent parameters into special system configuration files. These include kernel parameters and device configuration information. The configuration data may be specified at any one of three stages by coding them into files used by the configuration program with a text editor, such as **vi** or by specifying the configuration information while the UNIX system is actively running (in such cases the configuration tables are modified dynamically by the kernel). The kernel is also capable of reading hardware configuration switches for devices supporting this option.

When the configuration parameters have been specified, the administrator executes a special configuration procedure that modifies the kernel by generating the necessary code from the appropriate updated tables. From that point until the next configuration process, the kernel will include the new configuration. When making changes to the kernel, it is usually required to re-boot the system before they take effect.

Device Driver System Calls

There are a few system calls available for device drivers to use for performing I/O operations. Not all of these system calls, however, are required to be included by the driver in order to function.

open( ) System Call

This system call is used to open files. It works by returning a file pointer that is actually a positive integer value known as a *file descriptor*. All subsequent manipulative references to the file are made through the use of the file descriptor. Device drivers regard their peripheral devices as special files that require a file descriptor, even though they are actually devices.

close( ) System Call

This system call is used to close files. It works by closing a file descriptor returned from a previous **open( )** system call. Only a previously opened file may be closed.

read( ) System Call

The **read( )** system call is used to obtain data (bytes) from a file. The file descriptor from a previous **open( )** system call is used to identify from which file to get the data. The address of a buffer that will store the data being read and the number of bytes to obtain (usually the same as the size of the buffer where the data is being read into) must be specified.

write( ) System Call

The **write( )** system call is used to write data to the file specified by a file descriptor returned from a previous **open( )** system call. The address of a buffer containing the data being written and the number of bytes to write (usually the same as the size of the buffer containing the data) must be specified.

ioctl( ) System Call

The **ioctl( )** system call is used by character device drivers to perform operations other than standard reads or writes. It is frequently used to set the device mode by setting internal device driver flags or by writing commands to device registers. It can also be used to provide information to the user about the current state of a device. The following informational parameters are specified for the **ioctl( )** system call:

- **File Descriptor**: Returned from a previously specified **open( )** system call; used to identify which device is to be affected.
- **Function Code**: Indicates the device specific function that is to be performed.

233

- **Buffer Pointer**: A pointer to a buffer containing any data to be used while performing the stated function.

- **Mode Values**: Set when the device was first opened.

Block Driver Strategy Routines

Block driver strategy routines are called by the UNIX kernel to do blocked reads and writes. The kernel calls a block device strategy routine when there is a data block, which is required to be read or written, in its block buffering cache. It calls the routine with a pointer to identify a data structure indicating the buffer and the data block to be affected.

This data structure is called the *buf structure* and contains information and data that describe the request, a pointer to the data, and other information used by the kernel to maintain the block buffering cache.

All the necessary information to perform blocked I/O is provided in the buf structure because blocked I/O requests are not necessarily related to the current process. For this reason the block driver strategy routine must not use the *u structure* (associated to a particular process).

Interrupt Handlers

The kernel will execute an interrupt handler routine upon the occurrence of a specific interrupt. An offset within the interrupt vector table points to the routine to be called by the kernel when a device presents a corresponding interrupt. The device specific interrupt handler is invoked by the kernel and is provided with informational parameters (including the device number) that identify the particular device causing the interrupt.

It is possible for several devices to be associated with an interrupt vector table entry, such as tty (serial) communications ports. Because of this, the device driver must be able to distinguish which device caused the interrupt. This is accomplished via the major/minor device numbers. The minor number is correlated to the hardware unit number by the driver. The device number used by the interrupt handler routine references a hardware unit and a minor number (in the device file), identifying the specific interrupting device to the kernel.

Device Drivers

A device driver is a collection of subroutines and data within the UNIX kernel, that make up the software interface to a physical I/O device, such as a disk drive, printer, and terminal.

The UNIX kernel will call the necessary driver routine if it recognizes that such an action is required. It is only the device driver routine, and no other kernel code, that makes direct contact with the device. Device drivers are an integral part of the UNIX kernel; they are usually written in C language, compiled to object modules and are linked into the kernel using the loader (**ld**).

A new UNIX kernel image must be generated (linked) and the UNIX system must be re-booted before a new device driver added to the kernel can become effective.

Driver Components and Routines

The interface between the UNIX kernel and a device driver is a set of standard entry points in the driver. There are certain rules and conventions that must be adhered to regarding the naming of these entry points and the operations they perform. The entry points that may be present in a driver are:

- Initialization Routine: Called during the kernel boot sequence.
- Driver OPEN and CLOSE Routines
- READ and WRITE Routines: To effect data transfer to and from the device.
- Start Routine: For miscellaneous driver management functions.
- Interrupt Handlers: To respond to device interrupts.
- Special I/O Control Routines: For character mode drivers.

Prologue

When writing a device driver it is necessary to create a *prologue*, that may be a header file containing the following:

- #include statements (system declarations and definitions)
- #define statements (addresses and contents of registers used by device)
- driver's internal global variable declaration list

Driver Routine Naming Conventions

Not all of these routines must be included as entry points in a driver, only the applicable ones for the particular driver type (character/block). A system configuration file provides information on which entry points are included for every driver. A driver's entry point names must follow certain conventions. A unique alphanumeric prefix (a generic name describing the driver routine) is concatenated with a more descriptive name indicating the type of routine.

For example, if driver routines were being named for a project called "RDS" (Rates Distribution System), the name for the initialization routine might be *rdsinit*. The open and close routines might be called *rdsopen* and *rdsclose*; the read and write routines might be named *rdsread* and *rdswrite*; and a block device strategy routine for this system might be named *rdsstrategy*. The interrupt handler routine might be called *rdsintr* and a character device for this system that requires special control might have a routine named *rdsioctl*.

Initialization Routine

If a device driver has an initialization routine, it is called at system startup (boot) time by the UNIX kernel. It performs initialization of the driver by clearing or setting flags and counters to their initial values and may allocate other necessary resources (such as memory). One of the most important function of the initialization routine is to determine if the device in question is actually available (as in *online*).

A device bus timeout can be detected by the initialization routine via kernel facilities, and is interpreted as an *offline* condition for the device. The device is declared offline when the initialization routine zeroes out its base address.

In doing this, the kernel is relieved from unnecessary interrupt polling for offline devices and other driver routines may also avoid attempting to access the device's registers. The initialization routine also may issue device initialization commands to make the device ready to handle subsequent I/O operations. An example of this might be sending an initialization string that performs setup operations for a laser printer.

OPEN Routine

A driver's open routine is called when a user process issues an **open()** system call for the device being handled. The open routine's responsibilities include: verification of device access permission for the user process; validation of the device number; any additional initialization necessary; and any initialization of the driver's local variables.

The device driver open routine is not mandatory, in fact, many simple device drivers do not use them. A frequent use of the device open routine is to ensure exclusive access to the device. This is done by setting a flag on the first device open call and clearing it when the last user process issues a **close( )** system call.

CLOSE Routine

This routine is effective only when the last user process accessing the device has issued a **close( )** system call. The device close routine's responsibilities include: performing a device shutdown (if applicable); disabling further interrupts from the device; and setting the appropriate internal indicator flags when closing the device. Drivers that don't have exclusive use of a device cannot use the **open( )** and **close( )** system calls to keep track of the number of processes which have the device open.

Strategy Routine (Block Mode Drivers Only)

The strategy routine is called by the kernel when performing block mode read and write operations to the device. The kernel calls the strategy routine with a pointer to a data structure (called the *buf structure*) that describes the buffer and the block to be read. The buf structure contains information describing the I/O request, data pointers, and other relevant data for the kernel to use to maintain the block buffering cache. The strategy routine's responsibilities include:

- Verification that the I/O request is valid.
- Queuing of I/O requests.
- Checking for device busy conditions, and if not busy, initiate I/O.

WRITE Routine

The write routine is used to write data from a memory buffer to the device, via a **write( )** system call. The main tasks that the write routine must perform are:

- Validation of the argument list for I/O operations.
- Copying data from the calling process to driver's internal buffer.
- Initiation of I/O by calling the start routine when the buffer is full (or if there is no more data to copy from the process). If, however, there is additional data to copy from the process, it sleeps until the buffer is empty.

READ Routine

The read routine is used to read data from the device to a memory buffer, via a **read( )** system call. The main tasks that the read routine performs are:

- Validation of the read request.

- Verify the device is ready for the read operation.

- Obtaining read operation information (number of bytes and read buffer location).

- Setting up a direct transfer to the calling process data buffer.

- Should appropriately set the device registers and start the read operation.

- Waiting for the read operation to complete (or set up the interrupt routine to complete the read operation).

- Performing some error handling functions.

START Routine

This routine is the workhorse of the read and write routines. It makes sure there is work to perform and, if necessary, will set the *busy* flag. It fetches the next data element to handle for the I/O operation and will appropriately set the device register to indicate that either a read or write operation is in progress. If necessary, it will also wake up the write routine.

INTR (interrupt) Routine

The interrupt routine (also called the interrupt service routine or ISR) is called to handle device interrupts for devices that are interrupt driven; that is, devices that cause a hardware interrupt to signal that an event has occurred. ISRs are specific to a particular device.

Generally, the ISR services the device by reading or writing its hardware registers and will notify the calling processes associated with the device when the I/O operation is complete. Interrupt routines come in basically two types: *polled* or *vectored*. A polled interrupt occurs when a cycle of time has elapsed and it is time for the ISR to check in with the device to see what new developments have transpired.

Vectored interrupts occur by setting an interrupt vector to point to the address of an interrupt handler routine to be executed if and when a device generates the interrupt associated with the vector address.

It is sometimes more advantageous to use the polled approach as opposed to the vectored approach, though generally the vectored approach is considered more efficient. If a device generates an interrupt, the ISR must service the interrupts; otherwise, interrupts could get lost. For polled devices, a separate routine may actually perform the polling function and call the real interrupt handler only when it becomes necessary. The tasks that the interrupt service routine must perform include:

- Verification that the last operation completed without errors.

- Tagging the previous operation as completed and remove it from the request queue.

- Checking to see if there is any more work to be done.

- Starting the device if there is more work.

IOCTL Routine (Character Mode Drivers Only)

This routine is used only for character mode drivers, usually terminal devices, although they may be any character mode device. The **ioctl( )** system call is the programmer's equivalent of the UNIX **gtty** and **stty** commands and is used to get or to set the device's characteristics such as line speed, parity value, and word length. The specific usage depends upon the device being manipulated.

The basic function of the IOCTL routine is to perform handling of any special requests for the device driver, such as rewinding a tape drive and specifying virtual circuit addresses and numbers for networks like Starlan and Ethernet. This is accomplished by using a file descriptor, provided from a previous **open( )** system call, and the device specific command and arguments as the parameters used in the **ioctl( )** system call. The programmer must know the details of how the device works in order to make use of this function call.

Driver Creation, Installation, and Debugging

A device driver is actually only a C language program and is created the same way any other C program is written: using a text editor, such as **vi**. Installation is accomplished by incorporating the driver code with the UNIX kernel, which must be regenerated by the System Administrator.

There are several debugging methods and aids available. A good place to start would be with the C language preprocessor. By effectively using the preprocessor, it is possible to incorporate debugging aides directly into the source code and to remove them later with minimal effort.

The simplest way to trace activity of the driver is to use **printf( )** and **fprintf( )** statements placed at strategic points within the program, so that it reports what activity is going on. The output may be sent to a terminal device or to a log file, or both, for easy tracing of events.

A variant of this method is to construct an internal trace table within the program's memory that keeps track of program events and periodically writes out the trace table contents to a disk file. The major drawback to this method is, should the program fail, part of the trace table data still in memory may become inaccessible. A variant of this method is to have another independent process that receives messages from the driver being debugged, running in memory. The independent process can store the trace data in its own memory areas, write them out to disk, display them on a control terminal, or any combination of these.

The UNIX **ps** command may also be used to determine the state of a process (if it is actually executable or sleeping) and may be of help in debugging problems. This is possible using the -l or -v flags for the command. The **crash** command may also be used in determining the state of a process. This command is an interactive utility that allows examination of physical memory locations within the operating system. It is described in detail in the UNIX System V Programmer's Reference.

The **adb** command may also be used to obtain a kernel backtrace. This handy little utility is also described in the Programmer's Reference.

Nothing, however, beats old fashioned digging into the source code to find bugs. Debugging tools make the job easier, however, it takes patience, intuition, and experience to become really good at debugging.

STREAMS

STREAMS is a set of C functions intended for the development of system communication services ranging from complete network protocol processes to individual device drivers that are hardware independent.

STREAMS defines standard interfaces for character input/output within the UNIX kernel and between the kernel and the rest of the system. The associated mechanism consist of a set system calls, kernel resources, and utility routines that allow modular, portable developement, and integration of higher performance network services and their components. It does not rely on any specific network architecture, but provides a framework with a consistent user interface that is compatible with the currently available character input/output interface.

The basic components in a STREAMS implementation are kernel resident modules that offer a set of processing functions and associated service interfaces. These modules may be selected dynamically and interconnected to provide any rational processing sequence without the need for kernel programming, assembly, and link editing. They may also be patched dynamically into existing connections from the user level.

STREAMS can be used to create, use, and dismantle a *stream*, which is a full-duplex processing and data transfer path between a driver in kernel space and a process in the user space. Streams have three parts:

- **The Stream Head**: This provides for the interface between the stream and a user program. Its main function is to process STREAMS related system calls originating from an application and also to perform the bidirectional transfer of data between the application and messages from the kernel.

- **The Module(s)**: The module(s) is/are optional and process data between the stream head and the driver. Modules can be inserted between the stream head and the stream end to perform intermediate processing of data being passed between the stream head and the driver. Any two modules can be connected anywhere in a stream, but relational sequences are built by connecting modules with protocol service interfaces.

- **The Stream End**: The stream end (also known as a STREAMS driver, because it may be a device driver) provides the services of an external input/output device, or it can be an internal software driver (sometimes referred to as a pseudo-device driver). Drivers must transform all data and status/control information between STREAMS message formats and the external representations.

System Calls

The **open( )**, **close( )**, **read( )**, **write( )**, and **ioctl( )** system calls all support STREAMS basic operations. There are additional new system calls to support advanced STREAMS functionality:

- **poll( )**: Enables application programs to poll multiple streams for various events.

- **putmsg( )** and **getmsg( )**: These routines allow applications to interact with streams modules and drivers via a STREAMS service interface.

Summary

The UNIX I/O file subsystem is quite intricate and designed to insulate the application from the inner workings of the access methods that actually communicate with the hardware. These access methods are called device drivers. They are generated by a UNIX system administrator using conventional C language development methods and special configuration files that are used as inputs to generate a new kernel image. The device drivers become extensions to the kernel, which must be rebooted before any of the changes become effective.

There are two main types of device drivers supported in the UNIX system: character mode and block mode. Character mode drivers handle byte streams of individual characters of data, while block mode drivers handle fixed blocks of data (usually 1024 bytes) in a single I/O operation. File systems may exist only on block devices.

The system calls **open( )**, **close( )**, **read( )**, **write( )**, and **ioctl( )** calls may be used to perform the necessary I/O for device drivers. Which calls are used depend upon the type of driver: blocked or character. Block drivers use a strategy routine to perform I/O operations when invoked by the kernel. A special data structure called the buf structure contains the necessary information for blocked I/O requests so the kernel may perform buffer cache management.

Device drivers may also have an interrupt handler routine that responds to interrupts generated by the device. There are basically two types of interrupts: polled or vectored. For polled devices, an interrupt handler routine is called when the polling mechanism has determined the need to do so. For vectored interrupt handlers, whenever a device generates an interrupt, an interrupt service routine is called to handle the interrupts by associating the address of the ISR with the interrupt number. When such interrupts occur, the ISR must service the interrupts, otherwise interrupts for a device could be lost.

CHAPTER 10

UNIX INTERPROCESS COMMUNICATION

In multitasking environments where several processes execute concurrently, it becomes necessary sooner or later for them to communicate, especially when multiple processes all perform important parts of the whole job by working together. The multiple concurrent process approach is more desirable than the conventional monolithic program approach (used in earlier days on the big mainframes).

Smaller programs are easier to write, easier to maintain, and easier to debug. They can become highly specialized so that duplicity between modules is reduced or eliminated. One example of processes cooperating with each other is when a server process communicates with several client processes, as they do in X Window applications.

When multiple processes are executing and cooperating with each other, they need to share data. For example, files may be shared between processes, but this can be inefficient as the demand for access to a file increases. For this reason, UNIX System V provides a wealth of interprocess communication methods. The most widely used of these methods are *signals* and *pipes* (also called FIFOs).

Signals

The most common interprocess communications facilities in the UNIX system are referred to as signals. They are most often used to communicate occurrences of specific events between related processes, mostly by the UNIX kernel, as the result of some kind of exceptional event. Signals are sent by one process and received by another. The receiving process performs some action appropriate to the signal received, or it may even ignore the signal.

Sometimes during the execution of long running processes, such as a program compilation or file system search for data, it may become necessary to interrupt the process and to abort it (in order to perform some other more pressing need). This is easily accomplished by using the BREAK key (also called the current interrupt key.)

The BREAK key is actually a special key sequence, usually the CTRL-C or the DEL keys. The actual key may be user specified during login execution and is usually part of the user's *.profile* shell script. When such a key is depressed on the keyboard, the currently active process immediately terminates execution and the user is returned to the command line prompt of their shell.

A portion of the kernel that is responsible for handling keyboard input, detects the special interrupt character sequence. A special signal (called SIGINT) is sent by the kernel to the process(es) associated with the terminal that owns the keyboard (also called the *control terminal*).

When active processes receive a SIGINT signal, they immediately perform some default action associated with the SIGINT interrupt and terminate any further execution. Although the shell process associated with the control terminal also sees the SIGINT interrupt, it is ignored because the shell must remain active to service further terminal I/O from the user.

Processes may be required to intercept a SIGINT interrupt and perform some special interrupt handler routines.

The kernel also uses signals when performing error handling for serious errors. For example, an executable program that has somehow become damaged (such as a hardware error on disk, data check, or memory parity check) might attempt to execute illegal op-codes (machine instructions). The kernel would detect this and send the offending process the SIGILL (illegal instruction) interrupt and cause it to terminate. The most likely outcome of this is a core dump of the failing process' memory areas to a special file called *core*.

Process-to-process signals are also supported in UNIX System V. An example of this is when a long running process is seemingly hung or looping endlessly, another process may terminate it by using the SIGTERM signal—such as when the UNIX **kill** command is entered by a frustrated user to terminate a process he or she had started and owns (unless they have superuser privileges.) The **kill** command uses a SIGTERM signal to interrupt and terminate another active process, unless some other action has been previously arranged for when a SIGTERM interrupt is received by a process.

Signals provide a simple method of communicating software interrupts between UNIX processes. A signal may be thought of as an electronic tap on the shoulder of an active process to interrupt whatever it is doing. A SIGTERM type of signal can be thought of as a direct order from the process' owner to immediately and unconditionally terminate, regardless of the circumstances. When a process receives a SIGTERM signal, the usual result is that the process immediately terminates.

Signals are normally used to handle abnormal or error conditions, rather than for communicating data between processes. This is because signals cannot carry information directly; thus limiting their usefulness for general purpose interprocess communications.

A special file called signal.h, a header file in the /usr/include/sys directory, contains the standard definitions for the various signals supported in UNIX System V. There are 19 standard mnemonic names for these signals, and two special ones (SIGWIND and SIGPHONE) that are supported only for the AT&T 7300 (UNIX PC). Although most of the signals provided are for use by the UNIX system kernel, this file makes interesting reading for the curious as there are some signals that are for specific use in process-to-process communication. The mnemonics are described in detail in the UNIX System V Interface Definition.

A process may terminate either normally or abnormally. When a process receives a signal it usually terminates normally; that is, it appears to have taken an early but orderly exit. When this happens, the child process notifies its parent process of its exit status. Sometimes a process will terminate abnormally, as when a program attempts to execute an illegal op-code (in which case a memory dump results.) The UNIX debugger **sdb**, can be used to read the core dump file and obtain the details of what caused the abnormal termination. Signals that will cause abnormal termination and a core dump file are:

- SIGQUIT
- SIGILL
- SIGTRAP
- SIGSYS
- SIGFPE

Signals may be caught or ignored by a process by handling them through software, with one exception: SIGKILL. When a process receives this signal, it knows it is time to die and there is no way to prevent this. The process simply complies and terminates immediately. Since all other signals may be ignored, it is necessary to provide at least one that would guarantee positive termination, hence SIGKILL. The SIGKILL signal differs from the SIGTERM in that SIGTERM is a request for the process to terminate, while SIGKILL is an order that cannot be refused.

It is quite easy for a process to ignore a signal. For example, if it was desirable for a process to ignore the SIGINT signal, the **signal( )** UNIX system call could be added to the program's source code in the appropriate place:

```
signal( SIGINT, SIG_IGN );
```

Moreover, it is possible to ignore multiple signals at the same time:

```
signal( SIGINT,  SIG_IGN );
signal( SIGTERM, SIG_IGN );
signal( SIGQUIT, SIG_IGN );
```

A process may not ignore the SIGKILL signal, so the following would be invalid:

```
signal( SIGKILL, SIG_IGN );
```

Programs anticipating a signal usually provide some sort of graceful exit routine to be called in the event the signal is received. A process also may send a signal to another process through the **kill( )** system call, as indicated in the following example:

```
kill( pid, SIGTERM );
```

In this example, pid is the process ID number of the process being interrupted by the SIGTERM signal that is issued by the **kill( )** system call. The **kill( )** function is almost solely used in parent/child process relationships because the process issuing the **kill( )** function must know the pid for the process to be terminated. In the **kill( )** function, the pid number can have other special meanings.

If the pid is a value of zero, this means that the signal will be sent to *all* processes belonging to the sending process, including the sending process itself. As a result, the sender and all of its children are terminated.

If the pid value is -1 and the effective user ID of the sending process is *not* the superuser, the signal is sent to all processes that have a real user ID equal to the effective user ID of the sending process. This includes the sending and non-child processes as well.

When the pid value is -1 and the effective user ID is superuser, then the signal applies to all processes except certain special system processes.

Lastly, when the pid value is less than zero (but other than -1) the signal is sent to all processes that have a process group ID equal to the absolute value of the pid value. Table 10-1 highlights the signals used in UNIX System V.

Table 10-1: UNIX System V Signals

```
SIGNAL      NAME            DESCRIPTION
01          SIGHUP          hang up
02          SIGINT          interrupt
03          SIGQUIT         quit
04          SIGILL          illegal instruction
05          SIGTRAP         trace trap
06          SIGIOT          IOT instruction
07          SIGEMT          EMT instruction
08          SIGFPT          floating point exception
09          SIGKILL         kill
10          SIGBUS          bus error
11          SIGSEGV         segmentation violations
12          SYGSYS          bad argument to system call
13          SIGPIPE         write on pipe with no one to read it
14          SIGALRM         alarm clock
15          SIGTERM         software termination
16          SIGUSR1         user defined signal 1
17          SIGUSR2         user defined signal 2
18          SIGCLD          death of a child
19          SIGPWR          power failure
```

Pipes

Another basic form of interprocess communication is through the use of pipes. Pipes can be used to connect processes together so that they may communicate. The most familiar form of pipes is in the UNIX shell using the | symbol to connect commands together on the command line, as in the following example:

```
who | sort | more
```

In this example there are three separate processes connected by two pipes. When commands are piped together in this fashion, it is referred to as a *pipeline*. The data generated as the output of the **who** command is passed on as input to the **sort** command. After sorting the data, the output of the **sort** command is piped as input to the **more** command.

Assuming the output is long enough, the **more** command breaks up the display on screen into segments that fit the display area and then waits for the user to strike a key on the keyboard before it proceeds. The process is repeated until all of the data from the **who** command has been displayed.

The data flows only in one direction, in this case the precedence is from left to right. These are known as directional pipelines. There are two types of pipes, *named* and *unnamed*.

When the pipe character is used on a command line, it invokes the **pipe( )** system call. The **pipe( )** system call is used to create and initiate *unnamed* pipes. The **mknod( )** system call is used to create FIFO (first-in, first-out) files. The UNIX shell treats the data piped from one command to another as files. All pipes are actually FIFO files written to by one process and read as input by another.

A pipe is created within a program by issuing the **pipe( )** system call. The **pipe( )** system call returns two file descriptors if successful. One file descriptor is for the process sending the data (writing down the pipe) and the second is for the process to receive the data (reading from the pipe).

Messages travel down pipes in a "first in, first-out" arrangement, hence the term FIFO. The data that is placed into the pipe first is read first at the receiving end. The **lseek( )** function will not work with pipes.

The following code example illustrates how pipes are used:

```
#include <stdio.h>
#define MSG 16
char *Msg_1 = "hello world, #1";
char *Msg_2 = "hello world, #2";
char *Msg_3 = "hello world, #3";
main()
```

```
{
char buffer[MSG];
int   p[2], x;
/* open the pipe */
   if( pipe(p) < 0 ) {
      error("pipe failed to open\n");
      exit(-1);
   }
/* write data down the pipe */
write( p[1], Msg_1, MSG );
write( p[1],Msg_2, MSG );
write( p[1], Msg_3, MSG );
/* read from the pipe */
x=0;
   while( x < 3 ) {
      read( p[0], buffer, MSG);
      printf( "%s\n", buffer );
      ++x;
   }
exit(0 );
}
```

The output from this example should read:

```
hello world, #1
hello world, #2
hello world, #3
```

Processes do not necessarily have to read pipes in the same size segments as they have written. For example, a process may write data down the pipe in 512 byte blocks and then read from it a character at time, like an ordinary file. There are, however, certain benefits to reading in blocked segments.

Processes may open multiple pipes; this establishes two way communications between processes. It is possible to operate the pipes in different directions — this is how the two-way communications link is possible. To operate pipes in only one direction, a pipe must be opened either read-only or write-only.

This example illustrates how a pipe connects two processes:

```c
#include <stdio.h>
#define MSG 16
char *Msg_1 = "hello world, #1";
char *Msg_2 = "hello world, #2";
char *Msg_3 = "hello world, #3";
main()
{
char buffer[MSG];
int p[2], x, pid;
/* open the pipe */
if( pipe(p) < 0 ) {
  perror("pipe failed to open\n");
  exit(-1);
}
/* call fork process */
if( (pid = fork()) < 0 ) {
  perror( "fork failed\n" );
  exit(-2);
}
/* write data down the pipe if we are the parent
process */
if( pid > 0 ) {
  write( p[1], Msg_1, MSG );
  write( p[1], Msg_2, MSG );
  write( p[1], Msg_3, MSG );
  wait( (int *)0 );
}
/* read from the pipe if we are the child process */
if( pid == 0 ) {
  x=0;
  while( x < 3 ) {
    read( p[0], buffer, MSG);
    printf( "%s\n", buffer );
    ++x;
  } /* end while */
} /* end if */
  exit( 0 );
}
```

Pipes have a few drawbacks as interprocess communications vehicles. For example, pipes can only be used to connect processes that share ancestry, such as a parent process and its children processes. If one were attempting to develop a server program that remains in permanent existence, the drawbacks may become readily apparent.

An example is a printer spooler program or a network control server. In an ideal situation, a client process that communicates with an unrelated server process by using a pipe and then terminates from existence could be created. This can't be done using a conventional pipe.

Pipes are not permanent entities; they must be created each time they are necessary and they are terminated when the processes that access them have terminated. To overcome these deficiencies, another interprocess communications mechanism was devised, called a FIFO or *named pipe*.

To the **read( )** and **write( )** functions, FIFOs are the same as ordinary pipes. FIFOs are permanent entities and are given UNIX file names. FIFOs also have owner, size, and access permissions attributes. A FIFO may also be opened, closed, and removed like an ordinary UNIX file; however, it possesses properties identical to pipes whenever written to or read. A FIFO is created using the **mknod** command (which in turn issues the **mknod( )** system call) as demonstrated in the following command:

```
/etc/mknod another_FIFO p
```

The named pipe is called "another_FIFO", and may have been given any valid file name that conforms to the standard UNIX file naming conventions. The file name may also include fully qualified path names. The second argument to the **mknod** command, the character 'p' (for pipe), is used to tell **mknod** to create a FIFO. This is necessary since the **mknod** command can also be used to create special files that represent devices. The **ls** command may then be used to identify newly created FIFOs by specifying the **-l** option:

```
ls -l another_FIFO
prw-rw-r--     1     tsm    usr       0     Sep
00:53     another_FIFO
```

The FIFO has access permissions, an owner and group owner (tsm and usr), a file size (0 bytes if currently empty), and a creation date/time stamp. FIFOs may be read and written to using standard UNIX commands, as the following example illustrates:

```
$ cat < another_FIFO &
106
$ ls -las /usr > another_FIFO; wait
total 37
1 drwxrwxr-x   24 root    sys     384    May  1    18:31    .
1 drwxrwxr-x   16 root    sys     432    May  1    18:30    ..
1 drwxrwxr-x    2 root    sys      32    Jan  4    1988     3bnet
1 drwxrwxr-x    5 adm     adm     112    May 10    1988     adm
1 drwxr-xr-x    7 root    sys     304    Oct  7    1987     admin
1 drwxrwxr-x    3 gibbo   other    59    Jan  3    04:10    afg
1 drwxrwxr-x    2 bds     other    48    May 12    1988     bds
1 drwxrwxr-x    2 bgv     other    48    Jan  7    01:11    bgv
5 drwxrwxr-x    3 bin     bin    2544    Jan 13    00:54    bin
1 drwxrwxr-x   10 root    root    224    Apr  2    22:20    bwk
1 drwxrwxr-x    3 crm     other    59    Jan  3    04:10    rm
1 drwxrwxr-x    2 root    root    112    Jan  3    22:22    dmr
5 drwxr-xr-x    2 ggc     other   560    Nov  6    1987     ggc
1 drwxrwxr-x   10 root    root    160    Jan 13    00:55    gww
3 drwxrwxr-x    3 bin     bin    1088    Jan  8    07:52    include
1 drwxrwxr-x    3 bully   other    59    Jan  3    04:10    jdb
1 drwxrwxrwx   10 kdb     other   208    May  1    18:40    kdb
2 drwxrwxr-x    2 bin     bin     608    Jan  6    1986     lbin
3 drwxr-xr-x   24 root    sys    1456    Jan  8    07:52    lib
5 drwxr-xr-x    2 root    root   2560    Jan  6    1986     lost+found
1 drwxrwxr-x    3 root    mail     96    Apr 28    23:45    mail
1 drwxrwxr-x   10 root    root    224    Apr  2    22:20    mickey
1 drwxrwxr-x    2 mlh     other    48    May 12    1988     mlh
1 drwxrwxr-x    3 mmb     other    39    Jan  3    04:50    mmb
1 drwxrwxr-x    2 root    sys     496    Jan 13    00:57    options
1 drwxrwxr-x    2 pati    other    48    May 12    1987     pati
1 drwxrwxrwx    2 bin     bin      32    Jan  6    1986     preserve
1 drwxrwxr-x    2 bin     bin      32    Jan  4    1986     pub
1 drwxrwxr-x    9 slan    slan    144    Jan  8    07:54    slan
1 drwxrwxr-x   10 root    bin     160    Jan 13    00:55    spool
1 drwxrwxr-x   10 root    other   224    Apr  2    22:20    src
1 drwxrwxrwx    2 sys     sys      48    May  1    18:31    tmp
1 drwxrwxrwx   10 tsm     other   208    May  1    18:40    tsm
1 drwxrwxr-x    2 wbu     other   112    Jan  3    22:22    wbu
$
```

In this example, assuming that a FIFO called "another_FIFO" was created earlier using the **mknod** command, the **cat** command is started as a background task to read from the FIFO as indicated by the process identification number that is returned as the response.

Next, the /usr directory is listed by the **ls** command and its output is redirected down the pipe. The awaiting **cat** command reads from the FIFO, displaying the data onto the screen. When a FIFO is no longer open for writing, reading it will return a zero value like an ordinary pipe. This zero return value is interpreted by the **cat** process as an end of file indication. The **wait** command causes the UNIX shell to wait for **cat** to exit before the ready prompt is displayed.

For programmers, programming with FIFOs is almost identical to programming with ordinary pipes. The main difference is in the initialization. Instead of using the **pipe( )** system call, the **mknod( )** system call is used. To signify that a FIFO is to be created, an octal value of 010000 must be added to the mode value as illustrated by the following code fragment example:

```
if( mknod("another_FIFO", 010600, 0) 0 ) {
   perror( "mknod for FIFO failed\n" );
   exit( -1 );
}
```

In this example, the file permissions assigned to the FIFO is the value 600 (read/write by the owner.) The UNIX header file called stat.h defines S_IFIFO as the value 010000. Once the FIFO is created, it must be opened using the **open( )** system call, as the following code fragment illustrates:

```
#include <fcntl.h>
.
.
.
fd = open( "another_FIFO", O_WRONLY );
```

This example will open the FIFO for write-only. A non-blocking open for a FIFO is possible by bitwise ORing the value O_NDELAY (defined in fcntl.h) with O_RDONLY, O_WRONLY, and O_RDWR, as demonstrated in the following example:

```
if( (fd = open( "another_FIFO", O_RDONLY | O_NDELAY)) 0
) {
  perror( "open for FIFO failed\n" );
  exit( -1 );
}
```

Message Queues

Messages are a sequence of characters or bytes, not necessarily terminated with a null character, and are passed between processes by using *message queues*. Message queues are created (or accessed) using the **msgget( )** function. A process may place messages onto the queue, assuming the appropriate queue permissions were given and that the queue is already established.

Other processes may then read the message queue by using the **msgrcv( )** function, which also removes the message from the queue. It may be apparent that there is a similarity between message passing and the read/write calls for pipes. The following code fragment example illustrates how to establish a message queue using the initialization function **msgget( ):**

```
#include <sys/types.h>
#include <sys/ipc.h>
#include <sys/msg.h>
int iMessage_Queue;
int iPermission_Flags;
key_t Key;
  .
  .
  .
iMessage_Queue= msgget( Key, iPermission_Flags );
```

This action may be thought of as the equivalent of the **open( )** or **creat( )** system calls. The "Key" parameter is used to identify the message queue by means of a unique identifier called a *facility key*. Keys are numbers that identify IPC objects on UNIX systems in a similar fashion as a file name identifies a file. The actual data type for the key is determined by the type "key_t", defined in the UNIX header file "types.h" and is implementation dependent. For UNIX System V, key_t is defined as a long integer.

Once a message queue has been established, there are two message operations, **msgsnd( )** and **msgrcv( )**, that may be used to send and receive data to and from the queue. The **msgsnd( )** function is used to send messages to the message queue. The following code fragment example illustrates how to use the **msgsnd( )** function, and assumes that the **msgget( )** function from the previous example has already been performed:

```
#include            <sys/types.h>
#include            <sys/ipc.h>
#include            <sys/msg.h>
#define  MAXVALUE           161;
int      iRc = 0;
int      iFlags =IPC_NOWAIT;
struct   The_Message {
                    long     lMsg_Type;
                    char     szMsg_Text[MAXVALUE];
            } Message;
.
.
.
iRc = msgsnd( iMessage_Queue, &Message,
(sizeof(iMessage)), iFlags );
        if( iRc != 0 ) {
            perror("Failed to send message to queue\n"
)
            .
            .
            .
        }
```

The **msgrcv( )** function is used to read messages from the message queue. The following code fragment example illustrates how to use the **msgrcv( )** function, and assumes that the **msgget( )** function from the previous example has already been performed:

```
#include  <sys/types.h>
#include  <sys/ipc.h>
#include  <sys/msg.h>
#define   MAXVALUE           161;
int       iRc = 0;
int       iFlags = IPC_NOWAIT;
long      lMessage_Type=0;
struct    The_Message {
                    long      lMsg_Type;
                    char      szMsg_Text[MAXVALUE];
          } Message;
.
.
.
iRc = msgrcv(iMessage_Queue, &Message,
(sizeof(iMessage)),
lMessage_Type, iFlags);
          if( iRc == 0 ) {
              perror( "No data read from message queue\n"
)
              .
              .
              .
          }
```

Note that this time the Message structure is used to contain the data read from the message queue (identified by iMessage_Queue); and that a new parameter (lMessage_Type) is used to identify what type of message to read from the queue. If the value of iMessage_Type is zero, then the first message on the queue is read.

In both the **msgsnd( )** and the **msgrcv( )** functions, the return code is checked to determine if an error has occurred. One reason that either function may fail is that the process which calls the program containing either of these functions may not have sufficient access permissions to manipulate the message queue. It would therefore be wise to include an error handler to correctly process such a condition.

The **msgctl( )** system call may be used to manipulate message queues for the purposes of obtaining status information about a message queue, changing limitations associated with a message queue, or simply deleting the message queue entirely. Using the assumptions made in the preceding examples, the following code fragment example illustrates how to invoke the **msgctl( )** system call:

```
#include  <sys/types.h>
#include  <sys/ipc.h>
#include  <sys/msg.h>
int       iRc = 0;
int       iCommand = 0;
struct    msqid_ds Msq_Stat;
  .
  .
  .
  iRc = msgctl( iMessage_Queue, iCommand, &Msq_Stat );
        if( iRc != 0 ) {
           perror( "msgctl function failed\n" )
              .
              .
              .

        }
```

The iCommand parameter specifies the action for the **msgctl( )** system call to perform and IPC_STAT places status data into structure pointed to by &Msq_Stat. IPC_SET is used to set control variable values and IPC_RMID is used to remove the message queue from the system. A message queue may be removed or modified only by its owner or by someone with superuser privileges.

Semaphores

Semaphores provide a solution to problems associated with process synchronization. Using signals for interprocess communication may present problems in that they can be difficult to handle correctly. Race conditions may occur, for example, if two processes send each other a request for data. If the messages are (near) simultaneous, each process goes to sleep, suspending further processing until the other provides the requested data. In UNIX System V there is a way to deal with the possibility of such synchronization problems: semaphores.

The concept of semaphores was first introduced by a Dutch theoretician, Edsger W. Dijkstra, and may be thought of as an extension to the concept of signals.

Essentially, semaphores are integer values used to ensure mutual exclusion, where only a single process may use an interprocess facility (such as a message queue) at a time. It helps in avoiding the consequences that can arise from synchronization problems. On a railroad, a semaphore would prevent two trains from colliding with each other when they are on a shared section of track; and so is the intended purpose of semaphores when used in interprocess communications on computers.

Semaphores are purely advisory; this means that if a process (or railroad engineer) doesn't observe and obey the semaphore, there is no built-in mechanism to prevent the collision of shared objects (on computers or railroads). For this reason, semaphores are used to prevent the chaotic consequences that might otherwise occur. There are two kinds of semaphores: *binary* and *general*.

As previously stated, on computers semaphores are implemented as integer values. Binary semaphores may only have a value of 0 or 1. General semaphores, however, may have an infinite number of states. A semaphore may be used as a counter of sorts. It is decreased by 1 when it is acquired by a process (indicating "locked" status), and it is increased by 1 when a process is finished (indicating "unlocked" status). If the semaphore value is zero (negative values are illegal), a process has to wait until another process releases it, thus incrementing it by 1.

In UNIX System V a semaphore is a data structure that can be shared by several processes. An example of why and how a semaphore may be used is when several processes may require read/write access to a shared file. In such a scenario it would be catastrophic to write to the same file at the same time with more than one process. Each process desiring to update the file must synchronize with all other processes using the file before accessing it. A process should operate on the file only after synchronization and after exclusive access has been gained.

Processes are suspended (sleep) until they have synchronized and gained exclusive access to the shared resource. After a process has finished using the shared resource, it must release exclusive use of it and increment the semaphore value by 1 so that other awaiting processes may use it. There are three steps that must occur for proper semaphore processing:

- Obtain exclusive access to the shared resource.

- Process the shared resource.

- Release exclusive control of the shared resource.

The processing of the shared resource is referred to as a *program's critical region*. Semaphores are an advanced interprocess communication mechanism; they are not an easy concept to understand, nor are they easy to describe in simple terms to novice UNIX developers. (In some cases, even experienced UNIX developers may have some difficulty understanding or explaining semaphores.) In any case, an attempt will be made here to describe how semaphores are implemented in UNIX System V.

Semaphores are implemented as structures consisting of four elements:

- semval: The semaphore value.

- sempid: The pid of the last process to use the semaphore.

- semncnt: Number of processes waiting for semaphore value to increase.

- semzcnt: Number of processes waiting for semaphore value to equal 0.

The *semval* is decremented by each process when it gains exclusive access to the shared resource and is incremented when the process releases the shared resource. The *sempid* is the process ID of the last process to gain exclusive access of the shared resource and is provided automatically when the process receives exclusive control. The semaphore structures described above are allocated, deallocated, and managed just like memory.

There are three system calls that a process may invoke in the use of semaphores: **semget( )**, **semop( )**, and **semctl( )**. The **semget( )** system call is similar to the **msgget( )** system call, and is used to create a semaphore set that is an array of semaphores. The **semget( )** function translates a key to a value (ID) that represents a set of semaphores. The semaphore set is created if the IPC_CREAT bit of the option flags parameter is on; otherwise, the set already exists.

The **semop( )** system call is used to acquire or to release the semaphore, according to the parameters that were specified. The **semop( )** system call has three arguments:

- semid: semaphore identifier returned by a semget( ) system call.

- semop: pointer to an array of semaphore operation structures.

- sem_n: number of entries in the array pointed to by semop.

The **semop( )** system call is illustrated in the following pseudo code example:

```
semid = semget( key, 1, flags ); /* create a semaphore
*/
while( not done ) {
   semop( -1 );  /* lock the shared resource */
   ManipulateTheSharedResource();
   semop( +1 );  /* unlock the shared resource */
} /* end */
```

The **semctl( )** system call is used to manipulate the values of a semaphore. The **semget( )** system call doesn't allow for initialization of a semaphore, only for the creation of it. One important use of the

263

semctl( ) system call is to set the initial values for the semaphore. An example of how to use the **semctl( )** system call is illustrated by the following code fragment:

```
int iRc;
.
.
.
iRc = semctl( semid, 0, SETVAL, 1 );
```

This example assumes that a **semget( )** system call had previously returned a valid semaphore ID as the variable *semid*, and performs the function of setting the initial value for the newly created semaphore. This system call can be used to get or to set the semval parameter of the semaphore structure; return the values of **sempid**, **semncnt** and **semzcnt,** in the semaphore structure; obtain the statistics of each member of the semaphore structure; or to remove the semaphore from the system.

Shared Memory

The last new UNIX System V IPC facility is *shared memory*. The fastest way to move data between processes is not to move it at all, but simply to provide a means for one process to access data within another. One reason for this capability might be that the volume of data is quite large, and accessing it through FIFO's may prove to be slow and inefficient.

Shared memory, as the name implies, permits the same physical memory to be accessed by more than one process. It is the most efficient of the IPC mechanisms. A process may create a shared memory area, called a *segment*, and make it available to other processes.

The process that creates such a shared memory segment is sometimes called the *sender*, while a process that requires access to the shared memory segment is sometimes called a *receiver*. All of the data within the shared memory segment is instantly accessible by the receiving process. It is possible for a process to create several shared memory segments at once; on the other hand, a process may also access several shared memory segments (from the same or many other processes) at the same time.

This is accomplished when a process creates a shared memory segment outside of its own address space and a receiving process makes a system call that maps the shared segment into its own address space. The mapping of shared segments is very fast on most modern computers because of multiple hardware segmentation registers that are used to address data segments.

Once the system call has been made and the shared memory segment has been mapped into a receiving process, all subsequent access to the data is made using normal machine instructions to fetch and store the data. Access to data within a shared memory segment, after it has been mapped into a receiver process, is just as fast as access to its own local variables and locally allocated memory areas. This is what makes shared memory a powerful and attractive feature of UNIX System V.

The only constraints on the number of shared memory segments accessible to a process are the limitations imposed by the particular hardware in use. Only one segment should be mapped at a time, for portability reasons. All shared memory operations require special hardware support; if they aren't available, shared memory operations are not available either. The types of special hardware support required are those necessary to implement protected memory regions, such as those found in the Intel 80386 architecture.

Shared memory techniques should be used only when efficiency is important or if there are other compelling reasons to do so. If the techniques are used for other purposes, the range of machines the application is capable of running on will be limited. In UNIX System V, shared memory is implemented as a set of system calls:

- **shmget( )**
- **shmat( )**
- **shmdt( )**
- **shmctl( )**

The **shmget( )** system call is used to create or obtain access to an already existing shared memory segment. An interesting feature of shared memory segments is that they may be created using access permission masks for reading and writing data, identical to the way in which UNIX files are accessed. These permissions are enforced only if there is hardware support for the ability to designate read-only data segments. For 80386-based systems, the UNIX system operates in full 32 bit protected mode, meaning that the requirements for enforcing shared memory segment access permissions are met.

The **shmat( )** system call is used to map the shared memory segment into a process' own address space. Mapping a shared memory segment is another way of saying that the shared memory segment is attached to a process's address space. The **shmat( )** function provides the caller with a pointer to the number of bytes requested. Ordinary C language operators are used to read and write data to the shared memory segment as if it were a locally allocated memory buffer. Since several processes may use System V IPC concurrently, semaphores or messages are used to prevent all of the multiple processes from writing to the same shared memory segment at the same time.

When a process has finished using a shared data segment, **shmdt( )** is called to detach the segment. This function may also be called if the receiver process requires the use of the segmentation register for another shared memory segment. The physical shared memory area remains intact, it is merely made unavailable to the process that issued the call to **shmdt( )**. A shared memory segment that has been detached via **shmdt( )**, may be reattached by making a subsequent call to **shmat( )**.

The process that originally created the shared memory segment may remove or destroy the segment by invoking the **shmctl( )** system call using the IPC_RMID command parameter. Unsavory results will occur if a shared memory segment is removed and there are still receiver processes attached to the shared segment. *This is a major problem!* The kernel only provides access to shared memory, it does not enforce the correct use of that memory.

The most common use of shared memory is as a message passing medium. This is more efficient than the kernel provided **message( )**

system calls because data doesn't need to be copied from the sending process' data area to the kernel and back to the receiving process. It is also more efficient because, when using shared memory, the kernel's involvement is limited to processing semaphores, thus eliminating the overhead of message queue processing.

If, in a given application, there will never be more than two processes using shared memory, and one process is always going to access the shared memory segment as read-only, the overhead of semaphores may be eliminated as a method of increasing performance. This is not recommended, but is mentioned only as a way to increase processing speed if it becomes critical.

CHAPTER 11

BASIC COMMUNICATIONS AND NETWORKING

UNIX offers a rich set of networking and communications facilities, supporting the widest range of facilities for an operating system environment.

UUCP

The name *uucp* is an acronym for UNIX-to-UNIX copy. To novice users it may first be perceived as merely a command used to copy data between UNIX systems. It is, in fact, much more. Uucp is an entire data communications subsystem, powerful and sophisticated. The uucp subsystem provides the ability to move both ASCII and binary data between UNIX systems without much attention from the end user. In addition to providing the ability to transfer files, uucp also provides a means to control command execution on a remote machine.

The uucp subsystem provides a facility to queue jobs for later transfer, it will automatically retry transmission of a file if a transfer should fail. Many user commands are also provided so that inquiries can be made to get the latest status of a uucp job. These commands provide users and administrators the capability to perform control functions on their uucp jobs, such as canceling or resending a file, reporting the status of a file, and increasing or decreasing the execution priority of a given job. The uucp subsystem also provides customization facilities for different communication networks, has good built-in security features, provides complete logging and debugging tools, and supports several different data transfer protocols with error checking matched to the network type.

The uucp subsystem is not limited to the **uucp** command, but is a set of several tools. An example of a UNIX application that uses the uucp subsystem extensively is the UNIX electronic mail facility, implemented through the **mail** or **mailx** commands. Users need not know the low level details of the uucp subsystem and are free to focus their attention on the **mail** command.

UNIX provides high level routines for communications that work independently of the particular transport medium. With this arrangement, where the UNIX system handles low level detail involved with communications, users are free to get their work done.

The persons most likely to be involved with the lower levels of communication details are UNIX system administrators or programmers.

The UNIX System V release material consists of a collection of distribution media that are divided into several components. The uucp subsystem's formal name as it is distributed in the release package is the **Basic Networking Utilities**, also referred to as BNU. The installation of the BNU package is the responsibility of the UNIX system administrator and is accomplished by using the system administration utility, called **sysadm.**

The BNU is basically made up of the following three categories:

- Communication with remote users (**mail**, **mailx**).
- File transfers between local and remote users.
- Execution of commands remotely from the local machine.

The BNU package consists of the following programs:

uucp: Copy a UNIX file to another remote UNIX system.

cu: The *call UNIX* command establishes a session with another remote UNIX system.

uux: UNIX-to-UNIX Execution, this executes UNIX commands on remote UNIX systems.

uuname: Lists all known remote machines with which the local machine is allowed to communicate with.

uulog: Queries a summary log of uucp and uux transactions.

uustat: Used to obtain a status of, or to kill, previously spooled uucp jobs.

uuto: Sends a local source file to the public directory on the remote UNIX system.

uupick: Accepts or rejects the files transmitted to the user.

There are actually two major versions of uucp: BNU and HDB. HDB uucp is vastly superior to the BNU version and is to be included as a standard part of the UNIX System V distribution set in upcoming releases. It may not be available for all UNIX variants. This version of uucp provides the same functionality as the BNU version at the user level, however, there is quite a difference in the internals.

HDB uucp also eliminates problems that still exist in the BNU version and is also far more flexible. For more detailed information on the BNU version, readers should reference the Basic Networking section in the UNIX System V Release 3 System Administrator's Guide.

There are three directories owned by the uucp subsystem:

```
/usr/lib/uucp
/usr/spool/uucp
/usr/spool/uucppublic
```

The /usr/lib/uucp directory contains the control files that uucp uses to determine how to connect to other machines. This directory also contains the executable programs owned by the uucp subsystem, as well as uucp administrative *daemons* to perform clean up tasks.

The daemons use a naming convention where *uudemon* is the first part of the name, a separating period follows and the last part is the daemon name. This signifies that these daemons are actually shell scripts and may be browsed to determine what functions they actually perform. The last part of the daemon name also provides some clue as to its functionality.

The following is a sample directory listing of /usr/lib/uucp:

```
$ ls -las /usr/lib/uucp
total 531
    1 drwxr-xr-x   4 uucp    bin        496   Oct  2 23:49 .
    3 drwxrwxr-x  16 bin     bin       1104   Apr 25 00:19 ..
    1 drwxrwxrwx   2 uucp    bin         32   Jan  1  1970 .OLD
    1 drwxrwxrwx   2 uucp    bin         48   Oct 26  1987 .XQTDIR
    7 -rw-------   1 uucp    bin       3148   Apr 12 01:20 Devices
    7 -rw-r--r--   1 uucp    bin       3118   Oct 28  1987 Dialcodes
    6 -rw-r--r--   1 uucp    bin       2830   Nov 22  1987 Dialers
    1 -rw-r--r--   1 uucp    bin         41   Nov 19  1987 L-devices
    1 -rw-r--r--   1 root    users        1   Nov 19  1987 L.sys
    1 -r--r--r--   1 uucp    bin          2   Oct 28  1987 Maxuuscheds
    1 -r--r--r--   1 uucp    bin          2   Oct 28  1987 Maxuuxqts
    3 -rw-------   1 uucp    bin       1063   Oct 28  1987 Permissions
    1 -rw-rw-rw-   1 uucp    bin        214   Oct 28  1987 Poll
    3 -r-xr-xr-x   1 uucp    bin       1518   Oct 28  1987 SetUp
    1 -rw-------   1 uucp    bin        264   Dec  9  1987 Sys.priv
  122 -rw-r--r--   1 uucp    bin      62162   Sep 30 23:06 Sys.uureg
    4 -rw-------   1 uucp    bin       1837   Oct 28  1987 Sysfiles
    1 -rw-------   1 uucp    bin          1   Oct 28  1987 Systems
    3 -r-xr-xr-x   1 uucp    bin       1278   Oct 28  1987 Uutry
    1 -r--r--r--   1 uucp    bin        133   Oct 28  1987 remote.unknown
   23 -r-x--x--x   1 uucp    bin      11424   Oct 28  1987 uucheck
  155 -r-s--x--x   1 uucp    bin      78902   Oct 28  1987 uucico
   42 -r-x--x--x   1 uucp    bin      21084   Oct 28  1987 uucleanup
    2 -r-xr-xr-x   1 uucp    bin        588   Oct 28  1987 uudemon.admin
    9 -r-xr-xr-x   1 uucp    bin       4369   Oct 28  1987 uudemon.cleanu
    1 -r-xr-xr-x   1 uucp    bin         81   Oct 28  1987 uudemon.hour
    2 -r-xr-xr-x   1 uucp    bin        914   Oct 28  1987 uudemon.poll
   26 -rwxr-xr-x   1 root    bin      13072   Oct 28  1987 uugetty
   25 -r-s--x--x   1 uucp    bin      12616   Oct 28  1987 uusched
   77 -r-s--x--x   1 uucp    bin      38996   Oct 28  1987 uuxqt$
```

The heart of the uucp subsystem is the **uucico** (UNIX-toUNIX-copy-in-copy-out) program, pronounced *you-you-ki-ko* or *you-you-seeko*. It is the component that actually makes the communication link and does the data transfer. The **uugetty** program is used by the **uucp** and **cu** programs when it is necessary to allow incoming and outgoing access over a single *tty* (serial/asynch) port. Most of the remaining files, the ones that begin with a capital letter, are the uucp control files that specify how connections are made on remote systems. (Note that these control files may specify other than only UNIX systems.)

The /usr/spool/uucp directory contains the log and status files used by several of the **uucp** commands. The following is a sample directory listing of /usr/spool/uucp:

```
$ ls -las /usr/spool/uucp
total 15
   1 drwxrwxrwx 14 uucp      bin     320 Oct   3 00:19  .
   1 drwxrwxr-x  5 root      bin      80 Oct  28 1987   ..
   1 drwxr-xr-x  2 uucp      bin     112 Jun  27 05:30  .Admin
   1 drwxr-xr-x  2 uucp      bin      32 Oct  28 1987   .Corrupt
   1 drwxr-xr-x  6 uucp      bin      96 Oct  28 1987   .Log
   1 drwxr-xr-x  2 uucp      bin     160 Jun  27 05:30  .Old
   1 drwxr-xr-x  2 uucp      bin     112 Aug  19 19:45  .Sequence
   1 drwxrwxrwx  2 uucp      bin      96 Jul  15 00:55  .Status
   1 drwxr-xr-x  2 uucp      bin      96 Sep  30 23:06  .Workspace
   1 drwxr-xr-x  2 uucp      bin      48 Mar   3 1988   .Xqtdir
   1 -rw-rw-rw-  2 root      root      4 Oct   3 00:00  LCK..ph0
   1 -rw-rw-rw-  2 root      root      4 Oct   3 00:00  LTMP.108
   1 drwxr-xr-x  2 uucp      users    96 Sep  28 01:54  left
   1 drwxr-xr-x  2 uucp      mail     80 Sep  30 23:06  mtbjc
   1 drwxr-xr-x  2 uucp      mail     96 Sep  29 18:38  mtune
   1 drwxrwxrwx  2 root      users    80 Jul  15 01:24  shop
$
```

The /usr/spool/uucppublic directory is a spool area set aside for use by uucp for normal file transfers, and for file transfers for which no specific destination was given. The permission settings for all files placed into this directory are open to all users on the system. Sensitive information should never be placed into this directory because it is so accessible. No sample listing is provided since its contents are not likely to be the same (or even close) on any two systems. This directory and the /usr/spool/uucp directory contain large subdirectories that are maintained by uucp administrative tools, and should never be modified or deleted by anyone!

The /usr/spool/uucppublic directory will contain subdirectories that are created as necessary whenever the **uucp** command is invoked.

These subdirectories are maintained and cleaned up by standard uucp subsystem utility programs, such as **uucleanup.**

All files and subdirectories in the /usr/lib/uucp and /usr/spool/uucp directories are owned by the administrative user ID. Any changes to the access permissions or ownerships of these files and subdirectories will eventually result in the gradual failure of the uucp subsystem. Should this occur, the best way of correcting the problem is to reload the uucp software from the original distribution media. (The current control files should be backed up first so they may be restored when the uucp subsystem has been restored. Also, make sure that when the control files are restored, they do not simply overwrite the newly recreated ones!)

Great care should be taken when editing any uucp control file. If any changes are made, be certain to keep the permissions and ownerships intact; otherwise the uucp subsystem may become disabled.

When uucp jobs are queued for transfer by one of the uucp programs or the **mail** and **mailx** commands, uucp references a list of the known remote systems with which it is permitted to communicate. If the remote system name is not in the list, the file is not transferred and the sender is notified. In the case where the remote system is in the list, uucp will create a file in the /usr/spool/uucp directory containing the data transfer request. If there is no transfer currently in progress to the remote system, **uucico** is executed to perform the connection and actual transfer of data.

The **uucico** program determines the best connection route to a target system by referencing the control files found in /usr/lib/uucp. If the connection is successful, **uucico** proceeds with the data transfer. The local **uucico** logs into the remote machine and starts another **uucico** process there. Upon completion of the data transfer, the control file in /usr/spool/uucp is deleted and the uucp log file is updated.

In the event the connection to the remote system should fail, **uucico** will make several attempts (trying the different connection paths defined in the control files) to deliver the data. After several attempts it may give up and the job will remain in the uucp job queue.

The uucp daemon is scheduled for execution (usually every hour) by the **cron** facility. The daemon searches the /usr/spool/uucp directory for queued jobs remaining to be sent and will execute **uucico** to do the job. If the transfer fails consistently for a week, the weekly uucp cleanup daemon sends warning messages (using the **mail** facility) to the original sender before deleting the job from the queue. This may be an indication that the remote machine is no longer in service or that serious problems exist for the communications channels.

The connection methods to remote systems are specified in uucp control files, which are referenced by uucp utility programs when there is data to transfer. If the target system is not defined in the appropriate control file, uucp aborts the transfer and issues the original sender an error message indicating this has happened. For a user to determine what the names of valid target systems, they may use the **uuname** command to produce a list of target system names.

The file /usr/lib/uucp/Sysfiles contains information about the other interlocking uucp control files that are used to determine the known systems, connection methods, and device types. The file /usr/lib/uucp/Systems is used to determine how a service may attempt connections to remote machines. These include modem, direct connect, and networked connections. The /usr/lib/uucp/Devices file provides information to **uucico** (or the **cu** command) about the device being used in the connection. The devices may be modems, direct connections, or networked connections. The /usr/lib/uucp/Dialers file specifies the *chat script* invoked for a particular device, such as the device control sequences for modems. The job of administering these files is complicated and may be difficult at first to novice UNIX system administrators.

uucp

This command provides the easiest access to the uucp subsystem for most data transfers and provides more control than other uucp data transfer utilities. The general format of the **uucp** command is:

```
uucp source.files target.files
```

The *source.files* may be on the local system or on a remote system, the same is true for *target.files*. *Source.files* and *target.files* are substituted with any valid UNIX path name, including the remote system identifiers that precede the path name with the *bang* (!) separator character. The resulting action is that a job is queued in the uucp execution queue and the source files are copied to the destination specified in target.files.

Multiple system names may be specified, separated by the bang delimiter. When such a specification is used, **uucp** attempts to deliver the file using the system names in the sequence entered as though they were routing instructions. Intermediate UNIX nodes in such a list must be capable and willing to forward uucp files, otherwise the data will not arrive at the ultimate destination.

Metacharacters, when used with **uucp**, are expanded by the shell on the remote systems. The tilde (~) character has special usage for uucp files. When *~username* is specified, (where *username* is the name of a user ID on the specified system), it is replaced by that user's home directory.

A special environment variable, JOBNO, when set (JOBNO=ON), produces a job number on the invoking user's terminal each time uucp is invoked by them. The **uucp** command associates a uucp job number with each uucp request, providing a method of tracking the status of any uucp request.

By convention, all UNIX machines have the directory /usr/spool/uucppublic, and it is set up so that anyone may access any file in it. It is a general catch-all directory available in case a sending user does not have the path name for an ultimate destination. On some UNIX systems, security rules may be in effect that require all uucp traffic to go through /usr/spool/uucppublic. The recipient on the destination end may be notified and can take the necessary steps to deal with the file. The following option flags are recognized by uucp:

-c: Bypasses copying the source file to the spool directory, instead it uses the source file directly as input. (Less overhead).

-C: Creates a copy of the source file to the spool directory.

-d: (default) Makes all necessary directories for the file copy.

-f: Specifies not to make intermediate directories for the file copy.

-j: If the JOBNO environment variable is not defined, the -j option is specified, then uucp will echo the uucp job number to the invoking user's terminal. If JOBNO is set (JOBNO=ON) and it has been exported, when the -j option is specified uucp will not print the uucp job number to the user's terminal. When JOBNO is set and the -j option is not specified, the uucp job number is echoed to the user's terminal.

-m: The -m option will send a mail message to the requesting user. Mail is sent only when uucp has actually completed the copy operation.

-nuser: The -n option notifies the specified remote user that the uucp file has arrived.

-r: This option notifies uucp to simply queue the job without actually starting the file transfer process.

To save on transmission time, files to be sent using uucp should first be compressed using the **pack** command, or the **arc** command. If the contents of the file are sensitive, the user may encrypt the transmission file using the **crypt** command. The following is an example of the **uucp** command:

```
$ uucp -msmikes -ntsm -j -c /usr/tsm/chapter11.txt
omega!~smikes
omegaN53d9
$
```

cu

This command establishes a session with a remote system.

This is the *call UNIX* or *call up* command, permitting users that are logged on to a UNIX system to call another system and log into it as though they were logged in locally. The **cu** command provides a primitive terminal emulator and communications program, although there is no functionality lacking. (The type of terminal emulated is specified in the TERM environment variable.) It provides telephone dialing services, terminal controls, and session management functions between systems. Even more useful is the ability for a user to **cu** through several UNIX machines in a daisy chain fashion.

The connectivity need not be limited to asynchronous serial communications. A system may be configured with networked connections such as Starlan and Ethernet. Additionally, virtual circuits provided by such systems as AT&T's *Datakit* may also be used to link the systems together (**dkcu**).

The following example demonstrates how to use the **cu** command to dial a telephone number and to call a system known as *rambo*.

```
cu -s 1200 -n 12012980161
cu -s 1200 -d -n 12012980161
cu rambo
```

The first line in the example uses a modem set at 1200 baud to dial the phone number that follows the -n flag (happens to be a good UNIX bulletin board system). The second line in the example has the -d option flag specified to provide a detailed trace of everything that takes place, it is useful for figuring out connectivity problems. The third example illustrates how another system by name (in reality, *rambo* is another UNIX system that uses a Starlan connection between UNIX machines).

When users have established a session using the **cu** command, they can execute commands locally or on the remote system. Once users have logged into the remote system, all commands entered at their local keyboard are passed through the local system as data and are then executed on the remote system, with the exception of lines preceded with the tilde (~) character. Any lines beginning with this character receive special treatement. The following listing is a synopsis of the ~ operator functions:

~! — Causes an escape to the local shell, during remote sessions,.

~!cmd — Executes the command on the local system without escaping.

~. — Terminates the **cu** session.

~$cmd — Executes a command locally and sends the output to be executed on the remote UNIX system.

~%break — Sends a BREAK character to the remote system.

~%cd — Executes a change directory command on the local system.

~%take s t — Copies a file specified by s from the remote system and copies it to the local system to the file specified by t. If t is not specified, the file name is derived from the value of s.

~%put s t — This command is the logical opposite of the ~%take command and will copy the file specified by s from the local system to the file specified by t to the remote system. If t is omitted, then the file name is derived from the value of s.

~%nostop — Toggles flow control protocol (on or off). This feature affects only DC3 and DC1 flow control characters and may be necessary in the event the remote system doesn't handle them properly.

~~cmd — This is a special command that sends ~cmd to be executed on the remote system.

It is possible to **cu** from one UNIX machine to another, creating a daisy chain effect. When logged on to a remote UNIX machine, ~cmd executes the command on the local system, while ~~cmd executes the command on the next UNIX machine in the communications chain. The -d option of the **cu** command serves as a way of debugging uucp connections. It prints out the details of every uucp action as they happen so that it may be determined exactly where in the connection attempt a failure occurred.

The **cu** command may be used to communicate with systems other than UNIX, such as CompuServe and GEnie.

uux

This command means UNIX-to-UNIX Execution and executes UNIX commands on remote UNIX systems.

This is the most powerful command within the uucp subsystem. It lets users specify command lines that are executed on a remote UNIX machine. It is capable of collecting files named in the command line from various systems, assembling the command on the target system and executing it there. One begins to see the possibilities when using the **uux** command, so its use is limited on most systems.

uux receives a normal command line as an argument; the command name may be prefixed with a remote system name and bang (!) delimiter character. This is interpreted by **uux** as the command is to be executed on the specified machine, or to collect the named files from that machine. An example of how the **uux** command may be invoked is as follows:

```
$ uux "omega!cat mtuxn!/usr/lib/Systems
mtuxo!/etc/passwd !/tmp/junk"
```

The consequences of this **uux** example are far reaching. First the /etc/passwd file from a system named *mtuxo* and the /usr/lib/Systems file from another system named *mtuxn* are collected and moved to another system named *omega*, where the **cat** command is invoked to type out their contents. The output is redirected to a file /tmp/junk on the local system. (If this were possible and sufficient access permissions were gained, it would be a serious security breach.)

uuname

This command lists all known remote machines with which the local machine is allowed to communicate with.

This command will print the list of uucp names of the systems known to the local UNIX system. This means those systems that have been defined in special control files which are part of the uucp subsystem. If the -l option flag is specified, then the name for the local system is echoed back.

```
$ uuname -l
rambo
$
```

uulog

This command queries a summary log of uucp and uux transactions.

The **uulog** command is a support utility for the uucp system. Its purpose is to provide information about uucp transactions. Listings can be produced for the entire log file, as well as information about individual or all systems and users.

```
$ uulog -sleft
$ uulog -utsm
$ uulog
```

uustat

This command obtains a status of, or kills, previously spooled uucp jobs

The **uustat** command allows users to obtain information about their uucp jobs. This command may also be used to cancel any job still awaiting to be processed by uucp, or any job that may already be in progress. In either case, only the user that initiated the job may cancel it, with the exception of root or any user having superuser privileges. The following options may be specified for the **uustat** command:

-kjobid: The -k flag is used to kill a uucp job in progress or queued for execution. The job ID must be owned by the user attempting to kill it otherwise, the user must have superuser privileges.

-q: This option flag is used to list all jobs queued for each machine.

-rjobid: The -r option flag is used to rejuvenate the uucp job specified by jobid. The jobs affected by this command have their timestamps modified to the current time in order to prevent the cleanup daemon from removing them, until they expire again.

-ssys: The -s option flag reports on the status of the system named by sys.

-uuser: The -u option flag reports on the status of all uucp jobs for the user specified.

The -k, -r, and -q options are mutually exclusive with each other as well as the -s and -u options. If no option flags are specified, then **uustat** will report the status of all uucp jobs for the requesting user.

uuto

This command sends a local source file to the public directory on the remote UNIX system.

The **uuto** command works much like the **uucp** command, except that only a single destination is permitted as the target system identifier. It supports multiple input files, but only one destination is allowed. This command does not actually perform any data transfer, instead it queues the job for the uucp subsystem to handle.

uupick

This command accepts or rejects the files transmitted to the user.

This command is used to retrieve files that have been sent to a user at the destination machine. When data files arrive, the uucp subsystem on the receiving machine notifies the recipient via electronic mail that the files have arrived. The receiving user may then use **uupick** to copy the data files from the directory where the uucp subsystem had placed them, into the receiver's current directory.

Remote File Sharing (RFS)

Remote file sharing, or RFS as it is usually referred to, is a relatively new feature introduced UNIX System V Release 3. RFS provides the ability for users to access file systems on remote machines as though they were part of the local file system. This is done by mounting directories of other systems to the local file system and accessing them as if they were local directories. The remotely shared files and directories may be operated upon using ordinary file system commands such as mv, cp, rm, and ls. Programs may write to the remote files; I/O may be redirected to them as well.

The main benefit to such a remote file sharing scheme is that the cost of disk space can be significantly reduced in multi-machine environments. Instead of loading the same copy of a large database management system onto all machines in a network, it may be available to all systems from a single server machine. (Better check the fine print on software licensing agreements before attempting this.) RFS also provides security features, administrative tools, and controls to make it a versatile and useful addition to UNIX System V.

RFS is built upon the **File System Switch** (FSS), another new feature of UNIX System V, that permits mapping between unlike file system types, such as UNIX and MS-DOS. An MS-DOS file system may be accessible from UNIX if it is set up as a foreign file system type. The FSS performs the necessary mapping to provide full access from the UNIX system, with the low level detail hidden from end users because the UNIX kernel handles it all. RFS is currently the only application to make use of the FSS in System V Release 3, because the FSS isstill under development.

RFS is functionally quite similar to Sun Microsystem's **Network File Sharing** (NFS) feature. NFS is implemented on a wide variety of UNIX system implementations, as well as directly on MS-DOS. RFS and NFS are mutually exclusive; they are not compatible with one another. A UNIX System V machine may run RFS or NFS, but not both at the same time.

Invoking RFS

To invoke RFS, all participating systems must have UNIX System V (base release 3) installed, since RFS is a new feature of SVR3 it is not supported in earlier releases. The RFS nodes must be connected together using some type of high speed local area network such as Ethernet or Starlan. Machines set up to allow uucp traffic over the network can invoke RFS too.

UNIX SVR3 systems that have been properly set up on the LAN may be configured into several *domains*, groups of systems permitting RFS activity between them. Other systems may be excluded from becoming domain members. A machine may participate in multiple RFS domains, however, systems in one domain do not usually access the files on systems in other domains. Every domain has a primary *name server*, that is responsible for the administration of that domain. Multiple secondary name servers may also be established for a domain. These systems are used mainly as alternative name servers, should the primary name server fail for any reason. The primary name server machine executes a daemon to manage the RFS domain.

Other machines in the RFS domain are called *clients* and may access files on other systems, but may not permit other systems to access their own files. Only a server machine may provide access to domain resources; client machines (non-servers) may only access the resources provided by the servers. All server machines in a domain enable the RFS facilities they are to provide. Domain servers may establish accessibility security limitations to other domain members (both clients and other servers). Setup and configuration of RFS domains and management processes on the servers is an administrative task usually performed by the system administrator of the server machine.

The server machine may *advertise* which specific facilities (directories) are accessible to RFS clients and other servers. A client system may use any of a server's advertised directories by mounting them locally. A permanent virtual circuit is created when the directories have been mounted over the local area network. To discard the advertised resources of an RFS domain server, a domain member need only unmount the directory and release it from the allocated resource list. When a client is finished using an RFS resource, it should be released so as to reduce the network load and to avoid the possibility of network related problems due to a LAN failure of some kind.

To use an RFS resource, after the resource has been mounted to a client machine, the only requirement is the use of normal file system access mechanisms. A remote file system may be mounted at any valid mount point within the local file system, just as if another local file system were being added. Not all devices may support remote access.

Only a superuser may execute any of the RFS administration commands. The **nsquery** (name server query) command may be used to determine what resources are available if RFS is already active for a domain member. To mount an RFS advertised resource, the UNIX **mount** command is used with the -d option flag signifying that the file system is remote. The -r flag may be specified (-dr) to indicate that the remote file system is to be read only.

To release the RFS resource the **umount** command is used with the -d flag indicating that the resource being dismounted is a remote file system. Before attempting to dismount the shared resource, it must not be in use by any user or process. The **fuser** command will report who is using the shared resource. To force a shared resource to be dismounted in an emergency, the **fumount** (force unmount) command may be invoked. When the **fumount** command is issued from a server that owns the shared resource, it causes a **rfuadmin** (remote file uadmin) process to be started on the remote system using the resource (or all remote systems using the resource) and forces the dismount.

It is possible to set up systems to perform automatic remote mounts for shared resources, by modifying the /etc/fstab file to include an entry for the shared resource. The -d flag is specified to indicate the resource is a remote directory. This is done by simply editing the /etc/fstab file with **vi** or some other text editor and inserting a line as follows:

```
name dir -d
```

In this example, *name* is the remote directory to mount and *dir* is the mount point within the local file system at which to mount. The -d indicates the shared resource is a remote directory, and may be modified to indicate read-only by specifying -dr. Before any remote shared resources can be mounted, RFS must first be active. Starting RFS may require changing the init state (init state 3) to permit RFS activity on both client and server machines. The local system may also join a domain, or several domains.

On RFS server machines, a local daemon must be started and its resources must be advertised before other machines may access them. RFS is started by using the **rfstart** command. The **rfstop** command stops RFS. Both commands require a password response before proceeding. Before RFS can start, the network must be active. Once started, RFS continues to execute after the system has been rebooted. This is because the **rfstart** command modifies the bootup procedure to make the system enter init state 3 rather than init state 2.

Once a system has been established as a server, its resources must be advertised. This is done using the **adv** (advertise) command that indicates the resource is available to the domain. When an administrator decides to let other computers in a network access resources, they are said to *advertise* those resources. The following example demonstrates how a database server might advertise a database directory:

```
adv INFORMIX /usr/bin/informix
```

The resource name, INFORMIX, is assigned when the shared resource is advertised; the resource to be shared is the directory /usr/bin/informix on the domain server. Client systems see the resource name, INFORMIX, as the resource that is advertised. The file /etc/rstab may be edited to include **adv** command lines so that resources can be advertised automatically at bootup time.

If it is decided that an advertised resource should no longer be advertised, servers may *unadvertise* a resource by using the **unadv** command. The **unadv** command prevents the resource from being mounted by new clients, but does not perform the **umount** command. As users dismount the shared resource, they too are prohibited from mounting it again until the resource is once again advertised.

RFS is terminated by using the **rfstop** command. When **rfstop** is entered, RFS is stopped only on the local system. Before RFS can be terminated, all clients must release any shared resources; if the machine on which RFS is being terminated is a client, then all shared resources must have been released. If the local system is a server, after all resources have been dismounted, they must also be unadvertised before RFS can stop. If the system leaves init state 3, all of these steps occur automatically.

The **rfstop** command invokes **fumount** to force any remote users from using the server's resources and returns the system to init state 2. This could cause system problems for any users of the server's resources; so it is courteous to provide users with the opportunity to release any resources necessary before stopping RFS without warning.

CHAPTER 12

WRITING APPLICATIONS FOR USE UNDER RFS

The Remote File Sharing (RFS) feature introduced in UNIX System V Release 3 allows for sharing of files among a network of computers.

Some applications may not work the way a user wants under RFS. In this chapter there are descriptions of ways to get around some of the problems. Programmers may be able to apply these *work arounds* to their benefit. Users of applications under RFS may consider themselves the customer.

As mentioned in the last chapter, Remote File Sharing lets one share files transparently among computers that are linked by a network. Each computer on the network controls which local resources are available to other computers and which remote resources its local users can access.

Sharing is done at the directory level. When one shares a directory, one shares its entire contents, including: files, subdirectories, named pipes, and special devices like terminals and printers. Because sharing involves more than just a directory or a file, the term *shared resources* is used instead of directory file.

Sharing Resources

A shared resource is owned by one computer and is remotely accessed by other computers. The administrator of an owning computer decides what resources they are willing to let other computers access. The administrator of the sharing computer decides what directories to share. Any computer can own several resources and can share several others. When advertising a resource, the administrator gives each resource a name, as is in this example using the **adv** command:

```
adv some-name some-directory
```

Once this has been done, the administrator of another computer in the network can mount the resource by referring to the same name:

```
mount some-name some-local-directory-name
```

The second administrator names the resource and gives a directory on their local computer where it should be mounted. The name of the local directory doesn't have to be the same as on the resource owner's computer.

This is like mounting a regular file system in UNIX System V. When mounting a file system found on a diskette; the contents of the resource are accessed just as any other files and directories are accessed. The difference is that mounting a remote resource on a computer simply makes it available to the people using that computer. These are the people who are really sharing the files with other people on other computers in the network.

Examples

Suppose Phil, as the administrator of the computer named *omega*, is willing to share a directory named /usr/share with other computers on a network of which omega is a member. To do this, Phil enters the following command:

```
adv omega_share /usr/share
```

Any other name could have been assigned in place of omega_share. Now suppose that Kurt, as the administrator of another computer named *rambo*, decides to share the resource omega_share. Kurt would then enter the following command on rambo:

```
mount -d omega_share /omega/private
```

The success of this command relies on the directory /omega/private already having been created for use as a *mount point*. (See UNIX System V Release 3 System Administrator's Guide, Mounting Filesystems for additional details regarding mount points.)

Consider the following example (on omega):

```
adv omega_usr /usr
```

and (on rambo):

```
mount -d omega_usr /omega/usr
```

Users on the system known as rambo can share all the files under the /usr directory of omega, including programs installed in /usr/bin and private files in omega users' $HOME directories. This may be useful when users have a login on both systems and want to access their other files, regardless of which computer they are using at any one time (on omega):

```
adv omega_lbin /usr/lbin
```

and (on rambo):

```
mount -d omega_lbin /usr/lbin
```

In this example, the /usr/lbin directories on omega and rambo will appear to be exactly the same because they are really one in the same directory.

Mapping User/Group IDs

As demonstrated, it may be feasible to give users a login on all the computers in a network and to share all the subdirectories of the /usr directory among the computers. What happens to the user and group IDs in such a case? What if user "tsm" logs in to omega as tsm, where his numerical user ID is 100, and creates a file; then logs in as "tsm" on rambo where his numerical user ID is 128? Can tsm access both files?

It depends. RFS provides a flexible means of mapping the user IDs from one system onto another. Numerical IDs can be mapped identically so that user ID 100 on omega is user ID 100 on rambo regardless of the associated user or, name arbitrarily so that one can make it so that user ID 100 on omega becomes, say, user ID 128 on rambo.

Alternatively, names can be mapped to relieve a network administrator from the burden of knowing numerical IDs. This means one could map tsm on omega to tsm on rambo, regardless of the numerical ID values. The same applies for group IDs. Even with this flexibility, though, some applications may have trouble.

Client-Server Relationships and Server Processes

What does "sharing" really mean? When an application opens a file that is in a shared directory, the opening of the file is really done on the computer that owns the shared resource. This computer is called the server, since it serves up its resources. If the application is running on the server, the opening is as for a normal, unshared file. If the application is not running on the server, it must be running on a client computer, and the opening is handled differently. A client computer is a user of a server's resources.

To open a remote file, the client sends the open request to the server and a server process does the actual open. This server process looks like a normal process, but is a UNIX kernel process whose job is to handle file access requests from clients. It takes on the user and group IDs of the process the client computer (appropriately mapped to the user and group IDs that are native to the server) so that file permissions are not circumvented. The server process sends back the results of the open attempt.

Read attempts are handled in a similar fashion, with requests going from the client to the server for handling by a server process; the server returning the results of the read attempt (including any data actually read) to the client. Write attempts are also handled in the same manner, except that the data to be written flow the other way.

One can see where a network might get really bogged down if the resources are improperly shared or if the wrong applications are run on client computers. For example, the simple application **diff**, that compares two files and reports the lines that differ, might run into difficulties by causing heavy network traffic if the files it operates upon are on different systems. Consider the following example:

```
diff file1 file2
```

Assuming that file1 is physically located on the local system, rambo, and that file2 is physically located on omega, a remote system, if the **diff** command is entered locally on rambo, then file2 must first be copied from omega to rambo before the comparison can take place. The network load would be increased even more if both files were located on different remote systems and the **diff** command was entered on yet another remote client.

There are seven features of RFS and UNIX System V Release 3 that could adversely affect an application running under RFS:

- Cannot nest shared resources
- User and group IDs may not be the same
- Device major and minor numbers are not the same
- PIDs are not unique across computers
- Computers in a network are unique
- Path names may change
- Some system directories are not good mount points

The inability to nest shared resources is a limitation that prevents bizarre behavior like infinite loops from occurring. This is unlikely to be a severe problem for any application. There are only a few known scenarios where this limitation is a problem. One is that it may be desirable to mount several file systems under a single shared directory and still provide public access to all the file systems. Under RFS this can be done only if all the file systems are owned by a single computer. This may mean, for instance, that several computers cannot pool their previously private databases under a single shared directory.

User and group IDs may not be the same. The RFS feature of mapping user and group IDs is about as flexible as could be expected, but this flexibility will do no good if an application subverts it. For instance, suppose two previously autonomous computers are now networked together and have RFS running. The user and group IDs on these two computers are probably not matched up, which means the administrators will probably choose to map IDs by name. For example, tsm on omega will be treated as being the same as tsm on rambo. Note that the numerical IDs are unlikely to match up.

Suppose now that an application keeps track of the ownership of files it creates. If it knows the owner of a file by name, then the application will work on the two computers. If the application knows the owner of a file only by the numerical ID, and it saves this numerical ID in a separate database, then it may fail to give access to a user's files on one computer. Note that this problem occurs because the *application* does not use the standard UNIX security mechanism, provided by the **stat( )** and **access( )** system calls. By storing numerical user or group IDs in a database and referring to that database to check access permissions, the application runs the risk of failing in an RFS environment.

Device major and minor numbers are not the same. Some applications may use the device major and minor numbers to refer to the file system that contains a file. Generally, these numbers are obtained from the **stat( )** system call. While using the **stat( )** system call this way is not a supported feature of UNIX System V, it has been worked in the past. When it is used this way with a file owned by a remote computer, it will fail to give the type of numbers expected.

Process IDs are not unique across computers. RFS does not share process information, such as PIDs, so any application that uses PIDs in communication between two processes may fail under RFS. There are several scenarios that are listed here.

Scenario One   An application uses the shell $$ value to name a temporary file. The usual reason for using PIDs in a temporary file name is to ensure that it is unique, so that concurrent executions of the same application use different files. If the temporary files are in a shared directory, there's a chance that two processes, running on separate computers but with the same PIDs, could attempt to use the same temporary file. This chance is small, although it increases if the shared directory is one often used for temporary files, like /tmp.

Scenario Two   A non-shell application uses the PIDs to name a temporary file. Note that the use of the **tmpnam( ), tempnam( ),** and **tmpfile( )** system calls make this problem insignificant, since they take care to avoid names already in use.

Scenario Three   An application uses a PID in a **kill** command or **kill( )** system call to alert a process. Since named pipes may be shared under RFS, it is possible for two processes to communicate with a pipe even though each is running on a separate computer. If they exchange process IDs to use in a **kill** command or system call to alert each other to new events, there will be trouble. There are other ways, of course, to exchange a PID, such as through a regular file.

Scenario Four   An application uses the PID in a *lock file*. This is really a special case of the preceding scenario. A process that creates a lock file does so to prevent another process from attempting to access the locked item indicated by the lock file. The best implementation of a lock file puts the locking PID in the file; another process that wants to check that the lock is still active will use the PID in a special **kill** command or system call to see if the original process is still around. If it is, but is on a different computer, then **kill** will fail; telling the new process that it may incorrectly ignore the lock file.

Note that this has nothing to do with the file and record locking feature. That feature invoked using the **fcntl( )** or **lock( )** system calls, will work with remote files. (When mandatory file and recording locking is used remotely, the automatic detection of deadlocks is not supported.)

Computers in a network are unique. Any information or data that are specific to a single computer will be unique to that computer and, in general, should not be shared. The non-unique PID problem and the UID/GID problem really fall into this category.

Scenario One   A process exchanges the file system identifiers and the inode numbers of files with a process on another computer. If an application uses these values to see if two files are actually the same file, it may fail if the values came from different computers. This problem doesn't occur if the application gets all the values from **stat()** system calls executed on the same computer; it only occurs when it is passed the results of the **stat( )** system calls executed on separate computers.

Scenario Two   An application references unshared system resources. Suppose that an application has been informed that /dev/tty10 is to be used for printing reports. If the application is shared, and runs on another computer, it will cause trouble since /dev/tty10 may not be shared and may no longer be the correct place to print reports on that system.

Scenario Three   An application gathers information or data about a computer, to be stored in a shared file. Any application that gathers information such as system resource utilization will report incorrect results if the information is stored in a file shared by other computers, unless care is taken to identify contributing computers. Logs of activity are also vulnerable here.

Scenario Four   An application gathers data from computers that have different byte ordering and data alignments. Initially, this is not a problem because a mixed computer network is not supported in UNIX System V Release 3.0. In the future, however, such networks may be allowed. Generally, only ASCII files will be directly sharable.

Path names may change. The administrator of a computer in an RFS network may choose to mount a shared resource on a different directory than the directory chosen by administrators of other systems. This means that an application cannot expect that the same path name will locate the item on every computer. This is true even without RFS, but the problem is amplified under RFS because the application may operate on both computers and share path names.

The worst thing an application could do here is use *hard coded* path names; that is, use fixed path names that can't be changed by users of the application. Most applications don't do this, but some have trouble when deriving path names from a shared resource, but when the path names aren't the same from one computer to the next.

Some system directories are not good mount points. This is not a limitation of RFS so much as a restriction that arises from the local use of system directories. Several standard UNIX System V utilities, like (BNU), the LP Spooler, and the scheduler (cron), keep programs and data in system directories. Other directories are used to store the programs and data needed by the RFS utility itself. Another directory keeps the entries for all devices used on a computer.

These utilities are run locally; that is, they don't or cannot be shared across computers in an RFS network. As mentioned, when data (and programs) are specific to a single computer, they should not be shared. Because the data and programs are stored in particular directories, it means that those directories and their parent directories cannot be the mount point used in a **mount** command for a remote resource. The directories disallowed by this restriction are:

/dev
/etc
/usr
/usr/net
/usr/bin
/usr/lbin

Any subdirectory of these is an acceptable mount point.

Use of Named Pipes

RFS supports the use of named pipes which means two processes, each on different computers, can exchange data directly. The problem with named pipes is that the data exchanged is sometimes used inappropriately.

In general, any data that is computer specific may cause a problem when used on a different computer. A terminal port number, for instance, is probably only correct if used on one computer. If an application on the computer omega expects to find a plotter attached to /dev/tty40, the application run on the computer rambo may fail if another identical plotter is not located on rambo's /dev/tty40. This problem is made worse if the application consists of multiple processes that communicate via a named pipe and exchange the port number.

Another computer specific data is a process ID. Multiple processes that communicate via a named pipe often exchange their PIDs so that one can alert others to new events via the **kill** command or the **kill( )** system call. This will fail if the processes are not all on the same computer.

There are other computer specific data whose exchange among computers are likely to cause an application to fail. Device major and minor numbers, inode numbers, usage statistics and numerical UID/GIDs are not unique in a network and should be used only on the computer from which they originated.

Path names may change from one computer to the next. A shared resource can be mounted on one directory on a computer and a different directory on another computer.

In the future, another variation to the use of named pipes will be that if the involved computers are a heterogeneous set — then the data structures passed among them may not be identical.

Can a user invoke separate parts of an application on different computers? Yes, but programmers should verify that doing so won't cause the application to fail. Or does the application start up all processes directly, using the **fork( )** and **exec( )** system calls or the shell command structures, and keeping all processes on the originating computer? If so, the application should not have a problem using named pipes. When developers test their application, if it is a multi-process application they should try to get the processes to run on different computers in an RFS network. Configure the shared resources so that the named pipe will be in a shared directory.

If the first step can't be done, then developers can assume the customer can't do it either. If the first step can be done, developers should do the second step and test the application to see if it fails. The test should cover the use by the application of:

- device major and minor numbers

- inode numbers

- process ID

- numerical User/Group IDs

- other system dependent information

- changing path names

The last one will require developers to set up an RFS configuration where a shared resource is mounted under different names on the systems.

Work Around

Remove the use of computer specific data. If this is not possible, then the customer can't share the directory where the named pipe is made, and thus probably cannot run the application with shared data. If the directory is a standard place like /tmp, /usr, or /usr/lib, then developers should see that the customer can direct the application to put the named pipe elsewhere. Otherwise the application will seriously limit the RFS configurations available to the customer for other applications.

Use of Data Files

From an application's point of view, there is little difference between using named pipes to exchange data between processes and using ordinary files—except for the mechanics. All the characteristics of named pipes apply to regular files if those files are used to exchange data between processes.

Use of Temporary Files

The safe use of temporary files under RFS is dependent on how the file names are constructed and where the files are found. Of course, if the files are not kept in a shared directory, there is no problem. Keep in mind that one cannot predict how a customer will choose to configure a network of sharing, so it is important to investigate the naming convention used by the application.

The **tmpnam( )**, **tempnam( )**, and **tmpfile( )** routines carefully insure that chosen names do not conflict with existing files — if the application uses only these routines in creating temporary files it should be safe. On the other hand, if it constructs names using a constant prefix or suffix concatenated with the PID, it is subject to occasional failure.

When Testing Applications

It is hard to build a test that checks for this problem; to do so would require running the application on two different computers in an RFS network, but each with the same PID. The only sure way to see if an application might have this problem is to thoroughly investigate the naming convention used for any temporary files it might create.

Work Around

None, unless it is easy to change the naming convention used by the application. Note that the best naming convention includes the computer name, as found from the **uname** command or the **uname( )** system call and the PID.

Use of Hard Coded Path Names

No application should use hard coded path names, since doing so removes flexibility from the application user. For instance, if an application always expects a user's data files to be found in /usr/data, then the user is not free to keep the data files in a private directory. Similarly, if an application expects to find all its executable parts in /usr/bin, it prevents an administrator from mounting a shared /usr/bin directory under a different name, such as /usr/share/bin.

When Testing Applications

Developers should try various RFS configurations that have the shared resources mounted under different names. For instance, if an application looks for a user's data files under their $HOME directory, then the test should set up separate $HOME directories, one on each computer in the network. Share one $HOME directory with the other computers, mounting it under a name like $HOME/shared and see if the application can correctly access the data in the $HOME or $HOME/shared directory. Also try sharing the /usr/bin directory of one computer under the name /usr/bin/share of another computer. See if the application can still find the correct programs or files.

Work Around

Probably none, if the path names involved are hard coded. An alternative to hard coded path names is the UNIX shell environment variables that a customer can set to the name of a directory or file where the applications will look for other files, other directories, or data.

Shared Resources With Different Names

Even if path names aren't hard coded, an application may get path names from a place that, when shared, could cause trouble. Suppose that an application looks in the file /usr/xyz/profile to find an environment variable that tells where to find data files, as in the following:

```
DATAFILES="/data/xyz"
```

Now suppose that the /usr/xyz directory is shared in an RFS network, as is the /data directory, except that on one computer the /data directory is mounted with the name /shared/data. The application running on this computer will not find the data files.

When Testing Applications

Watch for cases where an application might get its environment set from a shared profile or configuration file. Arrange an RFS configuration where such profiles or configuration files are shared.

Note that often an application expects to find a file in a user's $HOME directory. Suppose the user has two or more $HOME directories, and shares them from one computer, under names like $HOME/share1, $HOME/share2, and so on.

Note that $HOME/share1 is really the home directory for the user when logged into one remote computer and $HOME/share2 is the home directory on another remote computer, $HOME is the home directory on the local computer. See if the application looks for the particular file under just $HOME, or under $HOME/share1, as well.

Work Around

See if the application can determine, at run time, where to find all files of importance to it. One method of doing this is to have the application examine one or more UNIX shell environment variables for the names of the files. The $HOME variable alone may not be the best source. If these can't be done, then a customer may not be able to allow some of the RFS configurations that are more useful to them.

Use of Terminal Ports

An application designer may have taken the proper precaution of dynamically looking in an environment variable or configuration file for the name of the port it needs to use, but if the environment variable or configuration file came from a shared resource and the application is running on the wrong computer, the application may still fail. The problem arises because it is generally not advisable to share the /dev directory, and the administrator of each computer in a network will usually not assign the ports the same as on the other computers.

This means that a plotter, printer, or other device may be attached to /dev/tty40 on one computer and on different ports on other computers. In a network, special devices like a plotter will be kept on one server machine and access to the plotter by other machines on the network is accomplished only through the server.

When Testing Applications

If the application uses a special port to access a device other than the current terminal (also known as the *login terminal* or *control terminal*), developers should find out how it determines the name of the port each time it runs. If the port name is hard coded, the application is in trouble even without RFS. If the port name comes from an environment variable or a configuration file there are three steps to be taken:

- Set up an RFS configuration that shares the configuration file or the profile that produces the environment variable.

- Set up the device on a port on one computer.

- Run the application from another computer.

If the name placed in the environment variable of the configuration file is tty40 and the application appends that to /dev/ for the full name of the device, then the application is likely to fail because it won't be able to access the device. On the other hand, if the application accepts any reasonable name, like /dev/share/tty99, then it will probably work — if the name has been created properly.

Work Around

See if the customer is able to create a special directory that will contain the name of the port. For instance, while sharing /dev is generally not a good idea, sharing a subdirectory under /dev is acceptable.

Try to create a directory like /dev/share and use the **ln** or **mknod** commands to create a special file in that directory that refers to the port. If the port is /dev/tty40, developers could do the following:

```
mkdir /dev/share
ln /dev/tty40 /dev/share/tty40
```

Now set up an RFS configuration that shares the /dev/share directory, and have the configuration file or profile refer to the /dev/share directory.

Use of Lock Files

An application that uses lock files to control concurrent access to another file, a directory, or other resource, may have trouble under RFS. The best implementation of a lock file has the ID of the process that created the lock kept in the lock file. When another process checks the lock file, it can use the other's PID to see if the first process is still running. If it is not, the new process can ignore the lock file and access the resource.

The problem arises when the two processes are running on different computers in an RFS network, but the locked resource is shared. If the lock file is not kept in a shared directory, then neither process can ever know the other is accessing the shared resource. If the lock file is kept in a shared directory, the later process will see a lock file but, on investigating the process ID found in it, will not find the other process. The application will probably fail as the processes proceed concurrently to update the same data and possibly corrupt it.

When Testing Applications

If an application uses lock files, set up an RFS configuration to share the directory where the lock file is kept and to share the directory where the resource (file, directory, and database) resides. Then run the application on separate computers to attempt simultaneous access to the same resource.

If the application keeps the process ID in the lock file so that other processes can check the validity of the lock, then the application will fail under RFS. If the application doesn't keep the PID in the lock file, it should not have a problem here.

Note: Don't confuse lock files with mandatory or advisory *file and record locking*, which work under RFS.

Work Around

The best way to lock a resource is to use the file and record locking feature of UNIX System V. The application can use the **lockf( )** routine or the **fcntl( )** system call to impose and check a lock. If an application uses the cruder lock files, a customer will not be able to share data with the application.

Use of Numerical User/Group IDs

An application that stores the numerical user or group IDs (GID/UIDs) instead of storing user or group names may cause trouble unless a customer takes special precautions in setting up the IDs.

The administrators of an RFS network can arrange for UID/GIDs to be mapped in various ways. For instance, the most convenient way is to have all IDs mapped by name, so that the user "tsm" on one computer is the same as the user "tsm" on another computer, even if the numerical IDs are different. This allows users to access all of their shared files, regardless of where they may be logged in. This is a useful flexibility offered by the RFS feature. (This assumes, of course, that user IDs across systems are owned by the same person — tsm on one system is the same person as tsm on another.)

An application that attempts to provide data security beyond that provided by the standard UNIX file permissions may fail if it uses numerical IDs instead of names. Suppose, for example, an application arbitrates access to a database by numerical user ID and stores ownership information in a file called *access_allowed*.

Assume that user tsm, whose numerical ID is 102 on the computer named omega, creates a shared database on omega. The application saves the value 102 in the file access_allowed, as the owner of tsm's database. Now suppose tsm goes over to another computer named rambo, where tsm's numerical user ID is 145. The application, upon checking access_allowed on omega is not likely to let tsm access the database since tsm is now 145, not 102! What's worse, suppose the user wbu on rambo has the numerical ID of 102. While user wbu is on rambo, they have complete access to tsm's database on omega because the application thinks wbu is actually tsm. When testing applications developers should set up an RFS configuration that shares the directory where the application keeps a user's private files. This may be the user's $HOME directory. Then they should create a user on two computers with the same name but with different numerical IDs and log in as that user on one computer. They can then use the application to create some data (such as a file, directory, or whatever unit the application uses) and then restrict the access to the data to just that user. They could also log in to the other computer as the same user, but with the different numerical ID and attempt to access the data.

If the application doesn't give you access to the data while on the second computer, it has stored the numerical ID of the user on the first computer as the owner of the data. If the application doesn't hinder access on the second computer, it uses the standard UNIX permission structure or it stores and uses the user name. Sometimes it doesn't give access protection at all.

Work Around

An application with the problem presented here should not prevent it from being used under RFS. The customer, however, will have to fix the /etc/passwd and /etc/group files on all computers in the network, so that each user and each group has the same numerical ID on every computer. A better solution, of course, is to have the application save user names, not user IDs in the description of access permissions. (Again, this assumes that "tsm" on all systems is the same person!)

Use of the Kill Command or Routine

If an application uses the **kill** command or **kill( )** system call to remove another process or to signal another process to a new event, there may be a problem under RFS.

PIDs are not unique in a network, so if one process tries to kill or signal a process running on another computer, it will fail or worse, kill a different process. The *lock file* problem is a special case of this problem, and the *named pipe* problem describes another way that a process on one computer can get the ID of a process running on another computer.

When Testing Applications

Developers should see if the application runs as multiple processes, or tries to contact other processes run by other users. For example, the application may store the IDs of all the processes running the application in a shared place. If the processes are not all running on the same computer, the application will likely fail, perhaps killing an innocent process when it does.

Work Around

If the application can't be changed to avoid the use of the **kill** command or system call, then customers will have to restrict their use of it to a single computer. Even then, the application may still be able to access remote resources.

Storing Data in System Directories

An application that stores its programs or data directly under a few system directories is not likely to be sharable. The directories of concern are:

/dev
/etc
/usr

/usr/net
/usr/bin
/usr/lbin

Any subdirectory of these is a suitable place to store files.

When Testing Applications

See if the application stores any of its programs or data files in the above directories. If so, the parts stored in the directories cannot be shared in an RFS network. If any of those parts are necessary for proper sharing of data among separate computers, then the application cannot be used at all under RFS. An example of the latter is a lock file that must be seen by all invocations of the application in order to properly arbitrate access to shared data. If the lock file is kept directly under one of the above directories, then the same copy cannot be seen by applications on separate computers because the parent directory can't be shared.

Work Around

See if a different directory can be used. Note that subdirectories under the listed directories are acceptable. For instance, /usr/lib/xxx is a suitable directory, where xxx is replaced by the name of the application.

Use of System Dependent Information

If an application uses any system dependent information or resources, it may have problems under RFS.

There are other system dependent data and resources System usage measurements or system performance data might be gathered by an application. These data, if stored in a shared file, may produce invalid results if the application doesn't differentiate data from different computers. Device major and minor numbers and inode numbers are other data that should not be shared.

When Testing Applications

Try to arrange the RFS configurations to cause the application to mix system dependent data. Share the directories used by the application and run the application on separate computers. If the application runs as multiple processes, try to get the processes to run on separate computers.

Work Around

If an application expects to be used in an RFS network, but also collects system dependent data, it should segregate data from different systems and not try to use data from one to control or describe another. If it does, a customer will have to restrict their use of the application to a single computer.

CHAPTER 13

ETHERNET

DOS developers entering the UNIX world should investigate networking and communications since these areas are very much in demand and in need of polished products. So that DOS developers may pursue this avenue, this chapter describes the Ethernet networking environment and provides an understanding of what it is and how it works.

In today's modern business environment, the use of UNIX-based workstations is spreading. This is a significant event because it indicates a deviation from the tradition of centralized processing on large mainframes. These UNIX-based systems vary in size and computing capabilities, ranging from 80386-based microprocessors to the most powerful large scale mainframes and supercomputers.

Distributed processing in the IBM mainframe environment is not a new idea however, the integration of UNIX-based workstations into corporate computing facilities produced communication problems that had to be overcome. The term *workstation* has no standard definition that can be applied to all computing hardware in a universal manner. For the sake of discussion, "workstation" indicates UNIX-based systems, ranging from PC class machines to super-minis, and includes the latest reduced instruction set computer (RISC) technology available from several major vendors.

Two environments currently in the midst of large scale integration of UNIX-based workstations are the Banking and Financial Trading industries. In order for a distributed processing environment to be successful, all of the processing systems must have solid communications capabilities. One of the primary capabilities often required by the modern corporate data center using UNIX-based distributed processors, is the ability for the UNIX machines to communicate with IBM mainframe systems, usually using IBM's System Network Architecture (SNA) communications access methods. (It is only in more recent times that PCs have begun to play a major role in corporate mainframe computing, the majority of IBM mainframe communications involves extensive SNA-based networks. As a result, DOS based PCs have only a few micro-to-mainframe connectivity schemes, the most popular one is to emulate SNA devices over an SNA network.)

With the possible exception of one vendor, UNIX-based systems are not capable of *directly* communicating with IBM mainframes using SNA protocols, unless there is special software in place at both ends to help drive the SNA session. Even so, in most SNA links to UNIX systems the communication flow is awkward and inefficient, requiring tricky handling on the UNIX side. This is not to say that UNIX systems do not communicate with IBM mainframes using SNA; there are numerous methods, none of which have become standard.

The banking and financial trading industries have begun to develop standards. These emerging standards are considered such because the dominant business entities of those industries are all using similar technology.

The emerging standards center around two main components: *intelligent workstations* and *local area networks*. What makes a workstation intelligent are the applications developed for the purpose of easing the job functions of an end user, such as a financial trader. The intelligence is derived from the logic built into all of the applications that perform in a cooperative manner for a specialized purpose, similar in concept to turn-key systems.

For intelligent workstations, UNIX appears to be the operating environment of choice. Ethernet is the overwhelming choice for local area networks, and not surprisingly so. In the financial industry model, one likely reason for the acceptance of Ethernet may be the fact that there are few vendors of IBM Token Ring network hardware for the UNIX-based workstations being implemented.

Another reason for the general acceptance of the Ethernet networking standard may be that it is only recently that IBM has provided direct hardware support for non-SNA network interfaces, even their own Token Ring architecture.

A central communications issue seems to be the data transfer rate of a given network. Traditional SNA terminal connections normally operate at about 9,600 bits per second, although it is possible to operate them at higher rates. The IBM Token Ring local area network was designed to operate over limited distances at a data rate of 4 mega bits per second (Mbps). By contrast, today's Ethernet networks are designed to operate over significantly greater distances than a Token Ring network, and at a data rate of 10 Mbps.

Ethernet Background

Ethernet is the name given to a network originated by Xerox at their Palo Alto Research Center in 1973. The network medium was originally designed as a coaxial cable called *Ether*, named by one of the inventors, Dr. Robert M. Metcalfe, after the luminiferous element, ether.

Ethernet was one of the first local area networks to be standardized and marketed by multiple vendors. The Ethernet specification is the basis for the Institute of Electrical and Electronic Engineer's (IEEE) 802.3 specification, a multi-corporation standard. (The IEEE's 802 Committee was formed to develop local area network standards; the 802.3 standard and Ethernet are often used interchangeably, even though the original Ethernet specifications and modern 802.3 standards are different and incompatible.)

802.3 — CSMA/CD Systems

The 802.3 standard describes a network access method known as Carrier Sense Multiple Access/Collision Detection or CSMA/CD. CSMA/CD systems use a broadcast method of accessing the Ether.

Only one node can actually transmit onto the Ether at a time. In this scheme, before the sender transmits onto the Ether, it first determines if the Ether is "quiet" (no other transmissions in progress). This determination is made at the hardware level by the access circuitry. Voltage levels are used to determine the state of the Ether; if there are no other transmissions in progress then the sender transmits its message (without any guarantee of success). If the Ether is busy, then the sender waits for a random interval and attempts to transmit later; this process is called *collision avoidance*.

When collisions occur, they are detected by the circuitry of each transmitting node. In such cases, the transmission packets are aborted by all senders, leaving the Ether quiet. After random intervals, potential sending nodes attempt retransmission of their packets. The time interval from when the packet was transmitted onto the Ether, to the time it arrived at its destination, is referred to as the *end-to-end propagation delay*.

It is during this propagation delay that a packet is prone to a collision. As the size of the network increases, so must the minimum packet size, in order to minimize the end-to-end propagation delay and thereby reduce the possibilities of collisions. Unlike other network access methods, CSMA/CD uses a decentralized access control methodology.

The intelligence necessary to "direct network traffic" is built into the Ethernet connection hardware of each node. There is no control structure superimposed onto the Ether, it is a purely passive communication medium, designed to operate without a centralized control service to allocate system bandwidth to other nodes.

Ethernet Topology and Mediums

Ethernet employs a passive bus topology, originally designed for a coaxial cable medium. The topology of a network is the physical layout of the connecting cable. Newer technology permits Ethernets to be implemented over mediums other than coaxial cable, such as shielded twisted pair wire or fiber optic cable. In a bus topology, there is a central cable (the Ether) to which a number of nodes may be attached.

The bus is terminated by a special terminator device, a 50 Ohm resistor attached to the end of the coaxial cable. A break in the transmission medium would cause the network to fail because reflections from unterminated wires cause packets to collide with themselves. The terminator acts as a sponge to absorb electrical signals that have reached the end of the bus, preventing them from bouncing back down the Ether to cause signal interference. This is commonly referred to as *packet collisions*.

The passive bus structure is suitable for modular expansion and is considered highly reliable. The only consideration that must be adhered to is that there may be no circular return paths; meaning there can be no path from a node, around the Ether, and back again. Such a loop would constantly interfere with itself because the sending node would detect a collision for each packet it is attempting to transmit.

The original Ethernet was operational at Xerox in 1976. The prototype system was designed to operate at only 3 Mbps and to support a maximum of 256 nodes. The prototype Ether was limited to a maximum distance of one kilometer; the actual transmission medium used was standard CATV coaxial cable because it possessed suitable electrical characteristics and was available at a reasonable cost.

In comparison to the original Ethernet prototype, modern Ethernet specifications defined in the IEEE 802.3 standard indicate operation of the network at 10 Mbps, a maximum segment span of up to 500 meters (or a network span of 2.5 kilometers by combining segments and using packet repeaters), and a maximum of 1,024 network nodes. The transmission medium now includes the original coaxial cable (also known as *thickwire*), another version of coaxial cable known as *thinwire*, *twisted pair* wire and *fiber optic* cable.

An example of an Ethernet bus is illustrated in Figure 13-1 on the next page.

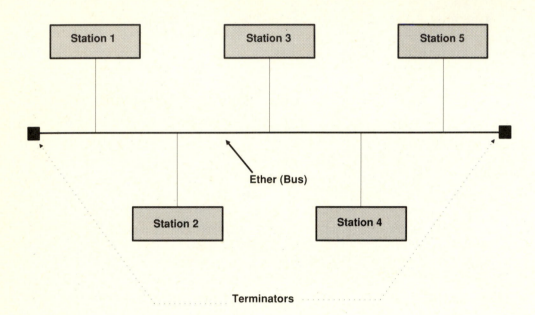

Figure 13-1: Sample Ethernet Bus

Ethernet Components

Each network node of an Ethernet is made up of several individual components. The individual components each perform specific portions of the Ethernet networking tasks. Figure 13-2 on the next page illustrates the components for each Ethernet network node.

The components of every Ethernet network node consist of the *Ether*, a physical connection to the Ether called a *tap*, a *transceiver*, an *interface cable*, an *interface unit,* and the *controller* that is attached to the host computer.

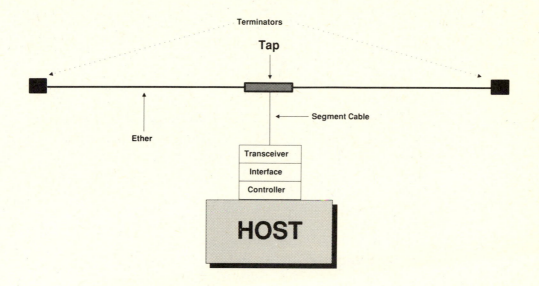

Figure 13-2: Ethernet Components

Twisted Pair

This is a very cost effective media, since it is easy to install, maintain and modify. Twisted pair cable derives its name from the fact that lengths of wire pairs are twisted around each other with a pitch calculated to reduce the electromagnetic interference generated by high frequency signals coming from the network electronics. Twisted pair cable can support network data transmission frequencies of up to 10 MHz without much attenuation.

Recently, IBM has announced the availability of Token Ring network hardware that operates with a bandwidth of 10 Mbps over twisted pair cable. AT&T has also recently announced the general availability of their StarLan-10 product, which also operates at 10 Mbps over twisted pair.

317

The data signal may be transmitted over several hundred meters. Amplifiers are used to strengthen the signal, sometimes incorporating methods of error reduction introduced by the amplified noise level. The major benefits of this type of media are that it is low cost and easy to install, and is already present in most buildings. Connecting additional nodes involves little more than plugging a modular jack into a control panel.

Coaxial Cable

This media is a dual conductor cable; the inner cable is enclosed by another to provide a shielded environment. Depending upon the quality of the cable, this media can be made to operate reliably at several hundred megahertz (Mhz). The original Ethernet cable was sometimes referred to as thickwire, and a new thinner version of the coaxial cable is also used today, known as *thinwire*. Coaxial cable has similar properties to twisted pair; it is relatively easy to splice in an additional node with minimal impact upon the network. This medium can span greater distances than twisted pair, without the need for signal regeneration. Also, the number of nodes it is possible to attach to this medium is greater than for twisted pair.

Coaxial cable was the medium selected for the implementation of Ethernet and is probably the most widely used communications medium in local area networks today.

Radio

The use of radio communications has many advantages, one being that no physical medium (cables) has to be installed. The Ether is the atmosphere, so the cost of installing this type of transmission scheme is limited to the setup of the transmitters and receivers. Atmospheric mediums have a few serious drawbacks, however. Using physical mediums, such as metal conductor cables, provides attenuation characteristics that are relatively constant.

Atmospheric mediums are not perfectly stable and there is no way to accurately predict weather conditions 100 percent of the time; in short, radio communications are easily disrupted by such things as lightning and the electromagnetic interference caused by the sun and other cosmic activity.

The best frequencies for data transmission over this medium are UHF (ultra high frequency) and microwave. Virtually every piece of space equipment such as satellites, missiles, and NASA space shuttle computer systems communicate over this type of transmission medium. U.S. government and military organizations have constructed packet radio networks in which transmitters and receivers are located on mobile vehicles. An intricate network of satellites (both commercial and governmental) are in place — communicating with ground stations around the world and forming large global networks.

Waveguide

A waveguide is a glass tube filled with dry inert gasses and which has a conductive inner surface. The transmission component is similar to radio transmission, but instead of sending over the atmosphere, the transmission is contained within the tube. This medium is suitable for very high transmission rates, often obtaining rates as high as 500 Mbps. The main drawback of the waveguide for use as a local area network transmission medium is that it is costly and difficult to install.

The tube is approximately five centimeters in diameter. Installation of this medium in an existing building would be about the same magnitude as attempting to install additional water piping.

Infra-Red Light Beam

Infra-red as a transmission medium is usually limited to the interior of buildings since the solar light spectrum is so intense that it would drown out exterior transmissions. Because infra-red is a light transmission medium there are no physical cable media, making it a low cost transmission medium to install and operate.

However, since infra-red does use the light spectrum, it is prone to problems when the light path is interrupted. For example, if an object is placed in the light path of the sending and receiving nodes, the transmission signal is effectively cut off. Placement of the infra-red transmitter on the ceiling of a room would reduce the possibility of breaks in the transmission path. This transmission medium is still in experimental stages.

Optical Fiber

During the mid-1980s, fiber optic cable was too expensive and difficult to use in order to be considered as a feasible network transmission medium. Recently, however, fiber optic cable as a transmission medium has become increasingly widespread. This is due, in part, to the falling costs of the fiber optic cable media and of the installation and maintenance.

Optical fibers are strands of non-conductive glass enclosed within a plastic insulator (this is to keep other light out and protect the fragile glass media). Since optical fibers are made of non-conductive materials, it cannot be accidentally grounded, is not susceptible to electrical interference and is not affected when submersed in water.

Information is transmitted over the fiber cable using optical techniques. A light source and detector is necessary at each end of the fiber cable for signal transmission and reception. Pulses of light at extremely high speeds are used to represent transmission data; by varying the light frequencies it is possible to have numerous "channels" for the data transmission path over a single fiber strand.

Transmission is limited to only one direction for each optical fiber, since any source of light other than the transmission source would obliterate the data. In order to provide simultaneous transmit and receive capabilities, two fiber strands are used for each node; one to send the data and the other to receive. Most vendors of optical fibers provide packaging that includes several fiber optic (send/receive) pairs over the same cable.

One of the major benefits of a fiber optic transmission medium is that it provides much higher data rates than are possible with coaxial or twisted pair wire media. Most fiber optic light sources use a light emitting diode (LED) capable of operating in the 50 Mhz range. For frequencies beyond this, semiconductor lasers are used and these are much more costly than LEDs. Compared to metal wire-based transmission mediums, the data rate possible over fiber optic mediums can go as high as several hundred Mbps. The length of fiber optic mediums is significantly greater than metal wire mediums, going into the tens of kilometers.

One drawback to fiber optic cable (aside from the cost), is that it is quite fragile. The glass element is prone to breakage either the cable somewhere in the run, or (more likely) at the exposed end that connects into the transceiver. Another drawback is that adding nodes to a fiber optic bus for Ethernet is not easy.

When tapping onto a fiber optic backbone Ether, the cable must be cut, the connecting ends must be spliced and properly polished — usually requiring a specially trained service technician. Finding breaks in a fiber optic Ether can also be very difficult. In contrast to metal cable conductors, fiber optic cable has very low transmission signal attenuation.

An installation consideration for this medium is that there may not be any sharp right angle twists in the cable as that may cause a break in the glass filament or cause other optical problems.

The Tap

The tap is the physical connection onto the Ether. For a coaxial cable Ether, this is a piece of hardware that has conductors designed to penetrate the protective covering of the cable and make contact with the wires inside. Once the connection is complete, the tap is then secured to the cable to prevent it from being moved. These types of *penetration taps* are sometimes referred to as *vampire taps*.

It is also possible to install several taps that run into a terminated patch panel centrally located in a communication closet. A new node is added by replacing a patch panel terminator with an interface cable running to the node's interface unit. This type of tap configuration calls for preliminary planning but could result in a significant savings later when it is time to add new nodes.

The amount of service interruption for the network is also reduced greatly using the patch panel concept; generally limited to the few minutes necessary to remove the terminator and replace it with the interface cable. Otherwise, the network down time due to connection interruptions would include the overhead necessary for installation of the vampire tap; a process that could take from a few minutes to several hours depending on the expertise of the service technician.

A fiber optic tap is slightly different. Instead of a penetration tap, the Ether must be cut all the way through. The tap device usually has connection ports for both pieces of the severed Ether cable, as well as one or more connection ports for the new node(s). Each connection requires a pair of ports.

The ends of the severed fiber optic Ether cable must be polished to a very close tolerance and be free of debris that would obstruct the optical properties of the cable, such as fingerprints or dirt. If the fiber ends aren't within tolerance, the light is diffracted and causes serious problems. The highest costs associated with fiber optic cables are those of installation and maintenance. For this reason, the use of pre-installed fiber optic taps running to terminated patch panel ports makes good business sense. Because fiber optic cable is so delicate and requires a high degree of technical skill to install and maintain, this medium is usually reserved for use as the network's backbone. Then other mediums (called *segments*) that are easier to install and to modify, such as coaxial cable, may be used to connect workstations to the network.

The Transceiver

The transceiver contains the line driver and receiver components of the network node and connects onto the Ether via the tap. The physical makeup of the transceiver is one or more electronic logic boards containing the necessary chips to implement its functionality at the hardware level. The circuitry includes a feature designed to make the transceiver extremely reliable. Since the transceiver comes into actual contact with the Ether, it was necessary to do this in order to prevent the network from failing if the transceiver fails. The reliability feature is implemented as circuitry designed to continually monitor the transceiver's performance. If the reliability monitoring circuit detects a fault, the transceiver is electronically disconnected from the Ether.

The transceiver also performs collision control through carrier detection, collision consensus enforcement and interference detection functions built into the circuitry. Prior to actually sending any packets, the carrier detection circuitry is used to determine if there is already activity on the Ether. If the Ether is in use by another station, then the logic to wait for the random interval before attempting to send onto the Ether is performed by the transceiver. Once an actual packet collision is detected, the transceiver stops sending and attempts to jam the Ether. When other stations that have not realized that other packets are present on the Ether, they will detect the jamming sequence and subsequently halt their transmissions. The transceiver is connected to the interface over twisted pair wire which carries signals and power supply voltages.

The Interface

The interface lies between the transceiver and the controller. It serializes and encodes data passing through to the Ether, and performs the logical opposite (decode and deserialize) data received from the Ether. The interface also performs the cyclic redundancy checksum (CRC) calculations of the packet contents that were sent and received. Should the results of the CRC calculation be invalid, the packet is aborted and the host is notified of the instance. Memory word sizes are different depending upon the type of computer in question; as a result, the interface component is host system dependent.

The Controller

The controller is also host dependent and manages the transmission and reception of network packets. The controller consists of both software on the host and a firmware attachment. The controller generates the retransmission delay for collision avoidance and recovery. The controller generates the delay by using a random interval, called a *slot*. The controller continues to generate the random delay until transmission of the packet is possible, according to the normal CSMA access protocol.

Open System Interconnect

In 1977, the International Standards Organization (ISO) began study-
ing the compatibility of network equipment, which ultimately led to
the development and publication of the Open System Interconnect
Reference Model, also known as the OSI model.

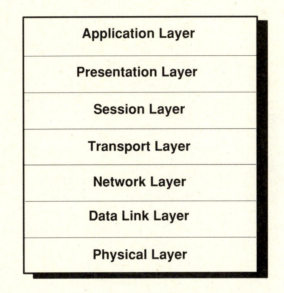

Figure 13-3: OSI Reference Model

The OSI model is useful for those involved with purchasing, designing, implementing, or managing local area networks because it
provides the necessary background and theoretical framework so that
networking issues may be better understood. In the OSI model, the
networking issues are divided into seven major functions called
layers.

Figure 13-3 depicts the seven functional layers of the OSI reference
model. Each of the OSI layers defines a level of functionality.

The Physical Layer

The physical layer is concerned with the hardware specifications for the transmission of data over the communication medium, such as the wire, network transceivers, and controllers. This layer defines the electrical (and mechanical) characteristics for the network connection hardware and electronic components.

The Data Link Layer

The data link layer is responsible for transforming a raw transmission facility into a line that appears to be free of transmission errors (to the network layer). This is accomplished by constructing data frames around the input data, transmitting them sequentially, and handling acknowledgements sent back by the receiver. The physical layer is designed to send bits without any regard to contents or structure, so the data link layer creates and manages transmission frame boundaries.

The transmission frame contains special bit patterns, placed at the beginning and end of each frame. It is possible for these special bit patterns to be produced accidentally, so special care is taken by the software at this layer to avoid problems that can be associated with the occurrence of such events.

A more precise term used to describe the transmission units handled by the data link layer is *physical layer service data unit*, and not the term *frame*. ("Frame" is a leftover from earlier communications methods.) The data link layer is also designed to handle the possibility of duplicate frames transmitted due to sudden line noise.

The Network Layer

The network layer manages the routing of packets (the unit of information handled in this layer) within the subnet. Modern networks provide interconnections to other networks and often there is the likelihood of concurrent communications with other networks. The message traffic can become quite busy, so the network layer software must be capable of handling the routing of packets to the appropriate hosts on the subnet.

Essentially, the network layer software accepts messages from a host, converts the message into packets, and then sends the packet to its destination. The network layer is also where network accounting and management routines are often included; mainly to keep track of the number of bits, characters, or packets being sent by users to produce billing information or administrative statistics such as network load factors.

The Transport Layer

The transport layer accepts data from the session layer and, if necessary, splits it into packets before passing them to the network layer, and ensures all packets arrived at the destination. The transport layer also determines what type of services to provide to the session layer, and eventually, to the end users of the network.

Discreet network connections, called *ports*, are created for each transport connection required by the session layer. In cases where high throughput volume is required, multiple ports may be opened simultaneously by the transport layer. The data is then divided among the ports to improve throughput. This multiplexing is made transparent to the session layer by the transport layer software.

The Session Layer

The session layer is the end user's primary interface to the network. This layer actually establishes the connection between the user and processes on another machine on the network. Connections between users are usually called a *session*. Sessions allow users to log into other machines remotely or to perform file transfers between machines. (Users are not limited to sessions between only two machines, they may in fact have multiple concurrent sessions with several machines.)

To establish a session, users must supply the address(es) of the machine(s) they want to connect to. The address(es) are usually some alias or mnemonic kept in a database accessible to the session layer

software on one or more of the network machines. The process of setting up sessions between machines is also referred to as binding.

The Presentation Layer

The presentation layer provides functions that warrant generalized
solutions instead of continually solving the same problem over and
over; usually library routines called by the end user. An example of
such a function is automatic compression and decompression of ASCII
data strings to improve communications throughput by reducing the
number of redundant characters.

Other conversions possible in this layer include data encryption for
security and character code conversions between ASCII and EBCDIC.
Terminal incompatibilities may also be dealt with by performing certain transformations within the presentation layer.

The Application Layer

The application layer is the least defined because it is up to the user.
For example, user programs executing on different machines communicating with each other must define which messages they will be
able to process and what actions must be taken to handle them.

CHAPTER 14

INTRODUCTION TO TCP/IP

Transmission Control Protocol/Internet Protocol (TCP/IP) is a set of network protocols that is transparent to the end user. Most UNIX users and programmers will never have to be concerned with the internals of TCP/IP, unless they are involved with the development of it. Some readers, however, may have heard the buzzword being used, so this chapter is included to satisfy the curious.

Although TCP/IP is not a standard part of every UNIX system, it is widely used in serious networking in most operating system environments. Ethernet Networks using TCP/IP have become an industry standard. For example, virtually every major brokerage institution on Wall Street has installed (or is in the process of installing) large scale Ethernet networks that use TCP/IP. Many of these networks are implemented on UNIX-based machines, significant because it is a departure from the traditional IBM mainframe environment.

Many vendors have developed customized products such as intelligent Ethernet transceiver components with TCP/IP implemented at the hardware level. Eventually, these customized products may work their way to the marketplace. In Europe and in countries around the world, UNIX, Ethernet and TCP/IP have become standards. At some point, UNIX users are likely to encounter TCP/IP. It is important to understand what it is and how it works.

Basic Definitions and Concepts

TCP/IP protocols were developed by a group of researchers centered around ARPAnet to allow resource sharing by cooperating computers across a network. ARPAnet, (a network developed by the Defense Advanced Research Projects Agency, known by its former acronym ARPA) the best known TCP/IP network, started as a four node network in 1969 and has grown enormously in size over the years. ARPAnet is responsible for much of the world's early knowledge of networking.

TCP/IP is supported by over a hundred major vendors of network products, and is used by thousands of networks of all kinds. It is widely used on UNIX systems over Ethernet. The term Internet refers to a collection of networks that includes the ARPAnet, NFSnet, regional networks (such as NYsernet), many military networks, and local area networks in the business, research, and academic communities.

The Defense Department Network (DDN) is a prominent military network managed by the Department of Defense. The terms DDN and Internet are often used interchangeably, partially due to the funding that the Internet Protocol development project receives from the DDN organization.

All of the Internet networks are connected to one another. Messages may be transmitted between any user on any network (providing security guidelines are met). The Department of Defense has issued its own military specification (MILSPEC) definition of TCP/IP, while the rest of the TCP/IP community continues to adhere to Internet standards.

The family of TCP/IP protocols used for different applications include TCP, IP, and User Datagram Protocol (UDP). Others, such as File Transfer Protocol (FTP), perform specific tasks like file transfer between systems. Most serious network applications, such as networked electronic mail, use several of the TCP/IP protocols. A separate protocol for mail defines a set of commands exchanged by the machines on the network.

The commands include information that identifies the sender of the mail, the receiver, and the actual mail message text. Such a protocol assumes that there is already a reliable method of communication available to send the mail message between the source and destination machines on the network and it is oblivious to anything else. Mail and other application level protocols only define the commands and messages that are the object of the transmission and which are designed to be used in conjunction with TCP and IP.

TCP

TCP's job is to ensure that the mail (or other application protocol) commands reach their destination. In networking terminology, the term used to describe the unit of data being transmitted is called a *packet*. TCP keeps track of everything that is sent and will retransmit packets that did not arrive at their destination or arrived in an unrecognizable state.

When the message being sent exceeds the permitted size for a single packet (this is common in mail and file transfer applications), TCP splits the large message into several smaller packets, transmits them to their destination, and then reassembles them. TCP may be thought of as a set of library routines called by applications at both ends in order to perform reliable network communications between systems.

TCP doesn't do the entire job by itself, but calls upon IP services to handle the rest of the job. In this respect, IP may be thought of as a set of library routines for TCP to call upon. The process of constructing several levels of protocols is known as *layering*.

The applications (mail, TCP, IP, and others) are separate layers; each calling upon the services of the next layer below. Some applications may bypass an intermediate layer to access another directly. TCP/IP applications may use four layers:

- An application protocol (such as mail).

- Protocols providing services required by many applications (such as TCP).

- IP services to achieve delivery of application packets to their destinations.

- Protocols necessary for management of specific physical mediums (such as Ethernet).

Gateways are devices used to connect networks. In large networks connected by gateways, TCP/IP packets may pass through more than a dozen different networks before arriving at their final destination. This involves quite a bit of routing by IP, all of which is invisible to the end user. The end user only needs to know the Internet address of the target, in the form of a mnemonic.

An Internet address is actually a 32 bit number that is written out as four decimal numbers separated by periods. Each of these four decimal numbers represents 8 bits and is known in Internet terminology as an *octet*. Because TCP/IP is used on systems where a byte may be other than 8 bits, the term byte no longer holds universal meaning, and is therefore replaced by the term octet when describing elements of data.

This is not to say that octets are network addresses. TCP/IP uses the term octet as the standard unit of measure to describe the size of a data element. The term octet is used in place of byte because byte means different things on different systems.

Network addresses are assigned by a central authority in the Internet and have some structure providing information about the destination. An example of a network address is:

```
135.7.3.101
```

Attempting to remember the Internet network addresses of other nodes would be cumbersome, so a mnemonic or alias (name) is used instead. When connecting to another system, the network software responsible for completing the connection references a database of Internet addresses and converts the entry to numeric form.

In TCP/IP, information is handled in packets that are sent individually through the network and are treated by the network as completely separate items. For example, suppose that a message of

15,000 octets in size is to be sent. Since most networks cannot handle packets of this size, the various protocols (TCP, IP, and FTP) split the file into smaller units, perhaps 30 packets that are 500 octets in size, and send them to their destination.

When they all arrive, they are reassembled in correct sequence. During the actual transmission process, the network is unaware that the packets have any relationship with each other. It is quite likely that packets may arrive out of sequence; that is, packet number 10 may arrive before packet number eight. Sometimes packets may not arrive at all, in which case they are retransmitted.

There are two separate protocols involved in this process. TCP breaks the message into packets, reassembles the packets in the correct sequence in order to properly reconstruct the message at the destination, and handles the retransmission of any lost packets.

IP takes care of routing the packets through the Internet, and is responsible for keeping track of the routes to all destinations and handling any incompatibilities among different transport media. IP receives packets from TCP, along with a destination, and is unaware of any relationships between previous or subsequent packets processed. To IP, each packet is a single complete unit of work.

Most networks include multiple connections. TCP must not only know the destination, but also must know to which connection to send the message. The task of determining this is referred to as *demultiplexing*. The demultiplexing information necessary for TCP/IP is stored in a series of headers affixed to the beginning of the message packet by some protocol, usually only a few octets in size.

This is like placing a letter into an envelope with a destination address on the outside. In modern networks this is performed by the various protocols and occurs many times. Imagine a little envelope with an address on the outside being placed into a larger one with another address on the outside of it. Then the larger envelope is placed into yet another larger one and so on, until the packet is finally sent to its destination after which the process of removing all the envelopes takes place in the reverse order.

Here is a scenario of how data from a user is enveloped by various network protocol headers. First, a data file is created by the user and it becomes the object of a file transfer to another computer system on the Internet. The data stream is too large for a single packet, so TCP splits it up into a number of packets capable of containing the entire file. The packet size is not arbitrary, the TCP on both sides of the transmission agree on the packet size by determining the maximum size they each can handle. The smaller packet size of the two is used. Figure 14-1 illustrates some of the points made thus far.

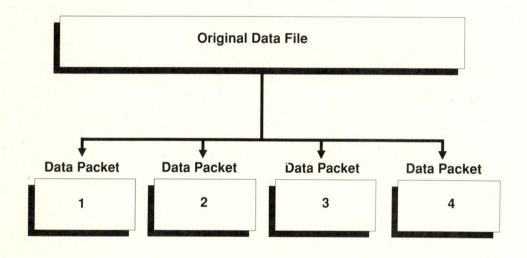

Figure 14-1: TCP Packets

TCP gives each packet a header that contains information about the source and destination port numbers, as well as the packet sequence number. Most systems that are part of a TCP/IP network are multiuser, and it is quite likely that more than one user may send data across the network at the same time. To deal with this situation, *port numbers* are used to identify the different conversations. The TCP at the destination reports its local port number and that number becomes the destination port number provided in the header that was affixed to the front of the source message data.

The header contains multiple fields: source port, destination port, sequence number, other information, and a checksum. The source port identifies the port address of the origination point, destination port is the receiving port address, and sequence is the packet sequence number. The packet numbers are not actually in sequence; instead, the sequence number is derived from the octets of data, see Figure 14-2.

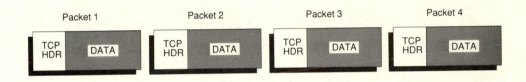

Figure 14-2: Packet Numbers

If each packet contained 1,000 octets of data, the first packet number would be 0, the next would be 1,000, the next would be 2,000, and so on. TCP computes the checksum field by adding up all the octets contained in the packet, after which the numeric value is placed in the header field. The receiving TCP then recalculates the checksum value, and if there is a discrepancy, the packet is discarded and retransmitted.

IP

When TCP has finished putting its header information on the front of each packet, it sends the packets to IP for transmission across the network, providing IP with the Internet address of the destination computer. IP doesn't require any additional information to send the packet, and is not concerned with any of TCP's header information. IP is concerned mainly with 32 bit source and destination Internet addresses, the protocol number, and another checksum. These items are contents of the IP header that is placed in front of each packet handled by IP.

The source Internet address is the address of the sending machine and the destination Internet address is the address of the IP packet receiver. The source Internet address is necessary so the destination machine knows where the point of origin was. The destination Internet address is necessary so that intermediate nodes (gateways) know the destination where the packet is to be sent.

The protocol number informs the receiving IP at the final destination to send the packet to TCP. Most IP transactions use TCP, but other protocols may be used. The IP checksum is used for the same reasons TCP uses a checksum; to verify that the contents of each packet were not garbled during transmission. Like TCP, IP will resend damaged packets if necessary; it should be noted that IP and TCP use separate checksums.

IP is unaware of the contents of the packets it is sending. For all intents and purposes the contents of the packets beyond IP's header are just a bunch of bits. For this reason, IP requires its own checksum to validate transmission packets received at the destination end.

Figure 14-3 on the next page illustrates how an IP packet may look after it has placed its header data in front of a packet received from TCP.

Depending upon what other communications links are involved, at this point there may be no reason to add any additional protocol transmission headers to a packet. If, however, one computer is linked to another via a gateway, then a few octets of additional header data may also be added by the appropriate protocol interface modules.

Ethernet

Most commercial business networks use Ethernet, an efficient high speed network originated by Xerox. Ethernet uses its own addresses, and was designed to avoid the possibility of network addressing conflicts such as duplicate or overlapping network addresses. This was accomplished by a centrally controlled addressing scheme that uses a

48 bit address, thus ensuring that enough addresses are available to avoid the reuse of network addresses. The addressing is implemented directly into the hardware of Ethernet controllers and is registered with a central controlling authority by each Ethernet equipment manufacturer.

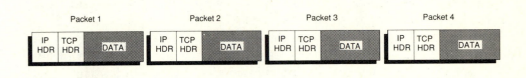

Figure 14-3: Packets with Headers

Ethernet is a broadcast medium, so its packet traffic is visible to every node on the network. To be certain that the correct destination machine receives the packet, Ethernet provides its own 14 octet header that includes Ethernet source and destination addresses, a type code, and a checksum.

Although Ethernet nodes are only supposed to "listen" for packet traffic addressed specifically for them, it is possible to monitor all traffic. There is no correlation between the IP Internet address and an Ethernet address. There is a table on each Ethernet node that maps Ethernet addresses to a corresponding Internet address. The type code in the Ethernet header provides for the use of many transmission protocols on the same network, such as XNS or DECnet.

This means that Ethernet may use several different protocol families at the same time over the same network. The type code field contains a different value for each of the transmission protocols used. The Ethernet checksum is calculated by the Ethernet controller (transceiver) and is recomputed at the destination end. If the checksums disagree, the packet is discarded and resent, much like the way IP and TCP handle checksums.

Ethernet will append the checksum at the end of the packet data. In this respect, the checksum is not part of the Ethernet header, but is a trailer; with the data sandwiched between the Ethernet header and trailer. Figure 14-4 illustrates this concept.

The Ethernet header data is removed by the Ethernet interface when the packet arrives at its destination. The type code field is checked and depending upon what the value is, Ethernet sends the remaining packet data to that protocol.

In the case of IP, for example, the packet is given to IP by the Ethernet device driver. The process is repeated for each protocol level involved in the packet transmission process. IP would strip the IP header information, examine the protocol field, and send it to the corresponding protocol handler, such as TCP. TCP then uses the packet sequence number and other information to reconstruct the original data file.

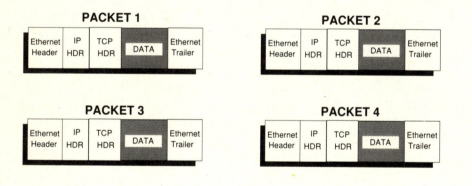

Figure 14-4: Packets with Various Headers

Well Known Sockets

An application protocol is said to run *on top* of TCP/IP. When an application protocol sends a message, the message is passed to TCP, which in turn makes sure the message is delivered to the destination.

The application protocols treat the network connection as if it were just a simple byte stream. This is because TCP and IP perform the details involving the actual transmission of messages.

Suppose, for example, that a user wanted to send a file to a particular destination. More action is necessary besides providing the destination node's Internet address. The file transfer server at the destination node must first be connected, by specifying the name of the network program to be executed (in this case the file transfer program). Network programs are usually specialized and provide a specific set of network tasks.

There are usually separate programs provided to perform file transfers, mail, and remote terminal login. Users accomplish the specification of which tasks to perform at the remote end by using well known sockets. Each network program requires a socket.

To keep track of concurrent, individual network conversations, TCP uses port numbers that are part of the Internet address contained in the TCP header data. Sockets are specific port numbers associated with certain network programs and are used to communicate with those programs. This sounds confusing, and it is. In most cases, user-written network programs require only random port numbers.

Specific port numbers must be assigned to network programs that await requests, like the file transfer program (FTP). FTP initiated on the local machine opens a connection to a random number for the local port number. On the destination end, however, port number 21 is always used since it is the official number reserved for the FTP server. In an FTP scenario, there are actually two programs involved.

First, there is the FTP on the local machine that accepts commands from the originating user's terminal, passing them through to the destination end. Second, there is an FTP program running on the destination end as the FTP server that accepts commands from a network connection instead of an interactive terminal.

User application programs do not require the use of well known socket addresses, since they generally do not provide services desired by everyone else. Servers, on the other hand, require well known sockets so that anyone can open connections to them and begin sending commands.

Describing Connections

A connection is described by a set of four numbers: two Internet addresses (one for each end), and two TCP port numbers (also one for each end). These connection numbers are included in every packet; the Internet addresses are contained in the IP header, and the TCP port addresses are in the TCP header. It is possible and likely that more than one user will send files to the same destination machine at the same time.

For this reason, no two connection numbers may be exactly the same, they must differ by at least one digit. For example, the Internet addresses would be identical for the same destination machine and, since the server application being described is a file transfer program, the well known socket numbers would also be the same. The port numbers for the user programs, however, must be different to achieve the required unique connection numbers. The following example illustrates this point. (These are not real connection addresses.)

```
CONNECTION        INTERNET ADDRESSES          TCP PORT

Connection 1      135.7.3.101, 135.7.3.135    2345, 21
Connection 2      135.7.3.101, 135.7.3.135    2346, 21
```

Usually, the network software at one end of the connection will assign a port number that is guaranteed to be unique. Since the server end must use a well known socket number, it is usually the user end that provides the unique number. Once the TCP connection is made, the communication session behaves similar to a hardwire connection between the machines. Although the most difficult tasks are handled by TCP and IP, another protocol is necessary to control the set of commands and formats used by the applications.

Using Connections

In a mail scenario for example, the local mail application opens a connection to a mail server at the destination machine and sends control information before it sends out the text of the actual mail message. The control information includes the originating machine's name, the sender's user ID information, and a list of all recipients for the message.

After the control information, the local mail application transmits a command indicating that the message text follows immediately. The remote mail server then treats the data stream as message text rather than application commands — until a special end-of-message character is received.

When the end-of-message character is received, both ends of the mail application resume command mode conversation, perhaps to receive another mail message, or perhaps to terminate the connection if there are no more mail requests. The mail scenario is used by many applications and is one of the simplest communications protocols.

File transfer involves more sophistication and requires two different connections. FTP begins in much the same way as the mail scenario. The user's program performs remote login by sending the appropriate command instructions along with the password. Once in, another command that includes the file specification is sent to initiate the file transfer. Like mail, there is a special command that instructs the remote FTP server to begin transmitting the file, but unlike mail, a second connection is opened for the actual data file.

Although it would be possible to send the data file across the same connection like the mail scenario, the second connection was designed to permit users to continue their session during the actual file transfer, This is because the transfer may involve large files and require a long time to send.

A user may perform inquiries, enter other commands, and even abort the file transfer if desired. The original connection is left intact for this purpose. It is also possible to open connections to different destination machines and send files between them. In such a scenario, a second file transfer would require a second connection anyway. (For multitasking systems like UNIX, a new process could be started as an alternative. TCP/IP is also implemented in non-multitasking environments, like DOS-based PCs, so this feature is necessary.)

Remote terminal scenarios use only a single connection and a different command processing strategy. This scenario normally sends data. When it is necessary to send a command, special characters are used to indicate what follows are character(s) that are part of a command. When any of these special character sequences appear embedded within the data text, the result is that two identical characters are sent, one as the special character and the other as the literal character.

Standard Representations

By convention, TCP/IP should be usable on any computer system regardless of the hardware or software. Data is not uniformly represented across the variety of machine environments. For example, most IBM mainframes use 8 bit EBCDIC character codes, while other machines use 7 bit ASCII.

There are differences in end-of-line conventions such as *carriage return* versus *line feeds* and whether or not a terminal device expects individual characters one at a time or blocked together in lines at a time (or a screen at a time). To overcome such problems, a standard representation is defined by each application protocol. This doesn't mean that binary files cannot be sent using FTP; any file may be sent.

Remember that neither TCP nor IP is concerned about representation, since they only send octets. It is the application programs receiving the octets that must know how to interpret them. Each application specifies its own standard representation in its RFC document, usually net ASCII. Net ASCII uses ASCII characters with carriage return line feed (CRLF) defined as the standard end-of-line delimiter.

There is also a definition for a standard terminal for the remote login application that is a half duplex terminal with local echo enabled. Applications may also agree on different standards as well. For example, a full duplex terminal may be used instead of half duplex. Each application has standard representations which must be supported by each machine that includes that application and which is on the network.

User Datagram Protocol

What about situations in which data will always fit into a single pack-et? There are applications that produce such packets, for example, a *lookup* application. When a connection is opened to a remote machine on the network, the machine's network name is used instead of its Internet address. Before the connection can be made, the destination machine's network name must first be translated to the Internet ad-dress. The database used for converting the machine names to Inter-net addresses is not available on all machines; it isn't necessary.

Instead, a query is sent to a machine where the database resides. The query message is quite short and will fit into a single packet, as will the response it generates from the remote machine. TCP could be used to handle this packet exchange, however, the overhead hardly seems worth the effort.

Should the response to the message take too long, a simple solution would be to send another query, which would not require TCP's over-head associated with ensuring end-to-end delivery of packets. For such message processing, the User Datagram Protocol (UDP) is a commonly used alternative.

UDP is perfect for applications that don't require sequences of pack-ets to be reassembled at the destination machine. UDP is similar to TCP in some respects. It has its own UDP header that is placed ahead of the packet data. Like TCP, UDP sends its packet to IP (while then adds its own header in front of the packet and places the value for UDP's protocol number in the protocol field, instead of TCPs).

The main differences between UDP and TCP are that UDP does not break the data into packets, nor does UDP keep track of packets that may require retransmission. It does, however, provide port numbers (like TCP) so that multiple connections are available to more than one program at a time. UDP also uses well known sockets for UDP ser-vers.

The UDP header is not as large as a TCP header; it has the source and destination port numbers and the checksum, but there is no pack-et sequence number since it isn't necessary. UDP may be used by any application protocol in which the message data is small enough to be contained within a single packet, such as in a lookup application.

Internet Control Message Protocol

Internet Control Message Protocol (ICMP) is another alternative to TCP. It is used for sending error and other messages to the TCP/IP software, instead of to another user application. As an example, the message "Host Unreachable" may be sent by ICMP to the local system if an attempt to connect to another host had failed.

There are several possible messages, usually of concern only to network administrators or developers, and they are completely transparent to the end user. The ICMP is similar to UDP, but is even simple. Its headers do not include port numbers; they aren't necessary because all ICMP messages are handled directly by the network software.

Packet Routing

As mentioned earlier in this chapter, IP is responsible for the routing of packets to the correct destination machines on the network. Routing is the task of determining how to deliver a packet to its destination address. The details can be implementation dependent, although some general characteristics always hold true. This section describes how IP performs its routing chores.

It is necessary, first of all, to understand upon which model IP is based. Generally, IP assumes that a system is part of a local area network. Another general assumption is that packets may be transmitted between any machine on the network. Ethernet, being a broadcast network, uses the Ethernet address of the destination machine and sends the packet down the network.

The destination machine "looks" or "listens" for any packet traffic that contains its Ethernet network address in the header, although it can retrieve a copy of any packet on the network. This is fine for packets being sent on the same network, but what about packets destined for machines on other networks?

The solution is to use a gateway. If, for example, a UNIX machine was connected to two Ethernet networks through the use of two Ethernet transceivers (one wired into example network address 135.7.3 and the other wired into example network address 135.7.1), then it could act as a gateway between the two networks. (In the previous statement only the first three octets of the network address are listed. Gateways don't use the fourth octet since their primary job is to provide access between networks.)

The network software on a gateway must be configured so that packets are forwarded automatically from one network to the correct destination network. (Gateways may exist into several networks from a single gateway server machine.) Many major communications centers support gateways into a number of different networks. The networks being connected through a gateway do not have to be the same kind of network. For example, Ethernet and Token Ring networks may be connected via a gateway.

Each machine has a table containing the network numbers. For every network, the associated gateway server is also listed, and is the gateway to be used to get to the specific network. Before sending the packet, the local machine determines if the destination address is on the local network. If so, the packet is sent directly. If the address is not on the local network, the network entry for the destination address is located and a packet is sent to the gateway server associated with that entry. The network address table can get very large; the Internet currently includes the addresses of several hundred networks. For this reason several ways have been developed to keep the size of the routing table under control.

One method is to use *default routes*. There is often only one gateway out of a network and it may connect into a local Ethernet, which in turn connects into a larger backbone network. For such cases, a separate entry for all known networks is not required. The only entry necessary defines the gateway as the default route. If no specific route is provided in a packet, it is sent using the default route to the gateway. A default gateway is usually established in networks with many gateways.

Gateways may also be configured to provide ICMP messages which indicate that a better route exists and should be used. When such messages are encountered, most networks are set up to add the information to their routing tables. It is not recommended for individual computers to keep track of the entire network. They should start by establishing a default gateway and let the gateways inform them of the new routes. The gateways themselves cannot depend upon this strategy and therefore, may require extensive routing tables. Gateways use something called a *routing protocol* to find each other in networks and to maintain up-to-date information on routing through the network.

Internet Addresses

Internet addresses must identify the network and the host within the network. For large networks, 24 bits may be necessary to represent all of their hosts. Logic would tell us that a 48 bit network address was required. However, the Internet designers decided to use only 32 bits. Based upon the assumption that most networks would be small, three different ranges of addresses were implemented. Table 14-1 should help you understand what the address ranges are and how they are used.

Table 14-1: Internet Address Ranges

CLASS	RANGE	TYPE
A	1-126	PRIVATE
RESERVED	127.1-127.254	NOT APPLICABLE
B	128.1-191.254	LARGE COMMERCIAL
C	191.1.1-223.254.254	SMALL COMMERCIAL
D/E	224.1-...	UNDEFINED

For "class A" Internet addresses, the first octet (ranging from 1 to 126) identifies the network number. The remaining three octets identify host numbers. For class A addresses, the problem is that there can only be 126 large major networks, of which ARPAnet is one. These large major networks are either private or reserved for use by government entities; very few commercial networks are given a class A Internet address.

"Class B" addresses were designed for large businesses. For class B addresses, the first two octets are used to identify the network number; so the range 128.1 through 191.254 are valid class B addresses. The addresses ranging from 127.1 through 127.254 are reserved for use by some systems for special purposes.

The last two octets of a class B network address (16 bits) are used to identify host addresses, providing a maximum of 64,516 nodes. (This should be enough for most organizations. Should an organization exhaust all available host addresses it is possible to obtain additional class B addresses.)

The final type of address is class C, which uses the first three octets ranging from 191.1.1 through 223.254.254. In class C addressing there is a limit of only 254 host machines on a network, but there may be many networks. The addresses beyond 223.1.1 are reserved for future use as class D and class E, currently still undefined.

Subnets

Many organizations divide their network numbers into a *subnet*. For example, a company with a class B address of 135.7 may find it convenient to use the third octet of the network number to identify on which Ethernet a particular host is. (This example assumes a company has more than one Ethernet local area network. Many of the large firms do use multiple Ethernet networks.)

The addresses 135.7.1 and 135.7.6 could be used to further identify two other networks. Assume that a fictitious company named Acme Brokerage, Inc., has several Ethernet networks throughout their new corporate headquarters on Wall Street.

If the class B address assigned to Acme Brokerage was 135.7 and packets are sent from another network outside of Acme Brokerage (like a news wire service, or real time market feed network), then those packets would be destined only for the address 135.7.

If Acme Brokerage has over 20 Ethernet networks connected together over a backbone network with their addresses ranging from 135.7.1 through 135.7.20, any packets from outside would only need to be addressed to 135.7. The addresses 135.7.1 and 135.7.6 would be treated as separate networks, but only internally at Acme Brokerage. Gateways used at Acme Brokerage would have separate entries for each internal subnet, while gateways external to the Acme Brokerage network would only have an entry for Acme's main network address of 135.7.

The same effect could be achieved using a class C address; however, then the rest of the outside world would require a separate entry for each Acme Brokerage subnet they wished to access. This would cause gateways to keep track of a very large number of networks, which can become cumbersome. Using subnets in class B networks is more efficient, more convenient for the outside world, and also hides the organization's internal network structure.

Readers will have noticed that the second octet of the network number ranges only between 1 and 254. Traditionally, in data processing, 0 is valid as the first number. In this case, the address 0 is used for machines that don't know their own address. Under certain circumstances it is possible that a machine doesn't know the number of the network it is on, or even its own host address. The address 0.0.0.14 would indicate that a machine knew its host number was 14, but did not know on what network.

The number 255 also has a special meaning in network addresses. It is used to indicate a broadcast message, a message every machine on the network sees. Broadcasts may be used in situations where it is not known with what system communication is desired. For example, if it were necessary to look up the Internet address of a particular host, but an application didn't know what machine on the network has the host database, the lookup request may be sent out as a broadcast message.

Going back to the imaginary company, Acme Brokerage, Inc., consider the following scenario, Acme Brokerage has 1,200 financial traders on several Ethernet subnets. Suppose that a news wire service, such as Reuters, provides constant news items and feeds them into the Acme Brokerage network. The trading community on the network could benefit tremendously if a news flash is broadcast to all traders regarding some key information relevant to the financial trading business.

It is more efficient to transmit a single packet as a broadcast than to send the same message as individual packets to a number of interested machines. For Ethernet, it is possible to broadcast a packet, while it is not possible on the ARPAnet or on point-to-point lines. When the Ethernet address has all of its bits on, every node on the network will read the packet.

An example of an Ethernet address indicating a broadcast packet is 135.7.1.255. This means that every machine on 135.7.1 would see the packet. Remember that in the previous example, 135.7.1 is the first of twenty subnet addresses for Acme Brokerage.

To send a broadcast packet to all nodes at Acme Brokerage, the address 135.7.255.255 would be used. The address 255.255.255.255 indicates all hosts on all networks. (Some older implementations of the network software use 0 instead of 255 for this purpose.) These will assume the network number to be the first two octets (135.7) and the broadcast address to be 135.7.255.255 or 135.7.0.0. This can be a dangerous feature to use until universal support for broadcasts has been properly implemented.

Network addresses are transparent and of no consequence to end users, except in a few rare instances. The end user may never need to know anything about a network address, except possibly when installing network software on a PC.

Programmers who develop network software components or products (such as network management software) would be among the most likely to know about or actually to use a network address. UNIX system administrators on UNIX machines who are responsible for setting up and maintaining the networking software, are also likely to know about and to use network addresses.

Network addresses are used by a database that contains a list of aliases for each network address. Such databases are used by the network protocols (TCP, IP, UDP, FTP, and mail) to obtain routing information so that connections to other machines can be achieved. The addresses 0 and 255 are used for unknown and broadcast addresses respectively. Normal hosts should never be given either of these addresses. Remember that 0, 127, and addresses above 223 are reserved for special purposes.

Packet Breakdown and Reassembly

Network designers have not yet agreed on how large a standard packet should be. Ethernet packets are 1,500 octets in size, while ARPAnet packets are about 1,000 octets. Some networks use larger packets and others use smaller packets. If IP were to settle on the smallest size available, this would cause serious performance problems.

For file transfer, especially for large files, large packets are more efficient than small ones and it would be desirable to use the largest possible packet size. The previous statement must be qualified; the larger a packet, the more chance there is of encountering a transmission error. If transmission errors are encountered, the entire packet is retransmitted, causing serious transmission performance problems. To deal with this, the appropriate network software can compute the optimum packet size based on the network's error rate. Networks with small limits must also be handled, there are provisions for this.

TCP is capable of determining what packet size to use according to network needs. When the connection is first opened, both ends may send packets of the maximum size they are capable of handling. Of the two initial packets, the smaller size is used for the rest of the connection. This permits TCP to use large or small packets that are dependent upon the implementation. This, however, is not the complete answer to the problem.

There may be events that occur between transmission of data from one TCP to another. If packets were sent from one machine to another, it is possible that both machines will be using Ethernet. In such a case, the packet size being handled would be 1,500 octets.

It is also possible that the connection may include a different type of network, such as ARPAnet, that cannot handle large packets. Because of this, packets are split into smaller components. Information is contained within the IP header which indicates that a packet has been split, along with the necessary reassembly information.

Gateways connecting Ethernets to ARPAnet, for example, must be set up to split Ethernet packets into pieces that can be handled by ARPAnet. All implementations of TCP/IP must also be capable of reassembling the pieces if necessary.

The approach that TCP/IP uses in deciding what packet size to use is implementation dependent. When there is uncertainty about the maximum size capable of being handled by any individual network in the connection path, a commonly used packet size is 72 octets. Because of bugs in the reassembly code, the developers of the various implementations of TCP/IP have taken different approaches to deciding when it is wise to use large packets.

Some of these implementations use large packets only for the local area network, while other implementations use large packets for any network on the same campus. The widely used 72 octet packet size is generally considered a safe size and is supported by every network.

Getting More Information

The amount of information available on TCP/IP is overwhelming. The Internet standards are first submitted as proposed standards called a Request For Comment (RFC), and then receive an RFC number. When the proposal is accepted, it is added to a document called Official Internet Protocols; and continues to be referenced by its RFC number. By convention, when an RFC is revised, the revised version receives its own RFC number. This convention causes confusion for two documents: Assigned Numbers and Official Internet Protocols. These two documents are continually revised, so their RFC numbers keep changing. The document called RFC Index keeps track of the latest RFC numbers.

Table 14-2 shows the RFCs that would be of interest to anyone serious about getting more information on TCP/IP.

Table 14-2: RFC Documents of Interest

```
RFC   INDEX    LISTING OF ALL THE LATEST RFC NUMBERS
RFC   1011     Official Internet Protocols
RFC   1010     Assigned Numbers, lists officially defined well known ports
RFC   1009     NSF Gateway Specs, review of IP routing and Gateway technology
RFC   959      FTP Specs
RFC   950      Description of subnets
RFC   882/2    Domains, describes Internet address conversion database
RFC   854/5    Telnet Specs, remote login protocol
RFC   826      ARP, protocol used to find out Ethernet addresses
RFC   821/2    mail
RFC   814      names/ports, concepts of well known ports
RFC   793      TCP Specs
RFC   792      ICMP Specs
RFC   791      IP Specs
RFC   768      UDP Specs
RFC   813      TCP, window and acknowledgement strategies
RFC   815      Packet reassembly techniques
RFC   816      Fault isolation and resolution techniques
RFC   817      Modularity and efficiency in implementation
RFC   879      TCP, maximum segment size option
RFC   896      Congestion control
```

A collection of the most important RFCs have been combined into a special three volume document called The DDN Protocol Handbook. This three volume set, as well as any RFC document of interest, is available by contacting the DDN Network Information Center at:

DDN Network Information Center
SRI International
Room EJ291
333 Ravenswood Avenue
Menlo Park, CA. 94025

CHAPTER 15

UNIX LOGS AND FILES

In this chapter, several important UNIX files and directories are described. These files include system administration files and certain logs used to keep track of events and errors.

The /bin Directory

The first directory is called /bin. This directory is where many of the user commands are kept. The following is a listing of these commands:

```
tsm: ls -las /bin
total 3351
3    drwxrwxr-x    2  bin   bin      1504  Apr  2  22:07  .
1    drwxrwxr-x   16  root  sys       432  Apr 25  23:33  ..
74   -r-xr-xr-x    1  bin   bin     37104  Jan  4  1986   ar
223  -rwxrwxr-x    1  bin   bin    112466  Jan  4  1986   as
2    -r-xr-xr-x    1  bin   bin       853  Jan  4  1986   basename
12   -r-xr-xr-x    1  bin   bin      5580  Jan  4  1986   cat
54   -rwxr-xr-x    1  bin   bin     27024  Jan  3  1986   cc
14   -r-xr-xr-x    1  bin   bin      6226  Jan  4  1986   chgrp
8    -r-xr-xr-x    1  bin   bin      3990  Jan  4  1986   chmod
14   -r-xr-xr-x    1  bin   bin      6490  Jan  4  1986   chown
6    -r-xr-xr-x    1  bin   bin      2696  Jan  4  1986   cmp
75   -rwxrwxr-x    1  bin   bin     37694  Jan  4  1986   conv
58   -rwxrwxr-x    1  bin   bin     28816  Jan  4  1986   convert
```

```
 31  -r-xr-xr-x   3 bin    bin      15100 Jan  3 1986   cp
 72  -r-xr-xr-x   1 bin    bin      36340 Jan  3 1986   cpio
 55  -rwxrwxr-x   1 bin    bin      27490 Jan  4 1986   cprs
 64  -r-xr-xr-x   1 bin    bin      32084 Jan  4 1986   crypt
 14  -r-xr-xr-x   1 bin    bin       6566 Jan  4 1986   date
 24  -r-xr-xr-x   1 bin    bin      11360 Jan  4 1986   dd
 17  -r-sr-xr-x   2 root   bin       7776 Jan  4 1986   df
  1  -rwx------   1 root   other       20 Jan  4 12:11  die
 16  -r-xr-xr-x   1 bin    bin       7630 Jan  4 1986   diff
  2  -r-xr-xr-x   1 bin    bin        653 Jan  4 1986   dirname
133  -rwxrwxr-x   1 bin    bin      67196 Jan  4 1986   dis
  6  -r-xr-xr-x   1 bin    bin       3010 Jan  4 1986   du
 96  -rwxrwxr-x   1 bin    bin      48428 Jan  4 1986   dump
  8  -r-xr-xr-x   1 bin    bin       3648 Jan  4 1986   echo
 62  -r-xr-xr-x   2 bin    bin      30752 Jan  4 1986   ed
 19  -r-xr-xr-x   1 bin    bin       9032 Jan  4 1986   env
 15  -r-xr-xr-x   1 bin    bin       7004 Jan  3 1986   expr
  1  -r-xr-xr-x   7 bin    bin        270 Jan  3 1986   false
 25  -r-xr-xr-x   1 bin    bin      12002 Jan  4 1986   file
 44  -r-xr-xr-x   1 bin    bin      21902 Jan  3 1986   find
  7  -rwxr-xr-x   1 bin    bin       3348 Jan  3 1986   gencc
 14  -r-xr-xr-x   1 bin    bin       6562 Jan  4 1986   grep
 27  -rwxrwxr-x   1 bin    bin      12922 Jan  4 1986   ipcrm
 72  -rwxr-sr-x   1 root   sys      36320 Jan  4 1986   ipcs
  4  -r-xr-xr-x   1 bin    bin       1846 Jan  4 1986   kill
260  -rwxrwxr-x   1 bin    bin     131224 Jan  4 1986   ld
  2  -r-xr-xr-x   1 bin    bin        748 Jan  4 1986   line
 66  -rwxr-xr-x   1 bin    bin      32806 Jan  3 1986   list
 31  -r-xr-xr-x   3 bin    bin      15100 Jan  3 1986   ln
 36  -r-sr-xr-x   1 root   bin      17662 Jan  4 1986   login
  4  -rwxrwxr-x   1 bin    bin       1929 Jan  4 1986   lorder
 35  -r-xr-xr-x   1 bin    bin      16972 Jan  6 1986   ls
 81  -r-xr-sr-x   2 bin    mail     40706 Jan  4 1986   mail
128  -r-xr-xr-x   1 bin    bin      64898 Jan  4 1986   make
  5  -r-xr-xr-x   1 bin    bin       2336 Jan  4 1986   mesg
 12  -r-xr-xr-x   1 bin    bin       5414 Jan  3 1986   mkdir
101  -rwxrwxr-x   1 bin    bin      51100 Jan  3 1986   mkshlib
 31  -r-xr-xr-x   3 bin    bin      15100 Jan  3 1986   mv
 23  -rwsr-xr-x   1 root   sys      11024 Jan  4 1986   newgrp
 31  -r-xr-xr-x   1 bin    bin      15168 Jan  4 1986   nice
 74  -rwxrwxr-x   1 bin    bin      37192 Jan  4 1986   nm
 33  -r-xr-xr-x   1 bin    bin      15982 Jan  4 1986   nohup
 28  -r-xr-xr-x   1 bin    bin      13778 Jan  4 1986   od
 25  -r-sr-sr-x   1 root   sys      12068 Jan  4 1986   passwd
  1  -r-xr-xr-x   7 bin    bin        270 Jan  3 1986   pdp11
 22  -r-xr-xr-x   1 bin    bin      10676 Jan  4 1986   pr
 64  -r-xr-sr-x   1 bin    sys      32060 Jan  4 1986   ps
  6  -r-xr-xr-x   1 bin    bin       2662 Jan  4 1986   pwd
 62  -r-xr-xr-x   2 bin    bin      30752 Jan  4 1986   red
 14  -r-xr-xr-x   1 bin    bin       6612 Jan  3 1986   rm
```

```
81 -r-xr-sr-x  2 bin   mail   40706 Jan  4  1986   rmail
12 -r-xr-xr-x  1 bin   bin     5474 Jan  3  1986   rmdir
97 -r-xr-xr-x  2 bin   root   49048 Jan  3  1986   rsh
33 -r-xr-xr-x  1 bin   bin    16144 Jan  4  1986   sed
47 -r-xr-xr-x  1 root  sys    23104 Jan  4  1986   setpgrp
97 -r-xr-xr-x  2 bin   root   49048 Jan  3  1986   sh
49 -rwxrwxr-x  1 bin   bin    24314 Jan  4  1986   size
 4 -r-xr-xr-x  1 bin   bin     1962 Jan  4  1986   sleep
25 -r-xr-xr-x  1 bin   bin    12182 Jan  4  1986   sort
77 -rwxrwxr-x  1 bin   bin    38422 Jan  4  1986   strip
35 -r-xr-xr-x  1 bin   bin    17364 Jan  4  1986   stty
50 -r-sr-xr-x  1 root  sys    24916 Jan  4  1986   su
24 -r-xr-xr-x  1 bin   bin    11704 Jan  4  1986   sum
 1 -r-xr-xr-x  1 bin   bin      408 Jan  3  1986   sync
 6 -r-xr-xr-x  1 bin   bin     2996 Jan  4  1986   tail
 5 -r-xr-xr-x  1 bin   bin     2140 Jan  4  1986   tee
12 -r-xr-xr-x  1 bin   bin     5328 Jan  4  1986   time
 9 -r-xr-xr-x  1 bin   bin     4394 Jan  4  1986   touch
 1 -r-xr-xr-x  2 bin   bin      260 Jan  3  1986   true
25 -r-xr-xr-x  1 bin   bin    12044 Jan  4  1986   tty
 1 -r-xr-xr-x  7 bin   bin      270 Jan  3  1986   u370
 1 -r-xr-xr-x  7 bin   bin      270 Jan  3  1986   u3b
 1 -r-xr-xr-x  7 bin   bin      270 Jan  3  1986   u3b15
 1 -r-xr-xr-x  2 bin   bin      260 Jan  3  1986   u3b2
 1 -r-xr-xr-x  7 bin   bin      270 Jan  3  1986   u3b5
46 -r-xr-xr-x  1 bin   bin    22928 Apr  2 22:07   umodem
 6 -r-xr-xr-x  1 bin   bin     2574 Jan  4  1986   uname
 1 -r-xr-xr-x  7 bin   bin      270 Jan  3  1986   vax
 4 -r-xr-xr-x  1 bin   bin     2046 Jan  4  1986   wc
30 -r-xr-xr-x  1 bin   bin    14552 Jan  4  1986   who
21 -r-xr-xr-x  1 bin   bin     9786 Jan  4  1986   write
tsm:
```

The /etc Directory

A full listing of the /etc directory is as follows:

```
tsm: ls -las /etc
total 2814
   4 drwxrwxr-x 14 root  sys    2016 Apr 25 23:33   .
   1 drwxrwxr-x 16 root  sys     432 Apr 25 23:33   ..
   1 -r--r--r--  1 root  sys      66 Apr 16 21:29   TIMEZONE
   0 -rw-r--r--  1 root  root      0 Apr 25 23:32   advtab
   1 -rwxr--r--  1 root  sys     415 Jan  4  1986   bcheckrc
   1 -rwxr--r--  1 root  sys     167 Jan  4  1986   brc
   2 -rw-r--r--  1 root  sys     840 Jan  4  1986   bupsched
   1 -rwxr--r--  1 root  sys     398 Jan  4  1986   bzapunix
   1 -rw-rw-r--  1 root  sys      17 May 21  1987   checklist
```

355

```
 39 -r-xr-xr-x   1 bin    bin       19066  Jan  4  1986  chroot
 22 -r-xr-xr-x   1 root   root      10398  Jan  4  1986  ckauto
 21 -rwxr-xr-x   1 root   sys        9828  Jan  4  1986  ckbupscd
  5 -r-xr-xr-x   1 bin    bin        2324  Jan  4  1986  clri
 13 -r-xr-xr-x   1 root   root       5856  Jan 13  1986  cmpress
  2 -rw-r--r--   1 root   sys         800  Jan  4  1986  coredirs
263 -r-xr-xr-x   1 bin    bin      133078  Jan  4  1986  crash
 53 -r-xr--r--   1 bin    bin       26538  Jan  4  1986  cron
 73 -r-xr-xr-x   1 root   root      36412  Jan 13  1986  ctccpio
 26 -r-xr-xr-x   1 root   root      12692  Jan 13  1986  ctcfmt
 31 -r-xr-xr-x   1 root   root      14952  Jan 13  1986  ctcinfo
 30 -r-xr-xr-x   1 bin    bin       14458  Jan  4  1986  dcopy
 17 -r-sr-xr-x   2 root   bin        7776  Jan  4  1986  devnm
 18 -r-xr-xr-x   1 bin    bin        8458  Jan  4  1986  dfsck
  2 -r--r--r--   1 root   sys         563  Jan  4  1986  disketteparm
 17 -rwxr-xr-x   1 root   sys        8078  Jan  4  1986  disks
 27 -rwxr-xr-x   1 bin    bin       13048  Jan  4  1986  drvinstall
  7 -r-xr-x---   1 root   root       3399  Jan  4  1986  editsa
 31 -rwxr-xr-x   1 bin    bin       15040  Jan  4  1986  edittbl
 12 -rwxr-xr-x   1 bin    bin        5612  Jan  4  1986  errdump
 33 -r-xr-xr-x   1 bin    bin       16134  Jan  4  1986  ff
 38 -r-xr-xr-x   1 root   root      18608  Jan 13  1986  finc
 12 -r-xr-xr-x   1 bin    bin        5504  Jan  4  1986  fltboot
 10 -r-xr-xr-x   1 root   sys        4796  Jan  4  1986  fmtflop
 24 -r-xr-xr-x   1 root   root      11660  Jan  3  1986  fmthard
 55 -r-xr-xr-x   1 root   root      27316  Jan 13  1986  frec
 57 -r-xr-xr-x   1 root   root      28174  Jan  3  1986  fsck
 56 -r-xr-xr-x   1 bin    bin       28144  Jan  4  1986  fsck1b
 40 -r-xr-xr-x   1 bin    bin       19604  Jan  4  1986  fsdb
 37 -r-xr-xr-x   1 bin    bin       18326  Jan  4  1986  fsdb1b
  5 -r-xr-xr-x   1 root   sys        2186  Jan  4  1986  fsstat
  1 -rw-r--r--   1 root   root         43  May 21  1987  fstab
  2 -r-xr-xr-x   1 root   sys         704  Jan  4  1986  fstyp
  1 drwxrwxr-x   2 root   sys          48  Jan  6  1986  fstyp.d
 10 -r-xr-x---   1 root   root       4984  Jan  3  1986  fsys
 23 -r-xr-xr-x   1 bin    bin       10894  Jan  4  1986  fuser
  9 -r-xr-xr-x   1 bin    bin        4532  Jan  4  1986  getmajor
 29 -r-xr--r--   1 root   bin       13946  Jan  4  1986  getty
  5 -rw-rw-r--   1 root   bin        2225  May 21  1987  gettydefs
  1 -rw-r--r--   1 root   sys         160  Jan  8  07:39  group
 10 -r-xr-xr-x   1 bin    bin        5066  Jan  4  1986  grpck
 87 -r-xr-xr-x   1 bin    bin       43914  Jan  4  1986  hdeadd
 98 -r-xr-xr-x   1 bin    bin       49398  Jan  4  1986  hdefix
 81 -r-xr-xr-x   1 bin    bin       40750  Jan  4  1986  hdelogger
  4 -rwxr-xr-x   1 bin    bin        1983  Jan  4  1986  helpadm
 75 -r-xr-xr-x   2 root   bin       37886  Jan  3  1986  init
  1 drwxrwxr-x   2 root   sys         224  May 10  1987  init.d
  3 -rw-rw-r--   1 bin    bin        1417  Jan  8  07:56  inittab
 12 -r-xr-xr-x   1 bin    bin        5524  Jan  4  1986  install
  1 -rw-r--r--   1 root   root         41  Mar 29  16:39  ioctl.syscon
```

```
 12 -r-xr-xr-x  1 bin   bin    5284  Jan  4  1986   killall
 12 -r-xr-xr-x  1 bin   bin    5524  Jan  4  1986   labelit
 13 -r-xr-xr-x  1 bin   bin    5734  Jan  4  1986   ldsysdump
  4 -r-xr-x---  1 bin   bin    1556  Jan  4  1986   led
  2 -r-x------  1 root  root    536  Jan  4  1986   link
  1 drwxrwxr-x  2 root  sys      32  Jan  4  1986   log
  6 -r--r--r--  1 bin   bin    2907  Jan  4  1986   magic
  2 drwxrwxr-x  2 root  sys     528  Jan  8  07:55  master.d
 99 -r-xr-xr-x  1 root  root  50064  Jan  4  1986   mkboot
 18 -r-xr-xr-x  1 bin   bin    8554  Jan  3  1986   mkfs
  9 -r-xr-xr-x  1 bin   bin    4470  Jan  4  1986   mknod
 77 -r-xr-xr-x  1 root  root  38886  Jan  4  1986   mkunix
  1 -rw-r--r--  1 root  bin     144  Apr 25  23:33  mnttab
  0 -rw-r--r--  1 root  sys       0  Jan  4  1986   motd
125 -r-xr-xr-x  1 bin   bin   63050  Jan  4  1986   mount
  4 -r-xr-xr-x  1 root  sys    1937  Jan  4  1986   mountall
  3 -r-xr--r--  1 root  bin    1125  Jan  4  1986   mvdir
  9 -r-xr-xr-x  1 bin   bin    4502  Jan  4  1986   ncheck
 14 -r-xr-xr-x  1 bin   bin    6244  Jan  4  1986   newboot
  0 -rw-r--r--  1 root  root      0  Apr 24  20:14  oadvtab
  3 -r--r--r--  1 root  sys    1335  Apr 11  21:36  opasswd
  3 -r--r--r--  1 root  sys    1206  Apr 16  16:26  passwd
 12 -r-xr-xr-x  1 bin   bin    5288  Jan  4  1986   ports
 10 -r-xr-xr-x  1 bin   bin    4766  Jan  4  1986   prfdc
  8 -r-xr-xr-x  1 bin   bin    3822  Jan  4  1986   prfld
 13 -r-xr-xr-x  1 bin   bin    6082  Jan  4  1986   prfpr
  3 -r-xr-xr-x  1 bin   bin    1172  Jan  4  1986   prfsnap
  4 -r-xr-xr-x  1 bin   bin    1776  Jan  4  1986   prfstat
  2 -rw-rw-rw-  1 root  sys     572  May 12  1987   profile
 43 -r-xr-xr-x  1 root  sys   21336  Jan  4  1986   prtconf
 22 -r-xr-xr-x  1 root  sys   10304  Jan  3  1986   prtvtoc
  9 -rw-rw-r--  1 root  sys    4596  Apr 25  23:33  ps_data
 17 -r-xr--r--  1 root  sys    8050  Jan  4  1986   pump
  6 -r-xr-xr-x  1 bin   bin    2668  Jan  4  1986   pwck
  1 drwxrwxr-x  2 root  sys      96  Oct 19  1987   rc.d
  2 -rwxr--r--  1 root  sys     846  Jan  4  1986   rc0
  1 drwxrwxr-x  2 root  sys      96  Jan 13  00:53  rc0.d
  3 -rwxr--r--  1 root  sys    1084  Jan  4  1986   rc2
  1 drwxrwxr-x  2 root  sys     224  Jan 13  00:53  rc2.d
  1 -rwxr--r--  1 root  sys     392  Jan  4  1986   rc3
  1 drwxrwxr-x  2 root  sys      48  Jan  8  07:52  rc3.d
  1 drwxrwxr-x  2 root  sys      48  Jan  6  1986   save.d
  7 -r-xr-xr-x  1 root  sys    3319  Jan  4  1986   savecpio
  6 -r-xr-x---  1 bin   bin    2886  Jan  4  1986   setclk
  2 -r-xr-xr-x  1 bin   bin     884  Jan  4  1986   setmnt
  5 -rwxrwxr-x  1 root  sys    2259  Jan  4  1986   shutdown
  1 drwxrwxr-x  2 root  sys      32  Jan  4  1986   shutdown.d
  1 -r--r--r--  1 root  sys     242  May 11  1987   stdprofile
 31 -r-xr-xr-x  1 bin   bin   14940  Jan  4  1986   swap
 42 -r-xr-xr-x  1 bin   bin   20890  Jan  4  1986   sysdef
```

```
   2 -rw-r--r--   1 root   root      965   Jan 18   07:55   system
  60 -r-xr-xr-x   1 root   root    30024   Jan  3   1986    tar
  75 -r-xr-xr-x   2 root   bin     37886   Jan  3   1986    telinit
 144 -r-xr-xr-x   1 bin    bin     71714   Jan  6   1986    termcap
   1 drwxrwxr-x   2 root   sys        32   Jan  4   1986    tm
   6 -r-xr-xr-x   1 root   root     2749   Jan 13   1986    tsavecpio
   7 -r-xr-xr-x   1 root   sys      3158   Jan  3   1986    uadmin
  19 -r-xr-xr-x   1 bin    bin      9144   Jan  4   1986    umount
   2 -r-xr-xr-x   1 root   sys       918   Jan  4   1986    umountall
   2 -r-x------   1 root   bin       522   Jan  4   1986    unlink
   1 -rw-r--r--   1 root   bin       360   Apr 26   00:26   utmp
  69 -r-xr-xr-x   1 bin    bin     34676   Jan  4   1986    volcopy
   1 drwxrwxr-x   2 root   sys        80   Oct 19   1987    vtoc
  26 -r-xr-xr-x   1 bin    bin     12468   Jan  4   1986    wall
  25 -r-xr-sr-x   1 bin    sys     12054   Jan  4   1986    whodo
 161 -rw-rw-r--   1 adm    adm     80820   Apr 26   00:26   wtmp
tsm:
```

The /etc/TIMEZONE File

The /etc/TIMEZONE file specifies the default time zone for a UNIX machine. The TIMEZONE value is an integer used as an offset from Greenwich Mean Time (GMT) so that the local time for the UNIX machine can be calculated. Certain values have mnemonic aliases, such as EDT for Eastern Daylight Time and CST for Central Standard Time. This file is used by the UNIX system to calculate the correct local time.

The /etc/bupsched File

This file is actually a text file input used to create a **crontab** for establishing a backup schedule.

The /etc/checklist File

The /etc/checklist file contains a list of device pathnames used by the **fsck** command. When the **fsck** command (file system check) is invoked without a device, this file provides the list of devices upon which to perform the file system checking.

A sample listing of the /etc/checklist file follows:

```
tsm: cat /etc/checklist
/dev/rdsk/c1d1s8
tsm:
```

The /etc/gettydefs File

The /etc/gettydefs file contains configuration information for the various tty devices defined on the system. The general format of the fields which make up the entries in this file is:

```
label # iflag(s) # fflag(s) # prompt # next-label
```

The first field is called label, and is usually the baud rate associated with the entry. The next field, iflag, defines the terminal characteristics in effect until the getty process executes the login sequence. The fflags define the terminal characteristics after a user logs in. For either of these fields there may be multiple values specified, separated by white space. The prompt entry is a character string (spaces allowed) which appears on the device while waiting for logins. The last field is the label name of the next gettydef entry to use when the BREAK key is pressed during a login attempt. A sample gettydefs file may look like this:

```
tsm: cat /etc/gettydefs

19200# B19200  HUPCL # B19200 SANE IXANY TAB3 HUPCL #login: #9600
 9600#  B9600   HUPCL # B9600  SANE IXANY TAB3 HUPCL #login: #4800
 4800#  B4800   HUPCL # B4800  SANE IXANY TAB3 HUPCL #login: #2400
 2400#  B2400   HUPCL # B2400  SANE IXANY TAB3 HUPCL #login: #1200
 1200#  B1200   HUPCL # B1200  SANE IXANY TAB3 HUPCL #login: #300
  300#  B300    HUPCL # B300   SANE IXANY TAB3 HUPCL #login: #19200
console# B9600 HUPCL OPOST ONLCR # B9600 SANE IXANY TAB3
#omega\nConsole Login: #console1
console1# B1200 HUPCL OPOST ONLCR # B1200 SANE IXANY TAB3 #Console
Login: #console2
console2# B300 HUPCL OPOST ONLCR # B300 SANE IXANY TAB3 #Console
Login: #console3
console3# B2400 HUPCL OPOST ONLCR # B2400 SANE IXANY TAB3 #Console
Login: #console4
```

```
console4# B4800 HUPCL OPOST ONLCR # B4800 SANE IXANY TAB3 #Console
Login: #console5
console5# B19200 HUPCL OPOST ONLCR # B19200 SANE IXANY TAB3 #Console
Login: #console
contty# B9600 HUPCL OPOST ONLCR # B9600 SANE IXANY TAB3 #login:
#contty1
contty1# B1200 HUPCL OPOST ONLCR # B1200 SANE IXANY TAB3 #login:
#contty2
contty2# B300 HUPCL OPOST ONLCR # B300 SANE IXANY TAB3 #login:
#contty3
contty3# B2400 HUPCL OPOST ONLCR # B2400 SANE IXANY TAB3 #login:
#contty4
contty4# B4800 HUPCL OPOST ONLCR # B4800 SANE IXANY TAB3 #login:
#contty5
contty5# B19200 HUPCL OPOST ONLCR # B19200 SANE IXANY TAB3 #login:
#contty
pty# B9600 HUPCL OPOST ONLCR # B9600 SANE IXANY TAB3 #PC login: #pty
4800H# B4800 # B4800 SANE IXANY TAB3 HUPCL #login: #9600H
9600H# B9600 # B9600 SANE IXANY TAB3 HUPCL #login: #19200H
19200H# B19200 # B19200 SANE IXANY TAB3 HUPCL #login: #2400H
2400H# B2400 # B2400 SANE IXANY TAB3 HUPCL #login: #1200H
1200H# B1200 # B1200 SANE IXANY TAB3 HUPCL #login: #300H
300H# B300 # B300 SANE IXANY TAB3 HUPCL #login: #4800H
conttyH# B9600 OPOST ONLCR # B9600 HUPCL SANE IXANY TAB3 #login:
#contty1H
contty1H# B1200 OPOST ONLCR # B1200 HUPCL SANE IXANY TAB3 #login:
#contty2H
contty2H# B300 OPOST ONLCR # B300 HUPCL SANE IXANY TAB3 #login:
#contty3H
contty3H# B2400 OPOST ONLCR # B2400 HUPCL SANE IXANY TAB3 #login:
#contty4H
contty4H# B4800 OPOST ONLCR # B4800 HUPCL SANE IXANY TAB3 #login:
#contty5H
contty5H# B19200 OPOST ONLCR # B19200 HUPCL SANE IXANY TAB3 #login:
#conttyH
tsm:
```

The /etc/group File

The /etc/group file contains the names of the groups recognized as part of the access permissions. Each line in the file identifies the name of the group, a group ID number, and all user IDs belonging to that group. A sample /etc/group file may look like this:

```
tsm: cat /etc/group
root::0:root
other::1:tsm,wbu,dkm,pati,kdb
```

```
bin::2:root,bin,daemon
sys::3:root,bin,sys,adm
adm::4:root,adm,daemon
mail::6:root
rje::8:rje,shqer
daemon::12:root,daemon
slan::57:slan
tsm:
```

The /etc/init.d Directory

This directory contains initialization and termination scripts used when changing init states. For details, the user should view the contents of the /etc/init.d/README file. Here is a listing of the /etc/init.d directory:

```
total 24
1 drwxrwxr-x   2 root    sys    224 May 10 1987     .
4 drwxrwxr-x  14 root    sys   2016 Apr 26 01:46    ..
1 -r--r--r--   2 root    sys    107 Jan  4 1986    ANNOUNCE
1 -r--r--r--   2 root    sys    113 Jan  4 1986    MOUNTFSYS
1 -r--r--r--   2 root    sys    157 May 10 1987    PRESERVE
4 -r--r--r--   1 root    sys   1896 Jan  4 1986    README
2 -r--r--r--   2 root    sys    541 Jan  4 1986    RMTMPFILES
1 -r--r--r--   2 root    sys    475 Jan  4 1986    autoconfig
1 -r--r--r--   3 root    sys    447 Jan  4 1986    cron
1 -r--r--r--   2 root    sys    191 Jan  4 1986    disks
3 -r--r--r--   2 root    sys   1025 Jan  4 1986    firstcheck
1 -r--r--r--   2 root    sys    398 Jan  4 1986    perf
2 -r--r--r--   2 root    sys    629 Jan  4 1986    sysetup
1 -r--r--r--   2 root    sys    177 Jan  4 1986    uucp
```

The /etc/inittab File

The file /etc/inittab (initialization table) contains information used when the UNIX system is being initialized during system boot, or any time the **init** command is entered. It specifies the processes to be started (or terminated) by **init**, for various run levels. The general format for an entry in the inittab file is:

```
id:run-level:init-action:process
```

The first field, is made up of one to four characters, which is a unique identifier for each entry. The run-level is a numeric value from 1 to 6 which corresponds to the various run levels. More than one level may be specified, there is no need for delimiters since the value is a single digit. Ranges may also be specified by placing a hyphen between the values. For example, 1-4 indicates run levels one through four. If there is no value specified, all run levels (1-6) are assumed. The next field, init-action, defines the action to be taken by init, that action may be any of the following:

- initdefault—The run level associated with this entry is established as the initial run level when the system is booted.

- off—Sends a process the SIGTERM warning signal, waits for 20 seconds and then kills the process using SIGKILL. The entry is ignored if the process does not exist.

- respawn—Forks the process if it does not exist. When the previous process dies, forks another. This entry is ignored if the process exists.

- wait—Forks the process and waits for it to die.

The last field, process, identifies the process that **init** is to take the preceding action upon. A sample inittab file is shown below:

```
tsm: cat /etc/inittab
zu::sysinit:/etc/bzapunix </dev/console >/dev/console 2>&1
fs::sysinit:/etc/bcheckrc </dev/console >/dev/console 2>&1
ck::sysinit:/etc/setclk </dev/console >/dev/console 2>&1
mt:23:bootwait:/etc/brc </dev/console >/dev/console 2>&1
pt:23:bootwait:/etc/ports </dev/console >/dev/console 2>&1
is:2:initdefault:
p1:s1234:powerfail:/etc/led -f              # start green LED flashing
p3:s1234:powerfail:/etc/shutdown -y -i0 -g0 >/dev/console 2>&1
s0:056:wait:/etc/rc0 >/dev/console 2>&1 </dev/console
s1:1:wait:/etc/shutdown -y -iS -g0 >/dev/console 2>&1 </dev/console
s2:23:wait:/etc/rc2 >/dev/console 2>&1 </dev/console
s3:3:wait:/etc/rc3 >/dev/console 2>&1 </dev/console
f1:056:wait:/etc/led -f >/dev/console 2>&1 </dev/console
of:0:wait:/etc/uadmin 2 0 >/dev/console 2>&1 </dev/console
fw:5:wait:/etc/uadmin 2 2 >/dev/console 2>&1 </dev/console
RB:6:wait:echo "\nThe system is being restarted." >/dev/console 2>&1
```

```
rb:6:wait:/etc/uadmin 2 1 >/dev/console 2>&1 </dev/console
co:234:respawn:/etc/getty console console
ct:234:respawn:/usr/lib/uucp/uugetty -r -t 30 contty 2400
11:234:off:/etc/getty tty11 9600
12:234:off:/etc/getty tty12 9600
13:234:off:/etc/getty tty13 9600
14:234:off:/etc/getty tty14 9600
15:234:off:/etc/getty tty15 9600
si:023456:wait:/usr/slan/lib/slninit > /dev/console
sl:023456:respawn:sh -c "sleep 20; exec /usr/slan/lib/admdaemon"
tsm:
```

The /etc/mnttab File

The /etc/mnttab file contains a list of all file systems currently mounted on the UNIX machine. It is not a normal ASCII file and should not be edited using any text editor. When the system is first booted, the **setmnt** utility initializes the mnttab file to contain an entry only for the root file system, mounted as /. Subsequently, every call to the **mount** and **unmount** programs cause updates to occur in the mnttab file. The mnttab file may be typed out using the **cat** command:

```
tsm: cat /etc/mnttab
/dev/dsk/c1d0s0/"u^/dev/dsk/c1d0s2/usr"u^
tsm:
```

The /etc/motd File

The /etc/motd (message of the day) file is used to display its contents to users' terminals when they first log into UNIX. This file is updated only by the UNIX system administrator and may contain anything they want. Traditionally, it contains a brief welcome message, or for the less serious, a bit of trivia:

```
tsm: cat /etc/motd
UNIX, it's not just a job, it's an Adventure!
tsm:
```

The /etc/passwd File

Of course, every user should know about the /etc/passwd file. This is where information is kept about all users of the UNIX system. There are several fields for the /etc/passwd records, which have the general form:

```
login-id:password:uid:gid:comments:home directory:shell
```

The first field is the text string that is the user's login ID, by convention in most UNIX environments, the user's initials (three letters). The next field is an ASCII string that represents the encrypted password for the user. This field is optional on less secure UNIX systems.

The third field is a numeric value which identifies the user's ID number. The root user is always 0 and most UNIX systems begin ordinary users with number 100. This number is arbitrarily assigned by the UNIX system administrator, or is automatically incremented when using tools such as the sysadm menu driven administration utility.

The gid field is similar to the uid field, except that this identifies the group to which the user belongs. The numeric values also have text string aliases as an alternative method of reference. The comments field is usually the full name of the user, or some other descriptive comment.

The home field identifies the user's home directory which becomes the user's current directory upon login. The last field, shell, identifies either the user's default shell, or the program which is executed upon login. If none is specified, then /bin/sh is the default. Restricted users are usually given /bin/rsh, the restricted shell. An example of /etc/passwd is:

```
tsm: cat /etc/passwd
root:W#hL((hX24-!:0:1:0000-Admin(0000) Steven Mikes:/:
daemon::1:1:0000-Admin(0000):/:
bin::2:2:0000-Admin(0000):/bin:
sys::3:3:0000-Admin(0000):/usr/src:
adm::4:4:0000-Admin(0000):/usr/adm:
uucp::5:5:0000-uucp(0000):/usr/lib/uucp:
```

```
nuucp::10:10:0000-uucp(0000):/usr/spool/uucppublic:/usr/lib/uucp/uucico
rje::18:18:0000-rje(0000):/usr/rje:
lp::71:2:0000-lp(0000):/usr/spool/lp:
setup::0:0:general system administration:/usr/admin:/bin/rsh
powerdown::0:0:general system administration:/usr/admin:/bin/rsh
sysadm:foolsonly:0:0:general system administration:/usr/admin:/bin/rsh
makefsys::0:0:make diskette file system:/usr/admin:/bin/rsh
mountfsys:pGBvbn7YT1Ecw:0:0:mount diskette file
system:/usr/admin:/bin/rsh
umountfsys:7HLXi.vmZhNzc:0:0:unmount diskette file
system:/usr/admin:/bin/rsh
tsm:iEpzUyJexcg06:100:1:Steven Mikes - Author:/usr/tsm:/bin/sh
listen:np:37:4:Network Admin:/usr/net/nls:
wbu:5FV9mNxacQiq2:101:1:William B. Urinoski:/usr/wbu:/bin/ksh
pati:WQsNdCt0eqlNs:102:1:Patricia A. Mikes:/usr/pati:/bin/sh
dani:WQsNdCt0eqlNs:103:1:Danielle K. Mikes:/usr/dani:/bin/ksh
bgv:vE299hX.CKJ2o:104:1:Bela G. Vegvary:/usr/bgv:
mlh::105:1:Maria L. Holz:/usr/mlh:
bds::106:1:Barbara D. Schwartz:/usr/bds:
crm::107:1:Clark R. McGranery - The Professor:/usr/crm:
gibbo:@zambia:108:1:Alan F. Gibbons - AccuMaster Master:/usr/afg:
bully::109:1:John Bullivant:/usr/jdb:
ggc:who_me?:110:1:Jerry G. Conte:/usr/ggc:
mmb:rukidding:111:1:Mark M. Barnett:/usr/mmb:/bin/rsh
gww:**ogosh**:0:0:Greg (Mr. DataKit) White:/usr/gww:/bin/ksh
bwk:$$guru$$:0:0:Brian W. Kernighan - UNIX & C
Demigod:/usr/bwk:/bin/ksh
dmr:$$guru$$:0:0:Dennis M. Ritchie - UNIX & C Demigod:/usr/bwk:/bin/ksh
kdb:vF34yKKlz@:112:1:Kurt D. Bauman - Learning Tree:/usr/kdb:/bin/ksh
mickey:@@2strange@@:0:0:Mickey Bauman - Learning Tree:/:/bin/ksh
slan:np:57:57:slan id:/usr/slan:
admin::36:1:MS-NET Administrator:/usr/net/servers/msnet/admin:
tsm:
```

The /etc/profile File

The /etc/profile file contains a script executed by the login shell, which is the first shell every user executes when they log into UNIX, before their own .profile shell script. The contents of this shell are determined by the UNIX system administrator. A sample script is listed here:

```
tsm: cat /etc/profile
#ident   "@(#)/etc/profile.sl 1.1 3.0 11/18/85 5081"
#                         The profile that all logins get before using
                          their own .profile.
```

```
trap ""   2 3
export LOGNAME

. /etc/TIMEZONE

#                           Login and -su shells get /etc/profile services.
#                           -rsh is given its environment in its .profile.
case "$0" in
-su )
                            export PATH
                            ;;

-sh )
                            export PATH

                            #          Allow the user to break the
                                       Message-Of-The-Day only.
                            trap "trap '' 2"   2
                            cat -s /etc/motd
                            trap ""  2

                            if mail -e
                            then
                                       echo "you have mail"
                            fi

                            if [ ${LOGNAME} != root ]
                            then
                                       news -n
                            fi
                            ;;
esac

umask 022
trap   2 3
stty echoe erase "^H"
tsm:
```

The /etc/shutdown File

The /etc/shutdown file is a shell script that is used by the system administrator when the UNIX system is being halted or rebooted. The command sequence insures an orderly shutdown of UNIX system services without causing inconveniences for other users who may be logged on.

The /etc/stdprofile File

The /etc/stdprofile file is a prototype used as the model .profile created when new user entries are made. A sample is shown below:

```
tsm: cat /etc/stdprofile
#ident   "@(#)/etc/stdprofile.sl 1.1 3.0 11/18/85 18386"
#          This is the default standard profile provided to a user.
#          They are expected to edit it to meet their own needs.

MAIL=/usr/mail/${LOGNAME:?}
stty erase '^H'
PS1='echo $LOGNAME'
PS2=>>
tsm:
```

The /etc/termcap File

Another file, /etc/termcap, for terminal capability, contains a list of assorted terminal devices and their specific characteristics. This file may or may not be present in UNIX System V machines, since it was replaced by the terminfo facility. If your UNIX system is any version of System V, this file is obsolete and may be ignored.

The /etc/vtoc Directory

The directory /etc/vtoc has files that contain the volume table of contents defaults for equipment such as disk and tape devices. The files in this directory are created and maintained by the system administrator. A sample directory listing might contain the following:

```
tsm: ls -las /etc/vtoc
total 8
1 drwxrwxr-x       2 root   sys        80 Oct 19   1987      .
4 drwxrwxr-x      14 root   sys      2016 Apr 27   00:08     ..
1 -r--r--r--       1 root   root      450 Jan 13   1986      ctc1dft
1 -r--r--r--       1 root   root      450 Jan 13   1986      ctc2dft
1 -rw-r--r--       1 root   other     496 May 21   1987      hd3dft
tsm:
```

A sample of the information contained for the hard disk on a UNIX system is as follows:

```
tsm: cat /etc/vtoc/hd3dft
*
* CDC Wren 32M Hard Disk VTOC defaults
*
* Dimensions:
*        512       bytes/sector
*        18        sectors/track
*        5         tracks/cylinder
*        697       cylinders total
*        695       user accessible cyls
*
* Flags:
*        01:       NOT Mountable
*        10:       Read-Only
*
* Partition       ID       Flag      Start Sector      Size in Sectors
            0       0       01        0                 0
           01       0       01        0                 0
           02       0       01        0                 0
           03       0       01        0                 0
           04       0       01        0                 0
           05       0       01        0                 0
           06       0       01        0                 62550
           07       0       01        0                 90
           08       0       00        90                62460
           09       0       01        0                 0
           10       0       01        0                 0
           11       0       01        0                 0
           12       0       01        0                 0
           13       0       01        0                 0
           14       0       01        0                 0
           15       0       01        0                 0
tsm:
```

The /usr Directory

This directory contains several subdirectories associated with UNIX services such as print spooling, mail, source code, and others; as well as the home directories for the users of the system. The following is a listing of the /usr directory:

```
total 37
1 drwxrwxr-x  24 root    sys    384 May   1 18:31  .
1 drwxrwxr-x  16 root    sys    432 May   1 18:30  ..
1 drwxrwxr-x   2 root    sys     32 Jan   4 1988   3bnet
1 drwxrwxr-x   5 adm     adm    112 May  10 1988   adm
1 drwxr-xr-x   7 root    sys    304 Oct   7 1987   admin
1 drwxrwxr-x   3 gibbo   other   59 Jan   3 04:10  afg
1 drwxrwxr-x   2 bds     other   48 May  12 1988   bds
1 drwxrwxr-x   2 bgv     other   48 Jan   7 01:11  bgv
5 drwxrwxr-x   3 bin     bin   2544 Jan  13 00:54  bin
1 drwxrwxr-x  10 root    root   224 Apr   2 22:20  bwk
1 drwxrwxr-x   3 crm     other   59 Jan   3 04:10  crm
1 drwxrwxr-x   2 root    root   112 Jan   3 22:22  dmr
5 drwxr-xr-x   2 ggc     other  560 Nov   6 1987   ggc
1 drwxrwxr-x  10 root    root   160 Jan  13 00:55  gww
3 drwxrwxr-x   3 bin     bin   1088 Jan   8 07:52  include
1 drwxrwxr-x   3 bully   other   59 Jan   3 04:10  jdb
1 drwxrwxrwx  10 kdb     other  208 May   1 18:40  kdb
2 drwxrwxr-x   2 bin     bin    608 Jan   6 1986   lbin
3 drwxr-xr-x  24 root    sys   1456 Jan   8 07:52  lib
5 drwxr-xr-x   2 root    root  2560 Jan   6 1986   lost+found
1 drwxrwxr-x   3 root    mail    96 Apr  28 23:45  mail
1 drwxrwxr-x  10 root    root   224 Apr   2 22:20  mickey
1 drwxrwxr-x   2 mlh     other   48 May  12 1988   mlh
1 drwxrwxr-x   3 mmb     other   39 Jan   3 04:50  mmb
1 drwxr-xr-x   4 root    sys     64 Oct   7 1986   net
1 drwxrwxrwx   2 bin     bin     32 Jan   4 1986   news
1 drwxrwxr-x   2 root    sys    496 Jan  13 00:57  options
1 drwxrwxr-x   2 pati    other   48 May  12 1987   pati
1 drwxrwxrwx   2 bin     bin     32 Jan   6 1986   preserve
1 drwxrwxr-x   2 bin     bin     32 Jan   4 1986   pub
1 drwxrwxr-x   9 slan    slan   144 Jan   8 07:54  slan
1 drwxrwxr-x  10 root    bin    160 Jan  13 00:55  spool
1 drwxrwxr-x  10 root    other  224 Apr   2 22:20  src
1 drwxrwxrwx   2 sys     sys     48 May   1 18:31  tmp
1 drwxrwxrwx  10 tsm     other  208 May   1 18:40  tsm
1 drwxrwxr-x   2 wbu     other  112 Jan   3 22:22  wbu
```

The /usr/adm/sulog File

This file contains a history of all attempts to become another user through the use of the **su** command, whether successful or not. Each entry contains the date and time of the attempt, the device location from where the attempt was made, the user ID making the attempt, and the user ID they wanted to **su** to. An example of the /usr/adm/sulog follows:

```
tsm: su
# tail /usr/adm/sulog
SU 04/27 23:08 + console root-sys
SU 04/27 23:11 + console tsm-root
SU 04/27 23:11 + console tsm-sysadm
SU 04/28 20:13 + console root-sys
SU 04/28 23:21 + console tsm-root
SU 04/28 23:22 + console tsm-root
SU 04/28 23:45 + tty??    root-uucp
SU 04/29 02:02 + console tsm-root
SU 05/01 18:30 + console root-sys
SU 05/01 20:58 + console tsm-root
# exit
tsm:
```

The /usr/adm/sa Directory

The /usr/adm/sa directory contains binary files created by the shell script /usr/lib/sa1, that is part of the System Activity Report package. The data in the files are system activity information about resource usage and are usually only of interest to UNIX system administrators. In a large multiuser installation, the files in this directory can become quite big. They are usually cleaned up by system administrators using an entry in their crontab file.

The /usr/admin Directory

The directory /usr/admin contains shell scripts and directories used by the unixadmin set of utilities.

The /usr/bin Directory

This directory contains the binary executables of more utility commands that many users use regularly, such as **vi**, **banner**, **cu**, **lp**, **mailx**, and **news**. Many of the optional add-on packages that are enhancements to the UNIX system may place their executables in this location.

The /usr/include Directory

For UNIX programmers the directory /usr/include is of special interest. It contains the standard header files (and directories) used to resolve external references for many system or subroutine calls used in C language. The files in this directory are gold mines of information to curious programmers.

The /usr/lbin Directory

The /usr/lbin directory is used to store the commands that are local to your system and that are not a standard part of the UNIX system. It may contain executables (binaries or shell scripts) and various files. The exact contents are determined by the optional packages the system has installed, and other user supplied executables.

The /usr/lib Directory

The /usr/lib directory is used as a kind of catch all for directories, commands, shell scripts, and various files, usually in some way related by groups, such as by activity or device. In UNIX system terminology, lib usually means libraries; archives of compiled program functions to be used for resolution of external references in programs. Besides object libraries, other files and directories are also to be found. The exact order or contents varies between UNIX systems, according to which options have been installed.

Consistency is not greatly enforced in the /usr/lib directory. For example, in the directory /usr/lib/uucp, many important files and programs used by the uucp facility may be found, yet for printers some programs may be found in /usr/lib while other printer programs may be found in the directory for the spooler. There are several interesting directories in /usr/lib.

The /usr/lib/cron Directory

The directory /usr/lib/cron contains the cron log file (/usr/lib/cron/log), and among other things, the optional files:

```
/usr/lib/cron/cron.allow
/usr/lib/cron/cron.deny
/usr/lib/cron/at.allow
/usr/lib/cron/at.deny
```

The /usr/lib/help Directory

This directory contains several files used by the UNIX system On-Line Help facility, which also includes a usage log of what help was asked for and by which user login.

The /usr/lib/mailx Directory

If the extended mail utilities are installed, this directory contains files used by the **mailx** command. The **mailx** command is an optional extended alternative to the standard **mail** command that comes as part of the standard UNIX system.

The /usr/lib/sa Directory

This directory contains commands and shell scripts used by the System Activity Report utilities.

The /usr/lib/spell Directory

The /usr/lib/spell directory contains commands and utilities used by the UNIX Spell package. In this directory, the /usr/lib/spell/spellhist file contains a list of every word which the **spell** command failed to match. The words in this directory should be reviewed and if necessary, added to the dictionary.

The /usr/lib/terminfo Directory

A most interesting directory is /usr/lib/terminfo, that contains several subdirectories (1-9, a-z, A,B,M, and P). Each of these subdirectories contains terminal information files that contain the characteristics of various terminals. Each terminal type is placed into a directory, according to the first letter of the terminfo file. For example, terminfo

files for VT100 terminals would be found in the /usr/lib/terminfo/v
directory:

```
tsm: ls -las /usr/lib/terminfo/v/vt1*

3 -rw-r--r--   2 root    root         1195 May 10   1987
/usr/lib/terminfo/v/vt100
3 -rw-r--r--   2 root    root         1195 May 10   1987
/usr/lib/terminfo/v/vt100-am
3 -rw-r--r--   2 root    root         1258 May 10   1987
/usr/lib/terminfo/v/vt100-bot-s
3 -rw-r--r--   1 root    root         1194 May 10   1987
/usr/lib/terminfo/v/vt100-nam
3 -rw-r--r--   2 root    root         1226 May 10   1987
/usr/lib/terminfo/v/vt100-nam-w
3 -rw-r--r--   1 root    root         1066 May 10   1987
/usr/lib/terminfo/v/vt100-nav
3 -rw-r--r--   2 root    root         1133 May 10   1987
/usr/lib/terminfo/v/vt100-nav-w
3 -rw-r--r--   3 root    root         1284 May 10   1987
/usr/lib/terminfo/v/vt100-s
3 -rw-r--r--   2 root    root         1258 May 10   1987
/usr/lib/terminfo/v/vt100-s-bot
3 -rw-r--r--   3 root    root         1284 May 10   1987
/usr/lib/terminfo/v/vt100-s-top
3 -rw-r--r--   3 root    root         1284 May 10   1987
/usr/lib/terminfo/v/vt100-top-s
3 -rw-r--r--   2 root    root         1217 May 10   1987
/usr/lib/terminfo/v/vt100-w
3 -rw-r--r--   2 root    root         1217 May 10   1987
/usr/lib/terminfo/v/vt100-w-am
3 -rw-r--r--   2 root    root         1226 May 10   1987
/usr/lib/terminfo/v/vt100-w-nam
3 -rw-r--r--   2 root    root         1133 May 10   1987
/usr/lib/terminfo/v/vt100-w-nav
3 -rw-r--r--   1 root    root         1179 May 10   1987
/usr/lib/terminfo/v/vt125
3 -rw-r--r--   1 root    root         1185 May 10   1987
/usr/lib/terminfo/v/vt132
tsm:
```

These files are used to control the user's terminal characteristics
for such things as proper cursor movement and display controls for
editing and graphics output.

The /usr/lib/uucp Directory

This is perhaps one of the most important directories in /usr/lib and it is used by uucp. The /usr/lib/uucp directory contains the files necessary for a UNIX machine to communicate with other UNIX systems. A listing of the files in this directory follows:

```
tsm: ls -las /usr/lib/uucp

total 689
    1 drwxr-xr-x    2 uucp    sys       448  Jan 13  03:13  .
    3 drwxr-xr-x   24 root    sys      1456  Jan  8  07:52  ..
    3 -r--r--r--    1 uucp    sys      1075  Jan 13  02:49  Devconfig
    8 -r--r--r--    1 uucp    sys      3756  Apr 12  01:10  Devices
    1 -r--------    1 uucp    sys       107  Jan 13  03:10  Devices.cico
    1 -r--r--r--    1 uucp    sys        76  Jan  3  1986   Dialcodes
    8 -r--r--r--    1 uucp    sys      3665  May 12  1987   Dialers
    1 -r--------    1 uucp    sys        98  Jan 13  03:13  Dialers.cico
    1 -r--r--r--    1 uucp    root        2  May 10  1987   Maxuuscheds
    1 -r--r--r--    1 uucp    root        2  May 10  1987   Maxuuxqts
    1 -r--------    1 uucp    sys       312  May 12  1987   Permissions
    1 -r--r--r--    1 uucp    sys       358  Jan  3  1986   Poll
    4 -r-xr-xr-x    1 uucp    sys      1544  Jan  3  1986   SetUp
    4 -r--r--r--    1 uucp    sys      1839  Jan 13  03:08  Sysfiles
    3 -r--------    1 uucp    sys      1048  Apr 12  01:11  Systems
    1 -r--------    1 uucp    sys        59  Jan 13  03:01  Systems.cico
    3 -r-xr-xr-x    1 uucp    sys      1309  Jan  3  1986   Uutry
    1 -r-xr-xr-x    1 uucp    sys       161  Jan  3  1986   remote.unknown
   51 ---x--x---    1 uucp    sys     25572  Jan  3  1986   uucheck
   89 ---s--x--x    1 uucp    sys    105380  Jan  3  1986   uucico
   91 ---x--x---    1 uucp    sys     45914  Jan  3  1986   uucleanup
    2 -r-xr-xr-x    1 uucp    sys       617  Jan  3  1986   uudemon.admin
    8 -r-xr-xr-x    1 uucp    sys      3718  Jan  3  1986   uudemon.cleanu
    1 -r-xr-xr-x    1 uucp    sys       109  Jan  3  1986   uudemon.hour
    2 -r-xr-xr-x    1 uucp    sys       944  Jan  3  1986   uudemon.poll
   68 -r-xr--r--    1 uucp    sys     33976  Jan  3  1986   uugetty
   69 ---s--x--x    1 uucp    sys     34516  Jan  3  1986   uusched
   42 ---s--x--x    1 uucp    sys     70990  Jan  3  1986   uuxqt
```

The /usr/mail Directory

This directory may be thought of as the UNIX system's post office. It is used by the UNIX **mail** command as a staging area for undelivered electronic mail, which is in the form of normal files. When users are notified they have mail, or if they just enter the **mail** command to see if they do, this directory is where the **mail** command searches.

If a file bearing the user's login ID exists in the /usr/mail directory, its contents are echoed to the inquiring user's terminal. File permissions and ownerships are set according to the login ID after whom the file was named. Only the owners of the file, the root user, or a superuser may view these files.

The /usr/news Directory

The /usr/news directory contains news files. The filenames are descriptive of the file contents and may be thought of as headlines of the topics contained. When a user reads a news item using the **readnews** command, a file called .news_time is created in their home directory, and can be used to determine if they have accessed the latest news files. UNIX systems which are part of USENET may have many entries in the /usr/news directory, making it quite large.

The /usr/options Directory

The /usr/options directory contains files that are used to identify which optional utilities are installed on the UNIX system. The files themselves contain the formal name of the package, as well as the release level. Examples of these are provided below:

```
tsm: ls -las /usr/options

total 31
1 drwxrwxr-x    2 root     sys      496 Jan  13  00:57    .
1 drwxrwxr-x   24 root     sys      384 May   1  18:31    ..
1 -r-xr-xr-x    1 bin      bin       40 Jan   3  1986     acu.name
1 -r-xr-xr-x    1 bin      bin       22 Jan   4  1986     calc.name
1 -r-xr-xr-x    1 bin      bin       42 Jan   3  1986     cc.name
1 -r--r--r--    1 bin      bin       34 Jan   4  1986     crypt.name
1 -r-xr-xr-x    1 bin      bin       25 Jan  13  1986     ctc.name
1 -r-xr-xr-x    1 bin      bin       40 Jan   4  1986     dfm.name
1 -r--r--r--    1 bin      bin       68 Oct   7  1986     dossrv.name
1 -r--r--r--    1 bin      bin       18 Jan   6  1986     ed.name
1 -r-xr-xr-x    1 bin      bin       58 Jan   4  1986     esg.name
1 -r-xr-xr-x    1 bin      bin       19 Jan   4  1986     graph.name
1 -r-xr-xr-x    1 bin      bin       15 Jan   4  1986     help.name
1 -rw-r--r--    1 root     other     22 May   9  1985     informix.name
```

```
1 -r-xr-xr-x   1 bin      bin       38 Jan   4  1986    ipc.name
1 -r-xr-xr-x   1 bin      bin       32 Jan   4  1986    lp.name
1 -r--r--r--   1 bin      bin       29 Jan   5  1986    nsu.name
1 -r-xr-xr-x   1 bin      bin       34 Jan   4  1986    perf.name
1 -r-xr-xr-x   1 bin      bin       30 Aug  17  1984    sccs.name
1 -r-xr-xr-x   1 bin      bin       49 Jan   4  1986    sgs.name
1 -r-xr-xr-x   1 bin      bin       28 Jan   4  1986    shell.name
1 -r--r--r--   1 bin      bin       76 Aug   1  1986    slnNAUd.name
1 -r--r--r--   1 bin      bin       72 Aug   1  1986    slnNPPd.name
1 -r-xr-xr-x   1 bin      bin       16 Jan   4  1986    spell.name
1 -r-xr-xr-x   1 bin      bin       33 Jan   4  1986    sys.name
1 -r-xr-xr-x   1 bin      bin       32 Jan   4  1986    sysadm.name
1 -r-xr-xr-x   1 bin      bin       27 Jan   4  1986    term.name
1 -r--r--r--   1 bin      bin       31 Jan   6  1986    terminf.name
1 -r-xr-xr-x   1 bin      bin       27 Jan   4  1986    usrenv.name
1 -rwxr-xr-x   1 root     sys       27 Jan   3  1986    uucp.name
1 -rw-r--r--   1 bin      bin       24 Jan   4  1986    windowing.name
tsm:

tsm: cat /usr/options/*
Advanced C Utilities: Issue 4 Version 0
Calculation Utilities
C Programming Language: Issue 4 Version 0
Security Administration Utilities
Cartridge Tape Utilities
Directory and File Management Utilities
AT&T STARLAN NETWORK 3B2 DOS Server Program: Release 1.01 Version 1
Editing Utilities
Extended Software Generation Utilities: Issue 4 Version 0
Graphics Utilities
HELP Utilities
INFORMIX              3.3      May 1985
Inter-Process Communication Utilities
Line Printer Spooling Utilities
Networking Support Utilities
Performance Measurement Utilities
Source Code Control Utilities
Software Generation Utilities: Issue 4 Version 0
Shell Programming Utilities
AT&T STARLAN NETWORK Access Unit Package: Release 1.1.0 Version 1
AT&T STARLAN NETWORK Program Package: Release 1.1.0 Version 1
SPELL Utilities
System Header Files: Release 3.0
System Administration Utilities
Terminal Filters Utilities
Terminal Information Utilities
User Environment Utilities
Basic Networking Utilities
ATT Windowing Utilities
tsm:
```

The /usr/spool Directory

The /usr/spool directory contains several important directories as well. The first is /usr/spool/cron. This directory is used by the UNIX cron facility, which in turn contains two directories, atjobs and crontabs. The /usr/spool/cron/atjobs directory is where any atjobs are stored when they are created by users. The /usr/spool/cron/crontabs directory is where the crontab files reside for users when created using the **crontab** command.

The /usr/spool/lp Directory

This directory is the heart of the UNIX print spooling system. It contains several files and directories that make it possible to spool files for printing on multiple output print devices. All of the files and directories found here are used by the lp system. A sample of the contents of this directory is listed below:

```
tsm: ls -las /usr/spool/lp
total 10
1 drwxrwxr-x   7 lp      bin    272 May   1  18:31   .
1 drwxrwxr-x  10 root    bin    160 Jan  13  00:55   ..
0 prw-------   1 lp      bin      0 May   1  18:31   FIFO
1 -r--r--r--   1 lp      bin      4 May   1  18:31   SCHEDLOCK
1 drwxrwxr-x   2 lp      bin     32 Jan   4  1986    class
1 drwxrwxr-x   2 lp      bin     32 Jan   4  1986    interface
1 -rw-r--r--   1 lp      bin     33 May   1  18:31   log
1 drwxrwxr-x   2 lp      bin     32 Jan   4  1986    member
1 drwxrwxr-x   2 lp      bin    160 May  10  1987    model
1 -rw-r--r--   1 lp      bin     67 Apr  29  02:03   oldlog
0 -rw-r--r--   1 lp      bin      0 May   1  18:31   outputq
0 -rw-r--r--   1 lp      bin      0 Jan   4  1986    pstatus
0 -rw-r--r--   1 lp      bin      0 Jan   4  1986    qstatus
1 drwxrwxr-x   2 lp      bin     32 Jan   4  1986    request
tsm:
```

The /usr/spool/lp/SCHEDLOCK File

The is a lock file, usually only of interest to UNIX system administrators and the lpsched daemon. When this file is present, it means the lpsched daemon is already active and causes a subsequent lpsched daemon to abort if an attempt is made to start one. It is intended to prevent possible damage to the already active lp system (lpsched daemon), due to reinitialization before it is properly quiesced.

If the lpsched daemon is not active and the SCHEDLOCK file is present, before the lpsched daemon will successfully start up this file must be deleted. This file must not be deleted if the lpsched daemon is already active!

The /usr/spool/lp/FIFO File

In this directory, the file FIFO is a named pipe that sets up communications between the lpsched daemon and the user command lp.

The /usr/spool/lp/class Directory

This directory contains information about printer classes. Printers can be assigned to a printer class, a group of printers that share a spool queue. When there are multiple printers servicing a printer class, the lp system manages the spool queue by sending print jobs to printers when they become idle. If a printer is busy, when it becomes idle it receives its next output job from the shared queue. Printers of the same or similar type are assigned to service one class, while printers of different types service other classes.

An example of this is the difference between laser printers and dot matrix or other impact printers. A UNIX system administrator assigns printer classes to printers during the configuration of the lp system by using the **lpadmin** command.

The /usr/spool/lp/interface Directory

This directory is where the executable interface programs for each printer (or class) reside.

The /usr/spool/lp/log File

The /usr/spool/lp/log file contains a listing of all files sent to printers that have been printed. The information includes the lp job request

ID, the sender's login ID, the device name of the printer, and a time and date stamp.

The /usr/spool/lp/member Directory

This directory contains files for each printer or class and is used only by the lp system.

The /usr/spool/lp/model Directory

In the /usr/spool/model directory, sample interface programs may be found for each printer or class. These programs provide an interface between the user command lp and the physical devices representing the printers.

The /usr/spool/lp/oldlog File

The file /usr/spool/lp/oldlog is the previous log saved after the lpsched daemon has been stopped and restarted. The log file is copied to oldlog by the lpsched daemon before starting a new log.

The outputq, pstatus, and qstatus Files

These three files are used by the lpsched daemon internally and are of little use to anyone else.

The /usr/spool/lp/request Directory

This directory contains subdirectories for each printer configured on the system. Text files that are spooled are placed into one of these directories by the **lp** command and are removed when the files has finished printing. The directories in /usr/spool/lp/request are the queues where print jobs await printing while a print device is busy or unavailable.

The /usr/spool/uucppublic Directory

The /usr/spool/uucppublic is a directory on each UNIX system for the purpose of being an open repository for undeliverable uucp files, as well as for many other things. If, for example, a user wanted to send some files to another user on a different UNIX machine, but did not know what directory to send them to, or did not have sufficient access permissions to place them directly into their home directory, then a good place to leave them might be /usr/spool/uucppublic.

This assumes, of course, that the data is not critical; for anybody may do anything with the data. (Encrypted data is useless to anyone without the correct decryption key.) On busy UNIX systems this directory often becomes quite large and is processed by the uucleanup utility.

The /usr/spool/uucp Directory

This directory contains directories owned by the uucp administrative login (also called uucp). The uucp subsystem is discussed later in more detail in the chapter on networking and also in the chapter on UNIX System Administration.

The /usr/src Directory

The /usr/src directory is usually where the source code for the UNIX commands and kernel reside. Most UNIX systems do not have the source code available, or at least not many have the kernel code.

Besides the source code for UNIX and its commands, by convention any source code for other packages is kept here. A sample directory listing follows:

```
tsm: ls -las /usr/src
total 40
   1 drwxrwxr-x    10 root    other     224 Apr  2  22:20   .
   1 drwxrwxr-x    24 root    sys       384 May  1  18:31   ..
  15 -rwxrwxrwx     1 tsm     other    6823 Mar 20  1986   :mkcmd
   3 -rwxrwxrwx     1 tsm     other    1128 Sep 30  1986   :mkhead
   2 -rwxrwxrwx     1 tsm     other     944 Aug 25  1986   :mksyshead
   4 -rwxrwxrwx     1 tsm     other    1903 Mar 20  1986   :mkuts
   5 drwxrwxrwx   129 tsm     other    2096 May 13  1987   cmd
   1 drwxrwxrwx     9 tsm     other     256 Dec 14  01:27   dts
   2 drwxrwxrwx     2 tsm     other     960 May 13  1987   head
   2 drwxrwxrwx     2 tsm     other     768 Dec 15  02:16   kermit4C
   1 drwxrwxrwx    11 tsm     other     176 May 13  1987   lib
   1 drwxrwxrwx    21 tsm     other     336 May 13  1987   scripts
```

```
1 drwxrwxrwx    2 tsm      other       80 Apr   2 22:48    umodem
1 drwxrwxrwx    3 tsm      other       48 May 13 1987      uts
tsm: ls -las /usr/src/cmd
total 177
5 drwxrwxrwx  129 tsm      other     2096 May 13 1987      .
1 drwxrwxr-x   10 root     other      224 Apr   2 22:20    ..
1 drwxrwxrwx    4 root     other       96 May 13 1987      .adm
1 drwxrwxrwx    3 root     other      112 May 13 1987      .cmd-3b2
1 drwxrwxrwx    2 tsm      other      128 May 13 1987      acct
1 drwxrwxrwx    2 tsm      other       48 May 13 1987      adv
1 drwxrwxrwx    4 tsm      other       80 May 13 1987      assist
1 drwxrwxrwx    2 tsm      other      208 May 13 1987      awk
1 drwxrwxrwx    2 tsm      other       48 May 13 1987      bbh
1 drwxrwxrwx    2 tsm      other      416 May 13 1987      bnu.admin
1 drwxrwxrwx    2 tsm      other       48 May 13 1987      cat
1 drwxrwxrwx    2 tsm      other       64 May 13 1987      chroot
1 drwxrwxrwx    2 tsm      other       80 May 13 1987      chrtbl
1 drwxrwxrwx    2 tsm      other       64 May 13 1987      ckbupscd
1 drwxrwxrwx    2 tsm      other       48 May 13 1987      clri
1 drwxrwxrwx    2 tsm      other       48 May 13 1987      cpio
9 -rw-rw-r--    1 tsm      other     8904 Jun 27 1986      cpset.c
1 drwxrwxrwx    2 tsm      other      304 May 13 1987      crash
1 drwxrwxrwx    2 tsm      other       80 May 13 1987      cron
1 drwxrwxrwx    2 tsm      other       64 May 13 1987      ct
1 drwxrwxrwx    2 tsm      other       48 May 13 1987      ctrace
1 drwxrwxrwx    2 tsm      other       64 May 13 1987      cu
1 drwxrwxrwx    2 tsm      other       48 May 13 1987      cut
1 drwxrwxrwx    3 tsm      other       64 May 13 1987      cxref
1 drwxrwxrwx    2 tsm      other       48 May 13 1987      date
1 drwxrwxrwx    2 tsm      other       96 May 13 1987      dbfconv
1 drwxrwxrwx    2 tsm      other       48 May 13 1987      dc
1 drwxrwxrwx    2 tsm      other       48 May 13 1987      dd
1 drwxrwxrwx    2 tsm      other       48 May 13 1987      devinfo
1 drwxrwxrwx    2 tsm      other       48 May 13 1987      df
1 drwxrwxrwx    2 tsm      other       48 May 13 1987      dfsck
1 drwxrwxrwx    2 tsm      other       48 May 13 1987      disks
1 drwxrwxrwx    2 tsm      other       64 May 13 1987      dname
1 drwxrwxrwx    2 tsm      other       64 May 13 1987      ed
1 drwxrwxrwx    2 tsm      other       48 May 13 1987      edittbl
1 drwxrwxrwx    2 tsm      other       48 May 13 1987      egrep
1 drwxrwxrwx    2 tsm      other       48 May 13 1987      errdump
1 drwxrwxrwx    2 tsm      other       48 May 13 1987      expr
1 drwxrwxrwx    2 tsm      other       48 May 13 1987      ff
1 drwxrwxrwx    2 tsm      other       48 May 13 1987      file
1 drwxrwxrwx    2 tsm      other       64 May 13 1987      find
1 drwxrwxrwx    2 tsm      other       64 May 13 1987      fltboot
1 drwxrwxrwx    2 tsm      other       64 May 13 1987      fmtflop
1 drwxrwxrwx    2 tsm      other       64 May 13 1987      fmthard
1 drwxrwxrwx    2 tsm      other       48 May 13 1987      fsck
1 drwxrwxrwx    2 tsm      other       48 May 13 1987      fsdb
```

```
1 drwxrwxrwx   2 tsm    other       48  May 13   1987 fstyp
1 drwxrwxrwx   2 tsm    other       80  May 13   1987 fumount
1 drwxrwxrwx   2 tsm    other       80  May 13   1987 fusage
1 drwxrwxrwx   2 tsm    other       64  May 13   1987 fuser
1 drwxrwxrwx   2 tsm    other       48  May 13   1987 getedt
1 drwxrwxrwx   2 tsm    other       64  May 13   1987 getmajor
1 drwxrwxrwx   2 tsm    other       48  May 13   1987 getopt
1 drwxrwxrwx   2 tsm    other       48  May 13   1987 getty
1 drwxrwxrwx   4 tsm    other       64  May 13   1987 graf
1 drwxrwxrwx   2 tsm    other       48  May 13   1987 grep
1 drwxrwxrwx   2 tsm    other       64  May 13   1987 grpck
1 drwxrwxrwx   3 tsm    other       48  May 13   1987 help
1 drwxrwxrwx   2 tsm    other       48  May 13   1987 id
1 drwxrwxrwx   2 tsm    other       64  May 13   1987 idload
1 drwxrwxrwx   2 tsm    other       48  May 13   1987 init
1 drwxrwxrwx   3 tsm    other      160  May 13   1987 initpkg
1 drwxrwxrwx   2 tsm    other       48  May 13   1987 ipc
1 drwxrwxrwx   2 tsm    other       48  May 13   1987 killall
1 drwxrwxrwx   2 tsm    other       48  May 13   1987 labelit
1 drwxrwxrwx   4 tsm    other      192  May 13   1987 layers
1 drwxrwxrwx   2 tsm    other       48  May 13   1987 led
1 drwxrwxrwx   2 tsm    other       48  May 13   1987 line
1 drwxrwxrwx   3 tsm    other      320  May 13   1987 lint
1 drwxrwxrwx   2 tsm    other      320  May 13   1987 listen
1 drwxrwxrwx   2 tsm    other       48  May 13   1987 login
1 drwxrwxrwx   2 tsm    other       64  May 13   1987 ls
1 drwxrwxrwx   2 tsm    other       48  May 13   1987 mail
1 drwxrwxrwx   3 tsm    other      352  May 13   1987 mailx
1 drwxrwxrwx   2 tsm    other      112  May 13   1987 make
1 drwxrwxrwx   2 tsm    other       64  May 13   1987 mcs
1 drwxrwxrwx   2 tsm    other       48  May 13   1987 mkboot
1 drwxrwxrwx   2 tsm    other       48  May 13   1987 mkfs
1 drwxrwxrwx   2 tsm    other       64  May 13   1987 mkunix
1 drwxrwxrwx   2 tsm    other       48  May 13   1987 mount
1 drwxrwxrwx   2 tsm    other       48  May 13   1987 mv
1 drwxrwxrwx   2 tsm    other       48  May 13   1987 ncheck
1 drwxrwxrwx   2 tsm    other       64  May 13   1987 newboot
1 drwxrwxrwx   2 tsm    other      112  May 13   1987 nlsadmin
1 drwxrwxrwx   2 tsm    other       96  May 13   1987 nserve
1 drwxrwxrwx   2 tsm    other       48  May 13   1987 nsquery
1 drwxrwxrwx   2 tsm    other      304  May 13   1987 oawk
1 drwxrwxrwx   2 tsm    other       48  May 13   1987 pg
1 drwxrwxrwx   2 tsm    other       64  May 13   1987 ports
1 drwxrwxrwx   2 tsm    other       48  May 13   1987 pr
1 drwxrwxrwx   3 tsm    other       64  May 13   1987 profiler
1 drwxrwxrwx   2 tsm    other       48  May 13   1987 prtconf
1 drwxrwxrwx   2 tsm    other       64  May 13   1987 prtvtoc
1 drwxrwxrwx   2 tsm    other       48  May 13   1987 ps
1 drwxrwxrwx   2 tsm    other       64  May 13   1987 pwck
1 drwxrwxrwx   2 tsm    other       64  May 13   1987 rfadmin
```

```
1 drwxrwxrwx    2 tsm     other       64 May 13  1987 rfpasswd
1 drwxrwxrwx    5 tsm     other      144 May 13  1987 rfs.admin
1 drwxrwxrwx    2 tsm     other       64 May 13  1987 rfstart
1 drwxrwxrwx    2 tsm     other       64 May 13  1987 rfstop
1 drwxrwxrwx    2 tsm     other       64 May 13  1987 rfuadmin
1 drwxrwxrwx    2 tsm     other       64 May 13  1987 rfudaemon
1 drwxrwxrwx    2 tsm     other       64 May 13  1987 rm
1 drwxrwxrwx    2 tsm     other       80 May 13  1987 rmntstat
1 drwxrwxrwx    3 tsm     other      192 May 13  1987 sa
1 drwxrwxrwx    8 tsm     other      144 May 13  1987 sadmin
1 drwxrwxrwx    4 tsm     other       80 May 13  1987 sadmin3b2
1 drwxrwxrwx    6 tsm     other       96 May 13  1987 sccs
1 drwxrwxrwx    5 tsm     other       80 May 13  1987 sdb
4 -rw-rw-r--    1 tsm     other    11655 Sep 30  1986 sdiff.c
1 drwxrwxrwx    2 tsm     other       80 May 13  1987 sed
1 drwxrwxrwx    2 tsm     other       48 May 13  1987 setclk
1 drwxrwxrwx    2 tsm     other       48 May 13  1987 setpgrp
1 drwxrwxrwx   14 tsm     other      256 May 13  1987 sgs
2 drwxrwxrwx    2 tsm     other      592 May 13  1987 sh
1 drwxrwxrwx    2 tsm     other       80 May 13  1987 shl
1 drwxrwxrwx    2 tsm     other       48 May 13  1987 sort
1 drwxrwxrwx    2 tsm     other       80 May 13  1987 spell
1 drwxrwxrwx    3 tsm     other       48 May 13  1987 streams
1 drwxrwxrwx    2 tsm     other       48 May 13  1987 stty
1 drwxrwxrwx    2 tsm     other       48 May 13  1987 sysdef
1 drwxrwxrwx    2 tsm     other       48 May 13  1987 tail
1 drwxrwxrwx    2 tsm     other       48 May 13  1987 time
1 drwxrwxrwx    2 tsm     other       48 May 13  1987 tplot
1 drwxrwxrwx    2 tsm     other       48 May 13  1987 unadv
1 drwxrwxrwx    2 tsm     other       64 May 13  1987 uname
1 drwxrwxrwx    2 tsm     other      512 May 13  1987 uucp
1 drwxrwxrwx    3 tsm     other       64 May 13  1987 vi
1 drwxrwxrwx    2 tsm     other       48 May 13  1987 vmkfs
1 drwxrwxrwx    2 tsm     other       64 May 13  1987 volcopy
1 drwxrwxrwx    2 tsm     other       64 May 13  1987 whodo
tsm:
```

Readers can see, almost all of the commands are kept in their own directories. In the next example, the /usr/src directory contains not only the commands, but the UNIX kernel and other non-system products as well:

```
tsm: ls -las /usr/src/uts/3b2

total 652
  1 drwxrwxrwx   11 tsm     other      240 May 13  1987 .
  1 drwxrwxrwx    3 tsm     other       48 May 13  1987 ..
  1 drwxrwxrwx    5 root    other       96 May 13  1987 boot
```

```
    1 drwxrwxrwx    2 root    other         80  May 13  1987 debug
    1 drwxrwxrwx    5 root    other         96  May 13  1987 fs
    1 drwxrwxrwx    2 root    other        448  May 13  1987 io
   61 -rw-rw-r--    1 root    other      30716  Oct 13  1986 lib.io
  566 -rw-rw-r--    1 root    other     286478  Oct 13  1986 lib.os
    1 drwxrwxrwx    2 root    other        176  May 13  1987 master.d
    1 drwxrwxrwx    2 root    other         80  May 13  1987 ml
    1 drwxrwxrwx    2 root    other        384  May 13  1987 nudnix
    2 drwxrwxrwx    2 root    other        576  May 13  1987 os
    2 drwxrwxrwx    3 root    other        688  May 13  1987 sys
    7 -rw-rw-r--    1 root    other       3208  May 27  1986 unix.mk
    5 -rw-rw-r--    1 root    other       2068  Jul 28  1986 vuifile
tsm: ls -las /usr/src/uts/3b2/*

   61 -rw-rw-r--    1 root    other      30716  Oct 13  1986 lib.io
  566 -rw-rw-r--    1 root    other     286478  Oct 13  1986 lib.os
    7 -rw-rw-r--    1 root    other       3208  May 27  1986 unix.mk
    5 -rw-rw-r--    1 root    other       2068  Jul 28  1986 vuifile

boot:
total 9
    1 drwxrwxrwx    5 root    other         96  May 13  1987 .
    1 drwxrwxrwx   11 tsm     other        240  May 13  1987 ..
    4 -rw-rw-r--    1 root    other       1537  May 27  1986 boot.mk
    1 drwxrwxrwx    2 root    other        208  May 13  1987 lboot
    1 drwxrwxrwx    2 root    other         64  May 13  1987 mboot
    1 drwxrwxrwx    2 root    other        112  May 13  1987 olboot

debug:
total 24
    1 drwxrwxrwx    2 root    other         80  May 13  1987 .
    1 drwxrwxrwx   11 tsm     other        240  May 13  1987 ..
    5 -rw-rw-r--    1 root    other       2178  May 27  1986 debug.mk
    7 -rw-rw-r--    1 root    other       3563  Jul 28  1986 prtabs.c
    9 -rw-rw-r--    1 root    other       4751  May 27  1986 trace.c

fs:
total 8
    1 drwxrwxrwx    5 root    other         96  May 13  1987 .
    1 drwxrwxrwx   11 tsm     other        240  May 13  1987 ..
    1 drwxrwxrwx    2 root    other        112  May 13  1987 du
    3 -rw-rw-r--    1 root    other       1083  May 27  1986 fs.mk
    1 drwxrwxrwx    2 root    other         48  May 13  1987 proc
    1 drwxrwxrwx    2 root    other        112  May 13  1987 s5

io:
total 968
    1 drwxrwxrwx    2 root    other        448  May 13  1987 .
    1 drwxrwxrwx   11 tsm     other        240  May 13  1987 ..
    8 -rw-rw-r--    1 root    other       3820  Jun 16  1986 clist.c
```

```
7  -rw-rw-r--    1 root      other     83709 Aug 29    1986    ct.c
2  -rw-rw-r--    1 root      other     10604 Aug 25    1986    drivers.mk
4  -rw-rw-r--    1 root      other     21589 Oct  1    1986    emd.c
4  -rw-rw-r--    1 root      other      1699 Mar 20    1986    gentty.c
1  -rw-rw-r--    1 root      other     25443 Aug 25    1986    if.c
3  -rw-rw-r--    1 root      other      1074 May 27    1986    io.mk
8  -rw-rw-r--    1 root      other      3586 Mar 20    1986    ipc.c
5  -rw-rw-r--    1 root      other      2297 May 27    1986    lib.io.mk
7  -rw-rw-r--    1 root      other     33432 Jun 16    1986    lla_ppc.c
7  -rw-rw-r--    1 root      other     13053 Mar 20    1986    msg.c
9  -rw-rw-r--    1 root      other     44598 Jun 13    1986    ni2.c
5  -rw-rw-r--    1 root      other     63300 Sep 30    1986    npack.c
2  -rw-rw-r--    1 root      other       969 Aug 25    1986    osm.mk
5  -rw-rw-r--    1 root      other      2051 May 27    1986    ports.mk
9  -rw-rw-r--    1 root      other     24476 Jun 16    1986    ppc.c
6  -rw-rw-r--    1 root      other      2591 Jun 27    1986    prf.c
3  -rw-rw-r--    1 root      other      1261 Jul 28    1986    sddrv.c
5  -rw-rw-r--    1 root      other     16959 Mar 20    1986    sem.c
8  -rw-rw-r--    1 root      other      8459 Jul 28    1986    shm.c
2  -rw-rw-r--    1 root      other     30900 May 27    1986    stream.c
6  -rw-rw-r--    1 root      other     22602 May 12    1986    sxt.c
6  -rw-rw-r--    1 root      other      7498 May 12    1986    tirdwr.c
2  -rw-rw-r--    1 root      other     10313 Jun 16    1986    tty.c
9  -rw-rw-r--    1 root      other     39715 Aug 25    1986    xt.c
3  -rw-rw-r--    1 root      other      1222 May 27    1986    xt.mk

master.d:
total 27
1  drwxrwxrwx    2 root      other       176 May 13    1987    .
1  drwxrwxrwx   11 tsm       other       240 May 13    1987    ..
3  -rw-rw-r--    1 root      other      1124 Aug 27    1986    du
1  -rw-rw-r--    1 root      other       340 Sep 30    1986    emd
2  -rw-rw-r--    1 root      other      5282 Aug 27    1986    kernel
1  -rw-rw-r--    1 root      other       350 Jun 13    1986    ni
1  -rw-rw-r--    1 root      other       477 May 30    1986    ports
1  -rw-rw-r--    1 root      other       250 Jun 27    1986    prf
1  -rw-rw-r--    1 root      other       249 Jun 13    1986    proc
4  -rw-rw-r--    1 root      other      1599 Oct 13    1986    stubs
1  -rw-rw-r--    1 root      other       241 Jul 31    1986    xt

ml:
total 101
 1  drwxrwxrwx    2 root      other        80 May 13    1987    .
 1  drwxrwxrwx   11 tsm       other       240 May 13    1987    ..
62  -rw-rw-r--    1 root      other     31134 Aug 25    1986    misc.s
 5  -rw-rw-r--    1 root      other      2356 May 27    1986    ml.mk
32  -rw-rw-r--    1 root      other     15601 Aug 26    1986    ttrap.s

nudnix:
total 559
```

```
 1 drwxrwxrwx   2 root    other       384 May 13   1987   .
 1 drwxrwxrwx  11 tsm     other       240 May 13   1987   ..
15 -rw-rw-r--   1 root    other      7101 May 27   1986   adv.c
38 -rw-rw-r--   1 root    other     18766 Apr 15   1986   auth.c
15 -rw-rw-r--   1 root    other      6857 Oct 13   1986   cache.c
34 -rw-rw-r--   1 root    other     16469 Aug 25   1986   cirmgr.c
38 -rw-rw-r--   1 root    other     18860 Oct  7   1986   comm.c
27 -rw-rw-r--   1 root    other     13150 Oct  7   1986   fileop.c
16 -rw-rw-r--   1 root    other      7490 Oct  7   1986   fumount.c
14 -rw-rw-r--   1 root    other      6599 Aug 25   1986   netboot.c
24 -rw-rw-r--   1 root    other     11683 Aug 27   1986   nudnix.mk
18 -rw-rw-r--   1 root    other      8256 Sep 30   1986   queue.c
29 -rw-rw-r--   1 root    other     14293 Oct  7   1986   rbio.c
 4 -rw-rw-r--   1 root    other      1932 May 27   1986   rdebug.c
34 -rw-rw-r--   1 root    other     16757 Oct  7   1986   recover.c
36 -rw-rw-r--   1 root    other     17591 Oct  7   1986   remcall.c
33 -rw-rw-r--   1 root    other     15917 Oct  7   1986   rfadmin.c
13 -rw-rw-r--   1 root    other      5669 Oct  7   1986   rfcanon.c
20 -rw-rw-r--   1 root    other      9388 May 27   1986   rfsys.c
33 -rw-rw-r--   1 root    other     15944 Aug 27   1986   rmount.c
19 -rw-rw-r--   1 root    other      9073 Oct  7   1986   rmove.c
 5 -rw-rw-r--   1 root    other      2541 Oct  7   1986   rnami.c
19 -rw-rw-r--   1 root    other      8720 Aug 27   1986   rsc.c
73 -rw-rw-r--   1 root    other     36404 Oct  7   1986   serve.c

os:
total 882
 2 drwxrwxrwx   2 root    other       576 May 13   1987   .
 1 drwxrwxrwx  11 tsm     other       240 May 13   1987   ..
 6 -rw-rw-r--   1 root    other      2600 Apr 28   1986   acct.c
24 -rw-rw-r--   1 root    other     11511 Jun 27   1986   bio.c
15 -rw-rw-r--   1 root    other      6905 Jul 28   1986   clock.c
44 -rw-rw-r--   1 root    other     21787 Oct  7   1986   exec.c
13 -rw-rw-r--   1 root    other      5768 Oct  7   1986   exit.c
 7 -rw-rw-r--   1 root    other      3212 Jun 27   1986   fio.c
32 -rw-rw-r--   1 root    other     15450 Jun 27   1986   flock.c
24 -rw-rw-r--   1 root    other     11541 Aug 27   1986   fork.c
19 -rw-rw-r--   1 root    other      9021 Jul 28   1986   grow.c
28 -rw-rw-r--   1 root    other     13670 Jun 27   1986   iget.c
24 -rw-rw-r--   1 root    other     11736 Jun 13   1986   machdep.c
10 -rw-rw-r--   1 root    other      4772 Aug 25   1986   main.c
18 -rw-rw-r--   1 root    other      8438 Oct  7   1986   nami.c
57 -rw-rw-r--   1 root    other     28614 Sep 30   1986   os.mk
37 -rw-rw-r--   1 root    other     18374 Aug 25   1986   page.c
 6 -rw-rw-r--   1 root    other      2655 Jun 27   1986   pipe.c
45 -rw-rw-r--   1 root    other     22230 Sep 30   1986   region.c
17 -rw-rw-r--   1 root    other      8157 Sep 30   1986   sched.c
12 -rw-rw-r--   1 root    other      5396 Oct 13   1986   sdt.c
29 -rw-rw-r--   1 root    other     14198 Oct  7   1986   sig.c
12 -rw-rw-r--   1 root    other      5376 Sep 30   1986   slp.c
```

```
 9 -rw-rw-r--    1 root      other        4112 Jul 28    1986 space.c
24 -rw-rw-r--    1 root      other       11269 Jul 28    1986 startup.c
29 -rw-rw-r--    1 root      other       65336 Aug 26    1986 streamio.c
 6 -rw-rw-r--    1 root      other        2906 Sep 30    1986 subr.c
25 -rw-rw-r--    1 root      other       12233 Jul 28    1986 swapalloc.c
 6 -rw-rw-r--    1 root      other        2570 Sep 30    1986 swtch.c
34 -rw-rw-r--    1 root      other       16603 Jun 27    1986 sys2.c
20 -rw-rw-r--    1 root      other        9246 Aug 26    1986 sys3.c
49 -rw-rw-r--    1 root      other       24366 Jun 13    1986 sys3b.c
21 -rw-rw-r--    1 root      other       10013 Sep 30    1986 sys4.c
12 -rw-rw-r--    1 root      other        5326 Jun 16    1986 sysent.c
20 -rw-rw-r--    1 root      other        9465 Sep 30    1986 text.c
45 -rw-rw-r--    1 root      other       22256 Sep 30    1986 trap.c
sys:
total 337
 2 drwxrwxrwx    3 root      other         688 May 13    1987 .
 1 drwxrwxrwx   11 tsm       other         240 May 13    1987 ..
 9 -rw-rw-r--    1 root      other        4507 Jul 28    1986 buf.h
 4 -rw-rw-r--    1 root      other        1900 May 27    1986 cirmgr.h
16 -rw-rw-r--    1 root      other        7290 Oct  7    1986 comm.h
 3 -rw-rw-r--    1 root      other        1443 Jul 28    1986 elog.h
 8 -rw-rw-r--    1 root      other        3996 May 27    1986 errno.h
 4 -rw-rw-r--    1 root      other        1684 Aug 25    1986 fcntl.h
 3 -rw-rw-r--    1 root      other        1283 Apr 15    1986 file.h
 1 drwxrwxrwx    2 root      other          48 May 13    1987 fs
 8 -rw-rw-r--    1 root      other        3870 Jun 13    1986 fstyp.h
 3 -rw-rw-r--    1 root      other        1521 Jul 28    1986 hdelog.h
 3 -rw-rw-r--    1 root      other        1503 Apr 28    1986 hetero.h
22 -rw-rw-r--    1 root      other       10626 Jul 28    1986 id.h
 3 -rw-rw-r--    1 root      other        1183 Apr 15    1986 idtab.h
13 -rw-rw-r--    1 root      other        5975 Jun 27    1986 if.h
10 -rw-rw-r--    1 root      other        4922 Jun 27    1986 inode.h
12 -rw-rw-r--    1 root      other        5472 Oct  7    1986 message.h
 5 -rw-rw-r--    1 root      other        2359 Jun 27    1986 mount.h
13 -rw-rw-r--    1 root      other        5678 Sep 30    1986 npack.h
 8 -rw-rw-r--    1 root      other        3645 Sep 30    1986 param.h
 3 -rw-rw-r--    1 root      other        1523 Jul 28    1986 pfdat.h
 5 -rw-rw-r--    1 root      other        2486 Jun 13    1986 ppc.h
13 -rw-rw-r--    1 root      other        5655 Sep 30    1986 proc.h
 8 -rw-rw-r--    1 root      other        3871 Aug 25    1986 rbuf.h
 5 -rw-rw-r--    1 root      other        2213 Jun 27    1986 rdebug.h
 3 -rw-rw-r--    1 root      other        1153 Oct  7    1986 recover.h
12 -rw-rw-r--    1 root      other        5491 Aug 25    1986 region.h
 2 -rw-rw-r--    1 root      other        1018 Apr 28    1986 rfsys.h
 4 -rw-rw-r--    1 root      other        1553 Mar 20    1986 sgs.h
29 -rw-rw-r--    1 root      other       13934 May 27    1986 stream.h
 6 -rw-rw-r--    1 root      other        2577 Jul 28    1986 swap.h
 9 -rw-rw-r--    1 root      other        4209 Jun 13    1986 sys3b.h
 9 -rw-rw-r--    1 root      other        4577 Jun 27    1986 sysinfo.h
 9 -rw-rw-r--    1 root      other        4290 Aug 25    1986 sysmacros.h
```

```
    4  -rw-rw-r--    1 root      other      1931 May 27  1986 systm.h
    9  -rw-rw-r--    1 root      other      4544 Mar 20  1986 termio.h
    5  -rw-rw-r--    1 root      other      2171 Aug  4  1986 timod.h
   15  -rw-rw-r--    1 root      other      6661 Aug  4  1986 tiuser.h
   10  -rw-rw-r--    1 root      other      4672 Mar 20  1986 tty.h
    3  -rw-rw-r--    1 root      other      1104 May 27  1986 types.h
   18  -rw-rw-r--    1 root      other      8550 Aug 26  1986 user.h
    5  -rw-rw-r--    1 root      other      2533 Jul 28  1986 var.h
tsm: ls -las /usr/src/umodem
total 208
    1  drwxrwxrwx    2 tsm       other        80 Apr  2  22:48 .
    1  drwxrwxr-x   10 root      other       224 Apr  2  22:20 ..
   98  -rwxrwxrwx    1 tsm       other     49158 Apr  2  22:31 umodem.c
  108  -rwxrwxrwx    1 tsm       other     54470 Apr  2  22:34 xmodem
tsm:
```

The /usr/tmp Directory

The /usr/tmp is another home for temporary files. The /tmp and /usr/tmp directories are usually placed on high speed devices, or sometimes they are areas of memory treated as a device. In the IBM PC environment, an analogy of this would be a virtual disk, also known as a RAM-disk. Both /tmp and /usr/tmp are used frequently as staging areas for network file transfer programs, such as Sun Microsystems' NFS package, ftp, and others.

CHAPTER 16

THE UNIX CRON FACILITY

/etc/cron

The *cron* process is initiated when the UNIX system is booted, and it is run when the UNIX system is in multiuser mode. Commands are executed on scheduled intervals that are specified in a special file called a *crontab*. The crontab is located in /usr/lib/crontab on some implementations of UNIX, or in the directory /usr/spool/cron/crontabs on machines with UNIX System V (Release 2 and later).

The **cron** command differs from the **at** and **batch** commands, in that commands executed by **cron** are executed repeatedly according to the cycle specified in the schedule. In contrast, commands executed by either the **at** or **batch** commands are executed only once, unless part of the command stream reschedules itself for subsequent execution.

The actual cron binary executable file is located in the file /etc/cron. **Cron** (short for chronograph) is actually the name of the UNIX clock daemon. A *daemon* (pronounced demon) is a process that continuously runs in the background and which is independent of a terminal. A daemon process usually performs specialized functions or services for other processes. The entries in /usr/spool/cron/crontab are instructions that specify what events are to occur at a particular scheduled time

389

and date. Although cron is running all the time, it requires minimal CPU resources and is not much overhead.

After the UNIX system has been booted, and the cron facility is functional, cron goes to sleep and wakes up every minute to check for any tasks that may require execution. If there are any jobs scheduled, then cron will execute them; otherwise, it goes back to sleep for another minute. It continually repeats this loop.

The cron uses control files that are located in the directory /usr/spool/cron/crontabs. Each control file contains a list of commands that are to be executed according to their schedule. Virtually any command or group of commands may be executed by cron; therefore, care must be taken so that only authorized users are permitted access to the cron facility.

One of the main uses of cron is using it to perform housekeeping chores by executing *cleanup* shell scripts designed to rid the system of old or unwanted data.

It should be understood that /etc/cron is not a user command, nor should it be executed by the superuser. The cron is automatically started during the UNIX initialization process when it is booted. If more than one instance of cron is active, it will produce undesirable results and may even cause serious system damage.

If the cron is not active immediately after the UNIX system has been booted, then something is most likely wrong and the system should be closely scrutinized and restarted. When there are problems with cron, a reinstallation of the system from the original UNIX distribution media may be required.

Whenever the system clock is changed, cron is aborted and then restarted so that the correct new time may be picked up.

Although the cron is primarily used for administrative and system related chores, regular individual users may invoke it as well. Before users are allowed access to the cron facility, they must have an entry in a special file called /usr/lib/cron/cron.allow. If users have an entry in the file /usr/lib/cron/cron.deny, then they are prohibited from using the cron facility. If a null cron.deny file exists, then no user is denied usage of the cron.

These files are optional, but if they are not present, only those users with superuser privileges are allowed to use the cron. The cron facility's services are invoked by entering the **crontab** command. This command looks in the directory /usr/spool/cron/crontabs for a crontab (cron table) file named after the invoking user's login ID (crontab files are limited to one per user). The crontab file is where users specify their control information for the cron facility.

When users create or modify a crontab file in the /usr/spool/cron/crontabs directory (using a text editor, such as vi), the cron will not recognize the crontab until either cron is restarted (as in a system reboot) or until a **crontab** command is entered. If no filename is given to the **crontab** command, the default is to overwrite the existing crontab file with a new one.

Any file created using a text editor may be specified as the input file for the **crontab** command. In all cases, the output file is always placed in the /usr/spool/cron/crontabs directory as the name of a user's login ID.

In older versions and implementations of UNIX, this file may also be called /etc/crontab, and may be modified only by *root* or other authorized superusers. In UNIX System V Release 3, however, regular users are permitted to create their own crontab files so they can also use the cron facility. The following example shows some entries in the /usr/spool/cron/crontabs directory:

```
tsm: ls /usr/spool/cron/crontabs
root
sys
adm
tsm
wbu
pam
dkm
kdb
tsm:
```

Record Format of the crontab File

All lines beginning with # (number or pound sign) are treated as comments. The crontab record consists of several positional fields. Any line not beginning with #, is treated as a request for cron to execute the associated command according to the schedule provided. Command strings can get quite sophisticated, so it is possible to continue lines by using a \ (backslash) just before hitting the enter key when the entry is being created. The general format of each line entry in a crontab file is as follows:

```
minute(s) hour day_of_month month day_of_week command_string
00-59     1-2  1-3          1-1   0-6         ... ... ...
```

In this example the first line shows the general format, while the second line specifies the permissible value ranges. The first field, *minute(s),* specifies the number of minutes after the hour that the command is executed, ranging from 00 through 59. The value 00 specifies execution on the hour, 30 would specify on the half hour, and so on. The * character has a special meaning in crontab field values. If specified, then the command is executed every period, for whatever field it appears in. For example, if the value for minute(s) was *, then the associated command would be executed every minute.

The next field specifies the *hour* that the command is to be executed, ranging from 1 (for 1 a.m.) through 24 (for midnight). A * value in this field would indicate execution *every hour.*

The third field indicates the *day of the month*, ranging from 1 through 31, for the number of days in a month. A * value in this field would indicate execution *every day.*

The fourth field specifies the *month* or range of months that the command is to be executed. The maximum valid range is from 1 through 12 for January through December. Subsets of this may be specified by using the - (hyphen) between the low and high numeric values, providing a smaller range.

For example, 2-7 represents February through July. Multiple ranges may also be specified by adding the comma separator character: 2-7, 9-12. This example would cause execution from February through

July, and September through December (omitting January and August). A * value in this field indicates execution *every month* and would be equivalent to 1-12.

The next field indicates which *day(s) of the week* this command is to execute, ranging from 0 through 6 for Sunday through Saturday. The same range subsets may also be given to this field as for the month field. If the command were to execute every other day, the entry would be 0,2,4,6 or 1,3,5. A * value for this field indicates execution *every day*.

Finally, the last field in the record are *any commands* to be executed when the cron goes off. The commands are subject to the access permissions allowed to the requesting user. Commands in crontab files belonging to superusers can do *anything*! One can imagine the possibilities here.

The * character may be specified for any or all of the scheduling fields. They are frequently grouped to create schedules such as every hour, of every day, of every month, of every day of the week; which would appear as follows:

```
00-15 * * * * /bin/date > /dev/console
```

The preceding example would execute the **date** command and print the results to the UNIX console device; every minute, starting on the hour and continuing for the next fifteen minutes, every day of every month. Any changes to ownerships of the files in /usr/spool/cron/crontabs do not affect the user ID selected when cron runs the job.

Usually, if there are any fatal messages causing termination, the cron daemon attempts to print them to the system console. Otherwise, messages may also be sent using the UNIX *mail* facility. When the cron daemon is not active, if the system is still up, users attempting to use the **at** or **crontab** commands will receive warning messages at their terminals.

The following examples show listings of the default crontab entries for the AT&T 3B2 and 7300 UNIX PC systems, respectively.

393

```
Sample crontab for sysadm user-ID (3B2)
#  ident  @(#)/usr/spool/cron/crontabs/sysadm.sl 1.1 3.0 08/14/85
33651
#  This file will be scheduled via the cron command
#
#  Format of lines:
#  min  hour daymo month daywk /etc/ckbupscd >/dev/console 2>/dev/tty0
#
#  mi.  - time(s) of day
#  hour
#  daymo - day(s) of month (1, 2, ... 31)
#  month - month(s) of the year (1, 2, ... 12)
#  daywk - day(s) of week (0-6, 0 = sun)
#
#  Example:
#  00  17 * * 1 /etc/ckbupscd >/dev/console 2>/dev/console
#
#  At 5:00pm in the evening on mondays during any month of the year,
#  check to see if there are any file systems that need
#  to be backed up.
#
#======================================================================
#
#  Default backup schedule calls for checks mon through friday
#  at 5:00pm.
#
00  17 * * 1,2,3,4,5 /etc/ckbupscd >/dev/console 2>/dev/console


The crontab file for a 7300 UNIX PC.
#sccs "@(#)fndcmd:crontab 1.5"
 0  4 * * * /bin/su uucpadm % /usr/lib/uucp/uudemon.admin >/dev/null
30  5 * * 1 /bin/su uucpadm % /usr/lib/uucp/uudemon.cleanu >/dev/null
30  5 * * 1 /bin/su root % /etc/cleanup.wk >/dev/null
 3  3 * * 0 /bin/su root % /etc/clockupd.wk >/dev/null
34  * * * * /bin/su uucpadm -c "/usr/lib/uucp/uudemon.hour >/dev/null"
30  3 * * * /bin/su root -c "/usr/bin/memo -m >/dev/null"
51  * * * * /bin/su uucpadm -c "/usr/lib/uucp/uudemon.hour >/dev/null"
30  3 * * * /bin/su root -c "/usr/bin/email -m >/dev/null"
 0 12 * * 2 /bin/su bin -c "/usr/adm/acct.week /dev/null"
```

Another interesting feature of cron is the log that is kept in the file /usr/lib/cron/log. In older versions and implementations of UNIX, this file may also have been known as /usr/adm/cronlog. If some rather strange things seem to have been happening on your system, this would be a good place to look for clues.

This file can get quite large when there are a lot of users with cron jobs being executed regularly, or in a system where there is heavy *uucp* activity. (Many UNIX systems do not truncate the log, creating the possibility of filling up all of the free space on disk.) The following example is the tail end of such a log, and is provided only as a sample. (For those interested in more detail, a look at your system's own cron log file is in order.)

```
tsm: tail -25 /usr/lib/cron/log
< tsm 535 c Mon Apr 25 02:10:00 1988
> CMD: /usr/lib/uucp/uudemon.hour >/dev/null
< root 537 c Mon Apr 25 02:11:00 1988
> CMD: echo 'date' >/dev/console
> tsm 540 c Mon Apr 25 02:11:01 1988
< root 537 c Mon Apr 25 02:11:01 1988
< tsm 540 c Mon Apr 25 02:11:01 1988
> CMD: echo 'date' >/dev/console
> tsm 543 c Mon Apr 25 02:12:00 1988
< tsm 543 c Mon Apr 25 02:12:00 1988
> CMD: echo 'date' /dev/console
> tsm 545 c Mon Apr 25 02:13:00 1988
< tsm 545 c Mon Apr 25 02:13:00 1988
> CMD: echo 'date' >/dev/console
> tsm 547 c Mon Apr 25 02:14:00 1988
< tsm 547 c Mon Apr 25 02:14:00 1988
> CMD: echo 'date' >/dev/console
> tsm 549 c Mon Apr 25 02:15:00 1988
< tsm 549 c Mon Apr 25 02:15:00 1988
> CMD: /usr/lib/uucp/uudemon.poll >/dev/null
> root 554 c Mon Apr 25 02:30:00 1988
< root 554 c Mon Apr 25 02:30:02 1988
> CMD: /usr/lib/uucp/uudemon.hou. >dev/null
> root 564 c Mon Apr 25 02:41:00 1988
< root 564 c Mon Apr 25 02:41:01 1988
tsm:
```

Lines that begin with > (right arrow/greater than) are written by the cron process itself, before executing the associated command. The lines beginning with < (logical opposite of >) are written by a child process started by the original cron process. It is the child process that actually executes the commands specified in the crontab files. The field entries are:

- Effective user-id (or CMD) indicates the command being executed.
- Process-ID (PID)
- Job Type: (a=atjob, c=cronjob)
- Entry's Time and Date Stamp indicates when the job was actually executed.

Summary

The cron is a powerful standard feature of the UNIX system that provides the capability of timed execution of any command. The **at** command uses cron to execute its scheduled commands, but differs in that **at** jobs execute only once. (An **at** job may also be designed to respawn itself. The cron will execute commands repetitively according to the schedule specified in a special control file called a *crontab*.

Crontab files are created either by invoking the **crontab** command, or by using a text editor (such as vi) to edit a text file containing the control information. If the editor approach is used, the **crontab** command must be executed before the edited file becomes effective. Also, be aware that crontab files will be truncated when the **crontab** command reads from the standard input.

The uses of cron are limited only by the imagination. Many UNIX gurus use it for such tasks as: driving an automated desk calendar for reminders, simplifying disk file maintenance, and automation of backups. The cron facility can be a very useful tool for UNIX developers and users.

CHAPTER 17

UNIX SYSTEM ADMINISTRATION

For most DOS developers, system administrative duties are limited to formatting disks, installing various software packages, and some system recovery because of failed hardware using the standard DOS tools such as **chkdsk** or **debug.** As a developer entering the UNIX system environment, there are numerous system administration duties to be aware of, some of which are already done by another person charged with administrative responsibilities.

If new developers' UNIX systems will be under their own control, it is likely that there will be some new duties to assume for which there was no DOS counterpart. On DOS systems, short of the initial setup of a machine, formatting disks, and performing backups, there are no formal ongoing administrative duties to perform.

There are no standard support utilities distributed with DOS to aid in the installation of software, perform file system maintenance, or administer user accounts. There is no standard facility in DOS to aid in the administration of system backup and recovery; this is also true for any system security concerns, since there are none in the DOS environment. The installation procedures for software packages vary from vendor to vendor. Because of the lack of standardization, they are often confusing and may at times conflict with the installation procedures of other vendors.

Prior to the use of subdirectories, it was not uncommon to overwrite the CONFIG.SYS or AUTOEXEC.BAT files in the root directory with a vendor-supplied version, resulting in frustration and the loss of these files.

One of the most important things to remember regarding system administration is that UNIX is a multiuser system. In instances where developers share machine resources with other users, the person acting as the system administrator must remember to be considerate of other users and perform administrative tasks when the system is in single user mode. The various initialization states of UNIX are described later in this chapter; one of these states is known as *single user mode*.

There are many system administration tasks; the most important ones for DOS developers acting as their own system administrators to know about are:

- How to start and stop the system.

- How to mount and unmount file systems.

- How to set access permissions.

- How to perform user account administration.

- How to do system backup and restore procedures.

Although UNIX system administration is certainly not limited to these areas, each of these procedures are discussed in more detail in the following sections.

Starting and Stopping the System

The first of the system administration chores that former DOS developers must become familiar with is how to properly start and stop their UNIX system. Improper system shutdown can have serious and undesirable results upon a UNIX file system, as will be explained later.

The actual steps that take place during startup and shutdown may vary not only between manufacturers of the hardware and software, but even between releases of the software from the same vendor. In fact, each machine may be customized for its own unique startup and shutdown sequence, even for the same releases of software. Additionally, dissimilar systems from different vendors may be customized to provide a uniform appearance for their startup and shutdown sequences. For these reasons, system startup and shutdown are described here in a general sense; any specific references pertain to AT&T's UNIX System V, the definitive UNIX model.

System Startup

There are a few general steps that most UNIX variants go through in order to bring up the system:

- Peripheral Equipment Is Powered On
- Computer Is Powered On
- Bootstrap Program Is Loaded
- UNIX Kernel Is Loaded
- System Date Is Set
- (Optional) Enter Single User Mode
- File System Is Checked
- System Enters Multiuser Mode

The first step involves turning on any external devices such as terminals, printers, disk drives, modems, network devices, and tape units. This is so that when the kernel is loaded, the appropriate device drivers can be loaded for the devices that are perceived to be present. Terminals must be active so that they can respond to the *getty prompt* issued by the system. (The **getty** process displays a **login:** message on terminal devices.)

After any outboard peripherals are powered on, the computer itself is powered up. What happens next depends upon the firmware for a particular system. Most systems perform some type of system self check diagnostics. Ultimately, all systems start the bootstrap program. The bootstrap is a very small program designed to read in another program from the boot disk. (Bootstrap programs vary from vendor to vendor because they are very device dependent.)

The program that the bootstrap reads in is designed to load and start execution of the UNIX kernel. Machines are booted either from a Programmable Read-Only Memory (PROM) chip, or from a peripheral device such as a floppy disk or cartridge tape. Some UNIX systems, such as certain models of Sun equipment, can be made to boot from the PROM by invoking a keyboard sequence, similar in concept to the CTRL-ALT-DEL key sequence on DOS machines. (This information is not general public knowledge and is intended for UNIX system administrators only. The exact key sequence is described in the system administration guide distributed with the Sun system.)

For systems that are being booted from a floppy disk, caution must be used not to power off the system during the boot procedure. This action could result in an erasure of the boot floppy.

Some boot sequences initiated from either PROM or diskette optionally prompt for a verification of the time and date. While this is usually considered important for DOS systems, it is extremely important in UNIX-based systems; primarily because of the UNIX cron facility's dependency on accurate time and date information. The time and date may also be reset after the UNIX system is already active.

After the UNIX kernel has been loaded and started, it starts the **swapper** and **init** processes. The job of the **swapper** process is to manage the available memory between subsequent tasks, swapping dormant processes out of memory and then back in as necessary.

The job of the **init** process is to create shells. The **swapper** is process 0 and **init** is process 1. All subsequent processes started in the UNIX system are spawned by **init**. Pre-System V machines would automatically come up in single user mode. Newer systems normally come up in multiuser mode; unless the system administrator interrupts the process and starts the machine in single user mode. How this is done differs between UNIX variants.

Initialization States

UNIX systems have the ability to run in one of several different modes, called *initialization states* (or init states for short). In UNIX System V there are nine init states, as indicated in the table below:

Table 17-1: UNIX Initialization States

STATE	DESCRIPTION
0	Machine Power Down State
1	Single User Mode
2	Multi-user Mode
3	Multi-user Mode (with RFS active)
4	Unused
5	Firmware Mode (shutdown and reboot mode on some systems)
6	Shutdown and Reboot Mode (firmware mode on some systems)
s	Single User Mode (an alias for init state 1)
S	Single User Mode (indicates a remote console)

The actual program used to keep the system running correctly is called **/etc/init**, which is what init states are named after. The **init** command is used to change the UNIX system's initialization state. (The **/etc/shutdown** command is actually a UNIX shell script that calls the **init** command.) The most commonly used state is multi-user mode, the state in which multiple users can access the system. Single user mode prevents more than one user from accessing the system, and is used mostly by the system administrator to perform administrative tasks. When the system is in single user mode, system administrators can make any necessary modifications to the system without worrying about affecting any active users, since they can't be logged on. Normally, only the system console device is active in single user mode, unless init state S has been specified (in which case the remote device used to access the system becomes the only active terminal).

Init state 0, power down mode, is used to bring the system to a graceful halt so that it may be totally shut down. Normally, most UNIX systems stay powered up and active around the clock. Reasons for init state 0 include hardware maintenance and physically relocating the system hardware. Init states 5 and 6 have different uses on different systems. For example, on some hardware, init state 5 is used to bring the machine into firmware mode. This means that the UNIX system is shut down andexecutes a PROM-based program, perhaps for the purpose of setting firmware options or to overcome problems encountered during an attempt to load and execute the UNIX kernel.

Init state 6 usually *bounces* the system; first shutting down all the way to firmware mode, then rebooting all the way back to multiuser mode. One reason why this may be necessary is if the UNIX system's behavior becomes deranged or erratic in any way, it is usually a good idea to reload a fresh copy of the kernel and restart everything anew. Another reason may be a requirement that the system be restarted after certain changes have been made, such as the addition of new device drivers or other software.

File System Checking

Before the system is available in multiuser or single user mode, the file system is checked for validity and consistency before it can be mounted. If the system was properly shut down during the last UNIX session, then the file system checking utility (**fsck**) simply terminates without any further activity. If **fsck** detects any problems with the file system, it performs the necessary operations to attempt repairs and make the file system valid and mountable.

The **fsck** command is the UNIX equivalent of the DOS **chkdsk** command. Its purpose is to test and, if necessary, repair the file system. This is done in a succession of passes, or *phases*. These phases are tests for blocks, sizes, reference counts, connectivity, the free block list, and path names. If and when errors are encountered, the opportunity to repair the file system is presented via a dialog between the **fsck** command and the system administrator. During the boot process, **fsck** is initiated automatically; if any problems are detected,

fsck automatically attempts to repair the file systems without any response required from the administrator.

The **fsck** command may also be run manually when the system is in single user mode. This dialog displays the diagnostics of the file in error, and suggests various fixes. The administrator may act on this if desired or may choose to ignore them, although this is usually not recommended. The general syntax of the **fsck** command is:

```
fsck  [-y]  [-n]  [-sX]  [-SX]  [-t  filename]  [-D]  [filesystem]  ...
```

The -y parameter tells **fsck** to check all files and if errors are found, to automatically attempt to recover the file system without the opportunity of human intervention. In some cases this may not be ideal, and in most cases the administrator will want to know if there is any file system damage. Discretion should be used with this switch, it is recommended to be used mostly as a time saver and not exclusively for all executions of this command. The equivalent of this switch for the DOS **chkdsk** command would be the **/f** parameter, which does the same thing for DOS files.

The -n parameter tells **fsck** to check all files and if errors are found, to report those errors but not perform corrective action. It assumes a *no* answer to all questions in the command/user dialog. This switch is useful for testing the file system integrity without taking additional action. The equivalent of this in DOS is to issue the **chkdsk** command with no parameters.

The -sX parameter tells **fsck** to ignore the free list and to initialize a new one, regardless of whether errors are found or not.

The -SX parameter tells **fsck** to ignore the free list and to initialize a new one only if errors are found.

The -t filename parameter tells **fsck** to use a temporary work file during execution, indicated by *filename*. This is used for systems with a small amount of memory, and the indicated filename cannot appear in the path of the files to be checked.

The -D parameter tells **fsck** to include extra consistency checks on directories — its use is highly recommended.

The *filesystem* parameter is the path and/or name of the file system to check.

After all file systems to be used have checked out successfully, they are mounted and the system is initialized to multiuser mode. At this point the UNIX system is ready to be used by anyone having a login account.

System Shutdown

System shutdown is another important administrative ritual that should be stringently observed, even in systems where the developer is the only user of the system. The reason is simple — following established procedures avoids (or at least reduces) the possibility of damage to the file system. Taking short-cuts sometimes results in damage to the file system, perhaps so serious that system recovery or reinstallation from scratch may be necessary before it can be used again.

Normally on most UNIX systems, according to the UNIX System V Interface Definition standards, the **/etc/shutdown** shell script is used to bring down the system. This shell script can be (and usually is) customized according to an individual system administrator's personal tastes. For this reason, it is not likely that two systems will have identical shutdown procedures, unless it is by specific design. Generally, the shutdown procedures are similar for all UNIX systems.

It is customary to send out a warning notice to any active users; this is done from within the **shutdown** script by invoking the **wall** command. After invoking the command, it is customary to wait some period of time, usually indicated as part of the warning notice and accomplished by invoking the **sleep** command. From this point on, the specifics of what takes place depends upon the rest of the **shutdown** script, as well as the implementation of UNIX.

If the local machine is part of a network and is providing services through network support software such as RFS or NFS, the remote machines need to be notified of the impending shutdown so that users on those machines will not be adversely affected. After the notice and grace period, any advertised network services are discontinued before proceeding with the local system's **shutdown** procedure.

Once the **shutdown** procedure has started, no new users may access the system. Smart users will heed the warning notices received earlier, terminate whatever they are doing, and log off; otherwise, they will be bounced rudely from their activities — without the opportunity to save any work they have done up to that point. (It isn't the system administrator that does this, it is part of the automated shutdown procedure, which is merciless about process termination.)

As the **shutdown** procedure continues, any active processes are terminated until process 1, the **init** process, itself terminates. Depending upon what options were specified as parameters to the **shutdown** command determines what initialization state the machine enters after **init** terminates.

File System Administration

Pulling the plug on a UNIX machine could have catastrophic consequences if the file system had not been properly closed prior to power down. The same is true of rebooting the system at will. DOS users are accustomed to simply hitting the CTRL-ALT-DEL keys on their keyboards, causing the machine to reboot. On most UNIX systems there is no equivalent for this ability. (Sun machines do have a hot-key break.)

The reason is that the UNIX file system is far more complex than DOS. DOS users do not have formal system setup utilities distributed as part of the operating system. To add a new hard disk to a DOS system requires only that the user execute the **fdisk** command and subsequently format the new disk. (There are no standard DOS utilities to perform low level formatting of a hard disk. The IBM Advanced Diagnostics disk is one possible way to do this, but is not part of the basic standard distribution of a DOS system; it is an optional add-on component.) Adding a new hard drive to a UNIX system is complicated and there are therefore, several support utilities provided to make the task easier. Besides adding hard disks, most UNIX users will at some time want to store information on floppy diskettes and ultimately retrieve that data later on.

Accessing data from floppy disks is quite different from the way it is done in DOS. Before any data can be written to a floppy disk, it must have a valid file system on it. It is also possible to make file systems on media other than floppy diskettes; cartridge tapes are one example.

Making File Systems

Whatever the media, floppy diskettes or tapes, it must first be properly formatted before a file system can be put on it. The commands and parameters used to do this are UNIX implementation dependent. Once the media has been formatted, it is ready to receive a file system. The **mkfs** command is used to make a file system.

File systems are necessary because the kernel requires that all superblock and inode information be initialized on the media prior to its writing any data. The size of the file system is specified when **mkfs** is invoked, otherwise certain defaults are assumed. The specific format and usage of **mkfs** varies slightly between implementations of UNIX. Readers should refer to the documentation distributed with their particular version of UNIX for a complete description of how to use **mkfs.**

Essentially, the **mkfs** command provides the opportunity to specify a *prototype* of a file system; a prototype is sort of like a template. The file system is written out on a special file defined as a parameter of the command line.

Exactly how the file system is created depends upon the rest of the command line. Either a prototype filename is provided or the number of blocks, inodes, and other file system information can be specified. A prototype file contains the necessary information to make a file system. There are usually several prototype files already defined, one for each of the many different types of disks supported by the implementation of UNIX.

Some versions of UNIX also have interactive menu-driven programs designed to assist system administrators with administrative chores, such as creating new disks and file systems. One example of this in older releases of UNIX System V is the **sysadm** utility. After the file system has been created on the media, it is ready to be mounted for access on the UNIX system.

Mounting and Dismounting File Systems

File systems are mounted only by authorized superusers. The UNIX **mount** command is used to do this. Earlier in this book the concept of *mount points* was presented. One standard mount point that should be present on all UNIX systems is /mnt. This directory, like any mount point, is simply an empty directory. Any empty directory may be used as a mount point; there is no special naming convention used, nor are there any other special requirements.

The following example demonstrates how a file system is mounted:

```
mount /dev/c1d1s8 /usr2
```

This example uses the directory */usr2* as the mount point. The */dev/c1d1s8* refers to a UNIX System V device commonly used on AT&T 3b2 hardware as the second drive, *c1d1* refers to the drive number (c1d0 is drive 0), and *s8* refers to section 8 which is a portion of the drive reserved for data and is usually mounted as /usr2. Of course, it is possible to use any mount point. Different implementations of UNIX refer to the /dev device by different names, this is highly implementation dependent.

File systems can be mounted from devices physically present on a system or they may be logical devices accessible over a network, such as in NFS or RFS. In either case, local or networked devices may be mounted automatically at boot time by creating an entry in a *mount table*. The mount table is a file containing the necessary information for the system to automatically mount a device, if it is ready, at boot time. Some implementations of UNIX use the file /etc/fstab (file system table), others also use /etc/checklist. Still, others use different names, but the purpose is the same. The exact format of the contents of any of these files varies according to the UNIX implementation.

File systems may be mounted or dismounted at any time, but only by authorized superusers.

If a file system is mounted, it may be dismounted by invoking the **umount** command. Like the **mount** command, only superusers can invoke **umount.** Before a file system can be dismounted it must not be in use. If a user's current directory is in the file system being dismounted the attempt will fail since the device will be busy.

Backup and Restore Operations

This is another area where the specifics of how to accomplish something in a UNIX system can be very implementation dependent. There are two types of backups, full and incremental. Full backups take a long time to complete, will likely require multiple storage media to write on, and are normally performed during hours when no users are logged on.

The type of media most commonly used are either various models of tapes (reel or cartridge) and diskettes. Diskettes are much slower and require greater interaction to do a full backup. In a typical modern small system, it would require upwards of 50 or 60 diskettes to do a full backup of a single file system approximately 70 megabytes in size, whereas most modern cartridge tapes could easily fit the entire 70 megabyte file system onto a single tape. Recent developments in tape backup technology have yielded storage capacities as high as 2.2 gigabytes on a single 8mm video cartridge.

Incremental backups are partial backups; they do not include the entire file system, only selected portions of it. Some implementations of UNIX have utilities that assist in the selection of which files to include for an incremental backup. For systems without such utilities, system administrators can build their own scripts. In such manually created scripts the **find** command can be quite helpful; it can be instructed to seek out only those files that have changed since a given time and date (since the last backup).

There are actually several ways to create backups of files, using commands and utilities such as **find**, **cpio**, **tar**, **ctccpio**, **tcio**, **store**, and **restore**. These commands represent only a few of the many different ways possible to copy data between the backup medium and a file system; they are also not standard across all releases of UNIX operating systems. Readers should reference the system administration documentation regarding the backup and restoration of files for their particular implementation.

One example of how a full backup might be implemented on UNIX System V might be:

```
find / -print | cpio -ocv > /dev/ctape
```

This example begins (recursively) finding files from the root directory, piping them to **cpio**. The **cpio** command writes its output to device named ctape, defined in the /dev directory, presumably a cartridge tape. Using this example, the restore operation might look like this:

```
cpio -icvudm < /dev/ctape > /
```

In this example, the **cpio** command reads input from the /dev/ctape device and writes its output to the root directory.

Normally, these commands are not entered at the command line when doing a backup, whether incremental or full. Instead, an elaborate backup shell script is usually developed and invoked automatically in conjunction with the UNIX system's cron facility. The specific contents of the script is up to individual system administrators, so there is no standard.

User Account Administration

Users access a UNIX system by means of a login account, an entry in a special file (/etc/passwd) used to determine who may access the system. The person responsible for administering login accounts is usually the system administrator, although some UNIX shops actually have separate persons associated with the system administration group who are responsible. Administering user login accounts involves creating new entries, deleting old entries, and making changes to existing entries in the /etc/passwd file. Besides entries in the /etc/passwd file, the user account administrator also oversees which group(s) a user may join or access. On some implementations of UNIX, such as UTS (the mainframe implementation of UNIX), there are utilities that users may execute to perform some of their own user account administration.

Different UNIX variants have different account administration tools, so the only universal standard way of doing administrative tasks is manually. For this reason, only the manual methods are described here.

Adding Users

New users may be added to the system by editing the /etc/passwd file with a text editor such as **ed**, **vi**, or **emacs.**

A line of data must be added to this file for each user that will be allowed to access the system. Only superusers can modify /etc/passwd. The format of this line of data is:

```
login:password:uid:gid:comment:home:shell
```

The login field is a short ASCII character string that specifies a unique user ID identifying the user. The login name can be a series of alphanumeric characters. The required minimum and maximum size of the login name may vary from system to system as well as between UNIX variants. It is recommended that the login name should be descriptive of the user to whom it is assigned, such as the user's initials. Login names must be unique; only the first login name is recognized in the /etc/passwd file, all subsequent duplicates are ignored.

The password field specifies the password the user will need to enter in order to log in to the system. The characters in this field are not the actual password, but are instead the encrypted form of the password.

This field may be left blank for no password, and may later be updated by the user or the system administrator via the **passwd** command. In UNIX System III and later, this field may contain parameters that force users to change their password before the system will complete the logon sequence. Depending on the parameter values used, the administrator can specify a password validity period, thus forcing a password change. A minimum retention period may also be specified to keep a user from changing the password and then immediately changing it back to the previous one. This ensures that the password change cannot be defeated if it is decided that users are required to change their password at regular periodic intervals in order to maintain system security.

When using the **passwd** command to change passwords, users will be prompted for the current password prior to any changes being effected. If a superuser enters the **passwd** command with a user's login name, they will not be asked for the password, but will instead be requested to enter the password twice before the change is made. Note that when editing the /etc/passwd file, this field will show up with unintelligible characters for security reasons. In the interests of system security, it is recommended that the system administrator require all users to have passwords, with mandatory periodic password change in force.

The uid field specifies a unique system user ID number, a positive integer value between 0 and 65,535. This number is used internally by the system to refer to the user with which it is associated, in almost all tasks relating to that user. Care must be taken to avoid assigning this ID to more than one user; if two or more users have the same uid, than all files associated with that uid will be fully accessible by any login that has the same uid.

The gid (group ID) field specifies an ID of a group of users related to one another in some way, such as project groups. The group ID may be alphanumeric, and the mandatory minimum and/or maximum size may vary from system to system. This field is optional and its use is recommended if there is more than one member of a group that needs access to one or more directories and/or files. If this field is omitted, than a default is assumed. The value in this field associates the login to a group; whatever the group, this becomes the effective group ID for the login and is the value used when testing for group access permissions.

411

The comment field specifies any comment that the administrator types in. It is recommended that the user's full name, telephone number, department number, and other informative data are entered here. There is no mandatory limit to the size of this field, however, this field must not contain the colon character. (Fields for entries in /etc/passwd are delimited by the colon (:) character.)

The home field specifies the user's default or *home* directory. This can be any path name, but it is recommended that path name given should follow established user home directory standards. If the directory provided in this field does not exist, it must be created. Note that the name entered here is also defined in the user's HOME environment variable.

The shell field specifies what command shell will be loaded for the user upon login. If the shell is not defined in the login entry for the user in the /etc/passwd file, the default shell is usually the Bourne shell, or whatever shell has been specified by the system administrator. Other shells such as the C shell, K shell, or a restricted shell may also be specified. A sample /etc/passwd entry may look like this:

```
htb:cfTdf8gEş.qk5ot:101:212:Homer  T.  Bedlow:/usr/htb:/bin/ksh
```

This would be interpreted as a user with the login name of htb. The password field (cfTdf8gEs.qk5ot) is not known since this field is encrypted. The internal system uid is 101, while the gid is 212. The comment field indicates that the user's name is Homer T. Bedlow. The home directory for htb is /usr/htb. The last field (/bin/ksh) indicates that the shell to be loaded upon login is the Korn or K shell.

After having edited a new entry into /etc/passwd, the next step is to create the home directory specified for the user. This is accomplished by entering the **mkdir** command with the appropriate directory name as its parameter:

```
# mkdir /usr/htb
```

The next step is to give ownership of this directory to the user via the **chown** command. After this, the **chgrp** command may optionally be used to change group ownership of the directory to a new group, if the one specified in their /etc/passwd entry is not appropriate:

```
# chown htb /usr/htb
# chgrp other /usr/htb            (this is optional!)
```

The next step is optionally to create the user's .profile script. Some UNIX administrators do not go as far as to write a new user's .profile script. This may be accomplished on most systems by copying a standard profile file to the user's home directory via the **cp** (copy) command. Finally, the ownerships of the .profile script must be reset to the user via the **chown** command. It may also be necessary to make the new .profile script executable by resetting its execution permissions using the **chmod** command:

```
# chown htb /usr/htb/.profile
# chmod +x /usr/htb/.profile
```

A step that should be taken (but is not necessary) is to create a mail file for the new user. This is accomplished by changing the current directory to the system's mail directory, which for UNIX System V is usually /usr/mail. The administrator creates the user's mail file via the **>** command, and then establishes ownership of this file to the new user using **chown** and **chgrp**. Note that the group ownership of this file must be set for *mail*.

```
# > /usr/mail/htb
# chown htb /usr/mail/htb
# chgrp mail /usr/mail/htb
# chmod 660 /usr/mail/htb
```

The final step is to change the file access mode to 660, indicating that only the owner and mail may read or write the file. After all of these steps, Mr. Homer T. Bedlow now has access to the system.

Removing Users

To remove a user is to reverse the steps necessary for adding one. (File access permissions need not be reset.) It is recommended that a backup be made of all of the user's directories and files before the removal process.

The next step would be to edit the /etc/passwd file and delete the line of data pertaining to the login account in question. If there is no need for any of that user's files and subdirectories to be kept then they may be deleted, although it is usually customary to reassign ownership of those files to another user responsible for keeping them until it is certain they no longer need them. To remove that user's home directory and all associated files therein, the superuser must make that user's home directory their current directory:

```
# cd /usr/htb
#
```

Before proceeding, it must be verified that the current directory is indeed, /usr/htb, the home directory specified earlier for Homer T. Bedlow:

```
# pwd
/user/htb
#
```

At this point, it is all right to begin the deletion process using the **rm** command:

```
# rm -r *
#
```

It cannot be over emphasized that extreme caution should be taken when using the **rm** command with the *-r ** options! *In the wrong directory, this command can have extremely devastating consequences from which there may be no easy recovery, if recovery is even possible.*

After the files in this directory have been removed, the superuser should get out of that current directory and remove it:

```
# cd ..
# rmdir /usr/htb
#
```

Because the home directory and files of former user htb have been removed doesn't necessarily mean that all of that user's files are gone. They may have created files in several other directories all over the file system, so it is necessary to seek them out and remove them as well. This can be accomplished with the **find** command:

```
# find / -type f -user htb -exec rm {} \; -print
# find / -type d -user htb -exec rmdir {} \; -print
#
```

If any files and directories belonging to htb had been missed before, these two command lines will take care of whatever ones are left. Note that in all of the examples associated with user account administration it is necessary to be an authorized superuser (as indicated by the # prompt) to carry them out.

To change any user account attributes simply requires a superuser to edit those changes in the /etc/passwd entry for the user. If the user's uid is changed, then all files formerly owned by that user are now owned by a non-existent uid, indicated by a uid number instead of the login name when such files are referenced using the **ls** command. To correct this problem and reassign ownership of those files back to the correct owner using their new uid it is necessary to find them and reset their ownerships as this example illustrates:

```
#find / -user 101 -exec chown steve {} \; -print
#
```

This example supposes that a user login named *steve* had been modified by changing the uid value from 101 to something else. By executing the **find** command it is easy to locate all occurrences of files

415

with ownership by uid 101 and reassign ownership to whatever the new uid value is for *steve*.

System Security Administration

Another feature present in the UNIX system, that is not present in DOS, is the built-in security for access to the system as well as to the file system. DOS, however, does have a limited subset equivalent to the file permissions available in the UNIX system, but they are extremely limited in their capabilities and usefulness.

Security on UNIX-based systems is a sensitive issue, especially in light of recent events. In November 1988, a sophisticated computer virus program was unleashed upon the Internet that caused an uproar. Although the damage done was not terribly serious, it could have been. This incident, as well as many day to day occurrences of similar, less publicized events have added to the paranoia and fears of system managers of all types, including UNIX systems in particular (since the virus in question used a UNIX mail facility to get around.) It underscores the need to implement good security measures on computer systems.

The first rule of security, regardless of what type of computer system or hardware is involved, is "if it's sensitive, don't keep it online!" The only truly secure system is one where there is no electronic access to it from the outside world and where personal human access is strictly controlled and supervised.

The UNIX system uses the concepts of logins, passwords, and encryption to provide a happy medium for implementation of reasonable security measures, but they are by no means totally secure. Some add-on measures for UNIX-based systems have been to implement another level of password challenging, the system access password.

There are even versions of secure UNIX currently in use and under development that use a shadow password file. The details on these systems are sketchy and they are used primarily by large corporations such as AT&T and the various government agencies with large UNIX-based networks, such as the U.S. Air Force and the Department of

Defense. For the average DOS developer, though, the likelihood of coming into contact with these ultra-security measures in their daily routines is small.

File System Security

The implementation of file system security begins with an understanding of how users are granted access to files.

The **chmod** command is used to change the *access mode* values associated with a file. The access mode value of a file defines, among other things, the access permissions granted to the file's owner, group, and the rest of the world (referred to as other). The access permissions are *read, write,* and *execute*, indicated by the r, w, and x.

Access mode values apply to directories and subdirectories as well as files, so the term "file" mentioned for this topic is interchangeable with either. (Please note that access mode values do not apply to superusers!)

Basically, there are three types of users who may access a file: the file's assigned owner, users belonging to the group associated with the file, and all other users. Within each of these categories of users, it is possible to define just how the file may be accessed: read, write, or execute. When a user lists the detailed information about a file using the -l option of the **ls** command, the information returned includes the file access mode permissions, depicted as:

```
rwxrwxrwx
```

This triad of rwx characters goes from left to right. The first group of these refers to the owner, the next refers to the group access, and the last refers to other (the rest of the world). Other information may also be provided such as an indication that the entry is a directory or a file. The following example illustrates how the groups are associated with the file access modes:

```
owner            group            other
r w x            r w x            r w x
```

417

Each access mode within each group has a numeric value associated with it, as indicated in Table 17-2.

Table 17-2: Access Mode Numeric Values

MODE	VALUE	DESCRIPTION
–	0	No Permissions
x	1	Execute Permission
w	2	Write Permission
wx	3	Write/Execute Permission
r	4	Read Permission
rx	5	Read/Execute Permission
rw	6	Read/Write Permission
rwx	7	Read/Write/Execute Permission

These numeric values may be used to set what access permissions each group has within the mode permissions triad may have. The **chmod** command uses numeric values for each of the triads; for example if the owner, group, and other permissions were to allow read, write, and execute permissions, the numeric value to specify when using the **chmod** command would be 777. If, instead of allowing full access for group and other, it were necessary to keep full access limited only to the owner with no other access allowed, the numeric value would be 700.

As can be seen, the three digit octal number has a positional relationship corresponding to the rwx triad group. The first number (left most) corresponds to the owner field, the second number (middle) corresponds to the group field, and the last number (right most) corresponds to field reserved for other. This may be confusing to some users of UNIX systems, so there is a different way to accomplish the same thing, but which is a bit easier to understand.

The alternative method of specifying the mode value to the **chmod** command is by using alphabetical characters. The alpha characters r, w, and x may be used in conjunction with the characters u, g, o, and a. The u character refers to the user that owns the file, the g character refers to the group, the o character refers to other (all other users), and a (all) applies the changes to all three groups (u,g, and o.)

The characters + (plus), - (minus), and = (equal) are also used in the assignment process. The + character means to *add* the permission value(s) to the right of it, the - character means to *remove* the permission value(s) to the right of it, and the = character means to *reset* (no permissions at all) the permission values for the users specified to the left of the character. Examples of this are listed below:

```
chmod a+rw filename
chmod uo-x filename
chmod a= filename
```

The first example line sets read and write permissions on for all users accessing filename. The second line turns off execution permissions for the owner and other, but not for group. The last line resets all attributes to off (no permissions at all) for the owner, group, and other. In order to manipulate this file, the owner must first **chmod** it to the appropriate permissions.

When a file is created, it is assigned certain ownership values, such as the uid of the owner (default is the creator of the file), the group ownership value (default is the group that the owner belongs to when the file is created), and certain other access permission values derived from defaults associated with the owner's *umask* values at file creation time.

There are many instances where it becomes necessary to change any of these values; the **chgrp** command is used to assign a new group ownership. The group must exist, otherwise a diagnostic message is returned. The group ownership value does not apply to superusers. In order to change the group ownerships, the user must be authorized; they must be a member of the group to which the file allows modification permissions.

The new group to which group ownership is being assigned may be any group, as long as it already exists (usually maintained by the system administrator.) Once the group ownership has been reassigned, access for the group level is restricted to members of the new group. The group level access permissions previously set remain in effect.

The **chown** command is used to reassign ownership of a file from one user to another. In order to change the ownership value of a file, the user must be authorized, they must own the file or they must have superuser privileges. For non-superuser authorized users, once the file ownership has been changed, they are bound to the access permissions defined for the file.

If a user accidentally changes ownership to another user, they must either get the new owner to change ownership back, or an authorized superuser may reset the ownership (usually done by the system administrator).

Directories

Directories are a special case with respect to access permissions. Directories must have read permissions (r) set to use the **ls** command on them; write permissions (w) to add, remove, or modify files within them; and execute permissions (x) to make it the current directory or to use it as part of the execution path. When the -l option of the **ls** command is used, directories are indicated by the d character:

```
$ ls -l /usr/tsm
 1 drwxrwxr-x    2 tsm users    32 Mar 21 1:21 memos
11 -rwxrwxr-x    2 tsm users 13799 Mar  1  09:31 mbox
$
```

Data Encryption

On most UNIX-based systems it is possible to render files completely unreadable by unauthorized persons invoking the **crypt** command. (Due to U.S. Government export restrictions concerning encryption/decryption technology, not all implementations of UNIX outside of the United States support the standard **crypt** command.) The **crypt** command uses the Data Encryption Standard (DES) encryption algorithm and when the decryption key is sufficiently complex, data encrypted in this manner are virtually impossible to decrypt without expensive supercomputers dedicated to the task, such as those used by the cryptography departments of the Department of Defense, U.S. Military Intelligence, and the National Security Council.

This means that for the most part, encrypted data on UNIX systems are relatively safe from the average snoop. Using the **crypt** command to encrypt a file is quite simple; a user must specify a key to be used later in decrypting the file to make its contents readable again. If this key is forgotten or lost there is no practical way to override the encryption and the file's contents will be lost until the decryption key can be remembered or found. This poses two serious problems inherent to encryption schemes.

First, because not everyone has a perfect memory, people tend to write their decryption keys down somewhere, in case they do forget. This security exposure creates the risk of the written key being found and used.

Second, in order to prevent the previously mentioned scenario, people tend to use decryption keys that they are not likely to forget, such as the names of family members, places, dates, or numbers they already know by heart. This security exposure creates the risk that the decryption key will be relatively easy to crack using programs running on nothing more powerful than the average personal computer (or even the resources of a power UNIX system) to which someone may have access; or just sheer ingenuity by logically guessing a person's decryption key based on personal knowledge of that person.

It is surprising how little time it may take a computer program to "guess" the 30,000 most used words in the English dictionary, their most commonly used foreign counterparts, or to use a sequential number generator as was the case in the fictional plot of the movie "War Games."

If encrypted data are of a sensitive nature, and there is a fear of it being compromised, then don't keep it online. If it is essential to keep it online, then sufficiently sophisticated encryption keys should be used.

A sufficiently sophisticated key is one that is at least eight characters in length, and that uses at least two numerics as part of the key.

Some encryption routines permit keys of up to 32 characters (or more) to be used; the longer the key, the less likely it is to be compromised.

The **crypt** command requires a key; if one is not provided on the command line, **crypt** will demand one from an interactive prompt before performing any encryption or decryption of the file. The key may be anything a user wants it to be; heed the information about decryption keys mentioned in this section. The following is an example of how to use the **crypt** command to encrypt a file:

```
$ crypt funny_99_bone < mbox > mbox.crypt
$
```

In this example, the file being encrypted is called mbox, a user's standard UNIX mailbox file. The original file is unaffected, it is the file mbox.crypt that is the encrypted version of mbox. The encryption/decryption key used in this example is funny_99_bone. The result is that mbox.crypt is totally useless to anyone without the decryption key. Note that this method of invoking **crypt** has a serious security flaw: the key is visible to anyone within sight of a user invoking the **crypt** command! To overcome this problem **crypt** should be invoked without specifying the key on the command line, it will prompt for the key without echoing back the user's response.

An example of how to decrypt a previously encrypted file is shown in this next example:

```
$ crypt funny_99_bone < mbox.crypt > mbox.decrypt
$
```

The decryption key was specified on the command line in this example for the sake of clarity; users should omit the decryption key be prompted for it instead. In this example, the previously encrypted file mbox.crypt is decrypted to the file mbox.decrypt which is readable. The original encrypted file remains intact.

Attempting to decrypt a file that was not previously encrypted will result in an encrypted output file. If a file that has already been encrypted is again encrypted, a different key must be used. This results in a double encryption; it also means that to get the contents back to a readable form, the process must be reversed in the correct sequence using the correct decryption keys. Although this is not a common practice, there is no reason why it cannot be done, nor are there any limitations as to how many levels of encryption a file may undergo.

Password Security

Most users should consider their login password sacred, giving it to nobody! Sometimes it may be necessary to give this password out, if this is the case it should be changed as soon as possible. This is especially so for the root login's password! The entire UNIX system is completely at the mercy of whoever has the root password. UNIX security operates on the premise that access to the root password will be kept confidential and that the minimum default file access permissions will be kept intact. Without these, a UNIX system could be rendered as unsecure as an ordinary DOS system, and fall prey to anyone.

Actually, the likelihood of deliberate damage to the system by unauthorized users is less than by accidental damage by authorized users. The important point to remember here is to be careful about what is being done when active as a superuser.

Passwords should be changed often, at least every three weeks or so. Some UNIX installations require password changes every week!

CHAPTER 18

X WINDOW SYSTEM

The X Window system is a network based graphics windowing system developed at MIT in 1984 by Bob Scheifler and Jim Gettys. X began as a windowing project, codenamed Athena, at MIT's Laboratory for Computer Science (LCS) and has evolved to become the preferred standard on UNIX and other systems.

Since its inception, X has been funded for further research and development by companies such as Digital Equipment Corporation, Hewlett-Packard, IBM, Sun Microsystems, and AT&T and a host of others. It has become the basis of commercial products from all of these funding companies. X Window is a public domain product distributed from MIT's Project Athena group, charging only for the actual cost and shipping of the distribution materials. Other products built on top of the X Window system, from the vendors mentioned above, may not be public domain and may involve substantial costs and licensing agreements.

The first widespread commercial release of X was Version 9, in 1985. It has since been upgraded through the years to the current Version 11 Release 3, as of November 1988.

The X Window system is different from most other graphic windowing systems because of the job it was designed to do. X provides a lot more functionality than merely painting color windows on a high resolution graphics screen.

The X Window system is network-based; it is *also network transparent*, meaning that applications running on one machine can be used on other machines scattered across a network — as though they were running locally. Perhaps more important than that, the machine hardware does not have to be of any particular type as is the case for many other windowing systems.

X provides hardware device independence; applications do not need to be rewritten, recompiled, or relinked to function correctly on different display hardware. The graphics capabilities of X are presently only two-dimensional, using lines, polygons, arcs, and points. This may change in future releases; a new graphical display standard known as *display PostScript* is currently being considered for incorporation into X. PostScript is a product of Adobe Systems that is used to draw graphics, primarily on printers. It has been adapted to draw graphics to video output devices. It has the power to provide three dimensional graphics, such as those found on the Apple Macintosh II and other systems.

System Fundamentals

The X Window system is based upon the concept of a *client-server* model. In this model, an X client is considered an application program and an X server is considered to be a program that provides screen display services.

In networking terminology, a *server* is a system (as in a computer) that runs network software and provides shared access to system services, such as shared resources (printers, disk, and other peripherals). A *client* in networking terminology is a system that requires the use of a network server's shared facilities. There is nothing that prohibits a program from being included as one of the services provided by a network server. In networked systems, a server can also be a client, but is considered a client only when using the services of another server. Servers are not usually considered clients of themselves.

In X, the server is a program running on a machine that provides screen display and other logical services to any X application programs connected to it. X application programs are called *clients*, because they do not perform screen display and input event manipulation functions directly; they require the services of the X server. X clients can run on the same machine as the X server, or they may connect to other X servers running on other machines scattered across a network. The machines may be of several different types as long as there is an X server that clients can connect to.

The type of network is also not of any consequence according to the design philosophy behind X. The X protocol uses the network that is in place as its transport mechanism, so there is no dependency on any specific network. For X11.3, however, only TCP/IP- and DECnet-based networks such as Ethernet and Starlan are supported. This is likely to change in the near future to include networks such as Token Ring and other PC-based products.

What this means is that when there is a network with several systems connected together, assuming they are all equipped with the correct X Window software (clients and servers), it is possible for X clients to execute on one machine and have the results displayed to multiple screens over the network.

Every window opened on an X server is a virtual screen capable of displaying an unlimited number (theoretically at least) of subwindows. Windows are considered to be an inexpensive resource. Applications are constructed that use hundreds of smaller subwindows. Scrollbars, buttons, and other objects used to control the user interface are actually subwindows within larger windows.

There is also discussion about incorporating a new object as part of X, called a *gadget* (actually a windowless entity). This would significantly improve X performance by reducing the program overhead that is currently required for making windows appear on screen.

The X Server

The primary function of the X server is to act as an intermediary between users and X applications. The server performs the job of collecting input such as mouse movements, pointer device input, or keystrokes from a keyboard and passes this information back to the appropriate X client(s). It also handles output from X clients that are destined for video display or other clients (as in interclient communications).

Usually, there is only one server for a display device. In the case of Sun workstations, however, there are two servers available; one to handle monochrome displays and one to handle color output. A server may be connected to several clients. A single client may also connect to several servers running on different machines over a network. The clients may be local or executing on a remote system connected over a network.

In order for clients to send their output requests to the server and for the server to send input information back to the appropriate client, a form of interprocess communications is required. This IPC is defined as a communications protocol (capable of being carried over networks) and is the basis of the X Window System Protocol: the dialog that takes place between a server and its clients.

X servers have been developed for devices ranging from ordinary PCs to powerful hybrid graphics display devices. The most commonly used device for X Window sessions are powerful microprocessor-based graphics workstations such as the Sun 3 and 4 family of workstations and the Hewlett-Packard 9000 series.

In networked applications, X clients are usually run on the more powerful processors, while the X servers are run on less expensive hardware designed to provide a good display rather than heavy duty CPU processing. There are some inexpensive display terminal devices that are designed for the sole purpose of being an X server by placing the X server and network interface code into a ROM.

X Clients

Several clients may execute concurrently in X, either locally to the X server or remotely on several systems. The server collects input data from the input device, typically a combination of a mouse and keyboard, and routes this data back to the appropriate client.

X uses the concept of *input focus*. A client has the input focus when the X cursor pointer is inside the boundaries of a particular client's window area. All input events that occur while the pointer is within this area are directed through the use of individual input event queues managed by the X server to the client that owns the window . When the focus is moved out of a window, it is shifted to the client owning the window to which the pointer has moved. If there is no window, the pointer is considered to be in the *root window*. If this is the case, the focus has shifted to another type of client, called a *window manager*, an optional client that may not necessarily be present.

Window Managers

A window manager is another type of X client, designed to manage the screen real estate of a display that is under the control of an X server. The window manager determines the placement of other client windows within the root window which is considered to be owned by the window manager (if one is present) or by **Xinit** (the X initialization process) if a window manager is not present.

If no window manager is present, then it is not possible to move windows around the screen — unless a client includes the necessary code to manage its root window operations. It would be terribly inefficient for every client to contain window management logic, which is why window managers were developed.

The window manager is also largely responsible for the *look and feel* of the user interface. The default window manager distributed with the X Window system is called *uwm*, for Universal Window Manager. It is customized by editing an ASCII file, called a *resource file*. It is possible to totally customize the X environment (including all clients, the X server, and window manager) by creating the appropriate entries in one or more resource files. Creation and maintenance of customized resource files are the responsibility of the user.

The ability to specify different window managers was provided to accommodate the changing the appearance and performance (look and feel) of the user interface.

Client windows can be moved and resized. Their stacking order, iconfy and deiconfy requests are all normally handled by the window manager. The stacking order is the order in which windows are stacked on top of one another, completely or partially overlaying one another.

Some window managers, modify the general appearance of client windows by enveloping them within specially designed borders that have attached icons. The window manager controls manipulation of the icons.

A window manager may be started and terminated at any time without any serious consequences to already running X clients. Only one window manager, however, may be active at a time. For that matter, only one X server can be active for a particular display, serious problems will occur if a second X server is started. Do not attempt to start the X server if another windowing system such as SunTools or NeWS is already active, and vice versa!

Standard X Clients

The X Window System is distributed with a few standard clients. These useful applications are provided with full source code and are intended to serve as examples of how to develop other X clients. (The source for the standard X window manager, uwm, is also provided.)

xterm - A Terminal Emulator

The client, xterm, provides a UNIX command shell in a window. It may be thought of as a window containing the more conventional command line interface familiar to UNIX users with experience. This is the most used client and serves as the basis for others.

bitmap - A Bitmap Editor

The bitmap editor is primarily of use to X developers and is used to create or modify bitmaps that will be used as screen icons. It is not likely to be used by ordinary end users unless their function includes graphical design.

xbiff - A Mailbox Flag

This sample X client displays a mailbox icon in the root window. When there is no mail for the end user, xbiff displays the mailbox with its flag down. When mail has arrived the mailbox has its flag up.

xcalc - A Scientific Calculator

The xcalc client is a scientific desktop calculator capable of emulating Texas Instruments TI-30 or Hewlett-Packard HP-10C calculators. It can also provide slide rule functions.

xclock - The X Window Time Piece

This X client displays an animated clock (digital or analog). The update interval may be user-specified, up to 1 second between updates.

xdpr - Dump X Window Screens To Printer

The xdpr client copies the contents of a window on a display directly to a printer, by running the commands **xwd**, **xpr**, and **lpr**. This is an easy way to print out screens.

xedit - An Editor For X

This is a simple full screen editor that uses combinations of keyboard and mouse movements for input. This is not like **vi** or **emacs**!

xfd - Display X Window Fonts

This client displays the ASCII character set for the named font in a window on screen. This handy for designing screens or checking what the many fonts appear like on different displays.

xhost - Server Access Control

This X client is used to add or delete X hosts to a list of systems permitted to the X server of the machine on which it is run. It can also be used to disable host access control.

xload - Measure System Load

Measures the process activity of a system and graphs the results into a window.

xlogo - Display The X Logo

Draws the X logo in a variety of sizes on the screen.

xlsfonts - Display Server Font List

This client displays information about fonts on a system.

xmodmap - Modify The X Keyboard

The xmodmap client is a utility used to display and modify the keyboard map for the specified server and host. This client is intended to be run from a user's X initialization script.

xpr - Print Output From xwd

The xpr utility reads in the output from xwd and formats the output for printing on PostScript printers or the IBM PP3812 page printer.

xprop - Display X Font Properties

This X utility displays window and font properties for the X server.

xrdb - X Server Resource Database Utility

This client normally is run from a user's X initialization script to get or set the contents of the RESOURCE_MANAGER property on the root window of screen 0 of the X server.

xrefresh - Refresh The X Screen

This X client repaints the screen.

xset - Set User Preferences In X

This utility is used to set various user preferences for the display and keyboard, such as mouse speed, screen saver time limits, and the search path for the directories containing the X screen fonts.

xsetroot - Change Root Window Parameters

The xsetroot client is used to customize parameters that affect the appearance of the root window, such as the background and foreground colors and background bitmap used for tiling.

xwd - Dump X Screen To File

This copies images from the screen into a specially formatted window dump that is used as input for the **xpr** and **xwud** commands.

xwininfo - Display Window Information

This client displays window metrics and other information. Useful for screen designers to see how windows differ in appearance and placement on other servers.

xwud - Display X Image From Dump File

This utility reads the output of the xwd utility and displays the image on the screen, instead of sending the output to a printer.

xinit - X Initialization Module

The xinit program is entered from the standard UNIX command line or from within a startup shell script (.profile or .cshrc) to start an X session. It starts the X server and the initial X client, usually the xterm or other terminal client.

Xserver - The X Server

This is the X window system server, with an alias of X. Usually, there is only one server for a machine, although there can be more. Only one server is active for an X session. The X server is terminated by xinit when X is stopped (when a user exits the last remaining xterm window or terminates the last X application).

uwm - X Universal Window Manager

The universal window manager distributed with X is called uwm. This client performs the window manipulation functions of all other clients. This particular window manager is designed to provide pop-up menus of action to the end user such as move, resize, iconify, refresh, and circulate.

The several documents distributed with the X Window release tape is another good source of information, mainly for X developers. These can be either printed locally or ordered directly from the X Consortium at a cost of $125.

Other Information

Members of the X Consortium and other X developers are reachable through network access to The Internet, or through USENET (sometimes referred to as *netnews*) in the special interest group known as *comp.windows.x*. Occasionally, there may also be postings in UNIX groups on CompuServe, GEnie, and EXEC PC.

There are also many user contributed programs with full source distributed as a courtesy by the X Consortium in special directories on the X release tape. These are not a standard part of the X Window distribution and are not supported by the Consortium.

APPENDIX A

UNIX SYSTEM CALLS

The following set of system calls are defined in the "UNIX System V Interface Definition," a set of documentation available from AT&T. This documentation is the definitive source of information regarding UNIX System V issues.

Table A-1: System Calls

FUNCTION	DESCRIPTION
abort()	forces abnormal process termination
abs()	returns the absolute integer value of its argument
access()	determines file accessibility
acct()	function to enable/disable the system process accounting routine
acos()	trigonometric arc cosine function
alarm()	sets an alarm clock for a process
asctime()	converts a time structure to a 26 character ASCII string
asin()	trigonometric arc sine function
atan()	trigonometric arc tangent function
atan2()	trigonometric arc tangent function (operates on 2 operands)
atof()	converts a string to a floating point number
atoi()	converts a string to an integer
atol()	converts a string to a long integer number
bsearch()	invokes a binary search on a sorted table
calloc()	allocates (and initializes) memory by number of elements
ceil()	computes the smallest number not less than its argument

Table A-1: System Calls (continued)

FUNCTION	DESCRIPTION
chdir()	changes the current directory
chmod()	changes file access modes
chown()	changes file and group ownerships
chroot()	changes the named directory to become the root directory
clearerr()	resets the error and EOF indicator for a file
clock()	returns amount of CPU time used since last clock() call
close()	closes an open file descriptor
closedir()	closes directory descriptor
cos()	trigonometric cosine function
cosh()	mathematic hyperbolic cosine function
creat()	creates new files or overwrite existing ones
crypt()	function to encrypt strings
ctermid()	creates a filename for the calling process' control terminal
ctime()	time conversion routine
dup()	creates a duplicate of an open file descriptor
encrypt()	function to perform encryption on a string
erf()	error function
erfc()	complementary error function
errno()	obtains error code and definitions
exec()	all forms of exec() execute a new process
exit()	terminates process execution
exp()	mathematical exponential function
fabs()	returns the absolute value of its argument
fclose()	closes an open file after writing out any buffered data
fcntl()	performs file control operations on an open file descriptor
fdopen()	associates a stream with a file descriptor
feof()	determines if an end of file condition exists for a file
ferror()	determines if I/O errors occurred while reading/writing files
fgetc()	gets a character from a file
fgets()	gets a string from a file
fileno()	gets the integer file descriptor for a file
floor()	computes the largest number not larger than its argument
fmod()	returns a floating point remainder value
fopen()	opens the specified file
fork()	creates a new child process
fprintf()	writes data to an open file
fputc()	function to write a character to a file
fputs()	writes a null terminated string to a file
fread()	buffered read from an open file
free()	free allocated memory
freopen()	attaches streams associated with stdin, stdout to other files

Table A-1: System Calls (continued)

FUNCTION	DESCRIPTION
frexp()	used to manipulate parts of a floating-point number
fscanf()	does formatted reads from an open file
fseek()	performs positioning within an open file
fstat()	retrieves information about open files
ftell()	returns current position within a file
ftw()	file tree walker function
fwrite()	buffered write to an open file
gamma()	mathematical gamma function
getc()	macro to get a character
getchar()	macro to get a character
getcwd()	get the current working directory
getegid()	gets the effective group ID of the calling process
getenv()	returns a pointer to an environment variable if it exists
geteuid()	gets the effective user ID of the calling process
getgid()	gets the real group ID of the calling process
getopt()	command line parsing function
getpgrp()	gets the process group ID of the calling process
getpid()	gets the process ID of the calling process
getppid()	gets the parent process ID of the calling process
gets()	gets a string from the standard input
getuid()	gets the real user ID of the calling process
getw()	returns the next word (integer) from a filE
gmtime()	converts a time value to GMT value
gsignal()	function associated with ssignal()
hcreate()	allocates space for a hash table
hdestroy()	destroys a hash table
hsearch()	performs hash table searching
hypot()	mathematical Euclidean distance function
ioctl()	performs various I/O control functions on devices
isalnum()	determines if a character is alpha-numeric
isalpha()	determines if a character is alpha
isascii()	determines if a character is an ASCII character
iscntrl()	determines if a character is a control character
isdigit()	determines if a character is a digit value
isgraph()	determines if a character is a graphic character
islower()	determines if a character is lowercase
isprint()	determines if a character is printable
ispunct()	determines if a character is a punctuation mark
isspace()	determines if a character is a space, CR, NL, FF, or tabs
istty()	macro to determine if its argument is a tty device
isupper()	determines if a character is uppercase

Table A-1: System Calls (continued)

FUNCTION	DESCRIPTION
isxdigit()	determines if a character is a hexadecimal value
kill()	sends a termination signal to processes
ldexp()	used to manipulate parts of a floating-point number
lfind()	linear search routine similar to lsearch()
link()	creates a link to a file
localtime()	returns the current time according to local time zone
lockf()	performs record locking on a file
log()	mathematical logarithm function
log10()	another mathematical logarithm function
longjmp()	performs a non-local jump (goto)
lsearch()	linear search routine
lseek()	repositions the file pointer in an open file
mallinfo()	provides information from the mallinfo structure
malloc()	memory allocation function
mallopt()	another way to allocate small blocks of memory quickly
matherr()	math error handling function
memccpy()	copies characters from one memory location to another
memchr()	character search routine for memory buffers
memcmp()	compare values in memory buffers
memcpy()	copies a fixed number of bytes between memory buffers
memset()	initializes a memory buffer to a specific value
mkdir()	used to make a new directory
mknod()	makes a new directory, FIFO, or special/ordinary files
mktemp()	constructs unique filenames
modf()	used to manipulate parts of a floating-point number
mount()	used to mount a removable file system
msgctl()	interprocess communications message control function
msgget()	IPC routine to get a message queue identifier
msgrcv()	IPC routine to read a message from a specific message queue
msgsnd()	IPC routine to send a message to a specific message queue
nice()	function to reset the execution priority of a process
open()	opens files for input and/or output
opendir()	open directory descriptor
pause()	suspends a process until it receives a signal
pclose()	closes the stream created by popen()
perror()	prints system error messages to the standard error output
pipe()	creates a pipe (FIFO) for interprocess communications
plock()	locks calling process' text and/or data segments into memory
popen()	creates a pipe between the calling process and a command
pow()	mathematical power function
printf()	writes data to the standard output

Table A-1: System Calls (continued)

FUNCTION	DESCRIPTION
profil()	enables or disables execution profiling
ptrace()	provides trace data for parent processes
putc()	writes a character to the specified file
putchar()	macro to write a character to the standard output
putenv()	adds or alters values in the environment
puts()	writes a null terminated string to the standard output
putw()	writes a word (integer) to a file
qsort()	quick general sorting routine
rand()	miscellaneous random number generation functions
read()	buffered read from an open file
readdir()	returns pointer to a directory structure
realloc()	reallocate already allocated memory
rewind()	positions to the beginning of a file
rewinddir()	resets directory position pointer to top of directory
rmdir()	removes empty directories from the file system
scanf()	reads from the standard input
semctl()	IPC semaphore control operations
semget()	IPC routine to get a semaphore identifier
semop()	IPC routine to perform user defined array of semaphore ops
setbuf()	assigns buffering to open stream before it's read or written
setgid()	sets real and effective GID of the calling process
setgrp()	sets the process group ID for the calling process
setjmp()	saves the stack for use by longjmp()
setkey()	function to generate a 56 bit encryption key
setuid()	sets real and effective UID of the calling process
setvbuf()	assigns buffering to open stream before it's read or written
shmat()	function to attach a shared memory segment
shmctl()	function to perform shared memory control operations
shmdt()	function to detach a shared memory segment
shmget()	gets a shared memory segment
sighold()	used in enhanced signal management
sigignore()	used in enhanced signal management
signal()	used to specify what to do when given signal is received
sigrelse()	used in enhanced signal management
sigset()	used in enhanced signal management
sin()	trigonometric sine function
sinh()	mathematic hyperbolic sine function
sleep()	suspends process execution for the specified interval
sprintf()	writes data to a buffer in the specified format
sqrt()	mathematical square root function
srand()	another random number generation function

Table A-1: System Calls (continued)

FUNCTION	DESCRIPTION
sscanf()	does formatted reads from a buffer
ssignal()	associates a procedure and action with a software signal
stat()	retrieves information about the specified file
stime()	used to set the system date and time from a program
strcat()	concatenates strings
strchr()	searches for a character within a string
strcmp()	compares two strings
strcpy()	copies one string into another
strcspn()	also returns number of matching characters in strings
strdup()	fast way to duplicate an existing string
strlen()	returns the length of a string
strncat()	concatenates the specified number of bytes to a string
strncmp()	compares only the number of characters specified
strncpy()	copies the specified number of bytes to a string
strpbrk()	searches for differences between strings
strrchr()	also searches for characters within a string
strspn()	returns number of characters in str1 that match str2
strtod()	converts a string to a double precision number
strtok()	used to separate tokens in a string
strtol()	converts a string to a long integer number
swab()	swaps bytes between strings
sync()	causes in core file system info to be written to disk
system()	issues commands by invoking the command interpreter
tan()	trigonometric tangent function
tanh()	mathematic hyperbolic tangent function
tdelete()	removes node from binary search tree created by tsearch()
tfind()	locate a key value in a binary tree
time()	obtains time in seconds from a fixed reference point
times()	gets elapsed times for processes
tmpfile()	creates a temporary filename using the tmpnam() routine
tmpnam()	generates a temporary filename
toascii()	macro to convert characters to ASCII
tolower()	macro to convert uppercase characters to lowercase
toupper()	macro to convert lowercase characters to uppercase
tsearch()	constructs and accesses a binary tree
ttyname()	finds the name of a terminal device
twalk()	walk a binary tree created by tsearch()
ulimit()	obtains and sets limits for processes
umask()	obtains and sets file creation mask for calling process
umount()	dismounts a previously mounted file system
uname()	obtains the name of the current operating system

Table A-1: System Calls (continued)

FUNCTION	DESCRIPTION
ungetc()	pushes a character back into the input stream
unlink()	removes directory entry or link from the file system
ustat()	gets statistics of a mounted file system
utime()	sets file access and modification times
vfprintf()	similar to fprintf, called with an argument list
vprintf()	similar to printf, called with an argument list
vsprintf()	similar to sprintf, called with an argument list
wait()	calling process waits for a child process to terminate
write()	buffered write to an open file
_exec()	immediately terminates process execution (no cleanup)
_tolower()	like tolower(), though more restricted (but faster)
_toupper()	like toupper(), though more restricted (but faster)

APPENDIX B

COMMANDS FOR ADVANCED USERS

This appendix contains explanations of commands often used by authorized superusers and advanced UNIX users.

The ar Command

The **ar** command is an archive utility used to group files together into a single archive file. It is especially useful for compressing files into data transmission The files may be of any type, such as object files, source code files, and executables. The **ar** command is similar to the DOS **arc** and **pkarc/pkxarc** public domain utilities.

Say, for example, a user wanted to archive all files in a particular subdirectory. The -r flag will add a file to the archive and, if it already exists, will replace it. Assuming the name of the directory was /usr/src/dts/rjesend.p, then the following example would generate an archive file named rjesend.arc:

```
tsm: cd /usr/tsm/src/dts/rjesend.p
tsm: pwd
/usr/src/dts/src/rjesend.p
tsm: ls
addtarg.c
addtrailer.c
```

```
gettargets.c
keymerge.c
makefile
rgetcmd.c
rjesend
rjesend.c
rmakedtf.c
rmakehdr.c
rmakejobs.c
rprocopts.c
rqueuedtf.c
rvalidcmd.c
tsm: ar -rv rjesend.arc *
a - addtarg.c
a - addtrailer.c
a - gettargets.c
a - keymerge.c
a - makefile
a - rgetcmd.c
a - rjesend
a - rjesend.c
a - rmakedtf.c
a - rmakehdr.c
a - rmakejobs.c
a - rprocopts.c
a - rqueuedtf.c
a - rvalidcmd.c
ar: creating rjesend.arc
tsm:ls -l rjesend.arc
329 -rw-r--r-- 1 tsm other 165976 Apr 11 01:01 rjesend.arc
tsm:
```

To get a listing of the files in an archive library, use the -t flag:

```
tsm: ar -t rjesend.arc
addtarg.c
addtrailer.c
gettargets.c
keymerge.c
makefile
```

```
rgetcmd.c
rjesend
rjesend.c
rmakedtf.c
rmakedtf.c
rmakehdr.c
rmakejobs.c
rprocopts.c
rqueuedtf.c
rvalidcmd.c
tsm:
```

Files may be extracted, one at a time, in groups, or all at once. This example extracts a single file, rjesend.c, from the archive file, rjesend.arc:

```
tsm: ar -xv rjesend.arc rjesend.c
x - rjesend.c
tsm:
```

Multiple file extraction is accomplished by specifying the name of each file to be extracted on the command line:

```
tsm: ar -xv rjesend.arc rjesend rjesend.c makefile
x - rjesend
x - rjesend.c
x - makefile tsm:
```

If no filename is specified, the default is to extract all files in the archive file. When a file is extracted from an archive file, it is not deleted automatically from the archive. A separate action is required to do this if you wish. The following example deletes the file called makefile from the archive file:

```
tsm: ar -dv rjesend.arc makefile
d - makefile
tsm:
```

Contents of the file may be sent to the standard output if desired:

```
tsm: ar -pv rjesend.arc rvalidcmd.c
<rvalidcmd.c>
#include <stdio.h>
#include "keystruct.h"
#include "dtsstruct.h"
/*
This routine examines the dtsstruct structure containing the
user's request and returns a count of the errors found.
*/
rvalidcmd(dtsp)
struct dtsstruct *dtsp;              /* user's request */
{
   int       errcnt = 0;
   if(dtsp->dtkeywds.dttarget[0][0] == 0
   && dtsp->dtkeywds.dtapp[0].dtapptype[0] == 0
      {
          fprintf(stderr,"no targets specified\n");
          errcnt++;
      }
   return(errcnt);
}
```

The at Command

The **at** command queues commands for execution at a later time. When the **at** command is entered, with the appropriate execution date as its argument, it reads lines entered from the standard input, queueing them in order until an end-of-file is encountered. The commands entered are then executed at the designated time. A simplified example that reads a file containing the commands to execute in sequence is shown below:

```
tsm: at 1500
$HOME/cmdfile
job 581402700.a at Sat Mar  7  15:00:00  1989
tsm:
```

This command has two option flags that may be specified. The first is the -l flag which is used to obtain a report on all **at** jobs scheduled by the inquiring user. The second is the -r flag, used to cancel any job(s) that may be awaiting execution. Users may only cancel their own jobs.

The input commands may be entered either at the terminal keyboard, or from a file with the redirection operator. The commands in the **at** file are executed a line at a time, much like a shell script, except that **at** files do not require execution mode permission. To use the **at** command, users must have their login ID entered in the file /usr/lib/cron/at.allow. Any user whose ID appears in the file /usr/lib/cron/at.deny is prohibited from using the **at** command, even if that user has an entry in the at.allow file.

When the **at** job has finished execution, a status message is sent to the issuing user via UNIX mail. Any output produced as the result of commands executed by **at** also appear in this mail message, unless those outputs had been redirected to other destinations within the script.

The **at** command itself may also be included within the script, creating the possibility for spawning other delayed commands, or even respawning itself regularly. For repetitive scheduling, the cron facility should be used.

The **at** command has a number of useful purposes — ranging from alarm clock style reminders, to automating processes such as file system backups. The following example illustrates the possibilities of the **at** command:

```
tsm: cat /usr/tsm/atfile
banner " `date|cut -d" " -f4|cut -d: -f2`" >
/dev/console
at now +1minutes /usr/tsm/atfile
tsm: at now +1minutes /usr/tsm/atfile
job 576825060.a at Tue Apr 12 01:11:00 1988
tsm:
```

This will result in the execution of the two lines in the file /usr/tsm/atfile one minute from the time the command is entered.

The first line will execute the banner command, which trims out a field from the date command. In this example, the output is directed to /dev/console, although it may be redirected elsewhere. The second line is an example of how an **at** command can respawn itself. The following example demonstrates how to terminate an **at** job:

```
tsm: at -l
576825060.a     Tue Apr 12 01:11:00 1988
tsm: at -r 576825060.a
tsm:
```

Every iteration of a self spawning **at** job creates a mail message and can cause a lot of overhead if left unchecked. The date specification may be an absolute date and time, as well as other relative execution increments: hours, days, weeks, months, or even years. Singular forms of these are also acceptable. The names of the weekdays may also be used as part of the time/date specification.

The df Command

The UNIX file system uses blocked I/O. Files are written onto the disk media in units called *blocks,* usually 512 or 1,024 bytes in size. An inode is a data structure used by the UNIX file system to define an individual file's existence. Inodes contain information about a file's attributes such as file size; creation, modification and last access dates; file ownership information; access privileges; and other information important to the UNIX file I/O system.

The **df** command is used to provide information about the number of free blocks (of 512 bytes), and also information on free file slots (inodes). Any user may execute this command, and it is useful to determine the amount of free space available on disk.

```
tsm: df
/        (/dev/dsk/c1d0s0 ):    1102 blocks   976 i-nodes
/usr     (/dev/dsk/c1d0s2 ):   66682 blocks 11499 i-nodes
tsm: df -t
/        (/dev/dsk/c1d0s0 ):    1102 blocks   976 i-nodes
```

```
                    total:        12636  blocks    1568  i-nodes
     /usr   (/dev/dsk/c1d0s2 ):   66682  blocks   11499  i-nodes
                    total:       126684  blocks   15824  i-nodes
     tsm:
```

The du Command

The **du** command is used to display the amount of space in use on the file system. There are only three option flags:

The -s flag produces a grand total count of 512 byte blocks in use, from the current directory on down.

The -a flag is the opposite of the -s flag; producing an entry for every file, starting from the current directory. It is likely to produce a lot of output, especially when the current directory is the root directory. When using the -a flag, redirection to a filename is recommended. If no option flag is specified, the listing contains an entry for each directory, beginning from the current directory on down.

When the -r flag is supplied, messages appear indicating the names of files and directories that cannot be read or opened, and so on. A target filename may be specified as an argument that identifies where to begin the utilization report; if omitted, in all cases, the default is from the current directory.

```
tsm: pwd
/usr/tsm
tsm: du /usr/spool
1          /usr/spool/cron/atjobs
6          /usr/spool/cron/crontabs
8          /usr/spool/cron
1          /usr/spool/lp/class
1          /usr/spool/lp/interface
1          /usr/spool/lp/member
1          /usr/spool/lp/request
30         /usr/spool/lp/model
38         /usr/spool/lp
1          /usr/spool/locks
1          /usr/spool/uucp/.Admin
1          /usr/spool/uucp/.Corrupt
```

```
1        /usr/spool/uucp/.Log/uucico
1        /usr/spool/uucp/.Log/uucp
1        /usr/spool/uucp/.Log/uux
1        /usr/spool/uucp/.Log/uuxqt
5        /usr/spool/uucp/.Log
8        /usr/spool/uucp/.Old
2        /usr/spool/uucp/.Sequence
2        /usr/spool/uucp/.Status
1        /usr/spool/uucp/.Workspace
1        /usr/spool/uucp/.Xqtdir
22       /usr/spool/uucp
1        /usr/spool/uucppublic
1        /usr/spool/msnet
5        /usr/spool/msnlog
77       /usr/spool tsm: du -a
1        ./.profile
1        ./bin
1        ./bantam
1        ./lib
1        ./shells/shifter
2        ./shells
1        ./osborne
1        ./src
1        ./addison-wesley
1        ./howard-sams
11       .
tsm:
```

The id Command

This command echoes back information about user and group IDs for the requesting user. It may be useful when executed from shell scripts, as a method of determining what user is executing the script, and to what group they belong:

```
tsm: id
uid=100(tsm) gid=1(other)
tsm:
```

The logname Command

This command obtains just the login name of the requesting user. It is also useful when executing from within shell scripts.

```
tsm: logname
tsm
tsm:
```

The lp Command

The **lp** command is used to send files to a line printer. When users want to print a file, this command is used to do the job. The **lp** system, normally started during system initialization, must first be active in order to process print jobs. Users should also read about the **pr** command described later in this text. Some option flags may be specified:

When -c is specified, the print file is copied rather than linked to. The -d option is used to specify the destination (name of the printer or print group eligible to do the printing for the current file. If the LPDEST environment variable is set, then the destination value is derived from it; otherwise, a previously established system default is used.

When the -m option is specified, the sending user is notified via UNIX mail. The -n option is used to indicate how many copies to print. The -o option is used to specify any printer specific options; multiple -o options with arguments may exist.

When the -s option is used, it causes **lp** messages to be suppressed. The -t specifies a title to be included as part of the banner page. Finally, the -w option notifies the user at the terminal when printing is done. If the user isn't logged on, the message is sent via UNIX mail. An example of how to send a file to a printer named *laser1* is shown below:

```
tsm: lp -dlaser1 -w -n3 /usr/tsm/addison/appndx_b/appndx_b.txt
```

451

This example sends a text file to a laser printer; three copies are to be produced, and when printing is complete, the user (tsm) is notified by a message to their terminal.

The lpstat Command

Once users have sent their files to print, they may wish to check on the status of their print job. The **lpstat** command provides information about the printer system. When no command line options are specified, **lpstat** reports on the status of all requests made by that user. A partial list of the option flags available are as follows.

The -a[*list*] option echoes the acceptance status of destinations for output requests. An optional list of printer names and classes may also be provided as the value for *list*. The -d option echoes back the default destinations for printer requests.

The -o option shows the current status for output requests. The -p[*list*] option shows the status of printers; *list* is a list of printer names. The -t option prints out all available **lp** status information.

```
tsm: lpstat -t
scheduler is running
tsm:
```

The passwd Command

This command is used to change or create a user ID password. When a new user is given a login account, on most UNIX systems it is customary for the system administrator to assign the user an initial password. After logging in, new users are expected to change their password to something that can be remembered.

The **passwd** command is used to change a user's password entry, which is actually a field within a record entry for the user in the /etc/passwd file. This field is encrypted and only the **passwd** command is capable of changing it by invoking the **crypt( )** system call.

When entered, the **passwd** command prompts the user for their old password (if there is one) and then prompts for a new password twice.

The second new password entry is compared against the first so that any typographical errors may be avoided, especially since characters entered at a terminal are not echoed back for security reasons.

Depending upon local system administrator, options such as password aging may have been invoked to prevent users from reusing the same passwords or to prevent someone from changing passwords too oftene. System administrators may also decide to enforce other password standards, such as minimum length requirements and mandatory inclusion of numerics as part of the string. The following is an example of how to change a password with the **passwd** command:

```
tsm: passwd
Changing password for tsm
Old password:
New password:
Password is too short - must be at least 6 digits
New password:
Passwords must differ by at least 3 positions
New password:
Password must contain at least two alphabetic
characters and at least one numeric or special
character.
New password:
Re-enter new password:
tsm:
```

This example illustrates some of the ways certain installations may enforce rigid password security. If the user continues to have problems in specifying the new password, the **passwd** command aborts the attempt and tells the user to try again later.

The pr Command

The **pr** command may be used to break files into pages in preparation for printing. The output is formatted with a page heading containing the filename, date and time stamps, and page numbers. The file to be printed is specified on the command line when the command is invoked. The output is usually redirected from the standard output and piped directly into the **lp** command for subsequent printing.

There are several options that may be specified which provide pagination controls. The -d option causes the output to be double spaced. The -h option, followed by a text string, may be used to specify page headings. (Strings containing blanks must be enclosed within quotation marks.) The page length may be specified using the -l option, the default is 66 lines per page. The page width may also be specified using the -w option, defaulting to 72 characters wide.

For a complete list of the other available options, readers should reference the UNIX System V User Reference Manual or the UNIX System V Interface Definition. Examples of the **pr** command are shown below:

```
tsm: pr /etc/passwd | lp
tsm: pr -w121 -l55 -h"/etc/passwd File" /etc/passwd | lp
```

The su Command

The **su** command (for set user) permits a user to switch to another user ID without first logging off. It also allows users to gain superuser status. If no user ID is specified as the name argument to **su**, then the default is to become the root user. All attempts, successful or failed, are recorded in the file /usr/adm/sulog, along with time and date stamps, as well as the ID of the user making the attempt; and which login they were attempting to **su** to.

If the user ID being changed to does not have a password assigned to it, then anyone may **su** to that ID. Otherwise, **su** will prompt for the appropriate password and allow the change only if the correct one is provided. In either situation, a record of the **su** event is made in the sulog.

Once a user has successfully changed to another user ID through the **su** command, any access permission available to the new user ID becomes available to the original user. If this sound a bit confusing, assume that user ID tsm has just attempted to **su** to root.

```
tsm: su
Password:
#
who am i
tsm         console         Apr 17 23:49
#
```

The previous example demonstrates that the user tsm has issued the **su** command from the command line prompt. Since no user ID was specified as an argument to the **su** command, the default of root was assumed (*su root* is the same as *su*).

Since root is usually a password protected ID, a password challange is made. After the correct password is supplied the new user's prompt is supplied, which in this case is the # sign. The **who** command is entered to demonstrate that the current user is still tsm, although for all intents and purposes tsm is now root and can do anything that root can do as well.

When users **su** to another ID without specifying the - (minus) flag, the shell retains their original environment. When the - flag is included, the shell temporarily abandons the normal environment and provides the environment of the ID **su**'d to. The following example should clarify this last point:

```
tsm: echo $HOME
/usr/tsm
tsm: su - root
password:
# echo $HOME
/
# who am i
tsm         console         Apr 17 23:49
# exit
tsm:
```

The tar Command

This command invokes the tape archiver utility. When it was original-ly written, **tar** was used to write disk files to 9 track reels of magnetic tape commonly found on larger machines. Today, it includes the popular tape cartridges found on micro computers as well. Additional-ly, the output of this utility may also be redirected to a file on disk, instead of being written out to a tape device. The general format of the **tar** command is:

```
tar [options] [file1, ... filen]
```

There are numerous option flags for the **tar** command, only some of which are listed here.

If the r option is specified, the named files are appended to the end of an archive. The x option flag extracts the named files from the archive. If the filename is that of a directory, then the entire directory and any subdirectories therein are extracted as well.

The t option prints a listing of all files contained in the archive. The c option overwrites an existing archive by creating a new one, instead of appending to the end of it. The v option produces the ver-bose information of **tar** activity, which is normally silent. This can be very helpful if redirected to a disk file, for backup logging.

When the m option is specified, this instructs **tar** not to restore modification times, and uses the time of the extraction instead. The o option causes **tar** to use the user and group identifiers of the user invoking it, rather than those originally associated with the files when they were backed up. (This is valid only with the x option.) The f option, when present, means that the next field indicates the disk file to be used instead of the normal tape device.

The tail Command

This command prints the specified number of lines from the end of the specified filename. If no name is specified, then the standard input is used. When the -f option is used, this command has the effect of constantly printing the last line of the specified file to the standard output, in an endless loop, but only if and when the file grows in size.

This command may be used to write some nifty little logging utilities that may run in background if entered with the & character appended to the command line. It is also helpful when looking at long files without the need to first **cat** out the entire beginning, or going into an editor.

By default, if no number is provided on the command line, then only the last ten lines of the file are displayed. Other useful features are the + and - arguments that specify the number of lines from the beginning of the file (+) to start the display; and the number of lines from the end of the file (-) to begin the display. When neither of these is present, the default is -10. Besides lines, characters or blocks may also be specified by using the c and b modifiers.

```
tsm: tail /etc/passwd
umountfsys:7HLXi.vmZhNzc:0:0:unmount:/usr/admin:/bin/rsh
tsm:iEpzUyJexcg06:100:1:Steven Mikes:/usr/tsm:
listen:np:37:4:Network Admin:/usr/net/nls:
wbu:5FV9mNxacQiq2:101:1:William B. Urinoski:/usr/wbu:
kdb:7HLXi.vmZhNzc:105:1:Kurt D. Bauman:/usr/kdb:/bin/ksh
pati:WQsNdCt0eqlNs:102:1:Patricia A. Mikes:/usr/pati:
bgv:vE299hX.CKJ2o:103:1:Bela G. Vegvary:/usr/bgv:
dkm:876dkE.Bi2o:104:1:Danielle K. Mikes:/usr/dkm:/bin/ksh
slan:np:57:57:slan id:/usr/slan:
admin::36:1:NETAdministrator:/usr/net/servers/msnet/admin:
tsm: tail -f /etc/passwd  /usr/tsm/passwd.log&
563
tsm: kill -9 563
563 Terminated
tsm:
```

The first example shows the last ten lines in the /etc/passwd file. The next example uses the -f option to continually monitor all additions to this file. The results are written to a log file; note that the command runs in background, until it is killed.

The tee Command

This is another very useful command, used to alter the flow of a pipeline. The output is not only redirected to another file, but to as many other files as are specified. The -i flag causes interrupts to be ignored and the -a option specifies that the output produced is to be appended to existing files. This is handy when a hardcopy listing or a log file are desired. The following example demonstrates how both can be achieved:

```
tsm: cat /etc/passwd | tee /dev/console | sort | tee
spasswd /dev/console | lp
tsm:
```

This command line does the following: first, it prints out the contents of the /etc/passwd file. Next, it **tee**'s the file to the device called console and also sends a copy to the **sort** filter. Then a sorted version is piped into another **tee** that in turn produces three outputs: a disk file in the current directory called spasswd, a copy of the sorted /etc/passwd listing to the console device, and a copy to the system printer via the **lp** command.

The touch Command

The **touch** command is used to set the date and time stamp information of the specified file(s). Wildcard metacharacters, expanded by the shell, produce very powerful and far reaching effects. The -a and -m flags indicate that the access and modification stamps are to be changed. Files have inodes that contain information on the last access to the file, regardless of whether the file was actually modified or not; as well as the date and time of the last modification.

The -c flag is used to prevent the specified file from being created if it didn't previously exist.

The date argument is optional; if omitted, the current date and time information is used. Otherwise, any time and date may be used, past, present, or future! To set the time and date stamps for all files in the current directory to the current date and time, the following command could be used:

```
tsm: touch -am *
tsm:
```

This is handy for software developers to set an exact time and date stamp for a product that is to be distributed. The date and time information you can specify using the **touch** command have the general form of mmddhhmm[yy]. The first mm is the month, dd is the day of the month, and hhmm are the hour and minute of the day in military time (0-24 for hh and 0-59 for mm). The yy (enclosed within square brackets indicating that it is optional) is the year with a valid range of 00-99. The following example touches the file /etc/passwd back to December 15, 1985, 2:37 pm.

```
tsm: touch -amc 1215143785 /etc/passwd
tsm:
```

The wall Command

The **wall** command is used to send messages to all users logged in to the system. It reads data from the standard input until an end of file (Control-D) and then prints out the contents that were entered to the terminals of all users logged on. The actual message is preceded by:

```
Broadcast Message from user-id
```

Usually, the system administrator will use the **wall** command to broadcast a message prior to bringing down the system for a shut down. Actually, the **shutdown** command is a special shell script that invokes the **wall** command to notify any active users of the imminent shut down.

More information on certain facets of UNIX System V may be found by referencing any of the following books:

On Interprocess Communications

UNIX System Programming; Haviland and Salama, Addison-Wesley, 1987.

Advanced UNIX Programming; Mark Rochkind, Prentice-Hall, 1985.

The Design of the UNIX Operating System; Maurice Bach, Prentice-Hall, 1986.

Advanced Programmer's Guide to Unix System, Thomas, Roger and Yates, Osborne McGraw-Hill, 1986.

UNIX System V Programmer's Reference Manual; AT&T, 1987.

UNIX System V Programmer's Guide; AT&T, 1987.

On Networking

Local Area Network Design; Hopper, Temple and Williamson, Addison-Wesley, 1986.

Data Communications For Programmers; Micael Purser, Addison-Wesley, 1986.

Local Area Networks — The Second Generation; Thomas Madron, John Wiley & Sons, 1988.

PC Lan Primer; The Waite Group, Howard W. Sams, 1986.

Internetworking with TCP/IP; Douglas Comer, Prentice-Hall, 1988.

On Device Drivers and STREAMS

Writing a UNIX Device Driver; Egan and Teixeira, John Wiley & Sons, 1988.

UNIX System V STREAMS Primer; AT&T, Prentice-Hall, 1986.

UNIX System V STREAMS Programmer's Guide; AT&T, Prentice-Hall, 1986.

UNIX System V Programmer's Reference; AT&T, Prentice-Hall, 1986.

INDEX

T